Mennonites in Europe

MENNONITE HISTORY

Volume I

MENNONITES IN EUROPE

MENNONITE PUBLISHING HOUSE

SCOTTDALE, PENNSYLVANIA

MENNONITE HISTORY

Volume I. *Mennonites in Europe*
By John Horsch

Volume II. *Mennonite Church in America*
By J. C. Wenger

Mennonites in Europe

By

JOHN HORSCH

MENNONITE PUBLISHING HOUSE

SCOTTDALE, PENNSYLVANIA

PUBLISHER'S PREFACE TO THE FIRST EDITION

Thirty years have passed since the need for a comprehensive history of the Mennonite Church was first felt keenly enough among the American Mennonites to give birth to the demand that such a work be prepared by a competent writer and published for the use of the brotherhood at large. In 1911 the Publishing Committee of the Mennonite Publication Board, upon the request of Mennonite General Conference, reported to the latter body, among other things, as follows:

> We need an authentic Church History; a book to which the Church everywhere can point and say, "We believe that this has been the record of the Church from the days of Christ to the present." As a hand-book of Church history, it should be written in simple style, pointed paragraphs, intended for all classes of readers, as exact and complete in its data as it is possible for such a book to be made, . . . to be published at a later date, subject to the order of some future General Conference.

A committee of ten brethren was appointed at the same time to promote this project. This committee has since become the Historical Committee of Mennonite General Conference.

In 1927 General Conference took further action based on recommendations from its Historical Committee. The plan as at first conceived and formulated called for a comprehensive history of the Mennonite Church in a single volume in two parts, one part dealing with the history of the Mennonite Church in Europe and the other part with the history of the Mennonite Church in America. The idea of producing a general Church History was dropped when these plans were made, and the scope of the proposed work was limited chiefly to Mennonite History.

Because John Horsch had already for many years been gathering materials on the history of the Anabaptists and Mennonites in Europe, it was to him that the task was assigned of writing that part of this work which pertains to the European side of Mennonite history. The preparation of the American part of the same work was delegated to Harold S. Bender. As the work of preparing this history progressed, it became evident that each of these segments of the history of the Mennonite Church was of sufficient scope to merit being published in a volume by itself. At the same time the unity of the work as a whole is being preserved by issuing the parts as two volumes of one work entitled *Mennonite History.*

PUBLISHER'S PREFACE

The volume before you is the product of the research and the labors of John Horsch in faithfully carrying out the part of the assignment given to him by the Historical Committee of Mennonite General Conference. It is a matter of keen regret that the author did not live to see this work in its final form. He passed to his reward on October 8, 1941. The manuscript for the book had been practically completed in 1940, before he was disabled through the illness which preceded his untimely death. The final task of editing the manuscript for printing was placed in the hands of Edward Yoder, of the editorial staff of the Mennonite Publishing House, who also prepared a brief bibliography and the index. The manuscript for the book as prepared by the author was read by all the members of the Historical Committee of Mennonite General Conference. The secretary of the Committee, Harold S. Bender, also read the proofs and offered valuable suggestions which have enhanced the accuracy of the volume. Some of the chapters of the book had earlier been published as articles in periodicals, particularly the *Christian Monitor* and *The Mennonite Quarterly Review.*

PUBLISHER'S PREFACE TO THE SECOND EDITION

We are happy at last to be able to issue a second edition of this popular volume which was sold out within two years after its original publication date. With the exception of a few minor changes to correct slight errors of fact, the addition of brief concluding paragraphs in chapters 17, and 27 to 32, and the insertion of one new appendix, only very slight revisions have been made in the text. It was thought better to reissue the volume at this time substantially as it left the author's hands initially, and to look forward to a completely re-written volume at a later date.

INTRODUCTION

The history of the Mennonite Church is associated with that of other Christian bodies which had their rise at the daybreak of the Reformation. Centuries passed before the true character of that group of believers, known as the Swiss Brethren, and the kindred bodies in the districts of the Rhine, Flanders, and Holland, began to be appreciated and the true worth of their leaders became better known. Because of their practice of "re-baptizing" upon confession of faith those believers who had before been baptized into the state church as infants, these bodies were called Anabaptists by their enemies. At a time a little later, because of the activity of one of their number, Menno Simons (a leader among them in Holland), they became known as Mennonites.

To the Mennonite people in general in the last century the records of their spiritual ancestors were unknown, save as they were briefly and infrequently referred to in the church literature of earlier times. A brief history of the faith was published in the booklet, *Confession of Faith;* the records of the martyrs were to be found in the great volume of the *Martyrs' Mirror;* the sermons of Dirck Philips contained expositions of the faith; and the writings and teachings of Menno Simons furnished a guide for the practice and faith of the church in worship and life.

It has been left to modern students of history to delve into the neglected and almost inaccessible records lying in vaults and libraries of Europe. Some of these records were even labeled as unimportant documents. Such materials have revealed the principles of the faith, the teachings and the character of our early church fathers. Those records confirm the character of the faith of our spiritual forebears, the character of which forms the basis for the Christian liberty now enjoyed by many Christian communities.

It is fortunate for the brotherhood that the author of this volume on the history of the Mennonite Church in Europe should have been born and reared almost at the doorstep of the birthplace of the Mennonite Church. John Horsch was born in Giebelstadt, Bavaria, December 18, 1867. His father, Jacob Horsch, was a Mennonite bishop at Giebelstadt. His mother was Barbara Landes. In 1871 the family moved to Gelchsheim and there engaged in farming, while the father continued his pastorate with the Giebelstadt congregation. It was here that John Horsch received his early education and also graduated from the Bavarian State Agricultural College. His interests, however, were not limited to agricultural pursuits. He became interested early in historical study and having learned of Dr. Ludwig Keller, a noted Anabaptist historian at Munster, he opened with him a correspondence on historical subjects, which continued for five years. This interest led to many late hours of study after days of labor on the farm.

The change of attitude regarding military service on the part of European Mennonite congregations was due to the changing and stricter requirements of the state authorities. John Horsch believed thoroughly in the principle of nonresistance as long held by the Mennonite Church, and this led him to leave his home in Germany and come to the United States. He arrived in New York City January 3, 1887, and from there continued his journey to Elkhart, Indiana. Through reading the periodical *Herold der Wahrheit,* printed by the Mennonite Publishing Company of that place, he had some acquaintance with the Mennonites of America. After spending a few months with relatives at Halstead, Kansas, he was engaged by John F. Funk to become assistant editor and German proofreader with the Mennonite Publishing Company at Elkhart.

Horsch continued his education at intervals and during the summer months, attending various colleges from 1888 to 1892. On September 26, 1893, he was united in marriage with Christine Funck of Schloss Neipperg, Germany, by John F. Funk at Elkhart. His connection with the Elkhart company continued until 1895. This contact with the Mennonite Church and its literature gave him an increased opportunity to search more widely into the history in which he became increasingly interested.

For several years Horsch was engaged in other enterprises, and in 1899 he was employed by J. A. Springer of the Light and Hope Publishing House. There he continued doing editorial work and also continued his historical research until 1908, in which year he was invited by the Mennonite Publishing House at Scottdale, Pennsylvania, to take a position on its editorial staff. This invitation afforded him the opportunity which he had long desired, and made it possible for the church to benefit from his years of study and labor and from the fruits of that labor in the publication of much of the historical material he had collected.

The Mennonite Church in America has had an awakening in historical interests through the writings of Horsch, and especially through his addresses earlier given at conferences and young people's gatherings throughout the church. As a result of the inspiration from these efforts numbers of young people found a new interest in the Mennonite Church and its doctrines, and some were inspired to engage in original historical research along various lines of Mennonite history, both in the early and the more recent records of the church.

INTRODUCTION

Because of the need for preserving the records of the church from the past and furnishing the church with a more complete and authentic record of its life and faith, the Mennonite General Conference in 1927 assigned to John Horsch the task of writing an extended history of the Mennonite Church in Europe. This work has now been completed. The sad part is that the author did not live to see this book which embodies the labors of so many years, for he passed to his reward on October 8, 1941. In the summer of 1940, just when the work was nearly ready for publication, due to the long strain and close attention he had given to the execution of this work, his health gave way and he was forced to relinquish most of his duties.

The product of Horsch's labors is the fruit of a lifetime of research and devotion. His writings have appeared in print in various publications and in several lands. They have met the criticisms of other historians, some of international repute. The value of these writings and the compilation of such records is not only a monument to the life of the author but a source of help and inspiration to the church which must continue its testimony in the light of the truth which has been sustained through the past centuries. The purpose of the author in writing this work was to produce a book on the history of the Mennonite Church in Europe that would be read by the members of the church at large. For that reason he has avoided learned discussion and omitted the mention of most of the original sources which he used in his studies. It was his fond hope that the members of the church today, old and young, would in reading this history of their brotherhood be inspired and feel challenged by the record of the devotion and the loyalty and the martyrdom of those who held the faith in the past.

It is with a deep sense of gratitude to God that we reflect on the fact that John Horsch, coming from so near the very birthplace of the Mennonite Church and her history, through his diligent research over a period of fifty-five years, has brought to us the light of the past. He inquired into the lives and the beliefs of the fathers of our faith; he searched out their writings and those of their contemporaries; and has been with them in their discussions with friends and enemies. He lived with the fathers through their trials and triumphs, and learned from them the secret of their faith and steadfastness—their simple faith in Jesus Christ and in the Word of God. He has laid down at the door of the present generation a challenge of faith, and has given to the church an inspiration and a new confidence in the faith of the saints of God, which they sustained and have passed on to us as our richest heritage.

INTRODUCTION

But the past may still have much in store for those who seek and who may yet be inspired to search. The true value of this history will be found in its confirmation of the faith of the gospel, which has come down to us from the past, and in enabling the church to live with sincere conviction and true devotion according to the Word of God and in the love of Jesus Christ. By this faith and devotion the church may continue to minister to the world the blessing of the gospel of peace among men and salvation through faith in Jesus Christ our Lord.

The Historical Committee wishes yet to thank the Mennonite Publishing House for the generous help given toward the production of this volume, both in providing funds for collecting rare historical materials and in giving the author opportunity and encouragement for doing his work in writing the same.

S. F. Coffman, Chairman
Historical Committee of Mennonite General Conference.

TABLE OF CONTENTS

PART ONE

BEFORE THE REFORMATION

PART TWO

RISE AND GROWTH OF THE MENNONITE CHURCH

xiii

TABLE OF CONTENTS

PART THREE

LIFE AND FAITH OF THE EARLY MENNONITES

PART FOUR

APPENDICES

LIST OF ILLUSTRATIONS

xv

PART ONE

Before the Reformation

CHAPTER 1

THE DECADENCE OF CHRISTIANITY

The history of the Christian Church from the days of the apostles to the Reformation is one first of glorious conquest in spite of persecution, but then, particularly after the beginning of the fourth century of notable decline and decadence even unto degradation at times. Gradually the church was transformed from a simple brotherhood of believers and disciples into a great mass institution which deviated markedly from its pristine character.

One of the early deviations from New Testament teaching was the supposition that the Christian ordinances are possessed, as it were, of magical power and are the means of salvation. Baptism in the course of time came to be looked upon as the instrument of regeneration, and the observance of the communion as the means of obtaining forgiveness for sins committed after baptism. Within a few centuries various other grave errors and unscriptural practices found their way into the church.

With the professed conversion to Christianity of Emperor Constantine of the Roman Empire, persecution ceased. There began an era of great outward growth and expansion for the church. Constantine and his sons, who succeeded him as rulers, made Christianity the religion of the state, to take the place of the old Roman religion. The Christian church was made a state church. Church and state were united and later the population was compelled to make a profession of Christianity. All preliminary conditions for church membership were abandoned, except baptism which was made compulsory. Since this ordinance was supposed to be the instrument of regeneration, the membership in theory consisted of regenerated persons. Infant baptism was introduced, which means that the church could no longer claim to be a body of believers. Scriptural church discipline ceased to be practiced. The consequence of this great decline in faith and practice was that the church all but lost what was yet left of the apostolic standard of life and practice.

Constantine did not undertake a sudden abolition of heathenism, however. He recognized the danger of political disturbances, and first granted general religious freedom (A. D. 313). Later he proceeded to forbid pagan worship. The amalgamation of the pagan masses with the church was in part responsible for the continuation of the paganizing process. The principle of nonresistance was abandoned upon the consummation of a union of the church with the state.

The idea of a literal priesthood was substituted for the spiritual priesthood of the believers. The priests of the established church were believed to be the mediators between God and man. Now, a priesthood in the literal sense required a literal altar and sacrifice. This was provided through the ceremony of the Mass, on the strange supposition that the host or bread in the communion service is changed into the body of the Lord Himself, and that He must be literally offered up again and again in the daily Mass, to atone for sin. Thus the sacrifice offered once for all on Calvary is supposed to be repeated on the altars in the churches, the place of the Roman soldiers being, strange to say, taken by the Christian priest. To Constantine belongs the doubtful honor of introducing sacerdotal vestments or peculiar, gorgeously wrought garments to be worn in saying Mass.

Prayer to Mary and the saints came to be looked upon as necessary. In the language of Scripture the saints are the believers. In consequence of the general decline of the Christian life this use of the word "saints" was abandoned. Only those were supposed to be saints who were canonized, that is declared to be saints after their departure from life. Images of Christ and the saints also in course of time became the objects of adoration and worship. In the Eastern (Greek) Church the use of images was restricted to paintings. Statues of stone or wood were forbidden, while the Roman or Western Church observed no such restriction. Among the most popular images were those of the cross and the crucifix. While the Greek church never sanctioned the use of musical instruments in public worship, no such restriction was in force in Western Christendom, where after the seventh century organs were used in the churches.

Among the evidences of departure from New Testament teaching were the doctrines of purgatory and indulgences, the use of holy water and holy oil, the practice of exorcism preceding the rite of baptism, the superstitions regarding relics, and other practices. Naturally not all the Christians assented to the gradual departure of the church from primitive Christianity. Many were keenly aware of the deviations made from the original faith. At least three early divisions took place in the church in consequence of the departure from New Testament Christianity.

The first of these divisions, of the Montanists, occurred toward the end of the second century. Their first leader was a certain Montanus of Phrygia in Asia Minor. Tertullian, a notable Christian writer of that period, was of this persuasion. The Montanists endeavored to maintain the purity and earnestness and church discipline of the apostolic age. Tertullian's writings indicate that they disapproved of infant baptism, the oath, and worldly conformity in dress. They defended the principle of nonresistance and the prayer veil. Some of their congregations existed on into the sixth century, as is proven by the fact that the emperor Justinian in that century repeatedly enacted laws against them. However, in some points the Montanists were heretical.

About one hundred years after the rise of Montanism the Novatian Church was first organized. The Novatianists differed but little from the Montanists. They withdrew from the general body of the church and were persecuted by Constantine.

The Donatists represented another movement having for its object the preservation of the apostolic purity of the church. They severely criticized the state church on various grounds. Notwithstanding persecution by banishment, confiscation of property, and death the Donatists existed until the seventh century. Augustine, who is considered the most prominent of the church fathers, approved of their persecution.

The general persecution of the Christian sects dissenting from the creed of the state church continued until over a half century after the beginning of the Reformation period. The leaders of the Protestant Reformation of the state church type —Luther, Zwingli and Calvin—did not approve the principle of general religious toleration. The Netherlands was the first Protestant country to grant toleration to the dissenters (principally Mennonites), and Switzerland the last.

CHAPTER 2

THE WALDENSES AND OTHER GROUPS

Uncertainty still prevails as regards the time and circumstances of the rise of the Waldensian Church. The name points to Peter Waldo (about 1140-1217) as their founder. But these believers were known by various other names as well, such as Poor Men of Lyons, Lyonists, Vallenses, Vaudois. The meaning of the two last terms is "people of the valleys." They were given this name for the reason that they were particularly numerous in certain Alpine valleys in Piedmont (northern Italy).

Shortly before Waldo's time the sect of the Petrobrusians, followers of Peter de Bruys, spread widely in southern France. In doctrine and practice there was close agreement between them and the Waldenses. Peter de Bruys was an eloquent evangelist, preaching against the foremost doctrines of Romanism. In 1126 he was burned at the stake as a heretic in St. Gilles. Like the Waldenses the Petrobrusians rejected infant baptism, the oath, prayer to the saints, prayer for the dead, adoration of images, and veneration of relics. They agreed with the Waldenses and earlier evangelical parties in giving a strong testimony against all forms of worldliness.

There is an old tradition of which mention was made even by some of the early opponents and persecutors of the Waldenses, that their origin goes back much farther than to Peter Waldo. A Roman Catholic chronicler, the inquisitor Reinerius, who died in 1259, wrote concerning the Waldenses:

Among all sects that have hitherto existed there has none been more pernicious to the [Roman] Church than that of the Lyonists, and this for three reasons. First because this sect reaches back the farthest, for some say that it exists since the time of Sylvester [who was bishop of Rome at the time of Constantine].

Peter Waldo was a wealthy merchant at Lyons in southern France. Through witnessing the sudden death of a friend he was aroused to a realization of the seriousness of life and at the same time to the incomparable value of the Word of God. About the year 1160 he engaged two learned men to translate large portions of the Bible from the Latin into the vernacular (the Romance dialect), and to make copies of the same (the art of printing being then unknown). As he obtained a knowledge of the Scriptures, he had the experience of a true conversion. He put the evangelical truth into practice and gave himself to the task of spreading it. In this work he was joined by some of those who had come under his influence. Peter Waldo was undoubtedly the most notable missionary of the primitive gospel in that period. Through his own and his assistants' efforts the Waldensian Church spread not only in France but also in other countries. Waldo died in 1217 in Bohemia.

The Waldenses held the Word of God in highest regard not merely in theory but in actual practice. Bibles, and even parts of Bibles, were not plentiful before the invention of printing, but of the Waldenses it may be said that for their use of the Scriptures they were to a considerable degree independent of the possession of copies of the Bible. They followed the usage of committing large portions of the Scriptures to memory. Many members of the Waldensian Church could recite whole books of the Bible from memory. Even such as were not able to read knew some of the most precious parts of the Scriptures by rote. They tested all teaching of the Roman church by the Scriptures and rejected that for which they found no foundation. Their antagonist Reinerius wrote: "They believe every point respecting God together with all the articles contained in the Apostle's Creed." He adds that on many points their teaching differed from that of the Roman Church.

The Waldenses believed that Christ, in the Sermon on the Mount, gave the rules of life for the Christian. They taught the principle of nonresistance and did not permit going to law before the civil courts. They would take no part in the civil government nor accept worldly offices. The swearing of oaths they held to be distinctly forbidden by Christ. Attending places of worldly amusement, such as the ballroom or theater, was not tolerated. Church discipline was as a rule strictly administered. "He who goes to a dance," says an old Waldensian church discipline, "is going in company with the devil." And again: "The jewelry worn by women is the stone on which Satan sharpens his sword." Dedication of churches, worship of relics, as well as belief in purgatory were rejected.

The Waldensian ministers were unsalaried, most of them followed some of the common occupations, but they were also well supported by the membership. Besides the ministers there were deacons whose special task was the care of the poor in the brotherhood. The missionaries (not the common ministers) of the Waldenses were as a rule unmarried, having neither family nor property. Commonly the missionaries went two by two, an older and a younger man. Their life was one of hardship and self-denial. It was impossible for them to labor publicly, and they often traveled as salesmen, the younger man carrying light wares, such as knives, needles, and the like. This was largely the means for providing points of contact in their work.[1]

Concerning their teaching on baptism Ermengardus wrote in his tract, *Against the Waldenses*: "They say that baptism is only for those who desire it with their own mouth and heart." The Waldenses pointed out that the Roman church first baptizes and then teaches, while in the primitive Christian church those who were baptized were first instructed (Matt. 28:19). They showed that the apostles baptized only those who believed and had come to years of understanding. The chronicler Sebastian Franck wrote in 1531 that the Waldenses do not baptize infants.

Concerning the doctrine and life of the Waldenses we have some striking testimonies from their antagonists. Reinerius, already mentioned, wrote further about them:

There is scarcely any land in which this sect does not exist. And while all other sects, through the enormity of their blasphemies against God, strike horror into the hearts of their hearers, the sect of the Leonists has a great semblance of piety, inasmuch as they live righteously before men.

Again the same writer says:

The Waldenses may be readily known by their quiet, unassuming life. They are modest in their attire and wear neither costly nor unclean clothing. They live by the labor of their hands, and even their preachers are shoemakers and weavers. They do not lay up riches but are content with that which is necessary. The Waldenses live pure lives and are temperate in eating and drinking. They do not visit drinking houses and do not attend places of amusement. They exercise self control and may be known by their considerate speaking, for they do not indulge in joking, slander, or gossip.

Claudius Seyssel, archbishop of Turin, wrote concerning the Waldenses:

They keep the Christian laws and rules better than many of our people. Leaving the things which they teach contrary to our faith out of consideration, they lead a better life than all others who call themselves Christians.

Notwithstanding the persecution which was waged against the Waldenses, they spread within a century over a wide territory including large parts of France and Italy. The persecution in this period was less severe than in later times, and yet there were many executions. Not less than eighty Waldensian men and women were burned at the stake in 1211 at Strasburg in Alsace. Seven were burned at Maurillac in Spain, in 1214. In the same century the Waldenses found a place of refuge in the Alpine valleys of western Piedmont (Italy), which later became their principal center. In Germany there occurred from 1231 to 1233 the first general persecution of the Waldenses.

Despite persecution the spread of the Waldenses continued. In Upper and Lower Austria Waldensian "schools," as their places for regular worship were called, were found in 1260 in upward of fifty places. In 1315 in a small political district in Lower Austria there were Waldenses in thirty-six villages and towns. In the whole dukedom of Austria the number of their adherents was calculated to be above 80,000. They also carried on successful missionary work in Bohemia, Moravia, Carinthia, Styria (Austrian provinces), also in Silesia, Brandenburg (modern Prussia), Pomerania, and Poland. According to a statement made by the Waldensian bishop Neumeister, who in 1315 was burned at the stake in Himburg near Vienna, they were very strong numerically in Bohemia and Moravia. In Schweidnitz a village in Silesia no less than fifty, among them a number of women and young people, were burned at the stake in 1315. Very many suffered martyrdom in Poland about the year 1330. Toward the end of that century the Waldenses were numerous in Hungary and had also spread into Transylvania. In Saxony and Mecklenburg they were found about fifty years later.

About a decade before the year 1400 a terrible persecution of the Waldenses began in the provinces and countries named above. The meagre extant remnants of the records of this persecution are sufficient to give an adequate idea of their strength in these countries. In southern Bohemia whole villages adhered to the Waldensian faith. In Moravia they were so numerous that the Roman hierarchy almost despaired of getting the mastery of the situation. In Brandenburg, Pomerania, and Mecklenburg no less than 443 persons were arrested in 1393 for the Waldensian "heresy," among them were persons whose parents already had been Waldenses. In Austria so many persons were accused as Waldenses and given a hearing that the minutes of the trials filled three thick volumes. Thirty-eight Waldenses were executed in 1393 at various places in Bavaria. Three hundred persons were burned at the stake in various parts of Saxony in 1416. In 1446 twelve persons were burned at Nordhausen, and in 1454 twenty-two persons at Sangerhausen in Saxony.

Hundreds of Waldensian refugees, in 1480, fled from Brandenburg to the Austrian provinces of Bohemia and Moravia, where they united with the Bohemian Brethren (Hussites). About a decade earlier, namely in 1467, the first bishop of the Bohemian Brethren had been ordained by the laying on of hands of a Waldensian bishop. In consequence many Waldenses in Bohemia and other provinces identified themselves with the Bohemian Brethren. There is no record of Waldenses in the German Empire after the year 1500. But they were numerous in this period in the so-called Waldensian valleys in northwestern Piedmont (Italy), and also in southeastern France and in the French provinces of Dauphine and Provence.

Chapter 3

THE QUESTION OF WALDENSIAN DESCENT

A number of historians, both Mennonite and others, among them Thieleman J. van Braght, have defended the opinion that the Mennonite Church descended from the ancient Waldenses. The similarity in their faith and practice is indeed striking. While it was naturally to be expected that the devoted study of the Scriptures on the part of the Waldenses and the early Mennonites would lead both to the same conclusion, in other words, that they would find in the Scriptures the same truths, it is also possible that Waldensian influences were active in the rise of the Swiss Brethren Church. There can scarcely be a doubt of this, although there is no record of personal contact between Waldenses and Swiss Brethren. The statement of van Braght's that Michael Sattler, Hans Hut, and other evangelical Anabaptists had formerly been Waldenses has been proved incorrect.

At the time of the Protestant Reformation the Waldenses were numerous in certain parts of Italy and France. In that period they came under the influence of the Reformed Church. Eventually they yielded fully to this influence and became one of the bodies which accepted the Reformed (Calvinistic) creed. Through the labors of certain Reformed Church leaders they gave up the principles and doctrines on which they until that time had differed from the Reformed creed. The story of how this change came about is worth noticing. It indicates a lack of adequate leadership among the Waldenses of that time.

The general Protestant reformation movement in its earlier years was principally under the leadership of Martin Luther and Ulrich Zwingli. The Reformation was on the whole a movement away from Rome and back to the Scriptures. For this reason it was naturally hailed with great interest and satisfaction by the Waldenses. After enduring the bitterest persecution for these centuries, it appeared to them indeed marvelous that the civil authorities of certain states, under the religious leadership of Luther and Zwingli, had broken away from Rome. So forcibly were most of the leaders of the Waldenses impressed by this movement that they were, so to speak, taken off their feet. They apparently lost sight of the fact that the leading reformers were men of human failings. A number of letters of Waldensian ministers to some of the leaders in the Reformed Church indicate an unquestioning acceptance of the opinions of these reformers and of the doctrines of the Reformed creed.

It is in this connection important to notice that the Waldenses of Italy and France had apparently at that time no information concerning the existence of the Swiss Brethren and of other Anabaptists nor of their doctrine, except possibly what they may have learned from some of the Zwinglian reformers and from their writings against the Anabaptists. The Anabaptists at that time (except in Moravia) were practically unable to make use of the printed page for the dissemination of their teachings. On the other hand the representatives of the state church type of the Reformation had opportunity for publishing and circulating their many books and pamphlets setting forth and defending their doctrines and at the same time denouncing the Anabaptists. It is improbable that any literature written by Anabaptists reached the Waldenses, and the missionary activities of the evangelical Anabaptists did not at that time reach the countries in which the French and Italian languages were used.

At an early date influences of the state church type of the Reformation found their way to the Waldenses in France and Italy. Through the efforts of William Farel, later a collaborator of John Calvin, some of the Waldenses were won for the Zwinglian type of the Reformation about the year 1527. The Zwinglian party among the Waldenses, in 1530, sent two of their ministers, Georges Morel and Pierre Masson, to Switzerland and South Germany, to confer with Zwinglian leaders and to ask for their instruction and counsel. They visited the Zwinglian reformers Johannes Oekolampad at Basel and Martin Butzer (Bucer) at Strasburg.

Why they did not go directly to Ulrich Zwingli in Zurich is unknown. It is not improbable that Zwingli's political endeavors and his warlike attitude toward the Roman Catholic cantons were offensive to them. The two delegates presented to both Oekolampad and Butzer a lengthy personal letter. This letter was written by Georges Morel in the name of the Zwinglian party among the Waldenses in France and Italy. The letter stated the Waldensian position on various points of doctrine and practice, and asked for criticism and instruction. The letter is written in a submissive tone, indicating the high esteem with which the Zwinglian party among the Waldenses regarded the reformers to whom it was addressed. The writer of the letter gave expression to their desire and readiness to receive instruction from them. In fact the writer or senders of the letter declared explicitly that they agreed with the reformers "in all things," and yet the letter indicated that they were not fully informed regarding their teachings, thus showing a readiness for an unquestioning, uncritical acceptance of their views.

Among the statements made in this letter is the mention of objections raised by the Waldenses to the denial of free will and to the doctrine of predestination, as taught by Luther and Zwingli. "Nothing has brought us such consternation," the writer of the letter of the Waldenses states, "as this doctrine." He adds that they had supposed that divine grace is offered freely to all, and that man himself is responsible for spurning or accepting the offer of grace.

Furthermore, the letter indicates that the Waldenses had until then defended the principle of nonresistance. It also states that "we do not permit our people to make oath under any circumstances." "Our ministers are from the ranks of those whose occupation is stock raising and farming." "In case of difficulty between church members we choose two or three of our ministers to adjust matters." "We do not permit worldly amusements and gambling or singing of empty or immoral songs, nor do we tolerate immodest clothing." "We expel such as decline to give ear to our admonitions and persistently refuse obedience."

Among the questions asked in the letter of the Waldenses are these: Is all swearing of oaths sin, according to Christ's words? Are the magistrates doing right in executing criminals, or should they punish them in another way, thus sparing them unto repentance? Are believers permitted to go to law before unbelieving judges?

After reading this letter of the Waldenses both Oekolampad and Butzer wrote letters to the Waldensian Church, complying with the requests they had received. Oekolampad, in his reply, says that he and his brethren do not rebaptize those who were baptized in the Roman church, "as do the Anabaptists," and he adds, "be it far from us to do such a thing." Of course, the membership of the Reformed state churches had been Roman Catholic. They had not been formally or individually received into the Reformed Church but had been required by the secular authorities to consider themselves members of the Protestant state church. Martin Butzer, in his reply to the Waldenses, wrote at length about the Anabaptists, asserting that they did not have the spirit of Christ, and warned against their alleged heresies.

Provided with the letters and instructions of Oekolampad and Butzer, and with Zwinglian literature, the two men started on their journey homeward. They had been won over to the doctrine of the Reformed Church, and considered it their task to persuade their brethren in the homeland of the orthodoxy of Zwinglianism. At Dijon, in France, Pierre Masson was arrested, condemned to death and executed by the Roman Catholic magistrates. Georges Morel reached the Waldensian center, Merindoll, and labored zealously and successfully for the spread of Zwinglian doctrine among the Waldenses. He attempted to point out in the regular meetings for worship "in how many and how great errors we [Waldenses] find ourselves." Two years later those who were of like persuasion with him decided to present their demands at a synod of the Waldensian ministers and to invite William Farel and other French Reformed leaders to this session of the synod. Farel complied with their request to visit and instruct them. He came with Antoine Saunier and Robert Oliveton to the synod which was opened on September 12, 1532, at Angrogne, located in territory which at that time belonged to France. This synod was dominated throughout by Farel, as is evident from the confession of faith which, after six days of discussion, was adopted by a majority vote of the ministers present.

In this confession all points of specifically Waldensian teaching are set aside. The Confession of Angrogne does not differ in doctrine and principle from other confessions of Calvinism.

This synod was not, however, fully representative of the Waldenses as a body. The resolutions were passed against the protests of a small minority of the ministers. At least two of the Waldensian ministers present refused to accept the new creed. But within a few decades the Waldenses of France were fully assimilated to the French Reformed Church (later called Huguenots). Of the numerous Waldenses of the Alpine valleys of Piedmont the majority for a time showed greater loyalty to their ancient creed and principles. However, a number of assistants of William Farel, called Guillermins (Williamites), labored among them with increasing success. Within a few decades the Waldenses of Italy followed those of France in accepting the Reformed (Calvinistic) creed and church polity. Like the French Waldenses they became one of the Reformed Church bodies, though they still retained the Waldensian name.

Thieleman J. van Braght in the *Martyrs' Mirror*[2] gives two Waldensian confessions of faith. These confessions were thought by van Braght to show a similarity to the Mennonite confessions. He believed that they at least do not contradict them. However, a close reading of these confessions shows that they do not teach the ancient Waldensian creed. They contain no statements concerning the baptism of believers. They do not mention infant baptism, war, or the oath. Both these confessions are of later date than the synod of Angrogne and the confession drawn up by that synod.

There exists today, in fact, no Waldensian confession of faith dating back to the time when the Waldenses yet stood for their primitive creed. The second confession printed in the *Martyrs' Mirror* was written in 1544. Article 4 of this confession, "On the Church," reads in part: "We believe in a holy Church, the congregation of all the elect (believers) of God from the foundation (or beginning) of the world unto the end." In the original Dutch edition of the *Martyrs' Mirror*[3] the words, which in this quotation are given in parentheses, are in brackets, indicating that they were added by the editor of this work. In the text of this confession as found in the great *History of the Waldenses,* by Leger, the sentence reads: "We believe in a holy Christian Church, and that the Church consists of the assembly of the elect of God whom He has chosen from the foundation of the world unto the end."

The confession of Angrogne thus teaches the Zwinglian (and Calvinistic) doctrine of predestination. Articles 2, 3, and 4 of this confession read respectively as follows: "We believe that God, before the creation of the world, has chosen those who are now saved and who shall yet be saved." "We believe that it is impossible that those who are predestinated to be saved may be lost." "We believe that those who believe in free will, deny God's grace and His eternal predestination of grace." Article 6 of this confession says that to make oath is in agreement with Scripture.

From the above facts it is apparent that at the time of the rise of the Swiss Brethren the Waldenses had not yet discarded their primitive Christian teaching. A historian of the Reformation period, Sebastian Franck, wrote in 1531 that the Waldenses do not baptize infants, and that there is in general extensive agreement between them and the Anabaptists. The Waldensian Church of the older type was for only a short period co-existent with the evangelical Anabaptists. The earliest leaders of the Swiss Brethren had apparently no reliable information about the Waldenses. On the other hand, it is, as already intimated, not improbable that the Waldenses had read some of the highly prejudiced controversial writings of Zwingli, Oekolampad, and Schmid against the Anabaptists, and that they supposed these writings to be reliable. In that case they were wholly misinformed about the Swiss Brethren.

The question of the Waldensian descent of the Mennonite Church may be considered from two aspects. As concerns personal succession, or the continuity of an unbroken line of ordained officials reaching from the Anabaptists through the Waldenses back to the apostolic church, such a claim cannot be substantiated. And even if a claim of this sort were based on fact, it would in itself not mean anything as an evidence of loyalty to the Scriptures, as witness the well-known fact that Romanism, despite its errors, can boast such succession. Ordained officials may be disloyal to the truth. Even among the apostles one was untrue.

However, as the author of the article "Anabaptists" in the *Encyclopedia Britannica* points out, "the continuity of a sect is to be traced in its principles."[4] Considered from this aspect, the continuity of the Waldensian denomination in the evangelical Anabaptists and Mennonites cannot be questioned. The two denominations represented a similar faith and practice. The question of an ordination of an Anabaptist minister or ministers by a Waldensian minister is unimportant. Indeed the rise of the Anabaptist movement is to be, at least indirectly, ascribed to Waldensian influences. Such is the opinion of a number of prominent historians, among them the late Professor Ernst Troeltsch of the University of Berlin, Germany. Following are a few facts to the point.

In the thirteenth and fourteenth centuries the Waldenses were numerous in some of those parts of Switzerland in which later the Anabaptist movement was exceptionally strong and where the Swiss Brethren maintained themselves from the beginning, notwithstanding all persecution. In the year 1277 a number of dissenters, obviously Waldenses, were burned at the stake as heretics in the city of Bern in Switzerland. A congregation of Waldenses numbering about one hundred and thirty members was discovered in 1399 at the same place. In 1430, or about a century before the rise of the Swiss Brethren movement in Zurich, there existed in the neighboring canton of Freiburg a large Waldensian congregation. Among those who were persecuted for the Waldensian faith at this place were men and women having the same family names as are found among the oldest Swiss Mennonite families, such as Stuckey, Treyer, Reiff, Bucher, Meyer, Nukomer, Huser, Rolet. From such facts it may be reasonably assumed that Waldensian traditions and influences contributed to the rise of the Swiss Brethren Church.[5]

CHAPTER 4

WYCLIFFE AND HUSS, EARLY REFORMERS

John Wycliffe (d. 1384), one of the notable predecessors of the Reformation, was a priest at Lutterworth in England. On a number of points of doctrine he deviated from Romanism. His teaching agreed to an extent with that of the Waldenses. The pope condemned nineteen points in Wycliffe's writings as heresies, but the English parliament protected him. His followers, the Lollards, took a more pronounced attitude against Romanism than Wycliffe himself, and were persistently persecuted. He died as a priest at Lutterworth. John Wycliffe translated the Bible into the English language, and yet even among his followers complete Bibles were rare, since this was before the invention of the art of printing.

John Huss (1369-1415), a professor at the university of Prague in Bohemia, was influenced by the reading of Wycliffe's books. He largely agreed with his teachings. Huss preached earnestly against the worldliness of the hierarchy and the corruption of the priesthood. The archbishop of Prague excommunicated him but he continued to preach under the protection of the king of Bohemia. John Huss wrote a book on *The Church,* pointing out that the believers are the church, and that the head of the church is Christ. The church could dispense with the pope, he said, for popery dates back only to the time of Constantine. Like Wycliffe, John Huss was a defender of the doctrine of predestination substantially as taught later by John Calvin.

John Huss was finally compelled to appear before the General Council of the Roman Catholic bishops which was in session at Constance in South Germany. Here he was condemned to death as a heretic and burned at the stake on July 6, 1415.

The followers of John Huss, in the first period of their history, took the sword to defend themselves against their persecutors; some of the Hussites engaged even in aggressive warfare. Later there arose among them, probably through Waldensian influence, a party known as the Bohemian and Mora-

16

vian Brethren which differed widely from the majority of the Hussites. One of their leaders, Peter Cheltchizki, wrote in 1440 a notable book on the principle of nonresistance, which was printed in 1521. Until the year 1465 these congregations were not actually separated from the Roman Church. The question of separation was agitated for some time and the Brethren determined finally to decide the matter through the use of the lot; such a decision was supposed to indicate the will of the Lord. The issue was stated in writing in two questions, namely whether it is God's will to separate entirely from the papacy and its priesthood, and whether they should institute a ministerial order of their own after the model of the primitive church. The lot was cast for each question and both answers were in the affirmative.

Ministers were then chosen by lot. A bishop was somewhat later ordained by a Waldensian bishop named Stephen. Like the Waldenses the Bohemian and Moravian Brethren rejected oaths, worldly offices, and warfare. Regarding baptism they were not a unit; some of them did not baptize infants. They were protected by some of the Bohemian and Moravian nobles. By 1488 the whole Bible was printed in the vernacular by the Brethren. Martin Luther took, on the whole, a sympathetic attitude toward the Bohemian Brethren; but they were offended by the lack of discipline in the Lutheran churches.

PART TWO

Rise and Growth of the Mennonite Church

CHAPTER 5

THE PROTESTANT REFORMATION

At the time of the rise of the Protestant Reformation Christendom consisted, in the main, of two sections, namely the western, or Roman Catholic, and the Eastern, or Greek Orthodox Church. The division between the Roman Catholic and the Greek Churches had taken place in the year 1054. Most of the European countries before the Reformation era adhered to the Roman Church. Within certain Roman Catholic countries the small denominations of the Waldenses and Bohemian Brethren had maintained their existence despite all persecution.

The Reformation did not touch the eastern wing of Christendom. It was, on the whole, a movement away from Rome and back to the Scriptures. The principal leaders in this movement were Martin Luther (1483-1546), Ulrich Zwingli (1484-1531), and John Calvin (1509-1564). Originally the Protestant Reformation movement stood for the vital restoration of primitive Christianity, but soon the leaders in this movement adopted the view that a union of the church with the state was necessary for the success of the church. They decided in favor of such a union. This decision on the part of the leading reformers was of a compromising nature, necessitating on various points a departure from their former position. It implied the persecution of any dissenters. The acceptance of this compromise by Luther and Zwingli, led to the rise of the evangelical Anabaptist movement.

The leaders in the Reformation of the state church type will now have our attention.

Martin Luther was born in 1483 at Eisleben in Saxony, a province of the German Empire. He was educated in the Latin school at Eisenach and the University of Erfurt. In 1505 he entered the Augustinian convent in the same city and became a monk, hoping to find peace of conscience through self-imposed penance. Eventually he was led to see that divine forgiveness and a change of heart are the result of faith in Christ and surrender to Him. In 1509 he accepted a call to a professorship in the University of Wittenberg in Saxony.

In 1517 the notorious Johann Tetzel was commissioned to sell papal indulgences in certain parts of Germany. Luther believed that Tetzel claimed too much for the efficacy of the indulgences, and that in this respect he acted contrary to the will of the pope and to the teaching of the Roman Catholic Church. In consequence Luther wrote ninety-five theses or statements, in Latin, on indulgences and affixed them to the door of the castle church in Wittenberg. In these theses he condemned the abuses of which he believed Tetzel was guilty from the Roman Catholic point of view.

In the course of the controversy which ensued, Luther became more and more convinced that various teachings and practices of Romanism are unscriptural. Even before writing the ninety-five theses he had advanced ideas on the doctrine of justification by faith, which from the Roman Catholic viewpoint were heretical. The ruler of Saxony, Elector Frederick the Wise, gave him all possible protection.[6]

Luther was finally excommunicated by the pope in 1520. Having obtained a copy of the papal declaration of excommunication, he treated it with contempt and burned it publicly. In the following year he appeared before the Diet, or parliament of the German Empire, at Worms, but refused to make the recantation which was demanded of him. Elector Frederick secretly arranged for him to be taken to Wartburg Castle near Eisenach in the interest of his personal safety. The elector decidedly favored the Reformation movement, but had conscientious scruples against ordering a change of creed for the whole population. He advised the postponement of actual church reformation.

Luther, during his sojourn of nearly a year in Wartburg Castle, made the important decision that the Mass (the most vital Roman Catholic practice) should be maintained until it could be discarded with the consent of the civil authorities. Such a general attitude on the Mass and other points of practical reformation naturally led to a close union of church and state. The Mass was finally abolished in Wittenberg and all Saxony after the death of Elector Frederick, by his brother and successor, Elector John, in 1525. The Lutheran Church was made the state church in Saxony and eventually in all provinces of Germany and the Scandinavian countries whose rulers accepted the Lutheran creed, while the Zwinglian or Reformed Church was made the state church of certain cantons of Switzerland.

Ulrich Zwingli was the leader in the Reformation movement in the German-speaking part of Switzerland, and the founder of the Reformed Church. In passing we may notice that Switzerland was a confederacy consisting of a number of states, called cantons, each of which was governed by a senate or council. Ulrich Zwingli was born in 1484 at Wildhaus near St. Gall, in Switzerland. He was educated in Bern, Vienna, and Basel and was consecrated a priest in 1506. At Einsiedeln he preached in 1518 against abuses in the sale of indulgences. In the same year he was elected head pastor of the city of Zurich, the capital of the canton Zurich and principal city of Switzerland.

Soon after his coming to Zurich an evangelical note became noticeable in Zwingli's preaching. Within a few years he in his sermons openly attacked certain Roman Catholic doctrines and practices. The attitude of the Council of Zurich toward the Reformation movement was decidedly favorable, but the Swiss federal government opposed the movement. The Council of Zurich gave Zwingli full liberty to preach whatever he could substantiate from the Scriptures. Nevertheless, from political motives, the Council took an attitude of compromise, forbidding for the time being all actual deviation from Roman Catholic practice. In consequence Zwingli was permitted to preach against Romanism, but not to abandon Roman Catholic practices. The further development and progress of the Reformation movement in Zurich will be treated in the following chapter in connection with the story of the rise of the Swiss Brethren Church.

Luther and Zwingli were not entirely at one in their teaching. The principal point of controversy between them concerned the doctrine of the Lord's Supper. Luther defended the doctrine of the Real Presence, or the view that the bread and the fruit of the vine are in reality the body and blood of Christ, while Zwingli considered them as emblems or symbols. Zwingli also rejected the doctrine of regeneration through baptism, which Luther retained. It is important to observe that Zwingli, according to his own confession, was led through his controversy with the Swiss Brethren to see the scripturalness of the Anabaptist's teaching that neither baptism nor the observance of the communion is a means of cleansing from sin. Zwingli's teaching on this point was due largely to Swiss Brethren influence.

In a number of states and countries the Reformation, as led by Luther and Zwingli, resulted in the establishment of Protestant state churches. In every instance the rulers who accepted the Lutheran or Zwinglian creed established a Lutheran or a Zwinglian state church. The membership of these churches consisted of the whole population. The rulers tolerated among their subjects no dissent from the creed of the established church.

Establishing a new state church was a simple matter. It was accomplished by the rulers giving orders to the priests within their realm to conform in doctrine and practice to the new creed. The priests were willing to accept these orders of the rulers. The people had no voice in the matter. They saw themselves compelled by the rulers to consider themselves members of the new state church. And it is a noteworthy fact that the abolition of the Roman Catholic creed was to the personal advantage of the rulers. It placed them largely in control of the church and of much of its wealth, in particular the wealth of the cloisters. In the Lutheran provinces and states the ruling prince was recognized as the *summus episcopus* (supreme bishop) of the church in his state. Luther referred to these princes as emergency bishops.

The people in general readily consented to the acceptance of the new faith and practice prescribed by the state. The general attitude of the population was given forceful expression in the second disputation of Zurich (October, 1523) by the prior of the Dominican cloister in Zurich, who said with reference to the pending changes in creed and practice: "Whatever my lords [the Council] may decide and order will be perfectly satisfactory to me, and I shall willingly obey them." Martin Butzer, a leader of state church Protestantism, said on this point: "The people follow the orders of the civil ruler or burgomaster alone [instead of Scripture], and in place of one pope there are now many popes." "Every one fashions his faith to please the crowd and the authorities," said the chronicler Sebastian Franck in 1534; "one must not open his mouth but to worship the god of the country." The same chronicler complains that "no one [besides a comparatively small number of Anabaptists] is willing to bear persecution for his faith."

The readiness with which the Roman Catholic population discarded their creed upon the command of the civil authorities is remarkable, but is to be explained partly by the fact that many were led to see things in a different light, having received pertinent instruction. More surprising is the failure of the populace, in the states in which Romanism had been discarded, to prize the new creed more highly. They showed a like willingness to discard the newly accepted Protestant creed, when commanded to do so by the civil authorities. In Switzerland and Germany the populations of a number of territories and states changed their religious profession again and again upon the command of the rulers.

After the second war of Cappel (1531) certain districts in which Zwinglianism had been introduced by the civil authorities, came again under Roman Catholic governments, and the population of these districts re-accepted the Roman Catholic creed. The inhabitants of the Upper Palatinate were compelled to change their profession four times during the Reformation period. The last change was from the Lutheran to the Roman Catholic faith. "Not less than seven times within a few decades," says J. R. Dieterich, "the population of Oppenheim changed their profession, being compelled to do so." In the large territory of the Electorate of Cologne, under Elector Herman von Wied, a beginning was made in the introduction of Protestantism; but in consequence of political complications the elector was deposed and his work undone. This territory has remained Roman Catholic to this day. The people in general, whether Protestant or Catholic, did not take their faith with sufficient seriousness to be willing to endure persecution for it. The number of Lutheran and Zwinglian martyrs, after the rise of Protestant state churches, is exceedingly small. The Anabaptists complained bitterly that they were ridiculed for their willingness to suffer persecution for their faith.

As previously stated, all dissent or deviation from the creed of the state churches was severely punished and persecuted. Menno Simons wrote concerning the prevalent religious tyranny:

The foundation of the faith and religion of the preachers of the state churches are the mandates of the emperor, kings, princes, and magistrates. Whatever the governments order, the ministers teach; what they forbid they leave undone. . . . It is demanded that one must disregard the teachings of Christ and His holy apostles, and give ear to the princes and official theologians and believe their word—all on pain of being executed on the wheel, or burned at the stake, or killed and murdered in some other tyrannical way, just as if the preachers were to be guided by the orders of the princes instead of following Jesus Christ.

From the writings of both Luther and Zwingli it is clear that in the earlier years of their reformatory labors they defended the principle of voluntary church membership, the need of church discipline, and the independence of the church from state control. It was through obvious compromise that they later consented to the establishment of churches of the kind described above. In plain fact, Luther always recognized that the promiscuous church in which the whole population was compelled by the civil authorities to hold membership, was not a church in the New Testament sense. Often he spoke of the people of the state church as "the rabble" or "the multitude" instead of the church. He frequently said that the general condition of the people (who were identified with the state church) was deplorable, and that he had abandoned the hope for their Christianization.

In the earlier period of his labors as a reformer Luther realized the need of organizing a church whose members from personal choice took Christianity seriously and were determined to walk in newness of life. In April of the year 1522 he expressed this hope, "May we who at the present are well-nigh heathen under a Christian name, yet organize a Christian assembly" in which discipline could be practiced. In the following year he said in a sermon that a separation of the church from the indifferent masses was necessary. Again he stated in the same year that he could not undertake such a separation (or the assembling of a New Testament church), for he had not the people for it. After the new state church, comprising the whole population, had been established (1525), he continued to entertain the hope that true Christian congregations, which consisted of believers and practiced discipline, could yet be organized, though for the time being he consented to the union between church and state.

In December, 1525, he had an important conversation with Caspar Schwenckfeld concerning the establishment of a New Testament church. At that time Schwenckfeld visited him in Wittenberg and called his attention to the fact (admitted by Luther) that the establishment of the new state church had failed to result in spiritual and moral betterment of the people. Schwenckfeld added that in his opinion such betterment could not be looked for unless those who confessed themselves to be in earnest in their Christian profession were gathered into congregations in which scriptural discipline was exercised. Otherwise, he said, things would go from bad to worse, as was even then noticeable.

Schwenckfeld relates further that "Luther regretted very much that no amendment of life was in evidence. As concerned the future organization of the church," Luther according to Schwenckfeld's report said, "he was not fully decided. But he was thinking of entering the names of those who personally confessed themselves to be in earnest in their Christian profession in a book. Among them discipline could be exercised, and he was thinking of preaching for them in the chapel of the former Augustinian monastery, while a chaplain should preach for the others at the parish church." Schwenckfeld says further: "I continued to question him regarding church discipline and asked him definitely what he proposed to do in this respect. He would not answer me on this point." In conclusion Luther said that he had not the people to make the plan of establishing such a church feasible. Schwenckfeld's main reason for pressing the need of church discipline and of the exclusion of unrepentant offenders was, that this was the most essential step toward the recognition of the principle of separation between the church and the world.

Within a few weeks after this discussion with Schwenckfeld Luther published a book in which he again stated the views which he had expressed on the above occasion. He said with regret that there was as yet no Christian church which was separated from the multitude, and pointed out that it would be fully in accordance with gospel principles, if "they who had obtained evangelical enlightenment and who were in earnest in their Christian profession (*die mit Ernst Christen sein wollen*) and who confess the gospel with their lives and tongues," would have their names entered in a book and have meetings separately from the multitude, and observe various evangelical practices including church discipline. He repeated the statement made to Schwenckfeld that he as yet had not the people for such a church.

In various other instances Luther gave expression to regret that such a church could not be organized, because of the difficulty of finding the people for it. In the spring of 1527 he again expressed the hope that such a church would become a reality. It may be observed that Luther's statement that he did not have the people for such a church must not be taken too literally. Obviously the statement means that in his opinion there were comparatively few who would be ready to unite with such a church. The evangelical Anabaptists proceeded to organize a church of such description, and found the people for it. But naturally the civil authorities would not have given permission for the organization of a dissenting church consisting of those who desired separation from the multitude.

On the whole the results of the Lutheran and Zwinglian reformation movements fell far short of what the promising earlier years of the movement would lead one to expect. This is a fact which was freely recognized by the reformers themselves. Luther (who outlived Zwingli a decade and a half) in his later years often expressed disappointment at the final outcome of the Reformation. He stated frequently that the people had become more and more indifferent toward religion, and that their moral condition was more deplorable than ever. His last years were embittered by the observation that the attempted wholesale reformation of the church was successful in only a limited sense. Even before the abolition of the Mass in Wittenberg Melanchthon, the most notable assistant of Luther, wrote: "The common people adhere to Luther only because they think that no further religious duty will be laid upon them. . . . Many believe themselves very pious and holy when they upbraid priests and monks, or eat meat on Friday." The

Lutheran church historian, Professor Karl Mueller, of Tuebingen, Germany, says: "The aggressive, conquering power, which Lutheranism manifested in its first period, was lost everywhere at the moment when the governments took matters in hand and established the Lutheran creed."

An early Anabaptist chronicler stated that a good beginning toward a true reformation of the church was made by the more prominent Protestant leaders in the earlier period of the movement. "However," the same writer says further, "in order to avoid the cross of persecution, these leaders soon joined themselves to the secular government, and thus they relied upon human assistance more than upon God. Therefore their work did not result in greater piety among the people. A change of life could not be observed in them. And although they had made a good beginning, the true light of the truth again became obscured to them."

CHAPTER 6

THE RISE OF THE SWISS BRETHREN

We have before intimated that the fathers of the Mennonite Church in Switzerland were for a number of years identified with the Zwinglian reformation movement. They parted ways with Ulrich Zwingli when, contrary to his former reformation program, he chose a course which would necessarily lead to a union of church and state. Such a union implied a far-reaching modification of his doctrinal position and the disapproval of certain Biblical practices which he had theretofore advocated. Before dwelling further upon the origin of the Swiss Brethren movement, we shall give attention to the fathers of the movement personally.

Conrad Grebel was the recognized leader among the founders of the first Mennonite (Swiss Brethren) church. He was born probably in 1498. His father, Jacob Grebel, a nobleman, was a senator, that is to say, a member of the Council of Zurich (after 1515). Conrad was the oldest of a family of eight or nine children. During his youth the family lived in the small town of Grüningen, the center of a political district of the canton Zurich of which Jacob Grebel was at that time the highest government official (*Landvogt*).

According to the testimony of Zwingli, Conrad Grebel's father was "a distinguished man, held among us in the highest regard." "Jacob Grebel was an honorable, prudent, and in the city of Zurich a very eminent, highly esteemed man," says Heinrich Bullinger, later the successor of Zwingli as the religious head of the Protestant state churches of German-speaking Switzerland. Another contemporary chronicler states that Conrad's father, in the earlier period of the Reformation movement, "supported Zwingli in all that he preached and taught, and assisted him in his efforts."

Conrad, as a boy and youth, attended the schools of Zurich. In the autumn of 1514 he became a student in the University of Basel, and from 1515 to 1518 he studied in the University of Vienna in Austria. While in Vienna he lived with Joachim

30

von Watt (called Vadian) of St. Gall in Switzerland, his intimate, fatherly friend, who was at that time professor of the classical languages in this institution, and who later married Conrad's sister Martha. From October, 1518, to July, 1520, Conrad was a student in Paris. After his return from Paris, he went to Basel to continue his studies, and then accepted a position as proofreader with the printing firm of Cratander in the same city, to assist in the publication of Latin books. The head of this firm, in a letter, referred to him as a young man of excellent talent whose presence was an honor to his establishment. Zwingli, in August, 1522, spoke of Conrad Grebel as a very noble and learned youth. Vadian and a number of others, who learned to know young Grebel, made mention also of his outstanding talents and uprightness of character.[7]

The scholarly attainments of Conrad Grebel and Felix Manz (of whom we shall hear more directly) are attested to by the fact that, as Bullinger states, Zwingli promised to recommend them for the respective positions of teacher of Greek and of Hebrew in the theological school that was planned for Zurich. This school was to be established as soon after the abolition of Romanism as circumstances would permit. Zwingli's recommendation assured their appointment. Before this school was opened, however, both Grebel and Manz had withdrawn from Zwingli's leadership. Bullinger states expressly that they were well qualified for these positions, but "they became possessed with the spirit of Anabaptism to such extent that they were no longer interested in anything whatever except to promote their Anabaptism." Again Bullinger says that they would have been appointed if they had not forsaken the state church and become Anabaptists. Dr. George Finsler, joint editor of the new edition of *Zwingli's Works,* states that Felix Manz was disappointed by the election of Jacob Ceporin as professor of Hebrew at the time of the opening of the theological school at Zurich, in June, 1525. Emil Egli also was of this opinion. Many writers have made similar assertions ignoring the plain fact that at the time of the opening of this school Grebel and Manz were leaders of the Swiss Brethren movement. It is absurd to suppose that Anabaptists could have been appointed to these positions. As just stated, Bullinger says that they would have been appointed, had they not withdrawn from Zwingli's leadership.

Conrad Grebel was a student of the humanities (that is, the liberal arts), and in this sense was a humanist. His letters of that period prove that he was not a religious sceptic, as were some of the humanists. However, he was before his conversion but slightly interested in religion.

In the autumn of the year 1522 Conrad Grebel experienced a religious awakening. Melchior Macrinus, of Solothurn, wrote on October 5, 1522, to Zwingli expressing his joy because Conrad Grebel had become "a distinguished patron of the gospel." On November 21 of the same year, Conrad Grebel in a letter to Vadian expressed deep interest in the study of the Scriptures. His awakening was followed by a thorough conversion which marked a great epoch in his life. He renounced all worldliness and became a zealous student of the Scriptures. In a letter to Vadian, dated July 28, 1523, Grebel wrote: "Pray Christ for me that I may be firm and steadfast in trusting in Him. I shall endeavor to do likewise for you. Further I feel to add that, strengthened by the gift of divine mercy and grace, I mean to bear humbly whatever may fall to my lot." He wrote to Vadian, on December 29, 1522, concerning his mother who was religiously disinterested: "I fear for her soul if she further delays 'putting on Christ' (Gal. 3:27) and becoming a new creature through the Holy Spirit." His later letters and the part which he had in the second Zurich debate show him to have been at that time a man of keen religious interest and deep convictions. Zwingli evidently expected much of him as an assistant in the great task with which he saw himself confronted.

Felix Manz[8] was born about 1490 in Zurich and was educated in the higher schools of Zurich; he also studied in Vienna. He had a good working knowledge of Latin and Greek and had made a specialty of the study of Hebrew. From the beginning he identified himself with the Zwinglian reform movement and frequently served as leader or "reader" in meetings for Bible study. When Zwingli decided in favor of a union of church and state, Felix Manz became a regular co-worker with Conrad Grebel in opposing the proposed establishment of a new state church.

George Cajakob, called Blaurock,[9] was born in the village of Bonaduz in the Swiss canton called the Grisons. He was educated at Chur (Coire), the principal town of this canton, and became a monk in St. Lucius' convent at the same place. When the Reformation movement reached these parts he left the cloister and, toward the end of the year 1524, went to Zurich, the center of the movement in Switzerland, to get in touch with Ulrich Zwingli. A contemporary chronicler relates that Blaurock showed great zeal and had many discussions with Zwingli but did not fully approve his reformation program. He then heard of Conrad Grebel and Felix Manz and was told that they were more thoroughgoing in their endeavors for establishing an evangelical church. After some effort he found them and conferred with them regarding matters of faith. He identified himself with the circle which had formed under their leadership. Blaurock was a man of deep convictions, of zeal and eloquence, "the second Paul" among the Brethren, as some referred to him.

Andrew Castelberger, of the Grisons, was a bookseller who from the beginning of the Reformation movement had assisted in spreading the writings of the reformers in Zurich and vicinity. He was also known as Andrew auf der Stülzen, since he was lame in one of his limbs and was compelled to use crutches. The fact that Conrad Grebel wrote to him in Latin shows that Castelberger was well educated. As early as the summer of 1522 he, with Zwingli's evident approval, held Bible meetings at Zurich. After the division in the reformation party had taken place, he became a zealous defender of the principles and doctrines of those who followed the leadership of Conrad Grebel.

Wilhelm Reublin was a priest at St. Alban's Catholic Church in the Swiss city of Basel where he began to preach against unscriptural doctrine and practice. Great crowds thronged the church to hear his sermons. In the great annual processions it was customary that the priest leading the procession through the streets carry relics consisting largely of what were supposed to be particles of the bodies of departed saints. In the procession held June 13, 1522, Reublin carried the open Bible, saying, "This is the true sacred thing; the other is only dead men's bones." He was banished by the Council of Basel, June 27 of the same year, and went to Zurich where he was appointed priest for the village of Wytikon near the city. In August, 1523, he married, the first of the priests of Switzerland to take this step. On account of a sermon in which he had spoken disapprovingly of infant baptism he was arrested and given a hearing at Zurich in August of the year 1524. Later he was baptized and united with the Swiss Brethren.

As intimated above, the fathers of the Mennonite (Swiss Brethren) Church were for a few years of one mind with Ulrich Zwingli and wholeheartedly supported his reformation program. By the time of the second disputation with the Romanists, on images and the Mass, at Zurich (October, 1523) both Zwingli and Grebel had made marked progress in evangelical enlightenment, nevertheless they still held at this time various Roman Catholic views which later they recognized as unscriptural. Zwingli, for example, intimated in this debate that there was no thought of repudiating the doctrine that the bread and the wine are the real body and blood of Christ.

In this second disputation in which the question of the abolition of the Mass and the images was discussed, a difference became distinctly noticeable between Grebel and Zwingli in their attitude toward practical church reformation. On the last day of the debate Conrad Grebel and his friend Simon Stumpf demanded the abolition of the Mass without further hesitation. Both in this debate and in the writings of Zwingli and his assistants this Roman practice was shown to be altogether unscriptural and contrary to evangelical conceptions. As the debate proceeded Grebel said: "The one thing necessary before all else is the abolition of the Mass. Much has been said [both in this debate and previously] about the Mass but none of the priests is willing to forsake this great abomination." To these words Zwingli replied: "The Council [the civil authorities] will decide concerning the Mass." Zwingli, in other words, indicated that the Mass would be discarded as soon as the Council gave orders to this effect. Thereupon Simon Stumpf addressed Zwingli with these memorable words: "Master Ulrich, you have not the right to leave the decision of this question to the Council. The matter is already decided; the Spirit

of God decides it." The latter expression of Stumpf is clearly
an appeal to the Scriptures as given by inspiration of the Holy
Spirit. Zwingli himself, on the same occasion, spoke repeatedly
of scriptural truth as the teaching of the Holy Spirit. For example, addressing the Council Zwingli said: "I admonish you
with all diligence that you submit yourselves to God in the
things which the Spirit of God teaches and commands." Simon
Stumpf concluded his remarks by stating that if the Council
rendered a decision contrary to the Word of God, that is to
say, if they demanded the further observance of the Mass, he
would not obey them.

With this statement Simon Stumpf, who was priest at
Hoengg near Zurich, gave expression to the attitude of Conrad Grebel and his friends, namely, since Mass is contrary to
the Scriptures and an abomination, there could be no excuse for
its further observance. Simon Stumpf never swerved from his
resolution to cease saying Mass. When after this second disputation the Council decided that all priests must continue saying Mass, he resigned his charge as a priest and served his people henceforth as a minister of the gospel. On November 3,
of the same year, 1523, he was ordered by the Council to leave
the village. A petition of his parishioners to the Council to
permit him to remain was not granted. On November 20 he
was formally exiled from the canton and territory of Zurich.
Simon Stumpf was the most straightforward character among
the Zwinglian priests of Zurich, a man whose conscience re-
volted against doing, for the sake of convenience and policy,
that which was recognized to be sinful, yea, idolatrous and
blasphemous. In point of conscientiousness and strict loyalty
to conviction he differed from all other priests who had accepted Zwinglian views.

We have indicated that a difference between the attitude of
Ulrich Zwingli and Conrad Grebel became noticeable on the
last day of this debate. From this time forward Zwingli began
to deviate in various respects from his former scriptural reformation program. Scarcely a half year previously he had
taught that the civil authorities should be obeyed only in so far
as their orders concurred with the teaching of Scripture. In
June of the year 1523, in his booklet *Of Divine Righteousness,*
he said that it would be an error to suppose that the Mass and

other unscriptural usages should be retained and practiced "until the civil government may give orders to the contrary." He said further at the same occasion: "One must not ask the government in such matters, for the civil authorities are not ordained to rule over the Word of God and Christian liberty, but only over things that are of a secular nature, as I have abundantly shown above."

As already indicated, the three days' disputation in October, 1523, (the second disputation) had been ordered by the Council of Zurich for the purpose of pointing out that the Mass and the images were unscriptural. Zwingli expected and believed that at the close of this debate the Council would order the abolition of these abuses which he declared to be sinful. That this was his expectation is evident from a number of statements which he made in the course of the discussions. He said, for example, that if "my lords" [the Council] further delayed the matter of the introduction of practical reforms, he would not obey them but would preach against them. But when, toward the close of the discussions it became evident that the Council was (for political reasons) not ready to permit the abolition of the Mass, and when at the same time it was seen that Conrad Grebel and others would not consent to the further observance of the Mass, Zwingli decided that a nominal unity of the church must be maintained by the Council.

Zwingli, in other words, thought it best to retrace his steps and to take the position that no changes from Roman Catholic practice must be made without orders from the civil authorities, and yet he recognized the great need of these changes. His final utterance on the last day of the debate was a solemn warning that, as concerned the Mass and the images, no change must be undertaken without the permission of the Council. He demanded that the Roman Catholic practices should be observed until the government would order their abolition. This was a fundamental shift from the position which he had formerly held concerning the relationship between church and state. While in theory he continued to defend the doctrine of the sole authority of the Scriptures, he in reality took the position that in matters of practical reformation the Council was the authority to be heeded. The Brethren declined to follow Zwingli in this departure from his former position.

Thus Zwingli virtually committed the task of church reformation to the civil authorities. The populace was placed under
obligation to accept the religious decrees of the Council as
authoritative and binding. This necessarily led to a union of
church and state, implying that the church, by force of the
civil law, must comprise the whole population. In other words,
this position precluded and frustrated the establishment of a
church of the New Testament type. This new attitude of
Zwingli was obviously at variance with the conception of the
church which he had theretofore defended. In a letter dated
July 24, 1520, he had, for example, written to his friend
Myconius:

Christ hath said to the Apostles, "In the world ye shall have tribulation," and again, "Ye shall be hated of all men for my name's sake,"
and "The time will come when whosoever killeth you will believe he
has rendered God a service." Also the children of Israel, though they
were finally permitted to live in the promised land, were not free from
oppression by the Philistines who tried to entice them to idolatry and
transgression of the divine law and make heathen of them. So also we
Christians will always have those who are persecuting Christ in us,
though they may make ever so great claims for themselves and may
say that they are acting in the name of Christ. For a Christian is only
he who has the characteristic by which Christ would have His own
known when He says, "By this, as by a distinct mark, shall all men
know that ye are my disciples if ye do what I have commanded you."
The question is, Are we striving for worldly glory, or for the glory
of Christ? The more cruel the persecution, the more fearlessly must
Christ's soldiers maintain their position. For I want to tell you frankly, I believe that, as the church came into existence by blood, so it can
be renewed only by blood, not otherwise. And we must not expect a
reward in this world. We must not be offended if men have displeasure in us, but should remind ourselves of the words of Scripture, "If
I yet pleased men, I should not be the servant of Christ," and, "Blessed
are they which are persecuted for righteousness' sake." Never will
the world be a friend to Christ. He sent His own as "sheep among
wolves."

It is readily seen that the conception of the church, as presented in the above quotation and elsewhere in Zwingli's earlier
writings, is not that of an organization united with and protected by the state. Zwingli's earlier conception of the church
was not that of an organization comprising the whole population of a given state without regard to the personal religious

attitude of the individuals. This was not by any means the conception of a church bearing the sword of persecution, a church such as was shortly afterwards established by the Council with Zwingli's consent and co-operation.

By the decision to establish a state church to take the place of the Roman Catholic state church, the immediate outward success of the Zwinglian reformation movement was assured in all cantons and states whose civil authorities favored and embraced the Zwinglian creed. Through this decision the success of the movement was reasonably certain, provided that the Zwinglian cantons were not overcome in a possible war with the Catholic cantons. For such and other reasons Zwingli was finally persuaded that a union of church and state would best serve the cause of Christ. He closed his eyes to the compromises which it involved. The first step in this direction was his consent to the Council's demand that the priests and people must be content with the observance of the Roman Catholic Mass until the Council saw best to abandon it.

Thus Ulrich Zwingli and his collaborators consented to an outstanding compromise which led to other compromises involving vital modifications of their position in various respects. We have already indicated the changes involved in Zwingli's new conception of the church. In his earlier writings he had expressed himself unfavorably about infant baptism. He had also recognized the need of scriptural church discipline, which he however found altogether impracticable in the state church. He had defended the principle of nonresistance and admitted that the swearing of oaths is contrary to the command of Christ. Regarding these points Zwingli now gradually changed his former position, as will be further shown later. It was his deviation from his earlier reformation program that was the cause of the parting of the ways between Zwingli on the one hand and Grebel and his friends on the other. "It must be admitted," says the Reformed (Zwinglian) professor Wilhelm Hadorn, of Bern, "that Zwingli and other Swiss and South German reformers, e. g. Oekolampad and Capito, originally held similar views as the Anabaptists [Swiss Brethren]."

Both Zwingli and Luther believed the Mass to be blasphemy and an abomination, and their collaborators shared this view.

Leo Judae, Zwingli's most prominent co-worker in Zurich referred to the Mass as "a grossly blasphemous practice." Wolfgang Capito spoke of it as "blasphemy against God" and "idolatry more abominable than that of the ancient Canaanites." Martin Butzer said that the Mass is idolatry and "the most grievous outrage against God." In Johannes Oekolampad's opinion the Mass was a greater abomination than any other vices and crimes that could be named. Nevertheless these reformers took a compromising attitude as regards the observance of the Mass before it was abolished by the civil authorities. In a letter to William Farel, dated February 6, 1525, Oekolampad stated that he had advised one of the priests of Basel who had scruples against the observance of the Mass, "to deceive the public" by saying Mass in appearance only, omitting the words which are the most important part of the Mass, and substituting some other words. Mass being said in Latin, and these particular words being uttered in a low voice, the deception would not be noticed. But this stratagem did not remove the offense, since the people were left under the impression that the priest engaged in that which he believed to be blasphemy. This particular priest, however (his name was Jacob Immler), found it impossible to overcome his scruples. He laid down his office and became a weaver.

Grebel and his friends felt the continuous observance of the Mass in Zurich, with Zwingli's consent, to be a violation of evangelical doctrine and principle, and an intolerable offense. This is clear from Grebel's letters to Vadian and to Thomas Münzer. Grebel wrote on December 18, 1523, to Vadian, complaining of Zwingli's inconsistent attitude on the observance of the Mass. Grebel indicated that such an attitude openly compromised the authority of Scripture. He stated that in Zurich God's Word was "compromised, thrust back, fettered," and in a letter to Thomas Münzer[10] he expressed himself similarly. And it was by no means the conscience of Grebel and his friends alone that was burdened by the compromises of which the ruling reformation party was guilty. Dr. Rudolph Stähelin, the author of the standard biography of Zwingli, says to the point: "The prolonged observance of the Mass was felt to be an unbearable burden of conscience after it had been spoken of by Zwingli and his associates in plain words as an insult to God." The historian C. A. Cornelius says: "As correct as was Zwingli's general attitude from the viewpoint of the state, and as great as were the political advantages it secured for his ecclesiastical work, just so inconsistent was it, on the other hand, considered from the evangelical angle, and so sure was it to lead to religious dissensions and conflicts within the reformation movement."

We have seen in a previous chapter that Martin Luther took an attitude similar to Zwingli on the question of a union of church and state. Conrad Grebel, in the name of the circle with which he was identified, wrote a letter to Luther in the autumn of the year 1524. Unfortunately this letter is lost, but Grebel, in his lengthy letter to Thomas Münzer, written about the same time, stated that they had addressed Luther in a letter and had "admonished him to desist from the false sparing of the weak," since Luther defended the view that, out of regard for "the weak," practical reforms should be deferred. To this letter of Grebel Luther never replied. Erhard Hegenwalt, a student at Wittenberg, upon Grebel's suggestion, called on Luther to ask him, whether he had received this letter. "I inquired of Luther," wrote Hegenwalt in his reply to Grebel, "whether he intended to answer your letter. He asked me to give you his regards lest you think him indisposed toward you. And he further said that he was at a loss to know what to reply to your letter." Obviously, then, Grebel's appeal to Luther was at least kindly received.

Of Conrad Grebel and those who stood with him on the great questions of the day, the contemporary Zwinglian chronicler Walter Klarer, of St. Gall, said: "They were for the most part precisely those who before had been the best with us in the Word of God [as interpreted by Zwingli]." So long as they could believe that Zwingli proposed to advance along strictly scriptural lines, they were his most loyal and devoted followers. This is stated by a number of Zwinglian (Reformed) church historians besides the above-mentioned Walter Klarer. Rudolph Stähelin says: "They were of his most faithful and resolute friends." Professor Wilhelm Hadorn, of Bern, states that "they were of the most faithful and zealous of Zwingli's adherents." C. A. Baechtold says: "They were originally the best friends of Zwingli."

The contemporary Zwinglian chroniclers, as also Zwingli himself, stated unanimously that Conrad Grebel, Felix Manz, and their associates insisted on the need of seceding from the Roman Catholic Church and establishing an evangelical church, without depending on permission by the government to do so. Zwingli said repeatedly that Conrad Grebel and others demanded immediate withdrawal from the Church of Rome, and Heinrich Bullinger made the same statement. The chronicler Wolfgang Haller says that Grebel and Manz urged that "the evangelical people should have no further fellowship with Romanism in order to have a pure, separate church." The Zwinglian chronicler Johannes Kessler, of the city of St. Gall, wrote: "Conrad Grebel, Felix Manz, and others were of the opinion that those who had received the Gospel and were now called evangelical, should first of all renounce Romanism and thus have a pure church." Kessler adds that "the ministers of the Word of God in Zurich, above all Ulrich Zwingli," would not permit any withdrawal from the Roman Church. Zwingli's program called for the establishment of a new state church to consist of the whole population just as the Roman Catholic Church comprised the people as a whole. The changes in faith and practice were to be brought about by decrees of the government. Thus an outward religious unity would be maintained, though not without great compromises, such as the continued observance of the Mass until the civil authorities would order its abolition. The heads of the state were determined to maintain the religious unity of the population by the use of force, and Zwingli supported them in carrying out this program.

Conrad Grebel wrote in September, 1524, that the preachers of Zurich (Zwingli and others) had pointed out the errors of Romanism, but, as concerns the true Christian life, there was no change for the better and the ceremonies of the Roman Catholic Church were still observed. "When we ourselves took to hand the Scriptures," he said further, "and studied them with reference to various articles, we were in a measure instructed and were led to recognize the existing lack." "The cause of the failure is the compromising attitude [on the part of the preachers], the setting aside the divine Word and adulterating it with the human word."

Heinrich Bullinger, the successor of Zwingli, in his larger work against the Swiss Brethren relates that Conrad Grebel, Felix Manz, and their friends often assembled themselves. In their opinion, says Bullinger, all that was done by Zwingli at that time toward establishing an evangelical church fell far short of scriptural requirements (the Mass being yet observed in all the churches). Grebel and his associates asserted that "it was necessary to show greater earnestness and determination in matters that concern the church and the kingdom of Christ." Bullinger says further that they came to Zwingli often to protest against the "lukewarmness" and inconsistencies of his general attitude. They felt that the continued observance of the Mass, with Zwingli's consent, was a grave offense. They indicated that God's Word was violated and denied by following the Council's decisions. Grebel and his associates showed that, in plain fact, the authority of the Council was substituted for the authority of the Scriptures.

Bullinger further states the reasons which Zwingli gave for disapproving the program of Grebel and his friends. Zwingli's principal argument was that "there are at this time many respectable people who do not oppose the Word, and concerning whom there is great hope, but who would by our withdrawal [from the Roman Catholic Church] become indignant and contrary-minded." Without question there were many who were at heart Romanists and did not favor any changes, but since the Council had declared itself for the eventual abolition of Romanism, they did not openly oppose Zwingli's preaching. Their practical attitude was one of virtual indifference.

Zwingli himself, in one of his books, gives an obviously correct statement of the plan which the Brethren suggested to him for the organization of a Christian church. He wrote to the point:

They addressed us in the following manner: It goes without saying that there will ever be those who will refuse to yield to the gospel requirements, even in communities which boast of the Christian name [in the so-called Christian states where the whole population consisted of church members]. Obviously it is not to be expected that all inhabitants of a given country would agree to live as Christians should live. The Acts of the Apostles indicate that those who believed seceded from the others. And then, as others believed, they were added to those who had already formed a church. In like manner, they said, we must now proceed. They begged us to make a public statement inviting those who had decided to be followers of Christ to stand with us. They expected that our forces would gain in strength after a separation from the multitude of those who do not believe. It was needful, they asserted, that the church elect its own leaders from the number of the devout. For it was clear that there were many ungodly both in the Council [which ruled the church] and in this promiscuous church [comprising the whole population without regard to their personal religious attitude].

The assertion that Grebel begrudged Zwingli his position of leadership, and therefore inaugurated a movement in which he could be leader, is unfounded. This assertion contradicts Zwingli's own statements. A number of passages in Zwingli's writings indicate that, after he had decided upon the establishment of a comprehensive state church, Grebel and his friends made persistent efforts to dissuade him from taking such a course. They earnestly entreated him to lead out in a movement for a reformation such as was in accord with his former program—a movement for establishing a church independent of the state and recognizing the authority of Scripture alone, disowning the authority of the state in matters of faith and practice.

We have Zwingli's testimony that Grebel and his friends, so far from seeking the honor of leadership, for a long period put forth earnest efforts to persuade Zwingli to become the leader in a thoroughly evangelical movement. Heinrich Bullinger says in particular that only after the failure of their determined efforts to win Zwingli, Grebel and his associates proceeded independently of Zwingli. In his *Book on Baptism* Zwingli wrote in this regard: "Those who among us have started the controversy concerning baptism have previously [namely before they organized themselves, renouncing Zwingli's leadership] often asked us to establish a new church [instead of waiting for the Council's permission for a reformation of the Roman Church]." Before the authorities of Zurich, Zwingli made a lengthy statement of the same import. In his last book against the Brethren, entitled *Elenchus,* he says: "You have asserted oftener than I can say that all will be well if I join you."

In at least three other instances Zwingli repeated and confirmed the statement that they urged him to lead out in a movement for establishing a church which did not recognize the authority of the state in religious questions, and this testimony is corroborated by Bullinger. Zwingli also stated that he was promised definite financial support (undoubtedly by the dissenters) if he would resign his office as a priest. Professor Walther Koehler, of the University of Heidelberg, says regarding Grebel and his friends, "Their pointed criticism of Zwingli's work and their personal attitude were not by any means due to ill will, much less to taking pleasure in strife and contention but rather to a deep religious earnestness." They held that the church should consist of believers, that is to say, of those who personally accepted Christ and whose lives show "fruits meet for repentance."

The principal point of controversy between Zwingli and Grebel was the question of baptism. Grebel and his friends conceived infant baptism to be unscriptural. On this point they upheld Zwingli's earlier views. Earlier Zwingli had entertained unfavorable views in regard to the baptism of infants. He wrote to Fridolin Lindauer, in Bremgarten, "God has commanded to baptize those who have previously believed." In the month of May, 1525, he wrote that "some years ago" (*vor etwas Jahren*) he had been "of the opinion that it would be far better not to baptize infants." Conrad Grebel stated that his own attitude as regards the rejection of infant baptism was due to Zwingli's influence in an earlier period, and Balthasar Hubmaier made a similar statement regarding Zwingli's earlier influence over him. Zwingli's earlier convictions against infant baptism were the result of the study of the Scriptures. He changed his mind on this point for reasons of expediency as will be further indicated. Even later he admitted that the Scriptures do not demand the baptism of infants; he held that the best interests of the church required it.

That Zwingli in his earlier period as a reformer took an unfavorable attitude toward infant baptism was widely known. Balthasar Hubmaier, commenting on Zwingli's printed statement that he had formerly believed it were far better to abolish the practice of infant baptism, says: "Yes, this was your opinion; you have set it forth in writing and have preached it from the pulpit; many hundreds of people have heard it out of your own mouth." Conrad Grebel wrote in December, 1524, to the Council of Zurich: "I am sure that Zwingli is of the same opinion concerning baptism as we, and I do not understand for what reason he does not admit it." "I do not know what to make of it," said Hans Hottinger concerning Zwingli; "today he preaches one thing and tomorrow he says the opposite. And particularly has he preached some years ago that infants should not be baptized, and now he says they should be baptized." A Zwinglian chronicler of Zurich also stated that Zwingli preached against infant baptism.

When Zwingli consented to the establishment of a state church in which membership was to be obligatory for the whole population, he realized that from this point of view the practice of infant baptism was essential. Within a short period he became the most zealous defender of the baptism of the infants. He held that all persons born within the boundaries of the state must be made church members in their infancy. Zwingli, as has been indicated, undertook a reformation of the existing Roman Catholic Church. Roman Catholic baptism and ordination (to the priesthood) were to be recognized. The Roman church was to be changed and "made over" into a new state church. As already indicated, this transition did not imply a change in the constituency, or membership, of the church. The whole membership of the Roman church, that is to say, the whole population of the state, was taken over into the new church without their having a voice in the matter.

The claim of the Roman Catholic population of being Christians was based on their being "christened" (made Christians) through baptism in their earliest infancy without their knowledge or consent. The Brethren realized this to be a deceptive claim. They believed the Christians to be those who personally accepted Christ and followed Him in newness of life. They believed that baptism and admission into the church should follow conversion. The rejection of infant baptism meant among other things that the Brethren would not stop at a reformation of the Roman Church; they proposed a renewal of the church after the apostolic pattern.

In the summer of 1523, when Grebel and Zwingli were yet in full accord, some of the more zealous friends of reform began, with Zwingli's approval, to hold meetings for Bible study. The leaders in these meetings were called readers, since they read and expounded the Scriptures. The readers labored in various parts of Switzerland and South Germany. The chronicler Herman Miles, of St. Gall, speaks of many who traveled through the land as readers, drawing large audiences. This was, he says, the origin of the Anabaptist movement. Another chronicler, Fridolin Sicher, also speaks of the numerous readers and the throngs of their listeners, and adds that such meetings were soon forbidden. In Zurich, Andrew Castelberger, Felix Manz and Conrad Grebel were the most prominent "readers." Meetings were well attended and were spoken of by the people as "schools." They were held at Zurich in the residence of Felix Manz' mother and at various other places. At St. Gall the regular attendants of these meetings called each other brothers and were commonly known as the Brethren, as is clear from the chronicles of Johannes Kessler. They were later called "Swiss Brethren," apparently by the Hutterites.

As early as August, 1524, it was discovered by the Council that among some of those who attended these Bible meetings the baptism of infants had been omitted since Easter of the same year, particularly at Zollikon and Wytikon, near Zurich. On August 11, 1524, the Council gave strict orders demanding the baptism of all infants within a short time after birth; transgressors must pay a fine. Nevertheless, the Bible meetings were forbidden by the Council only after the debate of January 17, namely on January 21, 1525.

The efforts put forth by the civil authorities to check the movement for establishing a truly evangelical church, free from state control, failed. Zwingli preached against the Brethren, denouncing particularly their attitude on the question of infant baptism. The Brethren demanded scriptural reasons for infant baptism, and petitioned the Council to suggest to Zwingli to overcome them with the Scriptures. Thereupon the Council ordered Zwingli to meet his opponents weekly on Tuesdays for discussion. The first of these debates took place on January 10, 1525. At its conclusion both parties claimed the victory. Then the Council decided to have a public debate on infant baptism. In consequence the position of the Council on this point was to be officially stated. True, the Council had, in August of the previous year, forbidden the omission of infant baptism as it had also prohibited the unauthorized removal of the images, although it was their intention to have the images removed at a later date. The Council had never committed themselves regarding infant baptism though it had become clear to them that it was indispensable for the maintenance of a state church. In consequence a mandate was published ordering that "all who held the error that infants should not be baptized" should appear before the council in the city hall on Tuesday, January 17, in the morning, to give reasons "from divine Scripture" for their opinion. This debate took place as planned. Grebel, Manz, and Reublin ably defended the baptism of believers against Zwingli. Heinrich Bullinger, later Zwingli's successor at Zurich, was present and was evidently impressed with the arguments of the Brethren.

Bullinger, in his *History of the Reformation,* gives the following statement of the defense of believers' baptism by Grebel, Manz, and Blaurock on this occasion:

Infants cannot believe nor can they understand the meaning of baptism. Baptism should be administered to believers to whom the Gospel has been preached, who have understood it and of their own accord desire baptism and who are willing to mortify the old man and lead a new life. Of all this the infants know nothing whatever, therefore baptism is not intended for them. Here they cited the Scriptures on baptism from the Gospels and the Acts of the Apostles and showed that the apostles did not baptize infants, but only those who had come to an age of understanding; therefore the same should not be done. And infant baptism, being not in accord with Scripture, was invalid and it was necessary to be baptized anew.[11]

Bullinger says further that Zwingli's arguments for infant baptism in this debate were the same as he afterwards set forth in his *Book on Baptism.* In the preface to this book, written by the editor of the new edition of *Zwingli's Works,* it is stated that Zwingli does not show strong conviction on the point in question; hence this book failed to evoke conviction in others. It is significant that neither Bullinger nor the Council, in their references to this debate, asserted that Zwingli successfully refuted the arguments against infant baptism. In a letter dated February 8, 1525, the Council of Zurich informed the authorities of Schaffhausen of the debate held on January 17. They stated further that Zwingli had shown that infant baptism was *nichts unrechtes* (nothing unlawful).

We have stated above that the Council ordered that for some time discussions should be held between Zwingli and the Brethren every Tuesday. However, a few days after the public debate the Council decreed in a mandate that no further debate would be permitted, and if any one of the dissenters had any question concerning matters of doctrine, they should go to the burgomaster or to the executive committee of the Council (instead of to Zwingli). Zwingli says expressly that he and all other pastors (of the state church) who had attended the public debate of January 17 believed "that it would be not only inadvisable but also *gfarlich* (dangerous) to have further debates with them."

On the day following the public debate the Council issued a decree demanding that all who failed to have their infants baptized within eight days after birth were to be exiled. Three days later another mandate was published ordering Conrad Grebel and Felix Manz to accept the decision of the Council on infant baptism and refrain from holding meetings. A number of men who were not natives of the canton Zurich, among them Andrew Castelberger, were banished. About a week later it was further decreed that baptism must not be administered in the homes of the people but "the new-born babes must be taken to the church and baptized by the priest." The Council having been informed that a number of pastors in the canton had preached against the mandate demanding infant baptism, the officers of the law were given strict orders to have a watchful eye over such and incarcerate in the Wellenberg prison any who would offend in this way.

It is worth noticing in this connection that the decree of the Council just mentioned demanded that all infants must be baptized *by the priests*. The pastors of the state church were the priests. About three months later the Mass was abolished and the ministers ceased to be priests, while even then various other Roman abuses were permitted to continue. Prayer to Mary, for example, was abolished in the state church a number of years later. The Brethren were severely reviled for rejecting this practice. In 1528 Conrad Schmidt, a collaborator of

Zwingli and minister in the Zwinglian state church of Zurich, preached a sermon against the Anabaptists in which he says: "To advance their Caiaphas-like knavery they preach first of all that one should not say the 'Hail Mary' [the well-known prayer to Mary beginning with these words]. Fie upon the devilish, impertinent Anabaptists that they are not ashamed to refuse due honor to the Virgin Mary." Heinrich Bullinger at a much later date severely criticized the Brethren because they believed it quite possible that Mary and Joseph had children after Jesus' birth. Until Easter of the year 1525 the state church of Zurich was the Roman Church.

We have indicated above that the Council decreed that all infants must be baptized and that the omission of infant baptism was to be punished by exile. Zwingli was of the opinion that a definite action of this kind on the part of the Council was all that was necessary for the suppression of the movement led by Conrad Grebel and his friends. Those of the population who were yet at heart Roman Catholic showed unmistakable signs of a willingness to obey the religious orders of the Council, and Zwingli expected Conrad Grebel and his associates to take a similar attitude. He evidently believed that they would submit to the mandate of the Council rather than to suffer persecution.

After the Council had decreed to punish the omission of infant baptism and suppress by the use of force the movement headed by Conrad Grebel, Zwingli intimated in a letter to Vadian, dated January 19, 1525, that the conflict with Grebel and his associates was over, and in the preface to his *Book on Baptism* he made the statement that after the public debate with them he had expected that the attitude of Grebel and his friends would henceforth be satisfactory. In this expectation Zwingli was wholly disappointed. He soon began to realize that the conflict with the dissenters had but fairly begun. A few months later he declared in a letter to Vadian (May 28, 1525) that nothing was accomplished by the measure of persecution taken against the religious party led by Grebel, and that their courage and power remained unshaken. In a later period Zwingli stated repeatedly that his struggle with Romanism was like child's play as compared with his conflict with "Anabaptism," and a similar statement was made by Leo Judae, his principal assistant in Zurich.

The Brethren declared, so Bullinger states, that the use of force and persecution did not solve the pending questions; it did not by any means prove that Zwingli's new program was scriptural. They were fully convinced that the new course pursued by Zwingli was indefensible from the scriptural viewpoint. They had shown prudence and consideration by patiently waiting, so long as such a course could be consistently followed. Eventually they fully realized that the church to be established by the Council would not be a New Testament church but a new state church to take the place of the Roman Catholic state church. The decision of the Council to suppress the dissenting movement convinced the Brethren that it would be vain to hope further for toleration by the civil authorities. They felt that their organization as a church could not be further deferred, and declared that "we must obey God rather than men."

A few days after the disputation of January 17 the Brethren organized themselves as a church. "Within three or four days [after the debate]," says Zwingli in his last book against them, "it was announced that they had baptized fifteen persons." The place where this organization was effected, was in all probability the village of Zollikon, near Zurich. Caspar Braitmichel, a contemporary chronicler of the early Hutterian Brethren, describes the inception of the Swiss Brethren Church as follows:

Conrad Grebel, Felix Manz and others came together and found that there was among themselves agreement in faith. They realized in the sincere fear of God that it was firstly necessary to obtain from the divine Word and from the preaching of the same a true faith which worketh by love, and then to receive the true Christian baptism upon the confessed faith, as the answer of a good conscience toward God (I Pet. 3:21), being resolved henceforth to serve God in all godliness of a holy Christian life and to be steadfast in affliction [persecution] to the end.

And it further came to pass, as they were assembled together, that great anxiety came upon them and they were moved in their hearts. Then they unitedly bowed their knees before God Almighty in heaven and called upon Him, the searcher of all hearts, and implored Him to grant them grace to do His Divine will, and that He would bestow upon them His mercy.

For flesh and blood and human forwardness did by no means lead them to take such a step; for they knew what would fall to their lot to suffer and endure on account of it.

After they had risen from their prayer George Blaurock arose and earnestly asked Conrad Grebel to baptize him with the true Christian baptism upon his faith and knowledge [in contrast to the baptism of the unknowing infants]. And entreating him thus he knelt down, and Conrad baptized him, since there was at that time no ordained minister to administer this ordinance. After this was done, the others likewise asked George to baptize them. He fulfilled their desire in sincere fear of God, and thus they gave themselves unitedly to the name of the Lord. Then some of them were chosen for the ministry of the gospel, and they began to teach and to keep the faith. Thus began the separation from the world and from its evil works.[12]

The event thus described took place as noted above, three or four days after the debate of January 17, 1525. The fact will bear repetition that the Reformed (Zwinglian) state church did not yet exist at this time. Romanism was finally abolished on Easter of the same year by a decision of the Council of Zurich, a bare majority of its members voting in favor of this momentous change. At the time of the organization of the first Swiss Brethren congregation the Mass was still observed in all the churches. Communion services in the state church were held only according to the Roman Catholic rite, the cup being withheld from the laity. Zwingli disapproved the introduction of evangelical communion services, and would not permit the establishment of a non-Roman Catholic church without orders of the civil authorities. The establishment of such a voluntary church by Grebel and Manz, contrary to the orders of the civil authorities and in the face of threatening persecution by the Council, could not fail to make a profound impression on the people in general, especially on persons of a deeply religious nature who were aware of the compromising position taken by the recognized religious leaders. In the light of these considerations it is not surprising that, as Vadian stated, "those who were of a pious, straightforward disposition" were the most susceptible to the teachings of the party led by Grebel and Manz.

CHAPTER 7

THE SWISS BRETHREN IN ZURICH

Twenty-four members of the Anabaptist congregation in Zurich were imprisoned in the Augustinian convent in Zurich early in February, 1525. They were given a hearing and after a short time were released under heavy bond. On March 16, of the same year, the Council of Zurich published a mandate decreeing that all who would henceforth be baptized should be exiled. Many were again arrested and imprisoned, among them Grebel, Manz, and Blaurock with whom Zwingli had a three-day discussion March 20-22. They were on that date called one by one before Zwingli and his assistants, where they were permitted to reply to certain questions of Zwingli.

Twenty-one persons—fourteen men and seven women—were at this time sentenced to imprisonment in the dark dungeon of the Witch Tower. A few of them had candles and materials for striking fire and were thus enabled to read the Scriptures in the dungeon. Grebel, Manz, and Blaurock led their fellow prisoners in their worship and admonished them to steadfastness. After about two weeks the prisoners found it possible to escape, probably with the aid of their friends and patrons among the councilors. Some of those who escaped from prison at this time entertained the thought of going to "the red Jews across the sea," having reference to America and the Indians, in the hope of finding a land of liberty. Blaurock, not being a native of Zurich, was soon after this imprisonment banished with the threat of severe punishment if he returned.

Between November, 1524, and June, 1525, Zwingli published three books against the Brethren, and early in November, 1525, another book[13] in which he defended the state church position and advanced various accusations against the Brethren which they felt to be slanders.

The Brethren had no adequate means for defending themselves and stating their position. True, there had been private and public debates early in the year 1525. The above-mentioned discussions which Zwingli had with them in March of the same year have also generally been considered debates, although on these occasions the leaders of the Brethren were merely brought before Zwingli and were permitted to answer such questions as he would ask them. Zwingli failed to give them the opportunity to express themselves freely and fully. This fact was admitted even by Bullinger, who says the Brethren were sometimes interrupted and stopped by Zwingli and others. Bullinger, peculiarly enough, gives this reason why the Brethren were thus interrupted. He says, it was "because they would say only what they desired to say, and not what they should say."

Conrad Grebel's ardent desire that he be given permission for a defense of the doctrine of the Brethren through the press was never granted. The Brethren asked for a public disputation worthy of the name, a debate in which they would be permitted to present and defend their doctrines freely, and to speak without being unduly interrupted and stopped by their opponents. Two written petitions of the Brethren to the Council are preserved in the archives of Zurich. Both petitions are touching appeals to arrange for a debate worthy of the name. "If it be found then by divine Scripture that we err," they say, "we shall gladly accept correction. . . . We desire nothing upon earth than to have these things decided according to the Word of God." Zwingli and his associates, on the other hand, held, as already stated, that it was dangerous to have public discussions with them. And yet the continuous spread of the Anabaptist movement was a matter of common knowledge. The Council was divided on the question of taking severer measures than imprisonment and banishment against the Anabaptists.

In the autumn of 1525 the Council of Zurich found themselves in a situation in which they were compelled to permit a public debate with the Brethren. In the principality of Grüningen, which was a part of the Canton Zurich and was governed by the Zurich Council, over one hundred Brethren were imprisoned. The magistrates of Grüningen were ordered by the Council of Zurich to send certain of these prisoners to Zurich to be tried and sentenced. This the magistrates of Grüningen

refused to do. They appealed to an old prerogative which gave
them the right to exercise supreme jurisdiction over the citizens
of the principality. The magistrates of Grüningen expressed
sympathy for the imprisoned Brethren who had the courage of
their conviction and had never had the opportunity of defending their faith publicly. Instead of sending the prisoners to
Zurich, the authorities of Grüningen decided to send a deputation of four men with a missive to "our gracious lords" (the
Council of Zurich) petitioning them earnestly and urgently for
two favors: to arrange for a public debate with the Anabaptists, and, if this be granted, to instruct Zwingli to "let the men
of the opposing party have their say in the debate and not to
interrupt or stop them, so that this question may finally be disposed of."

Under these circumstances the Council of Zurich could not
refuse the petition for a debate, but Zwingli was given the
privilege of formulating the topics or questions to which the
discussions were to be limited. None of these topics called for
a discussion of the scriptural reasons for or against infant baptism. One of the sentences presented for discussion contained
the statement that those who allow themselves to be rebaptized
crucify Christ afresh. This is all the more noteworthy since
Zwingli in his previous writings had repeatedly stated that the
points on which the Anabaptists differed from him were of
small importance. Bullinger informs us that four men were
appointed as judges to preside at the debate, that no one would
be interrupted or would be "permitted to speak contrary to
good rules of order." The four judges were leading representatives of Zwinglianism, among them Sebastian Hofmeister and
Joachim Vadian.

The debate began on November 6 in the city hall of Zurich,
but the hall proved too small for the throng of people attending. Hence the succeeding sessions were held in the largest
church of the city. Grebel, Manz, and Blaurock defended the
position of the Brethren against Zwingli and his associates. At
the close of the last session, on November 8, the three leaders
of the Brethren just named were again imprisoned in the Witch
Tower. Martin Link and Michael Sattler were banished from
the canton of Zurich. After a short time the Anabaptist prison-

ers were released with the threat that "if they persisted in their dissent, the most severe punishment would be meted out to them." Immediately after the debate complaints were again heard that in the disputation the Brethren had not been permitted to present their arguments, and were scorned and ridiculed. The Brethren felt that this discussion did not deserve the name of a debate.

Early in March, 1526, Grebel, Manz, and Blaurock and many other members of the Swiss Brethren, also Balthasar Hubmaier, found themselves again prisoners in Zurich. A terrible sentence was at this time pronounced over these men and fourteen other Anabaptists, among them the mother of Felix Manz and five other women who refused to recant. They were condemned to imprisonment for life in a dungeon, on a diet of bread and water. The sentence which was pronounced over them demanded that "they shall remain in the dungeon to die and rot, and in case of sickness no one shall have right to change their prison." This inhuman sentence had the approval of the heads of the established church. Zwingli in a letter made mention of the enactment of these cruel measures. "This day," he wrote to Vadian, "the Council has decided that the Anabaptist leaders shall be cast into the Tower to remain there until they either give up the ghost or recant." He says further that the death sentence would be pronounced over those who further rebaptized, and then adds: "Thus the long tried patience has come to an end." Balthasar Hubmaier who, as noted above, was one of the prisoners, complained in his reply to Zwingli's *Book on Baptism* of "the great severity and torment of this imprisonment."

On the same day when this sentence was pronounced, a mandate was also published by the Council of Zurich, decreeing that any one who would henceforth perform the act of rebaptism should be "drowned without mercy"—without trial or further hearing. The same punishment was to be executed upon those who, having once recanted, were again found attending Anabaptist meetings, and those who had given lodging or food to Anabaptists. Bullinger says: "When all measures proved fruitless and the Anabaptists, contrary to divine and civil rights, continued to promote their sect, Anabaptism was forbidden on pain of death."

Strange as it may seem, it is nevertheless a fact that the men and women who, as stated above, were condemned to the most cruel imprisonment for life, were within a few weeks released, as had also been the case on former occasions. One naturally asks, how is this extraordinary fact to be accounted for? A number of statements made by Zwingli in his letters to Joachim Vadian in St. Gall provide the key to the solution of this question. Zwingli, referring to the trial of the imprisoned Brethren at which the above-mentioned inhuman sentence was pronounced, wrote to Vadian: "In vain did your father-in-law plead for mercy [for the Anabaptists who were to be sentenced]." It may be recalled that Vadian's father-in-law was the councilman or senator Jacob Grebel, the father of Conrad Grebel. And Jacob Grebel did by no means stand alone in the Council of Zurich in favoring a policy of toleration toward the dissenters. A powerful minority in the Council took the same attitude toward the Brethren. This minority of councilmen, with the aid of the patrons of the Brethren outside the senate, found it possible to prevent the carrying out of the cruel mandates and sentences that were passed against them, and even to bring about their release from imprisonment.

The majority of the councilors were agreed upon the severe persecution of the Brethren, but, as stated, they saw their plans thwarted again and again by a small but powerful minority in the Council who stood for a policy of leniency and toleration. The head of this party was Jacob Grebel. Zwingli, in his writings at this time, complained repeatedly of the machinations of Jacob Grebel and "his accomplices," and of the leniency of the authorities in general in these things. And Bullinger, in his first book against the Anabaptists, made the interesting statement that he would present further evidence against them, if to do so were not contrary to the orders of "certain persons."

The "certain persons" whose desires Bullinger saw himself obliged to respect in this regard were obviously of the upper classes. Evidently some of them were members of the Council. They objected to spreading the damaging reports about the Brethren which were founded on mere hearsay. Clearly no one could have prevented Bullinger nor any one else from presenting actual evidence against them. Bullinger personally regarded the Anabaptists with pronounced disfavor. He refers to them as "an accursed sect." Again, in his books he spoke repeatedly of the influential patrons and friends of the Brethren. Both in Zurich and Grüningen the patrons of the Brethren made their influence felt. Zwingli himself stated that at the time "when the Council decreed that he who rebaptized another should be drowned," and when a large number of Anabaptists were sentenced to severe imprisonment "many of the brethren [his own followers] thought what had been done to them was too monstrous." Evidently some of Zwingli's followers looked upon the persecution of the Anabaptists with disfavor.

Conrad Grebel died within a few months after being released from the imprisonment referred to above. After his liberation from prison he went to Maienfeld in the canton called the Grisons where his sister Barbara with her husband and family had their home. He died of the plague at Maienfeld in July or August of 1526. While Conrad Grebel was not the founder of the Swiss Brethren Church in any such sense as Zwingli was the founder of the Reformed Church and Luther of the Lutheran Church, he was the most talented and prominent of the first leaders of the Brethren. As a talented young man of a prominent family, opportunities for a distinguished career in the world offered themselves to him, if he would stifle his convictions, as others had done, and remain with the state church party which enjoyed the favor and protection of the civil authorities.

Conrad Grebel had ardently hoped that the leading reformers would, in agreement with their earlier principles, organize voluntary churches of the New Testament type. He had hoped that, even if a Protestant state church were established, toleration would be granted the dissenters and the sword of the hangman would not be used against them. When these hopes proved disappointing, Conrad Grebel was ready to endure persecution for his religious convictions. For the sake of evangelical truth he counted not his life dear unto himself. He was willing to become an outcast, indeed virtually an outlaw. In consecration and "zeal for the Lord's house" he was clearly the equal of any of those who stood with him. Their ideal was the sincere acceptance and uncompromising carrying out of the whole of evangelical truth and its implications. Although Conrad Grebel's labors extended only over a period of less than three years, yet he accomplished much as a leader in one of the great movements in the history of the Christian church.

Despite the persecution, the cruel imprisonment and the heavy fines exacted, the Swiss Brethren movement spread, particularly in the principality of Grüningen in the canton of Zurich. Again the Council of Zurich sent a mandate to the authorities of Grüningen decreeing that the death sentence must be pronounced and carried out over such prisoners as had been rebaptized, as well as over those who attended Anabaptist meetings. This was a strange demand in the face of the plain fact that even in Zurich the prisoners had heretofore always been finally released. There is clear evidence that the authorities of the principality of Grüningen had conscientious scruples against the execution of Anabaptists. They persistently refused to stain their hands with the blood of the dissenters.

Zwingli and his associates in the work of the reformation of the church believed that the best interests of the church as well as of the state required the carrying out of their reform program, which included, as has been indicated, the establishment and maintenance of a state church comprising the whole population. Establishing such a church, in turn, necessitated the suppression of all dissent and in particular of the Swiss Brethren movement. However, as stated above, the Council of Zurich was not united in its attitude on the persecution of the Anabaptists. As long as a strong minority of the Council, headed by Jacob Grebel, did all in their power to protect the Anabaptists in their loyalty to their convictions, it proved to be impossible to carry out the program of the state church party. According to Zwingli's assertion, Jacob Grebel and others desired the toleration of both the Anabaptists and the Roman Catholics. They entertained the opinion that one of the churches of the city should be restored to the Roman Catholics. Zwingli was staunchly opposed to any such concession; nevertheless he demanded freedom for the preaching of the gospel in the Roman Catholic cantons.

Jacob Grebel was not an Anabaptist. He was a member of the state church and did not oppose the Zwinglian creed, but he disapproved of Zwingli's interference in political matters and of using the civil government to establish his creed and suppress all dissent. Jacob Grebel believed that a church should not, through the state or otherwise, exercise jurisdiction over those who do not voluntarily unite with it. His proposed policy of general religious toleration by the state, implying the abandonment of all persecution, was in direct opposition to the plans and policies of the state church party of which Zwingli was the head. Hence Jacob Grebel represented the great obstacle in the way of accomplishing what Zwingli conceived to be his life task. Grebel was the head of a political party opposing Zwingli's program for a state church. He was the leader of the opponents of the intolerance of the state church. Jacob Grebel deserves mention among the champions of the principle of liberty of conscience.

Jacob Grebel was one of the most prominent and influential councilors of Zurich. Both Zwingli and Bullinger stated that he was an influential, highly esteemed senator. No less than thirty-five times between 1521 and 1525 was Jacob Grebel sent as the official representative of the Council of Zurich to sessions of the *Tagsatzung,* the congress or central organization of the Swiss confederacy. In the first period of Zwingli's reformatory labors, before he decided upon the establishment of a state church, and before he came forward with his other ambitious political plans, Jacob Grebel was one of his most trusted friends and supporters. "Jacob Grebel," says a contemporary chronicler of Zurich, referring to that period, "aggressively assisted Zwingli in all his endeavors." In August, 1523, Zwingli spoke of him as a man who, on account of his integrity, had his full confidence. In a later period Jacob Grebel expressed the opinion that the reformer of the church should "teach the gospel and refrain from meddling in politics."

In various letters to Vadian, written in the second half of the year 1524, Zwingli denounced Jacob Grebel and his "accomplices" as adversaries of the Reformation movement and secret agents of the Catholic Church. He finally perceived that unless he could check and overcome the movement headed by Jacob Grebel, the establishment and maintenance of an all-inclusive state church would prove an impossibility. And not only was it apparent that in that case Zwingli's efforts toward this end would fail, but that he would lose his influence as a political leader as well. The late Professor Rudolf Stähelin said, in his biography of Zwingli, that Zwingli considered the victory over Jacob Grebel as absolutely essential not only to his success but to his existence in Zurich, and that he did not shrink from using any means that would secure for him this victory. Zwingli finally decided upon an extremely arbitrary course to make himself master of the situation.

In October 1526, Zwingli had Jacob Grebel and a few others of his party arrested and tried on the charge of having accepted monetary rewards ("pensions") from foreign potentates for promoting the voluntary enlistment of Swiss men in the armies of these potentates, the Swiss being considered the best fighters. Since the year 1503 the receiving of such "pensions" had been unlawful in Zurich. Nevertheless it was an open secret that many received them, not only previous to the year 1503 but in later years as well. Such fees were in fact sometimes accepted by the Council as a body, and were simply divided among the councilors. For many years the law forbidding pensions was a dead letter. In 1522, however, a strict mandate was passed by the Council, demanding punishment for such transgression. Zwingli now preached against taking pensions, though he himself had formerly (in 1519 and 1520) transgressed in this regard, receiving a pension from the Pope who desired Swiss recruits for his army. In a later period (after 1529) Zwingli openly defended the acceptance of pensions to win the favor of certain foreign potentates.

Jacob Grebel did not deny that he had received pensions, but this had been more than five years before his arrest, namely about the same time when Zwingli also was accepting pensions (previous to the year 1522). Incredible as it may seem, Jacob Grebel was condemned to death on this charge. A venerable old man but well preserved, "with a large snowy beard and snowy hair," as a contemporary chronicler describes him, he was beheaded on October 30, 1526, at the fish market in Zurich.

Jacob Grebel was not condemned to death by the courts of Zurich but by a dictatorial commission, as Zwingli himself speaks of it, consisting of eleven men. For several days during the trial the gates of Zurich were closed to all, except such as had obtained special permission to enter or leave the city. So great was the tension in Zurich that Zwingli's friends in Strasburg feared for his life. The sentence of death was executed immediately after it had been pronounced. Bullinger says that Jacob Grebel himself until the very hour of his execution had no thought at all that such a sentence was a possibility. To the last moment Grebel protested his innocence of any transgression worthy of death.

Again, Bullinger states that Jacob Grebel's execution caused a great commotion and many did not believe that the charge on which he was condemned was the real cause of his death. Bullinger says further: "It was the general opinion that, if he had not been put to death so suddenly, the sentence would not have been carried out." Precisely so, but were not his judges and antagonists aware of this? The last quoted expression of Bullinger means in plain fact that in the opinion of the people Jacob Grebel had done nothing deserving the death penalty. This is likewise the view of various Protestant church historians. It may be observed in passing that Heinrich Bullinger, at the time of Jacob Grebel's death, was a young man of 22, living at Bremgarten, a considerable distance from Zurich. He was evidently unaware of the actual situation in Zurich.

The way and manner of the suppression of the political party which favored a policy of religious toleration brought protests from Zwingli's friends in other cities. He defended himself in letters to his friends in Basel and Strasburg stating that the cause of the Reformation was at stake and a course such as he had chosen was necessary. Zwingli conceded that he had been the principal accuser of Jacob Grebel and had urged the need of severity, since, he says, "These men were to be feared more than the open enemies," that is, those who publicly opposed his teaching. Zwingli's victory over his political opponents was complete, but it was bought too dearly. His opponents on the political field were completely cowed. Nothing stood now in the way of the severest persecution of the Anabaptists.

When, a few weeks after Jacob Grebel's execution, Felix Manz and George Blaurock fell again into the hands of the authorities of Zurich, Zwingli wrote to Oekolampad in Basel: "I believe the sword will be put to their necks." He was right. Felix Manz was executed by drowning on January 5, 1527. The death sentence pronounced over him is an interesting document, giving various reasons for this cruel action. It is stated that he had assisted in causing dissent from the state church creed. "He and others have undertaken to bring together through Anabaptism such as were minded to accept Christ and were willing to give heed to His Word and to walk according to it, and leave the others undisturbed in respect to their faith." The thought is that he believed that people of various religious creeds could live under one civil government and should be tolerated by the authorities. Felix Manz was sentenced to be "handed over to the executioner who shall set him in a boat [on Lake Limmat], take him to the lower cabin, tie his hands with his knees between the arms, thrust in a stick between his arms and knees and, thus bound, throw him into the water and let him die and perish."

Heinrich Bullinger, in his *History of the Reformation*, describes Manz' heroic death. He was led by the executioner from the Wellenberg prison down to the lake, accompanied by two preachers who admonished him to recant and save his life. His mother and brother were also present and encouraged him to constancy and steadfastness to the end. He praised God for grace to give his life for the truth. When he had been tied and was about to be thrust from the boat he sang with a loud voice, "Into Thy hands, Father, I commit my spirit," and forthwith was held under the water by the executioner and drowned. According to the chronicler Wyss his martyrdom took place at three o'clock in the afternoon.

Bullinger states that the constancy of Felix Manz impressed many people. The execution of Manz caused a great sensation. Felix Manz was the first martyr executed by Protestants. The leading reformers, including Zwingli, had in the first years of their labors defended the principle of liberty of conscience and had severely censured Romish tyranny and persecution. Zwingli now saw himself compelled to defend this radical departure from his former reformation program; he was in fact called upon to do so. Wolfgang Capito, the Zwinglian reformer of Strasburg, wrote to Zwingli: "It is reported here that Felix Manz of your city has suffered death and died gloriously." He adds that the Zwinglian cause had greatly suffered on this account. And again, a few days later, Capito wrote: "I greatly desire to obtain information about the unhappy Felix Manz, whether he suffered punishment on account of transgression or because of obstinacy as regards his religious views, and also about the firmness which he manifested in meeting his death."[14]

George Blaurock escaped the fate of Felix Manz at this time because he was not a native of the canton Zurich. The sentence which was pronounced over Blaurock in Zurich demanded that "the executioner shall tie his hands together and strip him of his clothing down to the waist, and then lead him out of the city, striking him with rods until the blood flows as he passes along the street from the fish market to the Niederdorf gate." This sentence was carried out on the day of Manz' martyrdom. Zwingli, in his last book against the Brethren, mentions that Blaurock was beaten so severely that he was brought "near the door of Hades." We find Blaurock somewhat later in the Swiss cantons of Bern and Appenzell.

The governments of the cantons, both Catholic and Protestant, were now determined to take the severest measures of persecution against the Anabaptists. In the summer of 1527 Zwingli wrote letters to prominent persons in the Protestant cantons and states, urging them to give this matter more earnest attention. On August 2, 1527, the Council of Zurich, undoubtedly upon Zwingli's suggestion, invited the governments of Bern, Basel, Schaffhausen, Chur, Appenzell, and St. Gall (that is, all the Protestant cantons in Switzerland) to send delegates to a congress to be held August 11 in Zurich for the purpose of considering what was to be done to uproot Anabaptism. In the letter sent to these governments the Council stated that in the territory of Zurich even the severest measures had failed to check the Anabaptist movement, and that the authorities had received information of the continuous spread of Anabaptism in other cantons. The Zurich Council also addressed the magistrates of the cities of Ulm and Augsburg in South Germany in a similar way.

The proposed congress was held on the date mentioned. The governments of Zurich, Bern, and St. Gall agreed upon a concordat concerning the suppression of Anabaptism. A mandate was consequently published specifying the measures to be taken to this end. In this mandate Anabaptism is spoken of as a "vice," "an un-Christian, malicious, offensive, and seditious weed" which must be destroyed. Anabaptist leaders and ministers and all Anabaptists who once had promised to obey the religious orders of the government should be put to death without further effort to win them for the state church creed. All other Anabaptists should be admonished to recant. If they refused, they should suffer the death penalty. Every citizen was required to report to the authorities all persons who were under suspicion of being Anabaptists.

As indicated above, in the principality of Grüningen, in the Canton Zurich, where the Brethren were numerous, the officials persistently refused to condemn any one to death for his faith. The officials of Grüningen took such an attitude notwithstanding the most urgent orders to the contrary from the authorities of the Canton, the Zurich Council. The officials of Grüningen appealed to a particular prerogative granted this principality by the House of Hapsburg which gave them the right of pardoning criminals (and heretics) that were adjudged guilty of death.

Two ministers of the Brethren, Jacob Falk and Heinrich Reimann, were kept imprisoned in Grüningen for a long period in spite of insistent demands by the Council of Zurich for their execution according to the mandates. The magistrates of Grüningen tried to compromise by sentencing them to imprisonment for life, but the Zurich Council insisted on execution by drowning. The Council of Zurich finally consented to the proposal of the Grüningen authorities to submit the difference of opinion to the Council of Bern for arbitration. The Bern Council rendered a decision in favor of the opinion of Zurich, but even then the officials of Grüningen refused to consent to the execution of the two men. They delivered them to the authorities of Zurich.

Jacob Falk and Heinrich Reimann remained steadfast to the end. They were put to death by drowning in the Limmat River on September 5, 1528. In the archives of Zurich there is kept a brief account of a hearing given Jacob Falk. He refused to give the names of those he had baptized. "He would not be the cause of the persecution and death of his brethren," he said. To the question who had encouraged him to constancy, he replied: "No one has encouraged and comforted me except the Son of God who has redeemed me and will not forsake me."

Many other imprisoned members of the Swiss Brethren

Church in the principality of Grüningen were delivered up to the Council of Zurich in September, 1528. Some of them had been imprisoned for a year and fifteen weeks. Among them were Heinrich Karpfis, and Hans Hotz who later, in 1538, was one of the principal spokesmen of the Brethren in the great disputation held in the city of Bern. All of the prisoners confessed that they had encouraged and exhorted each other, sick or well, in the dungeon at Grüningen, to steadfastness. One of them had lain half a year in the dungeon, and was sick and swollen from his feet to his neck, so that he had to be carried; yet he preferred to die with his companions in the dungeon rather than to be taken to a less rigorous prison to die. In Zurich they all were placed in separate prisons.

Toward the end of the year 1529 Hans Müller of Medicon in the Aar valley was imprisoned at Zurich. "I ask you," he wrote to the Council of Zurich, "that you would not burden my conscience, since faith is a free gift of God; I implore you, ye servants of God, to grant me liberty for my faith."

Conrad Winkler, another minister of the Brethren, was executed by drowning in Zurich, on January 20, 1530. In his death sentence it is stated that he was "for a long time a prominent leader" of this sect. He had successfully labored in many places, particularly in the canton of Basel where in June, 1528, he was apprehended and sentenced to stand in the pillory and then to be beaten with rods while being led by the executioner through the streets of the city. This sentence was carried out. He was sentenced to death in Zurich because "contrary to rigorous mandates he had baptized so many persons that he did not know their number." Just before he was thrust into the water he sang with a clear voice one or two verses of a psalm. Two Brethren, Heinrich Karpfis and Hans Herzog, were executed in Zurich on March 23, 1532.

For about five decades following the martyrdom of these two men, there are but meager data on activities of Brethren in the Canton Zurich. In the great debate of Bern, in 1538, Hans Hotz of Grüningen in the canton Zurich was the principal spokesman of the Brethren.

A mandate of the year 1580, published by the Council of Zurich, states that among the membership of the state church "there are those who abet and give aid to the Anabaptists. They receive them and give them lodging, and thus become abettors to their erroneous doctrine and hedge-preaching." Those who give place to Anabaptists "in buildings, woods or fields, or on their property of any description" were threatened with a fine of ten pounds for every transgression. All who gave the Anabaptists any aid in holding meetings were to be severely punished without regard to person or station. The Brethren were to be sentenced to suffer capital punishment in agreement with the decrees formerly published.

Again, in a petition of the state church clergy of Zurich, addressed to the Council and dated July 31, 1588, complaint is made that "the pernicious sect of the Anabaptists is steadily increasing," not only in rural districts but in the city as well. It is stated in this petition that they have their meetings in both the country and the city. This document furthermore expresses regret that some of the clergy give grave cause for complaint, regarding things which are to be sincerely regretted by all well-intentioned people. The need of the dismissal of such clergymen is urged. "Countless pious, sincere people have been won for the Anabaptist sect." The petitioners personally offer to do all in their power to counteract Anabaptist influence.

In 1601, and again in 1612, the Council of Zurich published mandates against the Brethren. In the latter year, on December 30, a great Anabaptist Edict was published. The edict states that "the erring Anabaptist sect in some places continues to increase." Those who do not attend the worship of the state church, as well as those attending Anabaptist meetings are to be severely punished. All are warned against giving Anabaptists place or shelter in their houses, barns or fields, even if they are of their own families. To buy anything from Anabaptists is strictly forbidden, and all things or real estate thus bought will be confiscated by the government. Furthermore the edict states that any members of the clergy and other officers of the church "who are guilty of the vice of drunkenness, avarice, debauchery" are earnestly warned to abstain from everything that is inconsistent with their calling for "it is these things that give the Anabaptists occasion to withdraw from our church."

As an effort "to win the Anabaptists from their erroneous ways," the Council arranged for a debate with them. The debate was held in Wädenswyl, on January 26, 1613, and was attended by fifteen Brethren, including the bishop Hans Landis of Horgerberg. In the course of the discussions they were asked to render obedience to the Council. They in turn begged the Council to grant them liberty of conscience; in all things that are not contrary to their conscience, they said, they would be willingly obedient. Hans Landis made the statement that often persons came to him weeping and asking to be baptized. Shortly after this debate six Brethren were sentenced to the galleys. Three of them vacillated and yielded, the remaining three, among them Hans Landis, were delivered to the French ambassador in Solothurn. These three men escaped from prison at night, by the assistance of Bernese Brethren. They were let down from the city walls by ropes.

Hans Landis was again seized about a year later, and condemned to death. He was beheaded on September 29, 1614, in Zurich. While he was being led to the place of execution he was composed and calm. The executioner, who was personally acquainted with him, was in great distress. He lifted up his hands to heaven and exclaimed, "God have mercy! I make lamentation to Him that you, Hans, have come into my hands in such a way. Forgive me for God's sake that which I must do to you." Forgiveness was granted, and Hans Landis died "a hero of the faith"—the last martyr of the Brethren in Switzerland.[15] Again, in 1616 three Brethren were sentenced to the galleys.

The Antistes (head of the clergy) of Zurich was at that time Johann Jacob Breitinger who, while not favoring toleration of the Brethren, yet disapproved the most severe measures of persecution. In 1615 he protested against the confiscation of their property and against condemning them to the galleys. He wrote in the same year:

The Anabaptists have their peculiar ways but teach the faith in God the Father, Son, and Holy Spirit. They teach no errors which would exclude a man from salvation, but only such which were held by some of the ancient church fathers. And no one can deny that the Lutherans defend errors which are not of less consequence but are much more objectionable, and at the same time they grossly revile and con-

demn us, and we think nevertheless that we could hold them as brethren, if they would only take a friendly attitude toward us.

Again, Breitinger pointed out that many people are greatly
offended by seeing any one being put to death for his faith. He
said that even the executioners have compassion with such, and
that shedding blood in such a way will only serve to increase the
number of the Anabaptists. People who witnessed executions
have been heard remarking, "Would to God I were where these
Anabaptists are going."

Three Mennonite ministers were imprisoned in Zurich for
22 weeks in the year 1635, and in the same year discussions
were held with Mennonite ministers at three different places of
the canton. The ministers were summoned to appear before
the clergy of the city of Zurich on September 8, 1636, and were
then informed that, if they refused to yield to the demands of
the Council, all their possessions would be confiscated and they
must leave the country on pain of lifelong imprisonment. Many
were seized and consigned to prison, most of them in the dungeons of the monastery of Oetenbach, where they suffered from
the extreme dampness of the place and from undernourishment.
On November 19, 1637, a number of imprisoned Mennonite
men and women petitioned the Council "to be released during
the grievous winter months, because the dungeon is very damp
and unhealthful so that clothing turns gray with mould." The
records contain the names of over twenty persons, men and
women who within a period of nine years (1635-1644) perished
in noisome prisons in the canton Zurich. In this canton, as well
as in Bern, the arrest of the Mennonites was carried out by a
special police force, the infamous "Anabaptist Hunters" (*Täu-
ferjäger*).

As already intimated there were those among the state church
clergy and in other prominent circles who disapproved of the
severest measures against the Brethren. The government saw
the need of defending its course of action. This the authorities
did in a pamphlet which was freely distributed. The Brethren
in turn published a pamphlet in which they repudiated the
charge that they separated themselves from the Christian
church.[16] On the contrary, they said they were being persecuted for abiding by the clear Word of God. They pointed out
that the reformers of the state church type originally had in

many points been of the same mind as the Brethren, but had departed from their own primitive teaching. They made mention of the conflict of the earliest Brethren with Zwingli and Oekolampad and others of the leading reformers. Furthermore they complained of being left to perish in noisome, dark dungeons.

This defense failed of its purpose. The persecution continued. In a cold night in January, 1642, the officers surprised a Brethren prayer meeting, held in a stable, and arrested the participants. In their wet, frozen clothes they were thrown into prison. The minister Hans Müller, who was under suspicion of being the author of the pamphlet just mentioned, endured unmerciful imprisonment for two years. He was eventually liberated on account of failing health, but died soon after in consequence of the ill treatment to which he had been subjected. On February 19, 1660, the government of the Netherlands addressed a letter of intercession for the persecuted Mennonites to the Council of Zurich, asking for them permission to leave the country taking with them their possessions. This was refused. By about the last quarter of the century most of the Mennonites of the canton Zurich had fled, mostly into Alsace and the Palatinate. However, many of the first settlers in the Lancaster, Pennsylvania area, 1710-1727, came from Zurich.

CHAPTER 8

MICHAEL SATTLER AND HIS WORK

After the death of Conrad Grebel (1526) and Felix Manz (1527) Michael Sattler was the most noteworthy leader of the Swiss Brethren. His martyrdom took place only a few months after that of Manz.

Michael Sattler was born about 1495 at Staufen near Freiburg in Baden. Of his youth and early life nothing is definitely known. He was thoroughly versed in Latin, as well as in theology, having probably studied at the University of Freiburg. As a young man and a devout Catholic, he decided to become a monk. He entered the cloister of St. Peter near Freiburg in all sincerity of purpose, but found moral conditions in the cloister very disappointing. Yet, within a short period he advanced to the position of prior of the cloister. He read the ancient church fathers, and through the study of the Scriptures he sought and found enlightenment in evangelical truth. In 1523 he left the cloister and entered the state of matrimony.

In the summer of 1525 Michael Sattler arrived in the canton Zurich, Switzerland. Here he united with the Swiss Brethren and was active as a messenger of the gospel. Very probably he attended the disputation held on November 6 of the same year at Zurich, between the Brethren and the Zwinglian theologians. In consequence he was banished from Zurich on November 18, 1525, and then returned to the vicinity of Freiburg. For a number of months he labored at Horb and Rottenburg in Württemberg, where Wilhelm Reublin had previously been active. Later Sattler went to Strasburg in Alsace.

In this city the Protestant reformer, Wolfgang Capito, who at that time took an attitude of friendliness toward the Anabaptists, received Sattler into his home. Martin Butzer, the most influential of the reformers of Strasburg, had, together with Capito, a lengthy discussion with him. Butzer has been rightfully referred to as the diplomat among the reformers. He put forth every effort to persuade Michael Sattler to take a conciliatory attitude toward the Strasburg state church. Concerning infant baptism both Capito and Butzer could point to their own previous expressions of doubt and uncertainty. They naturally attempted to minimize the existing differences in faith and practice. Butzer made much of the fact that the magistrates of Strasburg had as yet not officially accepted or prescribed a definite creed and had not officially declared their position regarding baptism, though infant baptism was practiced in all churches of the city. He attempted to persuade Sattler of the possibility of the magistrates finally adopting a creed which would prove satisfactory, at least in a measure, from the Swiss Brethren viewpoint.

Nevertheless there existed important differences which could not be explained away. Martin Butzer, on the ground of the text: "The end of the commandment is charity,"[17] defended the view that Christian love should overlook and ignore the differences. More exactly, he urged that love on the part of the Brethren should create in them a willingness to unite with the state church despite the existing differences. But the question of love on the part of the state church leaders toward the Brethren he left entirely out of consideration. Butzer himself was the most persistent advocate of a policy of intolerance and persecution toward the Brethren in Strasburg. This fact he overlooked entirely, and he expected the Brethren to overlook it. He asserted that their refusal to consent to the proposed union with the state church indicated a lack of Christian love.

Some time after these discussions Michael Sattler wrote a letter to Butzer and Capito setting forth and defending his position. In this letter he spoke at length of the nature and function of the church. He showed that, on the ground of the principle of separation, which the New Testament teaches, a Christian church is not a promiscuous multitude, such as constituted the membership of the state churches. He showed that the church in the New Testament sense is a union of believers in Christ who are resolved to render obedience to Him as their Lord. It is not an organization of which every inhabitant is compelled by civil law to consider himself a member, regardless of his personal religious attitude. "True Christians," Sattler says in this letter, "are those who carry out Christ's doctrine in their lives." "They are fellow citizens with the saints and of the household of God; they are not of the world." "They are chosen out of the world; therefore the world hateth them."

"The kingdom of Christ is not of this world." Sattler shows further that the erring should be reproved in love, not persecuted.

Furthermore, Sattler in this letter explained that the existing differences concerned not only the nature or character of the church but also certain points of Christian practice, which are taught in the Word but were disregarded by the Strasburg state church, such as church discipline, the ordinances, nonresistance, and the oath. He repudiated the view expressed by Butzer that the divine commandments are of minor importance, and showed on the contrary that this question involves the authority of Christ and of the Scriptures. For the authority of the Scriptures Butzer and others would substitute charity or forbearance as the final authority.

After his short sojourn in Strasburg we find Michael Sattler again in the district of Horb and Rottenburg on the Neckar river, where he labored with success for a number of months. In the small town of Horb members of thirty-five families united with the Brethren. On February 24, 1527, Sattler presided over a conference of Swiss Brethren held at Schleitheim in Canton Schaffhausen. He presented to this conference a confession of faith which was approved and adopted without a dissenting voice, and was later printed under the title, *Brüderliche Vereinigung etlicher Kinder Gottes* (Brotherly Agreement of Some Children of God), as the confession of faith of the Swiss Brethren. Following is a synopsis of this confession:

1. Baptism shall be administered to all who have been instructed and give evidence of repentance and a change of life, and who believe of a truth that their sins have been taken away by Christ, and who desire to walk in the resurrection of Jesus Christ and to be buried with Him into death, that they may also rise with Him, and to all who desire baptism of us by their own decision with this understanding.

2. Discipline and expulsion shall be used toward those who have surrendered their lives to the Lord to follow Him in keeping His commandments, who have been baptized and profess to be brethren and sisters, and yet stumble and fall into sin or are unexpectedly overtaken. They shall be admonished twice and the third time reproved publicly before the church and expelled according to the command of Christ, Matt. 18. And

this is to be attended to before the communion service, that we may unitedly and in one love break and eat of one bread and drink of one cup.

3. All who partake of one bread in remembrance of the broken body, and of one cup in remembrance of His shed blood, shall be those who have been united by baptism into the one body, of which Christ is the Head.

4. Separation is needful from all evil and wickedness which Satan has planted into the world. This includes abstinence from all use of the un-Christian, yea, Satanic weapons of violence, such as sword and armor and the like. Such weapons shall not be used either for the protection of friends or against foes, on the ground of Christ's words, "Ye shall not resist evil."

5. Ministers shall have the qualifications mentioned by Paul. They shall teach and exhort and assist all the members toward advancement in their spiritual life. When a minister needs material support, he shall be aided by the congregation. If he be driven away, or imprisoned, or suffer martyrdom, another shall at once be put in his place.

6. The civil government is an institution of God outside the perfection of Christ, to punish evildoers and protect the good. In the Church of Christ no other means of correction are used than discipline through admonition and expulsion of him who has sinned. The question is asked, Can a Christian become an earthly ruler if he is elected to such an office? The answer is: Christ was to be made a king, and He fled (John 6:15). We should do likewise and follow Him, and we shall then not walk in darkness. He forbids the use of violence, and says (Matt. 20:25): "The princes of the Gentiles exercise dominion, etc., but it shall not be so among you." Again Paul says (Rom. 8: 29) that the believers are predestinated to be conformed to the image of His Son, and Peter wrote (I Peter 2:21) that Christ has suffered, not reigned, leaving us an example that we should follow His steps.

7. Christ, the perfect Teacher, forbade His disciples all oaths, whether true or false.

In the opening and concluding paragraphs it is stated that "these are the articles regarding which a few brethren have advanced erroneous views, for which reason it was needful for us to meet in conference and declare ourselves on these points."

This statement indicates that the Schleitheim Confession does not represent an attempt at a full statement of the faith of the Swiss Brethren. Those who are referred to as differing from them on these points had obviously caused disturbance in some of the congregations. They are in this document repeatedly spoken of as "false brethren." In all probability they were those who defended the policy of "standing still" as concerned the organization of churches and the observance of the New Testament commands. Michael Sattler, in his letter to the congregation at Horb evidently had these in mind when he says, "Let no one prevail over you to depart from the letter of Scripture which is sealed by the blood of Christ and of many witnesses of Jesus."

The Schleitheim confession was at first circulated in manuscript form. Within a short time at least two editions appeared in print. Ulrich Zwingli, in July, 1527, made the remark that scarcely could an Anabaptist be found who did not have a copy of this confession. The confession was sent Zwingli by a number of his friends, with urgent requests for help in refuting it.

Zwingli thereupon clearly recognized the urgent need for a refutation of the Anabaptist confession, for the benefit of the hard pressed state church clergy. He decided to publish a work quoting at length from the confession, together with his reply. But he feared that, by thus quoting extensively from this confession, he would give the people in general the opportunity to acquaint themselves with the contents of the confession, and would incur the risk of assisting in the spread of Anabaptist doctrine. Therefore he resolved to translate the seven articles of the confession into Latin and to publish them together with his refutation. He immediately carried out this plan. He addressed this book in particular to the clergy of the state church. A majority of the clergy had formerly been priests and had spent years learning the Latin language. Zwingli published the book in the autumn of the year 1527, under the title *Elenchus*. In addition to the refutation of the Schleitheim confession this book also contained a lengthy refutation of a booklet by Conrad Grebel.

Zwingli's translation of this confession, as he published it, is inaccurate. He attempted to show that the Swiss Brethren held insurrectionary, anarchistic views. On the ground of their doctrine of nonresistance he accused them of fomenting a conspiracy against the government. He also accused them of appalling immorality and crimes. Yet the Schleitheim confession itself constitutes a complete defense against any such charges. An American church historian, Professor Samuel Macauley Jackson, of New York University, says of the Schleitheim confession: "It is written in very simple language, showing a very honest and God-fearing mind, and is in itself a triumphant refutation of the charges of fanaticism and immorality which Zwingli brings against the Swiss Anabaptists. In fact, in this book Zwingli shows himself up in a very bad light."

John Calvin also published a refutation of the Schleitheim confession, written in Latin. An English translation appeared in 1544, entitled *A short instruction for to arme all good Christian people agaynst the pestiferous errours of the common secte of Anabaptistes.* He states that the confession was sent him "from a very great distance" with the request to refute it.[18]

During Michael Sattler's sojourn in Strasburg the Swiss Brethren congregation at Horb and Rottenburg was discovered by the authorities. Having returned to Horb he with his wife and a number of others were arrested and imprisoned by the Roman Catholic magistrates in a tower at Binsdorf. From his prison he found it possible to write a noteworthy "letter of consolation" to his beloved brethren and sisters at Horb. He admonished them to a pious walk, and warned them against those who are of a lukewarm, indolent disposition. "Use discipline against transgressors in all love, that the church may be an example in purity and piety, cleansed by the blood of Christ. . . . Be patient in tribulation and have a care that you may not fall short in love without which you can not be a Christian flock." He added that he knew what was waiting for him but that he was, with his fellow prisoners, fully resigned to the will of the Lord and ready to depart and be with Christ.[19]

The imprisonment continued for eleven weeks and three days. In this time the magistrates received various petitions in their favor, indicating that the people in general were impressed by the sincerity and piety of the prisoners. In the trial which took place on May 17, 1527, at Rottenburg, eight errors were laid to Sattler's charge. Sattler was asked whether he and his fellow prisoners desired a lawyer. His reply was to the effect that there had been no transgression of the civil law on their part, and as concerned their doctrines, they were ready to be corrected from the Scriptures. The answer given them consisted partly in the reading of nine articles in which their supposed heresies were laid to their charge. Sattler's defense was masterful. He admitted having taught that a Christian could not use carnal weapons even against the Turks. The Christian, Sattler said, had no other weapon against the Turks but prayer. Persecution was based upon Turkish, not Christian principles.

Sattler and his fellow prisoners were treated with the utmost rudeness and cruelty by the judges and officers, yet he addressed the judges as "ye ministers of God"[20] and in the course of the trial pointed out to them that it was the province of the magistracy to take wrongdoers to account, not those who differ from them in faith. He appealed to the Scriptures.

"Ye ministers of God," he addressed his judges, "if you have neither heard nor read the Word of God, we would suggest that you send for the most learned men and for the book of the divine Scriptures, and that they with us weigh these things in the light of the Word of God. If they show us from Holy Scripture that we err and are in the wrong, we shall gladly be taught, and recant."

Thereupon the officer who represented the state made the angry reply that no other discussion or disputation would be granted him than that which was to be given him by the executioner. Sattler retained a striking calmness of mind, which seemed only to enrage the officer the more. "I tell you," he cried, "if there were no hangman here, I would execute you myself, and believe that I was doing God a service thereby." Sattler's reply was, "God will be our judge." He stated that he and his brethren were ready to suffer what God would permit. They were determined to be steadfast to the end.

The judges then retired to an adjoining room, leaving Sattler to the mercies of the barbarous soldiers. An eyewitness, Claus von Graveneck, described the scene in the court room. He said that a murderer would have been treated with more consideration. One of the soldiers, turning to Sattler, cried, "If you will save your life and escape, I will believe in you." Another drew a sword from its sheath and holding it up, said, "With this they will dispute with you," a word which accords

The Great Council's Hall at Zurich, Switzerland
Important religious disputations were held here, 1523 and 1525.

The Great Minster, Zurich, Switzerland

Zwingli's Church, where he debated with the
Swiss Brethren, November 6 to 8, 1525.

Kehr Mennonite Meetinghouse

The Langnau Mennonite congregation of the Emmenthal, Switzerland,
worships here.

Kapelle Schänzli bei Basel

Schaenzli Mennonite Meetinghouse, near Basel, Switzerland

Etliche schöne

Christliche Geseng/ wie sie
in der Gefengkniß zu Passaw im
Schloß von den Schweitzer Brüdern
durch Gottes gnad geticht vnd gesun-
gen worden.

Psalm. 139.
Die.Stolzen haben mir strick gelegt/das garn haben
sie mir mit seilen auffgespannen / vnd da ich gehen solt
haben sie mir Fallen zugerüstet/Darumb sprich ich zum
HERREN: Du bist mein Gott/ ꝛc.

M. D. LXIIII.

**Exact Facsimile of the Title Page of the Original
European edition of the Ausbund**

Reproduced from the unique copy in the Mennonite Historical Library
of Goshen College

(From Geiser: "Die Taufgesinnten-Gemeinden," Karlsruhe, 1931)

Typical Figure of the Swiss Mennonites of the Eighteenth Century—A Preacher

(From Geiser: "Die Taufgesinnten-Gemeinden," Karlsruhe, 1931)

Typical Figure of the Swiss Mennonites of the Eighteenth Century—A Weaver and Preacher

(From Geiser: "Die Taufgesinnten-Gemeinden," Karlsruhe, 1931)

Typical Figure of the Swiss Mennonites of the Eighteenth Century—A Woman Spinning

with the expression of a certain Anabaptist writer: "The executioner is made the highest doctor who silences all opposition." The soldier found it incomprehensible that Sattler had given up his life of a "lord" in the cloister. His reply was, "According to the flesh I was a lord, but it is better so."

The judges entered the room after having been in retirement an hour and thirty minutes. Deep silence prevailed while the sentence was read. It was worded as follows: "Between the representatives of his Imperial Majesty and Michael Sattler judgment is passed that Michael Sattler shall be delivered to the executioner, who shall firstly cut out his tongue; then throw him upon a cart and with red hot tongs tear pieces out of his body twice, and on the way to the place of execution make use of the tongs five times more in like manner. Thereupon he shall burn his body to ashes as an arch heretic."

Michael Sattler even then did not lose his composure. The old chronicler Veesemeyer relates that his calmness, earnestness, and fearlessness never left him. The aforementioned Claus von Graveneck describes his martyrdom which took place on May 21, 1527. On the morning of that day this noble man of God, in sight of horrible torture, prayed for his judges and persecutors and admonished the people to repentance. He endured the inhuman torture stipulated in the sentence. Then his mangled body was tied to a ladder. He prayed again for his persecutors while the ladder was placed upon the stake. He had promised his friends to give them a sign from the burning stake, to show that he remained steadfast to the end, enduring it all willingly for Christ. The fire having severed the cords wherewith he was bound, he lifted up his hand for a sign to them. Soon it was noticed that his spirit had taken its flight to be with Him whom he had steadfastly confessed under the most excruciating torture, a true hero of the faith. On the same day four other Brethren were executed, and on the day following a number of others. Sattler's wife showed the same steadfastness and courage, and a few days later was drowned in the Neckar river.

Michael Sattler was an outstanding leader and minister of the Swiss Brethren, a man distinguished for his noble Christian character. This fact was acknowledged even by men who were of the state church party. Wolfgang Capito, when he heard of his martyrdom, wrote in a letter to the magistrates at Horb, that Sattler had been a man of great zeal for God and the Church of Christ, though he had been in error on a few points. Capito added that Sattler had stressed the need of consistent Christian living and abstaining from all appearance of evil. This, as already stated, was a characteristic of the evangelical Anabaptists in general. Michael Sattler's aforementioned letter of consolation to the brotherhood at Horb, together with the account of his martyrdom, was repeatedly printed in pamphlet form.[21]

CHAPTER 9

THE SWISS BRETHREN IN ST. GALL

The town of St. Gall, in eastern Switzerland, had for a short period a large Swiss Brethren congregation, exceeding in numbers by far any other of their congregations. The conditions under which the Swiss Brethren movement originated and developed in this town differed widely from conditions prevailing in Zurich and other Swiss cantons. The Council of St. Gall saw no reason for taking an attitude of intolerance and opposition toward the Swiss Brethren movement, therefore from the beginning the movement made rapid progress. The most prominent member of the Council was Joachim von Watt, called Vadian, who somewhat later was elected burgomaster. In this earlier period, before he came more distinctly under the influence of Ulrich Zwingli, Vadian agreed with the Brethren in their disapproval of infant baptism and of a state-controlled church.

As pointed out elsewhere, a movement for Bible study had been launched, with Ulrich Zwingli's approval, at Zurich, as early as 1523. The wave of interest in Bible study proceeding from Zurich reached St. Gall toward the end of the year 1523. In consequence a number of persons of St. Gall, who had been awakened to the need of the study of the Scriptures, asked Johannes Kessler, a well-educated layman who had been a student at Wittenberg, to act as leader in meetings for the study of the Bible. The first meeting of this kind, led by Kessler, was held on New Year's Day, 1524. Zwingli, as already intimated, was heartily in favor of these meetings. In a letter to Vadian he expressed satisfaction over these developments in St. Gall. Within less than two years this movement for Bible study developed into the Anabaptist movement.

From Zurich and St. Gall the movement for Bible study spread to other parts of Switzerland and to South Germany. A considerable number of "readers," men who read and expounded the Scriptures to interested groups of people, labored in various Swiss cantons and German provinces. In St. Gall those who regularly attended these meetings called each other

brothers and were commonly known as the Brethren, as is clear
from Johannes Kessler's chronicle. This was the background
for the later name "Swiss Brethren." In these Bible meetings
any one had the liberty to ask questions or to correct the "reader" from the Scriptures.

The Bible meetings led by Johannes Kessler were held in the
home of Beda Miles, who later united with the Swiss Brethren.
Soon quarters here proved inadequate to accommodate the
throng of interested people. Kessler expounded the first epistle
of John, and, after completing this book, the epistle to the
Romans. In one of these meetings, when Kessler, speaking on
Romans, chapter 6, referred to infant baptism approvingly,
one of his hearers, Laurence Hochrütiner, expressed the contrary opinion, questioning the scripturalness of infant baptism.

Laurence Hochrütiner was born and brought up in St. Gall,
but had for some time lived at Zurich. He had been an attend-
ant of the Bible meetings led by the "reader" Andrew Castelberger in Zurich. When Ulrich Zwingli had taught and preached against the "idols," or images, in the churches and other public places, Laurence Hochrütiner, together with Nicolaus Hottinger, in September, 1523, had removed a wooden crucifix at
Stadelhofen near Zurich. Contrary to Zwingli's advice both
these men were imprisoned and subsequently banished by the
Council of Zurich, because in removing the crucifix they had
acted without authorization. The Council of Zurich favored
the abolition of Romanism but had decided upon establishing
a state-controlled church; therefore they did not permit any
departure from Romish practices without their express consent.
Banished from Zurich, Hochrütiner returned to his native
town of St. Gall. At the time of his departure from Zurich both
Ulrich Zwingli and Conrad Grebel wrote letters to Vadian ex-
plaining that Hochrütiner had done nothing deserving punishment, and giving him warm recommendations. Zwingli, in the
letter to Vadian, said regarding him: "I beg of you to protect
him, a man good and innocent before God. Whatever you may
do for him, consider it as done for Zwingli."

As indicated above, Hochrütiner questioned infant baptism
in a meeting led by the "reader" Johannes Kessler. However,
this was not the first expression of opposition to infant baptism
in this town. In July, 1523, Benedict Burgauer, the head priest

of St. Laurentius Church in St. Gall, in a letter to Conrad Grebel, complained that some had asserted in his hearing that "infants who do not have personal faith should not be baptized." This was before Kessler had begun his Bible meetings. The Swiss federal government, on the ground that Kessler was a layman, objected to his "reading," to which they referred as "preaching." The Council of St. Gall therefore, in October 1524, asked him to cease "reading." He complied with this request. Shortly before Kessler's retirement Conrad Grebel wrote a lengthy letter "to the brethren" (to use Kessler's own words) on the question of infant baptism. Later Kessler became a leader in the Zwinglian state church and wrote an important chronicle entitled *Sabbata*.

The friends of these Bible meetings in St. Gall then asked Wolfgang Schorant, called Ulimann, to read for them. He did so, and the interest manifested by the people in general increased continuously. The meetings were held in the guild hall of the weavers which was probably the largest hall in the city. Ulimann was of a prominent St. Gall family. His father was the chairman of the large weavers' guild. Wolfgang had been a monk in the famous cloister of St. Lucius, near Chur in the Swiss canton of Graubünden.

The first congregation of the Swiss Brethren meanwhile had been organized in Zurich, in January, 1525. In February of the same year Ulimann met Conrad Grebel at Schaffhausen and was baptized by him, thus incurring the displeasure of those who desired the establishment of a Protestant state church. A number of prominent citizens of St. Gall approached Ulimann on March 18, 1525, and suggested that with the consent of the Council, he give his Bible readings henceforth in St. Laurentius church, the largest church of the city. The reason for this request is obvious. The Council of St. Gall had appointed a commission of four men for supervising all preaching and teaching in St. Laurentius church, thus aiming to prevent any teaching at variance with Zwinglianism.

In this church Ulimann would not have had the liberty to speak his convictions and teach the doctrine of the Brethren. He therefore declined the suggestion. Besides, the "idols," or images, which were adored by Roman Catholics, were still in the church, and the Mass was daily observed in it. These things were offensive to persons of evangelical convictions. Luther, also, had referred to a certain church in Wittenberg, in which the Mass was still observed, as a *bethaven* (idol house), and Johannes Kessler, at an earlier date, had spoken of the Romanists, who disapproved of his Bible meetings, as *Götzendiener* (idolaters).

About March 25, 1525, Conrad Grebel came to St. Gall and remained until after April 9. He preached in the guild hall of the weavers and baptized a considerable number. Another leader of the Brethren, Eberli Bolt, of Lachen in the territory of Appenzell, came soon after Grebel's departure. Johannes Kessler, in his chronicle, speaks of Bolt as "a good-hearted, pious man, very eloquent and well versed in Scripture." On Easter of 1525 and during the week following, Bolt preached in the open to large audiences from the town and surrounding regions. Many united with the Brethren through baptism. Kessler records that many were baptized in dwelling houses, others in the Sitter, a small stream near the town. The Council of St. Gall placed no obstacles in the way of these activities and developments. Among the councilors, so Vadian states, there were some "who were not displeased with all that the Anabaptists undertook to do."

However, it was finally agreed by a majority vote of the Council that, without resorting to the use of force, an attempt should be made to induce Eberli Bolt to leave the city. On Friday after Easter the Council decided that Bolt should be invited to the house of the burgomaster, "who should ask him to leave the territory of St. Gall." He complied with this request and left the city. Shortly afterwards he was seized by the authorities of the Catholic canton Schwyz and was burned at the stake in the town of Schwyz, on May 29, 1525, the first martyr of the Swiss Brethren. "He was very constant, patient, and valiant to the end and died gladly, calling upon the name of the Lord Jesus," says Heinrich Bullinger who was unaware that Bolt was an Anabaptist. Bolt's martyrdom took place more than eighteen months before that of Felix Manz who has been generally held to be the first martyr of the Swiss Brethren.[22]

From unbiased contemporary testimony it is clear that the Anabaptists of St. Gall took their Christian profession seriously, being determined to exemplify apostolic Christianity. Concerning their walk and life Johannes Kessler says, "Their walk and manner of life was altogether pious, holy, and irreproachable. They avoided costly clothing, despised costly food and drink, clothed themselves with coarse cloth, covered their heads with broad felt hats; their walk and conduct was altogether humble. [Contrary to the common usage] they carried no weapon, neither sword nor dagger, nothing more than a pointless bread knife, saying that these were wolf's clothing which should not be found on the sheep. They would never swear an oath, not even upon demand of the government. And if anyone transgressed, he was excluded by them." Another chronicler of St. Gall states that "their walk and life was quite humble, pious, and holy." The late professor Emil Egli, a prominent historian of the Swiss Protestant (Zwinglian) church, says, "The spiritual characteristics of the whole life of the Anabaptists made the deepest impression on the common people." Johannes Willi, also a Zwinglian historian, says, "They desired the purification of the faith from the many [Roman Catholic] abuses [as was also true of the Protestant state church leaders], but held piety of life to be essential to the Christian profession."

Wolfgang Ulimann continued the work at St. Gall which was begun by Grebel and Bolt. He preached regularly to great throngs of people in the open just outside one of the gates of the city. His message was well received by the people in general. On April 25, 1525, he was summoned to appear before the Council. There he defended the doctrinal position of the Brethren with marked ability. Baptism indicates, he said, that one is determined to die unto sin and live unto Christ and fully obey Him. The Council was divided on the questions involved in the controversy. Evidently the difficulty of refuting the doctrine of the Brethren from the Scriptures was keenly felt. Furthermore if the Swiss Brethren movement was to be suppressed by force and persecution, the Council had erred gravely by letting the movement grow to such proportions, instead of following the example of Zurich and taking an attitude of intolerance toward it from the beginning.

On the following day (April 26) Ulimann, upon request, appeared again before the Council. It was the government's desire, he was told, that he "for the sake of brotherly love should stand still in regard to the observances of baptism and the Lord's Supper until the questions at issue were further elucidated." After some discussion he was asked whether he was willing to comply with the Council's desire and "stand still," awaiting their final decision. He declined to give such a promise and was then threatened with banishment unless he changed his mind within three days. Thus the Council decided upon the persecution of the Brethren.

Four other men, Martin Bomgarter, Beda Miles, Nicolaus Swamberg, and Gabriel Giger's son, all assistants of Ulimann, were also summoned before the Council and given the same orders. Their attitude toward these orders was the same as that taken by the Swiss Brethren in Zurich and elsewhere. The leaders of the Anabaptists of St. Gall foresaw that the Council's final decision could be deferred almost indefinitely and, if given at all, doubtlessly would be a refusal of toleration. They realized that "standing still" under prevailing conditions meant disobedience to plain divine commands; it meant retraction and denial. They declared that, only if they were shown from the Scriptures that they erred, could they heed the orders to "stand still." They did not obey these orders. The Council nevertheless was wary of taking definite measures against them. Apparently the Council found itself unable to agree upon the actual steps to be taken toward the suppression of the movement, hence the threatening persecution was deferred for some time. Meanwhile the spread of the Swiss Brethren, so Kessler states, continued unabated.

About two weeks after the hearing given Ulimann, namely on May 12, the Council decided that the Brethren should present a written statement of their doctrinal position, and that the two most prominent clergymen, Burgauer and Wetter, prepare a written defense of the Zwinglian position. This they were to do within eight days, and meanwhile a general "standing still" should be observed by the Brethren, as concerned the practice of baptism and the Lord's Supper. Any one refusing to "stand still" was threatened with immediate imprisonment. However, the two clergymen just named were unwilling to take upon themselves the task of refuting the Brethren. This must have been disappointing and embarrassing to the Council. Thereupon, Vadian stepped in to act in their stead.

Vadian's decision to write the desired refutation of the doctrine of the Brethren indicates a decided change in his attitude. His biographer, Pressel, says that from the outset he was not disinclined toward the Anabaptists' doctrine and that he considered infant baptism an abuse. In a letter to Conrad Grebel, dated December 28, 1524, Vadian indicated that he had no objection to the position held by Grebel. Again, Grebel, in his letter of May 30, 1525, to Vadian, said that he (Vadian) approved the doctrine of the Brethren. These are indications of the earlier position of Vadian. Upon orders of the Council he now wrote a lengthy defense of the state church position. The Council granted the Brethren, upon their request, two weeks to prepare a reply, but they were again ordered "to stand still" during this period.

Meanwhile Zwingli's *Book on Baptism*,[23] containing his long expected and anxiously awaited defense of infant baptism, was published in Zurich early in June, 1525. Zwingli was fully aware that his former writings against the Brethren had proved inadequate. In a letter to Vadian, written in March, 1525, he remarked that in the defense of infant baptism a change in his own method of interpreting the Scriptures was necessary. Zwingli apparently had misgivings regarding Vadian's attitude toward the Anabaptists. In the same letter to Vadian he stated that Grebel was winning many. "Strengthen yourself," he warned Vadian, "lest you also be led astray by his teaching."

Zwingli dedicated his *Book on Baptism* to the burgomaster, councilors, and people of St. Gall. In the preface he addressed them, warning them not to permit a withdrawal of any portion of the population from the established church. He overlooked the fact that the state church in St. Gall, though nominally Protestant, was yet the Roman Catholic Church, and that he himself defended the right of withdrawal from the Roman Church. In Zurich, so Zwingli said further in the preface to this book, the Council saw themselves compelled to take definite action against the Anabaptists.

At the time when this book came from the press, Zwingli also wrote a letter to Vadian, calling attention to the book and asking him to do all that was in his power toward the suppression of Anabaptism. He refers to the Brethren as the enemies of the gospel, and says that he is engaged in a death struggle

with them, and that his conflict with Romanism was but an
empty show compared with his fight with the Anabaptists. He
adds that these people are spreading in all directions. "Warn
your Council in our name," he entreats Vadian, "that there
can not be greater opposition to the true gospel than this rebaptism."

In passing it may be noticed that Leo Judae, the most prominent associate of Zwingli at Zurich, in a letter to Vadian, stated
the reason why their struggle with the Anabaptists was so much
more difficult than the battle with Romanism. The Romanists,
he says, could be overcome with the Word of God, but not the
Anabaptists. Leo Judae says that the fight with the Anabaptists was by far the most difficult ever undertaken. After Zwingli's death he openly expressed grave doubts regarding infant
baptism.

When Conrad Grebel received word of developments in St.
Gall, that persecution was threatening the Brethren in this city,
he addressed Vadian in a letter dated May 30, 1525, to which
reference has already been made. This letter indicates that in
Grebel's view it was within Vadian's power to prevent actual
persecution in St. Gall and to prevail upon the Council to maintain their attitude of toleration toward the Brethren, if he so
decided. Clearly Grebel believed that the pending decision of
the Council was destined to influence very considerably the
further outward development of the Swiss Brethren movement.
So much the greater was his concern, as St. Gall was the only
place, until about that time, where there had been full toleration for the Brethren. Conrad Grebel entertained strong hopes
that the Council of St. Gall would maintain its attitude of tolerance, and that other Swiss governments would eventually fall
in line with such an attitude.

As stated, this hope hinged on the steadfastness of Vadian
in the attitude which from the first he had taken toward the
Brethren. When Grebel was informed of Vadian's change of
attitude toward the Brethren, he found it difficult to believe
that this change was due to sincere conviction. He was aware
that Vadian had recognized the Brethren as sincere Christians
whose doctrine was not unscriptural. Was it possible that he
now failed to realize the inconsistency of persecuting them?
In the letter to Vadian just mentioned he implored him to be-

ware of innocent blood; he reminded him that while he might misdirect the Council to commit acts of persecution, he could not deceive God.

It was early in June, 1525, that the Council of St. Gall rendered the decision for actual persecution. The Brethren were now definitely forbidden the teaching and practice of their faith in the city and vicinity, on pain of exile. It was decreed that their meetings must cease entirely, and that henceforth heavy fines were to be exacted from those who were baptized. Men were to be fined ten pounds and women five pounds.

Two hundred men, whose personal attitude was known to be satisfactory to the Council, were sworn in and ordered to be ready at any time to appear with their weapons at the city hall. Furthermore these men were charged with the duty to see to it that no religious meetings were held outside the churches and that all other religious orders and decrees of the Council were strictly observed. These precautionary measures, taken by the Council, may have been partly inspired by fear of an insurrection, since Zwingli and others charged the Brethren with seditious intentions, but these measures proved entirely unnecessary. The accusation that their teaching on nonresistance was but a cloak to hide sinister aims against the government was without any foundation.

The Swiss Brethren of St. Gall had accepted their faith with the silent consent of the Council. When the Council made the further profession and practice of their faith a crime, their disappointment and displeasure would be difficult to describe. According to Johannes Kessler's testimony their indignation knew no bounds. Recantation was not asked of them (as it was also not asked of the Romanists when the Mass was finally abolished and forbidden), but they were forbidden by decrees of the Council to practice the Christian ordinances, to hold meetings, and to maintain their church or congregation. Those who refused to conform to these decrees were arrested and exiled, unless they left the city on their own accord.

Vadian, who somewhat later was chosen burgomaster of the city, says that the Council of St. Gall found it an indescribably burdensome task to check the Anabaptist movement. The court records of St. Gall contain considerable material relative to the persecution of the Brethren. Hans Kern, called Krüsi, a minister of the Brethren, was banished from St. Gall on June 16, 1525. He was exiled with strict orders to keep silence regarding the treatment which he had received during his imprisonment. Apparently Laurence Hochrütiner and his family were also banished. We find them in August of the same year in Basel. Wolfgang Ulimann and Sebastian Ruggensberger were banished from St. Gall on July 17. Ulimann evidently returned to the city; with Martin Bomgarter he was banished again on September 6 with the threat of capital punishment if they returned.

Again and again Ulimann returned to St. Gall, being in every instance promptly arrested and exiled when he was found by the catchpolls. His father was a prominent man in the affairs of the city, and he had other influential friends and patrons whose intercession prevented severer punishment. After January 22, 1526, when he was again exiled after a long imprisonment, he seems to have avoided St. Gall. In March of the same year he just missed being executed at Chur in the canton of Graubünden. In April, 1528, he was banished from Basel. Two years later he was executed with the sword at Waldsee in South Germany while attempting to lead a number of his brethren from St. Gall and Appenzell to Moravia where there was less persecution than in any other country or province. Martin Bomgarter, apparently a minister of the Swiss Brethren, was sentenced by the Council of St. Gall, on November 19, 1526, to have his tongue cut out by the executioner. The records do not state whether or not this sentence was carried out.

Nicolaus Guldi, a prominent member of the Swiss Brethren congregation in St. Gall, wrote in a letter: "I am forsaken of all the world, of wife, father, mother and sister according to the flesh, and of all men, but it is well. Christ also was forsaken of all men and even of His disciples. It is enough that I be as He." Matthias Hiller, of St. Gall, we find in 1526 at Strasburg in Alsace. On May 21 of the following year he suffered martyrdom in Rottenburg on the Neckar, in Württemberg, with three other Brethren, one of whom, named Geiger, was apparently also of St. Gall. A contemporary chronicler described the execution of these men as follows: "The four men were led out to the place of execution on the same day that Michael Sattler, after enduring the most appalling torture, was burned at the stake. They manifested true Christian courage and stood loyally to the faith and to the Word of God to the end, encouraging and comforting one another. When they arrived at the place of execution, a mounted courier came with a message. The margrave offered them grace and release, if they recanted. They replied that they valued the grace of God more highly than the grace of men and of all the world. With cheerful hearts they knelt down and the hangman did his gruesome work. Matthias Hiller, when his three friends lay dead before him, was again implored to save his life, by recantation. He said quickly, 'By no means; this can never be the will of God. If I had seven heads, I would give them for the name of Christ.' With these words he knelt down, committed his soul to God, and thus ended his life with the others."

There is convincing proof that those Swiss Brethren who stood true to their convictions fled the city and territory of St. Gall. Many of the large numbers of those who had united with them failed in the test. They decided to follow the orders of the Council, to "stand still" as concerned the practice of the Christian ordinances, and to attend the services of the state church. In theory they approved of the faith of the Swiss Brethren, as formerly, but they abstained from teaching and practicing it. This was all that was asked of them by the authorities. The Council held, and quite rightfully, that these "still-standers" were not true Anabaptists. Clearly the faith of the Swiss Brethren would not be perpetuated through these people. We have noted that in Zurich and other cantons, where Anabaptism was persecuted from the beginning, the growth of the Swiss Brethren Church was by no means as rapid as in St. Gall. The consequent persecution brought to light the fact that many who had in this city united with the Brethren had done so in the expectation that the Council would maintain its policy of toleration and liberty of conscience. When the real test came, many joined the ranks of the *Halbtäufer* (Halfway-Anabaptists) who held the faith of the Swiss Brethren in theory, without publicly professing and practicing it.

After the second War of Cappel, in 1531, the Anabaptist movement showed unmistakable signs of increased strength in various parts of Switzerland. The Cappel War was a struggle between the Zwinglian and Catholic cantons, resulting in a crushing defeat of the Zwinglian forces and the death of Zwingli himself. Vadian, who in 1526 was chosen burgomaster of St. Gall, makes mention in his *Diarium* of the fact that in various places, particularly in the canton Zurich, the spread of the Anabaptists again claimed the attention of the civil authorities. In St. Gall also the Council was again called upon to deal with those who transgressed its orders as regards Anabaptism. Vadian states further that in a session of the *Tagsatzung,* or national assembly, held in the Swiss town of Baden, in 1532, the official representatives of Swiss states passed another decree demanding the arrest of all Anabaptists in every part of Switzerland, and the execution of those who declined to recant. Two men and four women suffered martyrdom by drowning in Baden about the time when this order was passed.

In June of the year 1532 the Council of St. Gall learned that a minister of the Brethren, Hans Marquart of Weissenhorn, had repeatedly preached in and near a private house in the vicinity of the city. Hans Marquart who, as Vadian says, was an eloquent speaker and had a thorough knowledge of the Scriptures, had formerly been priest in the city of Constance, then for about three years Zwinglian preacher at Reinach in the canton Bern, and had then united with the Swiss Brethren. His preaching near St. Gall was attended by large numbers, and resulted in the awakening of many. Among those who were reached and decisively influenced by him was Master Conrad, the executioner of St. Gall, who had led an evil life but now turned to God in sincere repentance. When a certain criminal who had committed murder was sentenced to death and was to be executed, Master Conrad handed in his resignation declaring that he would never again take human life. However he had not been baptized. The question how to deal with him was laid before the Council by the burgomaster. A strong minority of the councilors were of the opinion that a measure of toleration should be granted the Anabaptists, and that there was scarcely occasion for any action against them, but the majority sided with the burgomaster who took an attitude of intolerance toward the Brethren.

Hans Marquart was arrested and it was decided, before passing sentence, to arrange for a public debate between him and spokesmen of the state church, including Vadian. The de-

bate was held June 19 to 21, 1532. On the first day the meetings were held in a room of the town hall but, beginning on the
morning of the second day, in the large hall of the weavers'
guild. Vadian has given us a valuable account of this debate
showing the thoroughly evangelical position held by Marquart.
Within a few days he was banished from St. Gall. Three others, among them Otmar Roth, were exiled because they had
assisted in arranging for Anabaptist meetings and had given
lodging to Anabaptists.[24]

An indirect cause for the early rapid growth of the Swiss
Brethren Church in St. Gall was undoubtedly the course taken
by the Zwinglian leaders of the town, as well as by a majority
of the Council of the city, in matters of practical church reformation. They dealt with these questions in much the same
way as did the leaders and officials at Zurich. On April 4, 1524,
the Council of St. Gall had instructed the priests to preach only
what could be substantiated by the Scriptures. The meaning
of this order was that they should preach Zwinglian doctrine.
However for political reasons the Council did not yet permit the
practice of Zwinglian doctrine. Until the summer of 1525 the
priests of St. Gall were compelled to observe Mass, although
theoretically the Mass could be denounced by them as sin and
blasphemy. This inconsistent attitude on the part of the established church explains why many of those who were seriously
interested in religion felt themselves drawn to the Brethren.
After the summer of 1525 the priests had been permitted to
omit the Mass, although it was not officially abolished until
some time in 1528.

Without doubt these conditions were factors in preparing
the people for an uncompromising evangelical message, such
as the Brethren had to offer them. Small wonder that, as Vadian states, "none were more susceptible to the doctrine of the
Anabaptists than those who were inclined to piety and uprightness of life." When Zwingli's *Book on Baptism* appeared in
print, early in June, 1525, some of the more important parts
of this book were publicly read in St. Laurentius Church. Johannes Kessler, who recorded this occurrence in his chronicle,
says that the arguments presented in this book by Zwingli failed
to carry conviction to the hearers. The majority of those assembled in the church at the time, according to Kessler, believed

"that the truth of God was on the side of the Anabaptists." He states further that "the Christian [Zwinglian] congregation worshiping in St. Laurentius Church decreased daily, and those who withdrew united with the Anabaptists." The membership of the Anabaptist congregation in St. Gall was variously estimated at from 800 to 1,000.

The Anabaptist congregation was suppressed in St. Gall through the persecution described above. Those who stood true, fled the city. And yet there is interesting evidence that Anabaptist influence continued to live in St. Gall. It made itself felt even among some of the clergy of the city. When in 1528 the Romish communion service was finally discarded and the evangelical observance introduced in St. Gall, the Council of the city, as well as the clergy expressed the opinion that "church discipline, according to Matthew 18 and I Corinthians 5, should also be introduced." However, the opposition to discipline in the state church proved too strong for such an attempt. Dominic Zili, formerly schoolmaster, then preacher in St. Gall, was a zealous defender of the need of church discipline. In a synod of the Reformed state church, held in 1529 at Rheineck, the use of discipline was decided upon for St. Gall and some adjoining districts, but this decision was not carried out. Zili also demanded the prohibition of worldly amusements, such as dancing. In various successive synods he sharply contradicted and criticized Zwingli, who was personally present, for denying the need of church discipline. Evidently Zwingli was convinced that under the state church system, such as was in vogue in the various Protestant cantons, church discipline was an impossibility. The practice of church discipline had been tried at Basel by Oekolampad and had proved a signal failure. Dominic Zili also objected to the oath which was required for preachers of the state church at their ordination, because it contained the vow of obedience to the Council without making mention of the authority of the Scriptures.

CHAPTER 10

THE SWISS BRETHREN IN CANTON BERN

The canton Bern is one of the largest cantons, or states, of Switzerland. The history of the early Mennonites in this canton is from our point of view of special interest owing to the fact that the great majority of the Mennonite immigrants to Pennsylvania were Bernese or of Bernese descent.

Soon after the organization of the first congregation of the Swiss Brethren in or near Zurich we hear of Brethren in the city of Bern, the capital of the canton Bern. Within a decade this canton became the principal stronghold of the Brethren. In no other Swiss canton, or province of Germany, did the Swiss Brethren Church prosper and expand under the severest persecution as in the canton Bern, particularly in the Emmental (the valley of the Emme river).

The Council of Bern began to favor the Zwinglian reformation at an early date, but for a number of years did not give permission for abolishing Roman Catholic worship and practice. When the first Swiss Brethren came to the canton Bern, Catholicism was still the established church. The abolition of Roman Catholic worship was at that time not tolerated by the authorities, though the priests had been ordered by the Council to preach only what could be substantiated from Scripture as was done in Zurich and St. Gall. But within a few years Romanism was abolished by orders of the Council.

Berthold Haller, the most prominent Zwinglian reformer of Bern, reported to Ulrich Zwingli on November 29, 1525 that the doctrine of the Anabaptists was spreading in the city, and that Lienhard Tremp, Zwingli's brother-in-law, was in danger of being won for their doctrine. On January 13, 1526, the Swiss Brethren were for the first time given attention by the Council of Bern. In April of the following year eight Brethren from Basel, among them Hans Seckler and Jacob Hochrütiner came to Bern. Berthold Haller in a letter to Zwingli, dated April 25, 1527, reported that he had a three hours' discussion with the imprisoned Anabaptists, and had begged them not to take offense at the "idols" (images) which had not yet been removed from the churches and which were idolatrously adored by many.

Berthold Haller was evidently perplexed by the arguments advanced by the imprisoned Brethren. He confided to Zwingli in personal letters that he found himself unable to disprove their doctrine on scriptural grounds. The former lodgings of the Brethren were searched under the direction of a committee of the Council, and a booklet was found which turned out to be the Schleitheim Confession before mentioned, the recognized confession of faith of the Swiss Brethren. The Council committee handed this confession to Haller with the request that he examine and refute it.

Instead of attempting to comply with this suggestion of the committee, Haller immediately sent the booklet to Ulrich Zwingli and asked him most urgently for instruction on how the confession of the Anabaptists could be refuted. Twice in his letter he begged Zwingli to give this request prompt attention. In succeeding letters also Haller entreated Zwingli to assist him in the effort to refute the arguments of the Brethren. These letters indicate Haller's anxiety to meet the expectations of the Council of Bern in this regard. "Help us, dearest Ulrich," he wrote, "to frustrate the designs of these people." Needless to say, Zwingli was not only willing but anxious to act upon this request and give Haller all possible assistance in his conflict with the Anabaptists.

Zwingli now perceived that all he had written against the Brethren—including four books—had failed of its purpose. If Berthold Haller, the leading Zwinglian reformer of the canton Bern, and his associates were unable to cope with the situation and refute on scriptural grounds the teachings of the Anabaptists, evidently the rest of the state church clergy found themselves in a similar or worse predicament. For the benefit, not only of Haller but of the clergy generally, Zwingli decided to publish a refutation of the confession of the Anabaptists. To prevent the danger of thereby assisting in spreading their doctrine, he published the Schleitheim Confession in a Latin translation with a refutation in the same language.[25] He addressed this book to the clergy who had been educated for the priesthood and had a knowledge of the Latin language. The information contained in this book concerning the Anabaptists is even more unreliable and slanderous than his earlier writings about them.

Zwingli feared that the Anabaptists would win the day, unless the executioner was made, as it were, "the highest doctor," whose task it would be to silence all opposition. Reports reached Zwingli of a probability that Berthold Haller himself was being won for the cause of the Anabaptists. Indeed, Haller informed Zwingli that he had refused to approve of capital punishment in the persecution of these people. In another letter to Zwingli Haller remarked that the Anabaptists were taking a strict attitude against sin and immorality, while so much could not be said of many of those who were in authority in both state and church.

Differing decidedly from Zwingli in this respect Berthold Haller was burdened in conscience about the cruel persecution of devoted Christians. He recognized the piety and zeal of the Brethren, and continued to hope that ways and means would yet be found for suppressing the movement without resorting to further executions. In a letter to Martin Butzer, of Strasburg, Haller stated: "We realize that the best and the most sincere people are being seduced by the Anabaptists." In the same letter he speaks of the danger of being accused of shedding innocent blood. To Heinrich Bullinger Haller wrote: "The Anabaptists have meetings frequently. They shun open sin and take a strict attitude against it. They zealously adhere to their rules of conduct, and thus make an impression on the well-meaning." In a mandate of the Council of Bern, addressed to the district magistrates of the canton, it is stated that "the Anabaptists are easily recognized by their way and manner of life and conduct." Within a few years, however, Haller reversed his attitude in this regard. He decided to fall in line with the leading reformers of the state church type and to approve of the severest measures toward the suppression of the Anabaptists.

The Anabaptist movement spread notwithstanding persecution. Even a member of the Council, Vincent Spaeting, took sides with the Brethren for a time. The first martyrs executed in Bern were the ministers Hans Seckler, Hans Treyer, and

Heini Seiler who were drowned in the Aare river in July, 1529. Conrad Eicher, of Steffisburg in the Emmental, a minister of the Brethren, suffered martyrdom February 21, 1530. Of the large number that were banished about the same time many, upon orders of the Council, were "held under the water." This means they were submerged in the river by the executioner until life was nearly extinct—a form of punishment which, in the opinion of many, was even more barbarous and cruel than drowning. They were then released with the threat that they would be "drowned without mercy," if they were found again in the territory of the canton Bern. A herdsman at Othmaringen was even ordered not to reflect upon Anabaptist doctrine. Until the year 1534 all executions were carried out by drowning. In November of this year a mandate was published decreeing that Anabaptist men should be put to death by the sword, and women "by the water," as theretofore. In August, 1534, Berthold Haller remarked in a letter to Martin Butzer that the prisons of Bern did not afford sufficient room for the arrested Anabaptists.

A minister of the Brethren, Hans Pfistermeyer, of Aarau, was arrested in Bern in March of 1531. The leading ministers of the state church disputed with him for three days and finally prevailed upon him to recant—a notable victory for the state church. Yet the hopes of the authorities that Pfistermeyer's influence would be a help in opposing and overcoming the Swiss Brethren movement proved vain.

The disastrous religious war of the year 1531, in which the Protestant forces suffered a crushing defeat by the armies of the Roman Catholic cantons, proved a severe shock to Protestantism of the state church type. It created conditions that were distinctly favorable to the further progress of the Evangelical Anabaptist movement. Zwingli himself lost his life on the battlefield of Cappel, in October, 1531. He had been at that time not only the acknowledged head of the church but the recognized leader in the political field as well.

In consequence of this war Romanism was restored in a number of districts in which Zwinglianism had been established by the government. The people in general could not close their eyes to the fact that Zwingli's aggressive warlike attitude toward the Roman Catholic cantons had resulted in disaster. Even a number of influential clergymen of the Zwinglian state church now became completely discouraged. They were led to reconsider some of the questions on which the Brethren differed from the state church. Leo Judae, for example, a prominent Zwinglian minister in Zurich, now took a position favorable to the teaching of the Brethren. In private letters he expressed the opinion that the existing union of church and state was inexcusable. The establishment of a true Christian church, he said, necessitated separation from the indifferent multitude. He saw the need of church discipline and of the abolition of infant baptism. However, like hosts of others, he lacked the courage of his convictions. The attitude of the state church toward the Brethren remained the same.

Since severe persecution, including capital punishment, had utterly failed of its purpose, the Council of Bern after due consideration decided upon a great effort of another nature to check and overcome the Anabaptist movement. A debate was to be held with the ministers of the Brethren in the hope of convincing them of their alleged errors. The town of Zofingen in the district of Aarau in the canton Bern was chosen for the debate, since, as Berthold Haller stated, many of the Brethren would be disinclined to go to Bern, because not a few of their group had suffered martyrdom in the city. Haller, in a letter to Bullinger, referred to the proposed debate as a tragedy. He did not desire a debate. Repeatedly he had met imprisoned ministers of the Brethren, and, as above stated had confided to Zwingli in a personal letter that he was not able to refute their arguments. A general invitation to attend the debate was given the Brethren in public announcements. Four "presidents" and three secretaries were appointed by the Council. By order of the Council the topics to be discussed were chosen and arranged by Haller and his associates.

The Brethren were known to desire a public debate, since many unfounded reports concerning their teaching and life had been circulated, and they were denied the use of the printing press to set forth and defend their doctrine. However, it required some effort on the part of the Council of Bern to convince the Brethren that they could confide in the promise of a safe-conduct for this debate. A few years previously, namely in January, 1528, at the time of a great disputation at Bern between Zwinglians and Romanists, a safe-conduct had been guaranteed to all who desired to attend. A number of leaders of the Brethren, among them George Blaurock, had gone to Bern for this debate, only to find to their sorrow that they were not included in the promised safe-conduct. They were arrested and banished with the threat of execution, if they were again found in Bernese territory. Small wonder, then, that the Brethren hesitated at this time to take the promise of the Council seriously. However, the Council's decision in respect to the debate of Zofingen made mention of the Brethren in particular as included in the safe-conduct.

Twenty-three Brethren came to Bern for the debate, which was held July 1 to 9, 1532. Their principal spokesmen were Martin Weniger, of Schaffhausen, Hans Hotz, of Grüningen, canton Zurich, and Michael Schneider, of Stams near Innsbruck in the Tyrol. Simon Lantz and Christian Brugger, both of the canton Bern, also spoke occasionally. Martin Weniger was apparently the leading speaker on the Brethren's side. Berthold Haller, in a letter to Bullinger, refers to him as a learned, shrewd, and eloquent man. In scholarship Weniger was probably the equal of any of the opponents, and in his knowledge of the Scriptures he surpassed them. He presented his arguments pointedly and effectively.

On the state church side the leading spokesmen were apparently Caspar Grossmann and Sebastian Hofmeister, who were, besides Berthold Haller, the leading clergymen of Bern. Haller and others also took part in the discussions. The Zwinglian state churches of Zurich and Basel were represented in this debate, the latter by Simon Sulzer and others. Practically all state church preachers of the canton Bern were present, having been ordered by the Council to attend the debate or pay a heavy fine.

The first topic was, "Love to God and the neighbor [instead of the written Word of God] is to be the basis for adjusting all differences in this debate." The Brethren declared this statement to be acceptable provided it was not interpreted to mean that love should be made an excuse for sacrificing doctrine and principle to expediency. In other words, they should not be expected from motives of love to yield their scriptural convictions.

In their controversy with Romanism the state church theologians had always given the principle of the authority of Scripture particular emphasis. The Brethren stressed this principle even more than did the Zwinglian theologians against Romanism. Never would the Zwinglian leaders have given consideration to the idea of yielding to Romanism because of love. By now making love or forbearance, instead of the Scriptures, the final authority, the state church leaders hoped to defend the state church position successfully. Oscar Farner, a historian of the Reformed state church, says with reference to the Brethren: "They had in fact the letter of Scripture on their side."

The second topic was the authority for ministerial ordination. The spokesmen of the state church held that ordination must be with the consent of the civil authorities. Addressing the ministers of the Brethren, they said, "You have no right, or authority, to do the work of a minister of the Word; you are going without being properly sent." And again, "We ask of you to prove your authority, or refrain from preaching." They demanded that the Brethren, since they were not legally ordained, must prove their authority to preach by miracles, like the apostles.[26]

The Brethren replied that a Christian church has the right and duty to choose and ordain as ministers such as have the scriptural qualifications. After some discussion a spokesman of the state church stated that both parties agreed that a true church has authority to ordain and send forth ministers. "We will now see," he continued, "whether yours is the true church which has power to choose ministers, or is only a sedition and separation from the true church, and ours is the true Christian church." He proceeded to assert that theirs had the characteristics of a true church while the Brethren could not be recognized as a church. The Brethren pointed out that a church in which the whole population is compelled to hold membership, as was true of the state church, is not a church of the New Testament type. Scripture teaches, they stated, that to become a member of the church, certain well-defined conditions must be met. To consider the whole populace as church members, without regard to their personal standing and attitude toward Christ, is an unscriptural theory of the church. "The test of a true church," said the Brethren, "is that it is distinct from the world and subject to Christ. As long as it is identified with the world, we cannot recognize it as a true church." "A true church is not united with the state." "To establish a Christian church involves more than the abolition of Romish usages."

The Brethren said further: "The apostles first taught, and then baptized the believers." "At the time of the beginning of the Christian Church they who through faith submitted themselves to the obedience of the gospel, who showed by their lives that they repented, who believed that their sins were forgiven; these were received as members of the church."

Church discipline, including excommunication, was the next topic considered. The Brethren criticized the absence of discipline in the state church. The spokesmen of the state church in reply expressed great regret "that the vices which would call for excommunication are found among us." Nevertheless, under a Christian civil government, they said, the practice of excommunicating transgressors was neither possible nor necessary.

Among other topics discussed were civil government, the oath, paying taxes (which the Brethren declared to be a Christian duty), and baptism. Serfdom, or slavery, was defended by the representatives of the state church but disapproved by the Brethren. The spokesman of the latter said that in his opinion the bond servants mentioned in the New Testament Scriptures were not slaves in the ordinary sense, but persons who, on account of indebtedness, had been sold to their masters for a stated number of years, or until they had given service equivalent to the sum for which they had been bought.

On the evening of July 9 the debate was declared closed and the Brethren bidden to leave the town on the morning of the following day, since the safe-conduct was valid only to the end of the debate and until those who had attended it had returned home. Thereafter, it was declared, the mandates against them would be in force as formerly. Before the close of the final session the spokesman of the state church stated that the contrary doctrines of the Anabaptists "were all refuted with clear Scripture," an assertion against which the Brethren made solemn protest. The Council of Bern kept its promise, given at the beginning, to publish a report of the debate.[27]

The Council of Bern gave orders to have the report of this debate read from all pulpits within the territory of the canton Bern. Evidently the Council entertained the hope that the publication and distribution of the printed report would prove a help in accomplishing their purpose of checking the Swiss Brethren movement. This expectation was not fulfilled. In fact, many outside the Swiss Brethren Church had the impression that the outcome of the debate was more favorable to the position of the Brethren than of the state church. Among those who were of this opinion was Nicolaus Zurkinden of Sumiswald in the Emmental, who was the landvogt of that district. It was openly said, even by ministers of the state church, that "my lords [the Council] have arranged for a debate and have been shown to be in error." Six years later, when another great debate with the Brethren was held, the Council of Bern did not consider it best to have the report printed, and the request of the Brethren for a written copy was not granted them.

The report, or protocol, of the debate of Zofingen is one of the most important sources of information on the doctrine and practice of the Swiss Brethren. As a matter of fact, the report does not contain all that was said in the ten days' debate. Again, if there had been a representative of the Brethren among the secretaries, the choice of the material included in it would without question in some instances have been different. Yet there is no doubt as to the reliability of the report in its recorded statements.

The view that this was a debate with the Brethren of the canton Bern only, and that in other cantons the Brethren may have been of other opinion, is unacceptable, as has already been indicated. The two principal spokesmen of the Brethren were not of this canton; one of them was of the canton Schaffhausen and the other of the canton Zurich. Of the three remaining speakers on the side of the Brethren, one was from the Tyrol, and only two were of the canton Bern. At the time of this debate the Brethren in Switzerland (principally in the cantons Bern, Zurich, Schaffhausen, Appenzell, Basel, and St. Gall) were a unit in faith and practice.

"After this debate," wrote a historian of Bern, "the Anabaptists spread and increased in the canton Bern as never before. A number were executed by drowning, but since they suffered death without dismay, their sect continued to increase." "The number of the Anabaptists grows from day to day," wrote Berthold Haller in September, 1532, to Heinrich Bullinger. A few weeks later he again made statements of similar nature regarding them. Besides repeated complaints which Haller made in his letters in this period about the numerical increase of the Brethren in the canton Bern, he stated also that in the neighboring canton of Solothurn they were particularly numerous and had in fact the upper hand. Reports of their further spread came to the authorities of Bern also from the Emmental and other regions.

The Council of Bern, in a letter dated September 6, 1532, addressed to the magistrates of the various districts of the canton, said that "notwithstanding the great pains and expense we had recently with the Anabaptists through the debate at Zofingen," the sect was nevertheless spreading. The civil officers of the district of Aargau were severely threatened by the Council if they failed to show greater earnestness in carrying out the mandates against the Brethren. And not the Brethren only but all those who gave them food or lodging were to be arrested and dealt with according to the mandates.

For a period of a few years there was hesitation on the part of the authorities in Bern to pronounce the death sentence upon imprisoned Brethren. Berthold Haller, as already indicated, had scruples of conscience regarding the persecution of the Brethren. He had been informed that in the city of Strasburg in Alsace, where the Brethren had a congregation since the summer of 1525, none had suffered martyrdom. It was probably upon Haller's suggestion that the Council of Bern, in January, 1533, addressed the authorities of Strasburg, asking for information regarding the rules they had adopted for dealing with the Anabaptists. The Council of Strasburg replied that those Anabaptists who neither held nor attended separate meetings were tolerated in the city, and all others were exiled. In consequence Berthold Haller and Caspar Grossmann advised the Council of Bern that the Anabaptists should be left unmolested if they agreed "to keep their faith to themselves." Thereupon the Council of Bern decided to follow the example of Strasburg and try a policy of leniency. On March 2, 1533, they published a mandate ordering that all Anabaptists should be instructed and corrected by the preachers in a friendly way. "But if they refuse to recant," the mandate demands further, "they shall be ordered to observe silence and keep their faith to themselves. If they comply with this order, they shall not be molested, but shall be protected like others of the inhabitants. However, if they will not consent to this but will teach their error and further sow discord and error, we will not banish, or 'dip,' or execute them but will lay them into prison to be kept there until they die or recant." It was further stated in this mandate that these measures were decided upon because the enforcement of the former mandates against the Anabaptists had proved ineffective, and their number increased continually. This decree is one proof, among many, that the Brethren were not accused of an unsatisfactory attitude toward the laws of the land (excepting church laws).

However, the mandate just mentioned was virtually revoked within a few weeks. On April 4, 1533, a new decree was published by the Council of Bern ordering attendance at the worship of the state church and demanding the general practice of infant baptism. In August, 1534, Haller wrote to Martin Butzer that, since the Anabaptists are no longer exiled, the prisons of Bern were too small for all the arrested Anabaptists. He and his associates, he said further, had advised the Council to banish them. On November 8, 1534, a mandate was published by the Council, demanding that every individual of the population promise under oath to accept the creed prescribed by the Council.

Determined, country-wide attempts were now made to arrest every person who refused to take this oath and subscribe to the creed of the state church. The officers of the law were charged with the task of locating and arresting any Brethren who failed to appear before the authorities to take the required oath. Officers and others, sometimes in considerable numbers, undertook veritable drives ("Anabaptist chases," as the official records refer to these merciless measures) to apprehend the Brethren. A high premium was paid for every member of the Swiss Brethren brought in, and even if a drive proved without results, those who engaged in it were recompensed for their trouble by an ample reward. There are scarcely any detailed records of these inhuman proceedings, and yet there are unmistakable evidences of them.

The accounts of the treasurer of the Council of Bern contain frequent records of amounts paid out "for hunting down Anabaptists" (*Täufer jagen*), and for Anabaptists "brought in" or "delivered up." Not infrequently it occurred that Brethren living near the border of the canton when pursued fled across the border at the approach of the catchpolls or bailiffs. In June, 1535, the magistrates of Bern received word that about three hundred Brethren of Ried, in the canton Bern, had escaped into the canton of Lucerne which was Roman Catholic territory. The Council of Bern wrote to the authorities of Lucerne asking that measures be taken toward arresting them. In various other instances also Brethren when pursued fled from Bern into Roman Catholic territory.

These severe measures of persecution proved fruitless. And once more it was decided to give the method of persuasion a trial. Upon request of the Brethren another long debate was held from March 11 to 17, 1538, in the city of Bern. The list of the names of the Brethren who attended this debate is of interest. Among them were Brethren by the name of Lueti, Neuenschwand, Gerber, Rupp, Huser, Schellenberg, Huntzicker, Kraibill, Schuhmacher, Kolb, Aberly, Ryff, Schindler, Schneider, Sutter, Zougk, Fluggiker, Brugger. Five ministers of the Brethren from other cantons and from foreign countries took part in the debate; in fact these five men were the principal speakers on the side of the Brethren. All who desired to attend the debate were guaranteed safe-conduct.

On the evening of Saturday, March 16, the debate was declared closed and all *Täufer* in attendance were given strict orders to remain until the following day to hear the final decision of "our gracious lords" (the Council). On Sunday morning Bernhard Tillman, president of the Council, read a mandate in which it was stated that the *Täufer* had been found "unwilling to accept instruction from holy Scripture;" "they refused to confess their error and unite with us, the true church of God."

The mandate demanded further that the five men who had come from without the territory of Bern should be led over the border by the police, and if ever again found within the borders of the canton, they should be put to death without mercy with the sword. Those who were natives of the canton and had formerly been exiled, were again banished and sternly threatened with the same punishment if they ever returned again. They who refused to recant, and had never before been exiled, the mandate decreed, may return to their homes and families and sell their belongings and must leave the territory of the canton Bern as quickly as possible. If they return and are arrested, they shall not again be exiled but shall, like the other exiles, be put to death. At least four of the names of those who were present at this debate appear later in the list of the martyrs of Bern.

The report of this debate is kept in the state archives of the canton Bern, constituting a manuscript of 300 closely written pages. This manuscript was incorporated in a series of volumes designated by the collective name of *Unnütze Papiere* (Worthless Papers). The report of this debate is a very valuable source of information about the principles and doctrines of the Swiss Brethren. During the debate the state church representatives gave the Brethren the testimony that they had withdrawn from the state church "from a good zeal;" they said that the best people were won by them. Obviously this is a strong testimony to the falsity of the evil reports which were circulated about them.

In a decree of the Council published within a few months after the debate of 1538 the complaint is made that, despite the recent disputation, the Anabaptist sect increases, and in a mandate dated September 6, 1538, the same complaint is repeated. It was ordered that all ministers, teachers, and leaders of the Brethren should be "put to death without mercy with the sword." Imprisoned Brethren who would not recant should be subjected to torture, excepting women. The magistrates were ordered to hire men for the purpose of lying in wait for their leaders and ministers.

In the year 1541 Hans Franz Nägeli, a high official of Bern, addressed the Council, pleading for a more lenient attitude toward the Brethren. A few years previously he had been delegated by the Council to appear before the king of France to intercede for the persecuted Huguenots. Obviously this led him to make a comparison between the attitude of the Council of Bern toward the Brethren and that of the government of France toward the Huguenots. The Council then published a mandate which was somewhat less severe than the former decrees.

A noticeable increase of the "Anabaptists" in the whole Emmental region was recorded in 1551. In the year 1564 the decree was passed that those who give shelter and food to the Brethren should be punished "by burning down and utterly destroying their houses and barns." There is no evidence that the threat of destroying houses of the Brethren or of those who gave them lodging was carried out in any instance in the canton Bern as it was some other places. In 1567 the Council of Bern decided that children of married couples whose matrimonial bonds were not solemnized by a minister of the state church, were to be considered illegally born and could not be legal heirs of their parents. A new mandate demanding the persecution of the Brethren was issued in 1579.

In a general synod of the state church clergy held in Bern in 1581 the inconsistent lives of the clergy were censured by the Council of Bern. Many of the preachers, it was stated in a publication of the Council, were guilty of offensive sins: "fornication, adultery, blasphemy, drunkenness, avarice," and the like, and this in particular was mentioned as a cause of the spread of the Brethren. On the same occasion a number of leading clergymen rendered a noteworthy "Opinion" regarding the treatment of steadfast Brethren. They deemed it advisable to resort to execution of Anabaptists only in exceptional cases. "For when they are being led out," the clergymen of the canton said in this document, "and while at the place of their execution they speak and deport themselves in a way that many of the spectators are filled with pity and compassion, and marvel at their constancy; and all this has a tendency to predispose people favorably toward their doctrine. Past experiences have given abundant proof of this."

A lengthy mandate against the Brethren was published by the Council of Bern on September 3, 1585. Notwithstanding all efforts of the government, the mandate states, the Anabaptist sect has increased rather than decreased, and further attempts toward its suppression cannot be expected to succeed unless the cause of this evil be removed. "The main reason," this document states further, "why so many God-fearing people, who sincerely seek Christ, are offended and withdraw from our church, is the fact that vices such as adultery, avarice, cheating, usury, pride, profanity, and drunkenness are common among us." The mandate charges even the clergy of the state church with such transgressions. It was decreed that all "Anabaptists" shall be led over the border of the canton by the police. If they ever return they shall be executed without further sentence. Ministers and other leaders who have once been led over the border and are seized within the territory of Bern, have forfeited their lives. Ministers who are not natives of the canton Bern shall be put to the rack to exact confessions regarding their labors. To give shelter or lodging to Brethren, even to closest relatives, is forbidden on pain of a fine of 100 pounds.

Twelve years later, on July 29, 1597, the Council published another mandate against the Brethren. The complaints about offenses given by some of the clergymen of the state church are repeated and exemplary punishment threatened the offenders —one evidence, among many, of the salutary influence of the Brethren on practical Christian life in the state church.

The English *Martyrs' Mirror* contains a list of Swiss Brethren martyrs who were executed in Bern from the year 1529 to 1571. According to a statement attached to this list it was copied from the so-called tower-book, in 1667, by Hans Lörsch, a prisoner who was afterwards sentenced to the galleys and "in chains led down to the sea." When it is recalled that there are not a few cases on record where wardens of prisons were kindly disposed toward the Brethren, it appears quite probable that Hans Lörsch may have been given the opportunity to copy this list. The list was preserved by Christian Kropf, and was later incorporated into the Book of Martyrs.[28]

The list of martyrs just mentioned records nearly forty executions of Anabaptists in Bern. This list is apparently incomplete. According to a statement made by an executioner not a few Anabaptists were put to death secretly at night. In many instances no records of executions were kept. The only available source of information concerning the martyrdom of some of the Brethren are the records of the treasurer of the Council of Bern. These records show that in many instances sums of money were paid grave diggers for burying the bodies of executed Brethren. The names of the victims were not given. There are in these records, many entries, such as, "for burying an Anabaptist," "for burying two [or three] Anabaptists."

At an earlier date the Council of Bern had given orders that persistent Anabaptists should be put to death without trial or sentence, to save the cost of regular proceedings of law. In the territories of Switzerland which were under the direct rule of the Swiss central government a similar ruling was in force. Consequently court records contain no accounts of these executions. This scarcely explains the meagerness of the records, however. It is difficult to avoid the conclusion that the meagerness was intentional.

The authorities both secular and ecclesiastical attempted, as a matter of course, to persuade themselves that the persecution of the Anabaptists was necessary for safeguarding the best interests of the state church, and therefore it was excusable, even from the Protestant point of view. Nevertheless the magistrates, apparently, were determined to cover the tracks of their cruel mode of dealing with conscientious fellow Christians. And so well did they succeed in this attempt that less than a century after the execution of the last martyr it was denied by state church theologians that any Anabaptists were ever executed in Bern. Later this opinion was fully recognized as an error. The list of martyrs contains a greater number of executions in Bern than those found in the Book of Martyrs.

A special "Commission for Anabaptist Matters" was organized by the Council of Bern in 1659. This Commission asked the Council of Zurich for instruction regarding the steps to be taken toward the extermination of the Anabaptists. The Council of Bern in the same year published a decree containing a statement concerning the spread of Anabaptism. The decree states that, notwithstanding all efforts to the contrary put forth by the authorities, "this evil has increased rather than decreased." The Council of Bern in this decree forbids again, as they had done frequently, all persons to give food or lodging to Anabaptists. Every one was declared to be under duty to report to the governments the whereabouts of all Anabaptists known to them on pain of a fine of one hundred guilders. Thus the persecution continued, though by this time some of the councilmembers, as well as some of the clergy of the city, had conscientious objections against putting Anabaptists to death, and actual martyrdom did not take place in this period. Public sentiment against putting Anabaptists to death had grown too strong, hence selling them as galley slaves was used instead of the death sentence. This punishment was inflicted upon a considerable number of Brethren in Bern. Such extremely cruel measures of persecution resulted in general protests.

The clergy of Bern, in an "Opinion" rendered in 1659, declared that none of the articles of the Anabaptists' faith was of such nature as to justify capital punishment. Moreover they said that "the Anabaptists do not deserve being sold as galley slaves, because the life to which they are condemned on the galley is such that it were a thousand times better to be dead, and many people are greatly offended by pronouncing such a sentence against the Anabaptists." Nevertheless, as late as the year 1714 six Brethren in Bern were sentenced to the galleys.

The first information about the persecution of the Mennonites in Switzerland in that period reached the Mennonites of Holland in 1641. The Dutch Mennonites through a few of their leaders, interceded with the Swiss governments in their behalf. Their efforts were without results. The persecution continued unabated. On October 24, 1659, Hans Flamingh, a Mennonite merchant of Amsterdam, wrote letters of intercession to two members of the above-mentioned Anabaptist Commission of the Council in Bern. Again, the mayors of the Dutch cities of Rotterdam and Amsterdam addressed the magistrates of Bern, pleading for toleration.

In February, 1660, a number of prominent men of the Holland Mennonites assembled at the Hague and drew up a petition to the government of the Netherlands to intercede with the authorities in Switzerland on behalf of their persecuted brethren. Letters of intercession were then sent by the Dutch authorities to the governments of Bern and Zurich, in 1660, asking toleration for the Mennonites, and permission for them to leave the country without the confiscation of their property. These efforts were partly successful. A number of imprisoned Mennonites were permitted, in September, 1660, to leave Switzerland for Holland.

In the following decade the government of Bern laid various hindrances in the way of those who had decided to leave the land. The state government of Holland in a letter to the Council of Bern and of Zurich stated that they regarded these people as very desirable citizens. The adverse attitude of the Swiss Protestant governments is obviously to be ascribed to the fact that it was feared, if toleration were granted, multitudes of the state church membership would unite with the *Täufer* people. In certain sections of the canton Bern the number of the so-called *Halbtäufer* (Halfway-Anabaptists) was very great. While definite information regarding their number was not obtainable, some of the preachers of the state churches believed that in certain villages, particularly in the Emmental, the *Halbtäufer* constituted a majority of the population.

The state church minister of Langnau, for example, wrote in 1692 that almost every one in his parish was so favorably disposed toward the Anabaptists that they indicated strong displeasure whenever he said anything against the Anabaptists from the pulpit. Many other state church ministers made similar complaints. If toleration were granted, it was feared that the Anabaptists would in a few districts out-number the membership of the state church. In all probability many *Halbtäufer* joined the Brethren who left Switzerland for the Palatinate where they could profess the faith without persecution. The records indicate definitely that even members of the Reformed state church emigrated with the Brethren to the Palatinate.

Great "Anabaptist drives" were undertaken in the years 1670 and 1671. The prisons in Bern and the Orphans' Home at the same place, which was used for a prison, were again filled. In 1688 the Council of War of the canton Bern proposed that carrying a sword, a custom largely followed in Switzerland at that time, should be made obligatory for men and youths. This would enable every one, particularly officers of the law, to recognize a *Täufer* at sight, since they would refuse

to obey such a command. Furthermore in 1693 it was ordered
in various districts of the canton that all men and boys above
thirteen years must swear the oath of allegiance. They must
appear at a place indicated by the authorities and in groups
of about 20, give the oath. Those who refused to swear were
Anabaptists.

In 1671, the year of the great emigration of the Brethren
from the Canton Bern to Alsace and the Palatinate, peculiar
measures were taken to enforce the departure of all Anabaptists. In many parishes the population refused to assist the government in the task of driving them out. The authorities had
ascertained that even some of those who had migrated had returned again and that they were aided and supported by their
relatives and others. The Council in consequence decreed that
in every parish two or three of the most pious and most well-
to-do persons of the state church should be delivered to Bern
as hostages. This order was carried out and they were kept in
confinement at the expense of the parish until all the Anabaptists of the parish had departed.

A letter of Hans Moser, dated June 22, 1709, to Holland,
describes the terrible conditions in Switzerland. All houses
were searched for *Täufer*. The son must give information
about his parents, brother about his brother. A husband who
gave shelter to his wife who was a *Täufer*, was fined 300
pounds, a father who permitted his son to visit him had to pay
500 pounds to the "Anabaptist Chamber" of the Council.

Fifty-six Bernese *Täufer*, all men, were to be deported to
America in March of the year 1710. In a boat they were transported down the Rhine river. When the ship reached Nijmegen
in Holland it had only 24 of them on board. 32 were dismissed
from the boat at Mannheim in the Palatinate on account of
sickness and frailty. At Nijmegen the Mennonite passengers
were permitted to leave the boat. They all returned to the
Palatinate to seek their wives and children. The Mennonites
of Holland on May 2, 1710, sent 1200 guilders to the Palatinate for these and others of the refugees.

In the Palatinate the Mennonites were subject to various
measures of oppression. The King of Prussia, Frederick I, who
also interceded for the persecuted Mennonites in Switzerland,

wrote on July 5, 1710, to Bern, offering to receive all Swiss Anabaptists without exception to his land. He promised to assist "these good people" in every way possible to get a new start. The Mennonite refugees do not seem to have been enthusiastic to follow this invitation, though evidently some availed themselves of it, as is obvious from the Swiss family names found among the Prussian (and Russian) Mennonites, such as Funk, Schellenberg, Baltzer, Penner, Buller, Berg, Becker, Wedel, Marten, Peters, Bergthold, Rediger. Not a few Mennonite refugees settled in Holland upon the invitation of the Dutch brotherhood which in 1710 collected the sum of 50,000 guilders for relief among the refugees. For several generations a number of Swiss Mennonite churches existed and prospered at various points in Holland. An extensive migration of Swiss Mennonites, mostly of the Amish brethren, to Holland and America took place in the year 1711.

We have referred to the "Commission for Anabaptist Matters" in the canton Bern. This body was dissolved in 1699 to give place to a new organization, the "Anabaptist Chamber," whose duty was the management of the confiscated *Täufer* property and overseeing the work of apprehending and sentencing the *Täufer*. The so-called Anabaptist hunters were responsible to this organization which was called into existence because of the fact that, notwithstanding the emigration of many *Täufer,* their number kept increasing. The Anabaptist hunters might be designated as a special police force; they were not of the regular officers of the law, however. Their work was held in such general contempt that only men of low character were available for it.

As stated the population in general often sympathized with the Brethren, a fact which made their extermination an almost hopeless task. Every possible obstacle was by their sympathizers laid in the way of the Anabaptist hunters here as in some other places. Many of the general population were punished for their active opposition to the work of the Anabaptist hunters. Often an "Anabaptist drive" was frustrated through giving of signals of approaching danger, such as blowing horns, shooting or yelling, to warn the Anabaptists. On April 24, 1714 at Sumiswald in the Emmental, when Anabaptist hunters had seized a number of Brethren, a mob of from 60 to 70 persons snatched them out of their hands. Consequently the village of Sumiswald was sentenced to pay the Anabaptist hunters the sum of 100 thalers. In 1726 three women, fleeing from pursuing Anabaptist hunters, crossed the border into the canton of Lucerne. The officers followed them and were in consequence forced to pay a heavy fine.

Various new mandates against the Brethren were published after the year 1700. High rewards were offered those who made it possible to arrest any Anabaptist. The law was again published that children of Anabaptists whose marriage was not solemnized by a minister of the state church, were considered illegally born and could not inherit their parents' property. However about the middle of the same century an evident change toward partial toleration took place. The "Anabaptist Chamber" was dissolved, in 1743, implying the end of the institution of the Anabaptist hunters. After the French revolution Switzerland became a republic, an occurrence which marked the end of religious persecution, though not of all oppression of the Anabaptists. Until about the year 1812 the newborn children of Mennonites were by officers of the law carried into the churches for baptism.

Today most of the Mennonite congregations in Switzerland are located in the western part of the canton Bern, in the Jura Mountains, though there is a strong congregation also in the Emmental. In the Reformation period, and until about the year 1795, the Jura territory was not a part of the canton Bern, but was under the jurisdiction of the Catholic prince bishop of Basel. Nearly all the Mennonites of this region are descendants of refugees who fled here after the year 1690 from the Emmental, a district in the older territory of the canton Bern. The bishop of Basel in 1693 forbade Anabaptists to settle here, and on February 5, 1731, his successor prince bishop Johann Conrad published a mandate banishing them. Not a few Mennonites had rented farms in this region. The owners of these farms now, in a petition to the bishop protested that the banishment of these people constituted a real grievance, since as agriculturists they surpassed by far the mountain folk of these regions. A number of Mennonite families migrated

westward into the canton of Neufchatel. The decree of banishment was never enforced in the Jura district, however.

Today the number of the Mennonites in Switzerland is about
1,500—a small number as compared with that of the Mennonites of other countries who are descendents of Swiss refugees.
In the United States and Canada the number of Mennonites
of Swiss descent is estimated at above 95,000, including about
a dozen Swiss congregations which came to America from Russia and Austria. Also the great majority of the Mennonites
of France and South Germany are of Swiss descent.

CHAPTER 11

THE SWISS BRETHREN IN BASEL, SCHAFF-HAUSEN, APPENZELL

The city of Basel in Switzerland began to tolerate Protestantism at an early date. Johann Oekolampad, who became the leading reformer of this city, arrived in Basel in November, 1522, and within a short time was appointed professor of theology at the university of the city. In May of the following year the Council of Basel gave orders that only scriptural doctrine was to be preached in the city, but as yet the Council did not permit the abolition of the Mass. In February, 1525, Oekolampad became priest of St. Martin's Church. As such he was obliged to observe the Mass and other Roman Catholic ceremonies of which he personally did not approve.

As early as 1522 Ulrich Hugwald, professor at the University of Basel, wrote and published a booklet in which he declared himself against the practice of infant baptism. Oekolampad himself, in the autumn of 1524, confessed that infant baptism was to him an open question. He applied to Ulrich Zwingli for instruction on this point. At the same time Oekolampad wrote to Balthasar Hubmaier confessing that he did not know of any clear Scripture passages favoring the baptism of infants.

In August, 1525, the authorities of the city became aware of the presence of a small Anabaptist congregation in Basel. Laurence Hochrütiner, who had been driven from St. Gall, appears to have been their leader. He was banished from the city. In the course of the same year a number of others were banished. On July 6, 1526, the Council of Basel published its first mandate against the Anabaptists. The practice of infant baptism was commanded, and the repetition of the ceremony of baptism strictly forbidden, as were also all meetings of the dissenters. A second mandate was issued on March 14, 1528. All Anabaptists who would not "forsake their errors" were to be imprisoned, and those who would give them lodging should in every instance pay a fine of five pounds. This decree was

115

published in all political districts. A disputation took place in the city hall about the same time between some of the clergy of Basel and an Anabaptist minister of Zurich named Carlin.

Felix Manz was in Basel for a short time. Wolfgang Ulimann, of St. Gall, was banished from Basel in August, 1528; he was threatened with the death sentence if he returned. Hans Seckler, who later suffered martyrdom in Bern, and Conrad Winkler who met the same fate in Zurich, were punished in Basel by being placed in the pillory and beaten with rods. George Blaurock was imprisoned here in 1529. In February, 1529, the victory of the Zwinglian Reformation in Basel was gained by a revolution undertaken by the Protestant party leaders. By force of arms the Council was compelled to abolish Romanism in the city and territory of Basel.

Before the revolution the government had published a number of decrees against the Anabaptists. The observance of baptism, preaching outside the churches, and giving lodging to Anabaptist ministers was threatened with severe punishment. But since the Council at that time consisted in part of Romanists in whose eyes Zwinglianism was likewise objectionable, they were comparatively lenient in their dealings with the Anabaptists. Oekolampad, shortly before the revolution, complained that the Council was too slack in this matter. The new (Zwinglian) government took a stricter attitude against the dissenters. Article 22 of the new "Regulations" adopted by the Council demanded that all Anabaptists and those who give them shelter or attend their meetings, should be imprisoned and may be subjected to torture until they recant. Those Anabaptists "who persisted in their error" were to be held in prison until death.

Notwithstanding the persecution, Oekolampad, in January, 1530, reported to Zwingli a noticeable increase of Anabaptist influence in Basel. The Council decided to give a precedent of severity and sentenced the minister, Hans Ludi, to death. He was executed with the sword in the market place, on January 12, 1530, the first martyr of the city. Hans Ludi died in the triumph of an immovable faith. This cruel procedure of a Protestant government failed to have the desired effect; it proved on the contrary an aid to the Anabaptist cause, especially in the country sections of the canton Basel. In these districts, says Paul Burckhardt, the author of the most important work on the Anabaptists in Basel, the people had shown themselves disinterested when Protestantism was introduced by the Council, "but the preaching of the Anabaptists resulted in a true religious awakening." The majority of the people in certain country sections of the canton Basel took sides with the Anabaptists, as the same author says further. "They believed the Anabaptists to be sincere, pious people and Christian martyrs, as is indicated by their keen displeasure over the executions carried out by the government, and by the manifold aid they gave to these persecuted people."

At three various times Oekolampad had colloquies with Anabaptists. The first of these debates took place in August, 1525. Three Anabaptist ministers, Wolfgang Wissenburger, Thomas Geyerfalk, and Jacob Immelin debated with Oekolampad and other clergymen. A report of this debate, giving however the statements made by the three Anabaptist participants in very condensed form, was published by Oekolampad. Though the report is one-sided, it is of great importance, since it gives the arguments advanced by the state church theologians against the Anabaptists. Not a few of these arguments are curious indeed. Balthasar Hubmaier, subsequently wrote and published a masterly reply to this report under the title, *A Reply to the Ludicrous Debate of a Number of Clergymen at Basel*. He quotes literally from the published report of the debate, adding his comments and criticisms. This booklet of Hubmaier is of exceptional value, since it gives the arguments generally used by both sides in the Anabaptist controversy. As a refutation of the state church position it is equalled only by a few other booklets of the same author in his controversy with Ulrich Zwingli.

Another debate with Anabaptists took place on June 10, 1527, in St. Martin's Church. Particulars about it are not known. Again on December 29, 1529, Oekolampad had a debate with eleven imprisoned ministers of the Swiss Brethren. Hans Hersberger, a miller of the village Läufelfingen, appears to have been the principal spokesman of the Brethren. Hans Hersberger and Jacob Treyer were banished from the city somewhat later. Many Anabaptists were punished by being "ducked" thrice in the Rhine, to be drawn out only after they were nearly drowned. Two Anabaptists, Hans Madlinger and

Peter Liggenscher, were executed by drowning on February 10, 1531. There are no exact accounts of other executions, though in the records it is stated nine times within about five months that the executioner, generally accompanied by a grave-digger, was sent into country districts. On April 21, 1535, the Council of Basel in a letter to the Austrian authorities at En-sisheim, reported that they had executed many Anabaptists.

The bailiff of Homburg, in the Canton Basel, asked the Council, in case the Anabaptists imprisoned at Homburg were to be "ducked" or drowned, the executions should not be carried out in that district but in the city of Basel, since the population in the district were embittered on account of such proceedings. In March, 1531, Anna Hüdeli, and three other women were "ducked" and banished. The same sentence was meted out somewhat later to Anna Gysin. Many Anabaptists were imprisoned for long periods. Hans Hersberger was in prison from July, 1531, to December, 1533. Anna Gysin died in prison in March, 1533, having been incarcerated since the spring of 1532. Jacob Hersberger was placed in the pillory on July 11, 1535, and then his tongue cut out and two fingers cut off. Many were publicly beaten with rods. In the synod of the state church in 1538 the clergymen of the country districts reported that there were few Anabaptists left, and also that Christian piety was at a low ebb.

At a later date the Council of Basel decreed that all property of Anabaptists should be confiscated by the authorities. No one was permitted to purchase any property from Anabaptists. Yet the severest persecution failed to exterminate Anabaptism in Basel. There are today two Mennonite congregations in the city and canton of Basel.[29]

In the Swiss city of Schaffhausen on the Rhine the Anabaptist movement took a foothold in 1525. Conrad Grebel had important connections here. The nobleman Hans von Waldkirch, of this city, was married to Grebel's sister Gertrud. Von Wald-kirch was called to account by the Council of Schaffhausen for receiving Anabaptists into his house. His sister, Beatrice, the wife of the nobleman Ulrich von Fulach, later united with the Swiss Brethren. Hans von Waldkirch in later years became burgomaster of the city.

Conrad Grebel came to Schaffhausen in January, 1525. Soon after his arrival it was rumored that a public debate on baptism was to be held in this city, like that which had taken place in Zurich a few weeks earlier. The news that such a debate was planned in Schaffhausen caused consternation among the members of the Council of Zurich. The latter were obviously in grave doubt as to the results of such a debate held in Schaffhausen. They must have been informed of the position taken by the leading theologian of this city, Sebastian Hofmeister, who not only refused to have his own child baptized but preached publicly from the pulpit against infant baptism. In the course of the same year, however, Hofmeister became an outspoken Zwinglian and as such acted as president in the debate held at Zurich November 6 to 8, 1525.

On February 8, 1525, the Council of Zurich addressed the Schaffhausen Council, stating that they had a debate in Zurich on this question and had come to the conclusion that infant baptism was "nothing out of the way," and they had published a mandate that the infants must be baptized. Having now heard that a debate on infant baptism was to be held in Schaffhausen, they would inform them that their theologians had shown the doctrine of the Anabaptists erroneous. Furthermore they said in this letter that Ulrich Zwingli will immediately publish a book on the pending question. They asked the Council of Schaffhausen to postpone the proposed debate until after they had read Zwingli's forthcoming book. However, if they preferred not to wait, the Zurich Council asked to be informed of the date for the debate, so that they could send their representatives and theologians.

The reply of the Council of Schaffhausen to this letter is dated February 10, 1525. They stated that they had decided against having a debate on baptism, and furthermore that they intended "not to abolish at the present time the custom of baptizing the infants." The Council of Schaffhausen thereupon published a mandate to the effect that ecclesiastical unity was to be maintained and the young children baptized.

In the village of Hallau, canton Schaffhausen, Johannes Brötli, who had been banished from Zollikon near Zurich on January 21, 1525, preached and baptized many. Upon the protest of the Zurich Council to the authorities of Schaffhausen,

Brötli was apparently banished from this territory. In the year 1527 a number of persons were punished for holding Anabaptist views. On September 13, of the same year, the Council published a mandate against the Anabaptists, and on November 17 the first martyrdom took place, the execution with the sword of Hans Rüger. The second execution was that of Jacob Schuffel, on April 14, 1529. Early in the year 1530 many Anabaptists were imprisoned in Schaffhausen.

A noteworthy petition signed by eleven clergymen of the Zwinglian state church in Schaffhausen, was presented to the Council in 1532. The signers of this petition stated that the Anabaptists considered their separation necessary because "no amendment of life is detectable among us," but on the contrary "there is an increase in vices." The signers of this petition furthermore expressed regret because "we give them occasion for separation by our offensive life," and this, they say, "is indeed a great sin, for Christ says, Whoso shall offend one of these little ones which believe on me, it were better for him if a millstone were hanged about his neck and that he were drowned in the depth of the sea."

The Council thereupon published a mandate threatening gambling, profanity, drunkenness, and similar sins with punishment, and at the same time stressing the need of enforcing former decrees against the Anabaptists. "Those who give them food or shelter," the mandate demands further, "shall likewise be punished with such severity that they would regret to have given them any aid or succor."

In the succeeding years the protocols of the Council of Schaffhausen often treat of Anabaptists, no less than forty-one times in 1535. A new mandate against them was published on March 31, 1535. Many were punished in various ways, such as by public beatings with rods. "Anabaptist drives," that is, organized campaigns against Anabaptists for the purpose of apprehending and arresting them, were repeatedly arranged for by officers of the law. The clergy of the city complained repeatedly of leniency on the part of the Council in the persecution of the Anabaptists. The burgomaster, Hans von Waldkirch, in a letter to Heinrich Bullinger, defended himself against this charge. A debate between the clergymen of the city and the Anabaptist Laurence Rosenbaum took place on September 6, 1535. Also in the years 1543, 1559, and 1577 there were public debates between Anabaptists and state church theologians.

The canton of Appenzell was separated from St. Gall only by a narrow strip of territory which was ruled by the prince-abbot of the cloister of St. Gall. Eberli Bolt, of Lachen in the canton Appenzell, the first martyr of the Swiss Brethren, labored in this canton, as well as in St. Gall, with great success. After his execution in May, 1525, Hans Kern, called Krüsi, of Klingnau, who was mentioned above, preached and baptized in the canton Appenzell. At Gossau in this canton there was a large congregation of the Brethren. At Teufen Hans Kern won the majority of the adult population who apparently united with the Swiss Brethren and ceased to attend the church of the Zwinglian preacher Jacob Schurtanner. Johannes Kessler states that Schurtanner was "deposed" by his congregation (parishioners). This would undoubtedly mean that they refused to attend the services. Schurtanner seems to have continued the observance of the Mass, though he preached Zwinglian doctrine, and this doubtless offended his parishioners.[30] He left Teufen probably before the middle of April, 1525, when the Mass was abolished at Zurich. The first Protestant communion services in the canton of Appenzell were held two years later.

Hans Kern lived not in the canton Appenzell but at St. Georgen under the prince-abbot of the cloister of St. Gallen. Here he was arrested by an officer Melchior Tegen, and taken to Lucerne to be burned at the stake—the second martyr of the Swiss Brethren. George Blaurock was active in Appenzell in April, 1529.

In October, 1529, a disputation with the Brethren, arranged by the Council of Appenzell, was held in the church at Teufen, indicating that the Council took a comparatively mild attitude toward them. The leniency of the government of Appenzell toward the Brethren caused Zwingli and the Zwinglian governments of certain Swiss cantons to address this government, in 1531, urging the need of taking a more determined attitude and at least punish Anabaptism by exile. Zwingli also, and others, offered assistance in case another disputation was considered necessary. It is uncertain whether there was a second disputation. Many of the Brethren of Appenzell fled to Moravia, the land of comparative religious liberty.

Like the Swiss Brethren elsewhere, the Brethren of Appenzell were accused of various misdeeds and crimes.[31] Against the Brethren in Appenzell Ulrich Zwingli brought charges of gross immorality. These charges were of so serious a nature as to offend even the Council of Appenzell. The Council found it necessary to protest against the assertion that such things occurred in their territory. Zwingli made these charges in a sermon which he preached at Zurich in December, 1525. He denounced in this sermon the alleged misdeeds and crimes of the Anabaptists of Appenzell. Since these reports were questioned in Zurich, and St. Gall is located near Appenzell, Zwingli wrote a letter, dated January 17, 1526, to Vadian asking him for information. He said in this letter that in his sermon he had in a general way made mention of the shameless things which were practiced by the Anabaptists. He said further that reports of their crimes, consisting of the most offensive open practice of lewdness, had come to him. Again, in a letter, dated January 1, 1526, to Wolfgang Capito in Strasburg, Zwingli referred to these reports, and added, "There is nothing more foolhardy, deceptive, infamous, and shameful than these people."

Since the reported crimes were asserted to be openly or publicly practiced, and it was known that none of the offenders were taken to task by the authorities the reputation of the Appenzell Council was at stake for failing to punish the atrocities of which Zwingli had accused the Brethren. Within a few weeks it came to Zwingli's ears that the Council of Appenzell had received reports of his sermon and the accusations in question, and that they were greatly offended. He consequently wrote the Council a letter of apology. He admitted that he had preached a sermon in which he said that "at the present time the Anabaptists are making the good people of Appenzell a great deal of trouble and difficulty; they go to such lengths in their licentiousness that it is an open shame." This indicates that Zwingli admitted the seriousness of these charges, though the exact wording of his pertinent statements in the sermon is not known. Probably Zwingli himself did not recall the exact words he had used, yet his writings against the Brethren show that he was wont to use the strongest terms in accusing and denouncing them. In his letter of apology to the Council of Appenzell he stated that it had not been his intention to criticize or censure the Council of Appenzell. And yet the assertions which he had made concerning the alleged crimes of the Brethren were equivalent to a real censure of a government which would let such things go unpunished.

Obviously Zwingli took a lesson from his experiences with the authorities of Appenzell. In his last book against the Brethren, the *Elenchus,* which he wrote in 1527, he accused them repeatedly of every misdeed in the catalog of crimes. His accusations, however, are almost wholly of a general, indefinite nature, mentioning no names. Thus he made sure that his charges would not involve any government.

CHAPTER 12

STRASBURG, A SWISS BRETHREN CENTER

In the Reformation period Alsace, with Strasburg as its principal city, was a province of the German empire. Even before that era nonresistant dissenters had in various periods been numerous in this city. In the year 1212 a Waldensian congregation was detected there by officers of the law. No less than eighty brethren and sisters were burned at the stake in that year at Strasburg. Conrad Reiser, a Waldensian missionary, suffered martyrdom here, by burning at the stake in the month of January, 1458.

Early in the Reformation period Strasburg became nominally a Protestant city. Nevertheless the authorities were slow in abandoning Roman Catholic worship and practice. Preaching the gospel was permitted by the magistrates, but the Mass was not abolished until February 20, 1529. As we shall directly note, before the inception of the Anabaptist movement, Martin Butzer (Bucer) and Wolfgang Capito, leading Protestant reformers of the city, took an attitude of indecision and doubt regarding infant baptism. After the year 1525 they changed their views on this point, having been led to see that the baptism of the infants was indispensable for an all-inclusive state church. At the time when the Mass was abolished these reformers entertained strong hopes that infant baptism would be made obligatory by the magistracy. This expectation was not realized however. The definite organization of the Protestant state church of Strasburg was postponed by the civil authorities to a much later date, namely, until the year 1534.

In the meantime Martin Butzer and his associates continued their efforts toward the organization of a church by the magistracy. Butzer was fully decided to go hand in hand with the magistracy in this matter. The fact deserves notice in this connection that it was keenly and widely realized that the Reformation, in so far as it was state-made and stood for a union of church and state, had failed to bring such fruits as had been

124

hoped for. Even among the friends of the Reformation in the magistracy of Strasburg there were those who complained of a growing religious indifference among the population, though there had been Protestant preaching for about a decade. The Anabaptists, on the contrary, were known to take religion seriously and to emphasize practical piety. Owing to the ecclesiastical disorganization, before the year 1534, the people of Strasburg had full liberty to refuse to have their infants baptized. It is evident then that in this city the soil had been well prepared for the reception of the message of the evangelical Anabaptists.

The authorities of Strasburg took a position of comparative tolerance toward the Anabaptists. The famous burgomaster of the city, Jacob Sturm, regarded all persecution with disfavor and was supported in this attitude by a number of influential laymen, among them the knight Eckard zum Trubel. Matthias Zell, one of the leading reformers of the city, also disapproved of the persecution of dissenters. Two other state church ministers, Wolfgang Schultheiss and Anton Engelbrecht, openly defended the principle of full liberty of conscience, while Martin Butzer, on the contrary, did all in his power to prevail over the civil authorities to refuse the Anabaptists toleration.

A mandate against the Anabaptists was published by the magistrates on July 17, 1527, forbidding the populace to give shelter and food to Anabaptists, and this mandate was renewed in the autumn of 1530. In 1538 a new decree was issued requiring the banishment of all Anabaptists. In case any one of those who were banished would return, he was to be imprisoned for four weeks. An Anabaptist returning a second time would be punished by cutting off of fingers and by being branded on the cheek with a red-hot iron. Any one returning the third time was to be executed by drowning. In point of fact, however, the death sentence was never executed upon an Anabaptist in Strasburg. There was in evidence an inclination to leave Anabaptists unmolested if they refrained from attending separate meetings and from criticizing the state church. Nowhere outside Moravia, were the Anabaptists accorded such consideration as here. In consequence many refugees from surrounding regions sought shelter in Strasburg, swelling the numbers of the native Anabaptists.

In the spring of the year 1526 the attention of the authorities of the city was attracted by the presence of many Anabaptists. Michael Sattler was in Strasburg for some time in that year. In the autumn of 1528 Pilgram Marpeck fled from Augsburg to a village near Strasburg, and later moved into the city. The efforts of Martin Butzer to bring about Marpeck's banishment were unsuccessful for a considerable period, owing to the fact that he was a man of extraordinary skill as an engineer, and that the city authorities desired to avail themselves of his services. As a minister of the gospel he found Strasburg a fruitful field. Through Butzer's influence he was finally banished from the city in February, 1532. Other ministers of the Swiss Brethren as well as of other Anabaptist parties also labored in Strasburg.

In the spring of 1529 many Anabaptists were imprisoned in Strasburg, forty-four in the dungeons of the Wilhelm's Tower alone. About one hundred Anabaptists who had been banished from Augsburg fled to Strasburg in the same year. The Anabaptists and their sympathizers became numerically strong in the city. Of this there were numerous indications. Infant baptism fell more and more into disfavor among the population in general. The printers of the city hesitated to publish books against the Anabaptists, asserting that there was no sale for them; they preferred to issue publications defending the doctrine of the Anabaptists. Hubmaier's masterly defense of faith baptism, *The Christian Baptism of Believers,* was published here as early as 1525, and two books of Pilgram Marpeck were published later. Martin Butzer and his associates noticed with grave misgivings the spread of Anabaptist principles and the corresponding loss of the influence of the state church. The decadence of the state church type of Christianity was clearly in evidence. Church attendance decreased materially, as well as participation of the population in the communion services. There was great cause to fear that the dissenters would win the day in the city. The final success of the state church party was due to the fact that liberty of conscience was refused. Strasburg was one of the many places where the state church owed its final triumph to the strong arm of the civil authorities. About the year 1534 the number of Anabaptists in the city was estimated at two thousand.

As already stated, Martin Butzer and Wolfgang Capito before the rise of the Anabaptists had expressed serious doubts regarding infant baptism. In 1524 Butzer had published a book in which he made the statement that "in the first Christian congregations only those were baptized and received into the church who had fully surrendered to the Word of Christ." Capito held similar views regarding baptism, even in later years. In him the Anabaptists had for a number of years a warm friend. In letters to his friend Musculus Capito expressed the opinion that believers should be permitted to separate from the world (as did the Anabaptists). And again he wrote to the same person, "Those who under the greatest tyranny profess Anabaptist principles, err without evil intentions, if they do err. For they do not make use of baptism as a means for dividing the church but as a testimony that they believe the Word and are willing to give their lives for their Redeemer." In a letter to Zwingli, Capito spoke of "the praiseworthy sincerity of faith" of the Anabaptists. Again, in 1527, he wrote a letter of consolation to a number of imprisoned Anabaptists at Horb in Württemberg, admonishing them to steadfastness.

And not merely in private letters but also in some of his published writings Wolfgang Capito defended the Anabaptist position. In his *Commentary* to the book of Hosea he disapproved of infant baptism and defended the baptism of believers. He defined the Christian church not as a community of persons who were to be led to accept Christ (such was the state church idea) but as a union of obedient believers in Christ. He insisted that the Christian church consists of believers. Nevertheless he retained his office as minister in the state church. After a few years, however, namely toward the end of 1531, Martin Butzer and others succeeded in persuading Capito to make an entire change in his views on baptism and the nature of the Christian church. He now accepted a position that was entirely satisfactory from the viewpoint of the state church. Indeed he became a radical opponent of the Anabaptists. In 1535 he asserted that it was the foremost duty of the civil authorities to regulate matters of faith for the population. He denounced the principle of liberty of conscience.

For a long time the appeals of Butzer to use more stringent measures toward the suppression of the dissenters were disregarded by the authorities. After the first synod of the state church, held in 1533, however, the Council published a mandate ordering that no doctrine contrary to the Augsburg Confession was to be tolerated. Citizens holding contrary doctrines were to leave the city, with their families, within two weeks. Infant baptism in particular was made obligatory by the strict command that all infants must be baptized within six weeks after birth. Parents neglecting to bring their children for baptism were threatened with banishment. A mandate was published against "the common Anabaptists" (the Swiss Brethren), the Melchiorites (followers of Melchior Hofmann) and all other dissenters, ordering their banishment. Banished Anabaptists who returned to the city were threatened with capital punishment. Many now fled the city, and there was a consequent increase in the number of Anabaptists in many towns and villages of Alsace, especially in the vicinity of Strasburg. A committee, called *Täufer Herren* (Commission for Anabaptist Matters), was charged with the duty of apprehending and passing sentence on Anabaptists in Strasburg. Nevertheless, the city never stained its hands with the blood of those who would not accept the creed prescribed by the state church.

A description of a meeting of the Swiss Brethren was given at Colmar, Alsace, by a woman while under torture. She related that about thirty-six persons assembled at night in a forest near Kestenholz. One brother, named George Bastian, was reading the Scriptures and speaking for three hours. When he was done, they all knelt and prayed for a quarter of an hour for all authorities and for their persecutors. After that, all partook of a common meal for which some had brought food. Then one of them admonished those who were not yet baptized to lead a quiet Christian life. Some had need of clothing and tools, and were supplied.

In March of the year 1540 a meeting of the Swiss Brethren in Strasburg was surprised by officers. Thirty-nine persons were arrested, while about the same number made their escape. The most prominent of them were imprisoned for some time. Of two other Anabaptist meetings for worship in or near Strasburg, held in 1545 and in 1557, there are detailed reports. In the latter meeting two persons were received into the church by baptism. One of the questions asked the applicants was the following: "Whether they would, when necessity required it, give all they had to help their brethren, and would let none be in need, if they could help him."

Besides the congregation of the Swiss Brethren there were in Strasburg and vicinity also circles of Melchiorites and of followers of Hans Denck. The two last named parties differed in doctrine and practice from the Swiss Brethren. Both the followers of Melchior Hofmann and of Hans Denck practiced faith baptism only for a short period, and then abandoned this practice. Soon after 1540 both disappeared from the scene in Strasburg, while the Swiss Brethren continued to be as always the strongest Anabaptist party in the city. Strasburg was for centuries the center of activities of the Swiss Brethren in South Germany.

A number of conferences of the Swiss Brethren were held in or near the city of Strasburg. Of some of these conferences the records have been preserved. On August 24, 1555, the Swiss Brethren assembled here to take action regarding a particular doctrinal point, namely the peculiar view of the incarnation of Christ which was defended by the brethren in the Netherlands and northern Germany.

Another important conference held at Strasburg was that of 1557. About fifty bishops and ministers of the Brethren of the upper countries (Swiss Brethren) gathered for this conference from Alsace, Switzerland, Baden, Württemberg, and Moravia. Among them was the minister in whose house the conference had been held at which the Schleitheim confession was adopted, in 1527. The official report of the Strasburg conference of 1557 was given in the form of a letter to the brethren in the lower countries, namely, in the Netherlands and northern Germany. The churches in the lower countries had been directly under the influence of Menno Simons and Dirck Philips, and were the first to be named Mennonites. As stated in the report, the delegates to this conference represented about fifty churches, located from the Eyfelt (Eiffel) in southwestern Germany to Moravia, and a few of these congregations numbered 500 to 600 members.

One of the topics discussed was the avoidance of the excommunicated. This was a live question in the churches of the lower countries, not however in the congregations of the Swiss Brethren. Among the latter the strict avoidance was not practiced, but the report of the controversy on this point in the lower countries had caused disturbance in some of their congregations. The controversy was deplored by the Brethren assembled at Strasburg. They declared at this conference that the observance of avoidance in the case of married couples when one partner was excluded from the church, indicated an extreme view which was to them unacceptable. The report was in part addressed to "our dear brother Menno and all the ministers and bishops in the Netherlands who serve the churches of the Lord."

Previous to the general gathering of the bishops and ministers of the Swiss Brethren in Strasburg in 1592 they had been approached by the Socinians (Unitarians) of Poland, through Christoph Osterod to consent to a union with them. In reply to Osterod's proposal they declared emphatically that the Socinian teaching on the question of the deity of Christ was unscriptural and unacceptable. They went so far as to declare that they could not receive Socinians as brethren in the case of a visit by them.[32]

Other conferences of which records have been preserved in the form of regulations concerning discipline were held in Strasburg in 1568 and 1607. The rules of discipline of the year 1568 indicate that the Church in that period held to certain regulations in regard to attire. The pertinent statements as found in one record are:[33]

"Tailors and seamstresses shall hold to the plain and simple custom and shall make nothing at all for pride's sake."

"Brethren and sisters shall stay by the present form of our regulations concerning apparel and have nothing made for pride's sake."

A Mennonite congregation existed in Strasburg until well into the last century.

Concerning the persecution of the Anabaptists in Strasburg there is a noteworthy letter written about 1550 by Katharina Zell, widow of Matthias Zell, who had been a minister in the state church. The letter is addressed to the Protestant preachers of the city, and is in part as follows:

The poor Anabaptists about whom you are so enraged and incite the government against them as a hunter sets his dogs on wild pigs and rabbits, they nevertheless zealously confess Christ with us, and thus you persecute Christ in them. Yea, many of them have confessed Him notwithstanding exile, imprisonment, and execution by fire and water. Do you not realize that we, in doctrine and life, give them cause for separation? The government should punish those that do wrong, but should not use force in matters of faith, as you are doing. Strasburg, the Lord be praised, is yet giving today an example of mercy, sympathy, and hospitality for those that are homeless, harbors today many a poor Christian confessor whom you would desire to be driven out. Such things Matthias Zell never approved. He, on the contrary, gathered together the scattered sheep. He never consented to persecution, and at a time when the preachers urged the government to exile the Anabaptists he, with a sad heart and great earnestness, said publicly from the pulpit and in the convention of the ministers: "I call God, heaven and earth to witness at that day that I am innocent of the oppression and banishment of these poor people."

CHAPTER 13

PILGRAM MARPECK

Pilgram Marpeck was born about 1495 at Rattenberg on the Inn river in the Austrian province of the Tyrol. The Marpecks were an eminent family in this town; their son enjoyed distinct educational advantages. Pilgram wrote Latin fluently, having doubtlessly been trained in the Latin school at Rattenberg. He was a skillful mining engineer. In 1523 he was chosen a member of the Council, or governing body of the town, and in 1525 was entrusted with the position of inspector of mines. His parents were God-fearing Catholics who had come under the influences of the Lutheran reformation. As Pilgram stated in later discussions with Martin Butzer, he had observed however that the fruits of the general reformation movement were disappointing, because it gave rein to propensities toward carnal liberty. In consequence, Pilgram said further, he joined himself to the Anabaptists and received baptism as a witness of the obedience of faith, having his eyes fixed only on the divine Word and command.

Hence Marpeck saw himself compelled to flee the Tyrol, his property having been confiscated. He went with his wife and children to Augsburg in South Germany, in the spring of 1528. In October of the same year the family went to a village near Strasburg in Alsace, where they abode for over a year, and in the following year moved to Strasburg. There he rendered important services as an expert engineer. Under his supervision the excellent aqueducts which furnished the city with the needed water supply were constructed. The municipality of Strasburg benefited also from his knowledge of raftmanship. Upon his advice the city acquired timber lands in the Black Forest, and under his direction the lumber was floated down one or two tributaries of the Rhine to Strasburg.

Soon his religious activities attracted the attention of the authorities. There was a disposition, however, to leniency on their part, probably on account of the services he was rendering the community. Despite the opposing efforts of Martin Butzer he was tolerated in the city for a short time. Marpeck labored in Strasburg as a minister of the gospel with evident success. Those who learned to know him were impressed by his thorough knowledge of the Scriptures, his talents, and the nobility of his Christian character. This was recognized even by his most bitter opponent, Martin Butzer. The latter, in a letter to his friend Ambrosius Blaurer, remarked that Marpeck was a stubborn heretic, and yet he (Butzer) added that "otherwise he and his wife are of fine, irreproachable character."

At another time Butzer stated in a letter that Marpeck was leading a strict life and was free of the love of temporal things, which, he said, is "an old decoy of Satan" (to attract people to heretical teaching). Again Butzer stated that Marpeck "had received much of the Lord," being a man of extraordinary gifts. He complained in particular of the points in Marpeck's teaching which, from the state church point of view, were most objectionable, namely his teaching on baptism, and his opinion that *schwören und wehren* (taking oath and defense by force) were forbidden the Christian. Marpeck wrote and published two books in defense of the teaching of the Swiss Brethren. These books were suppressed by the Council and within a few weeks Marpeck was arrested with a few of his brethren.

On December 9, 1531, Butzer had a lengthy discussion with him before the Council of the city. Marpeck declared at the outset that these questions must be decided from the Word of God, not by any human authority. He said the fruits of the general reformation movement had proved disappointing. One of the reasons for it, he said further, was that the movement relied too much on the protection of the civil authorities. The ministers of the dominant Protestant church, he said, preached only in places where they had the protection of the magistrates, instead of "laboring freely under the cross of Christ." He mentioned that the Protestant church of Strasburg was as yet without a confession of faith. Marpeck spoke disapprovingly of preaching justification by faith without giving repentance and conversion their proper emphasis. Butzer replied at length with a defense of the practice of the state church, including an extensive apology for infant baptism. He accused Marpeck of failing to act from proper motives. In his opinion the dissent of the Anabaptists was due to a lack of love and forbearance.

Marpeck and Butzer had at least two more disputations. On December 18, 1531, Marpeck was formally exiled from the city. The order of expulsion contained the statement that he would be gladly tolerated if he would make common cause with the established church. On December 19, Marpeck wrote a letter to the Council, stating that he would accept their orders and leave the city but could not comply with their desire to give the promise never to return. If he, led by the Spirit of God, would come back to Strasburg, he would willingly endure what God would permit to be inflicted upon him. He humbly petitioned the Council to be granted a respite of a few weeks to enable him to dispose of his "little household furniture." This was granted him.

Before leaving the city Marpeck handed the Council his confession of faith.[34] He also addressed to them a letter which is notable for its simple, sincere tone. He said in this letter that in matters of faith no other judge was to be recognized than God alone, but in temporal things the magistrates must be obeyed. "The praiseworthy city of Strasburg," he wrote, "has every reason to contemplate the fact that of all places the Lord has thus far so graciously kept it from shedding blood because of matters of faith. This is truly not a small evidence of grace from God." He pleaded with them to desist from persecuting the distressed folk who in all the world have no place to stay and who flee to Strasburg. This plea, he said, he made not for his own sake but for theirs. He promised to pray for them, and stated that he could never forget their good deeds toward him.

After his banishment from Strasburg Pilgram Marpeck sojourned at various places in South Germany and the Tyrol. For a number of years, apparently, he lived at Ulm on the Danube river in Württemberg, the evangelical Anabaptist congregations in the territory between Ulm and the Neckar river being under his oversight. In 1544 he returned to the city of Augsburg. Here, as formerly at Strasburg, he rendered important services to the municipality by his mechanical skill. What he did for the city as an engineer was of such importance that the authorities showed an inclination to wink at his religious dissent. He was however repeatedly warned against Anabaptist activities, and on September 25, 1553, the Council decided that, since he does not refrain from propagating his error "he shall earn his bread elsewhere." Evidently the Council reconsidered this decision, however, for there is clear proof that he retained his position as engineer until his death. He died in the autumn of the year 1556.

For about a quarter of a century Pilgram Marpeck had a leading part in the work of the Swiss Brethren Church in various German provinces. He was their most prominent minister and leader. As a writer in defense of the doctrine and principles of the church he was outranked only by Menno Simons and possibly Dirck Philips. And yet he was practically forgotten until less than a generation ago. Two of Marpeck's books, printed in Strasburg, have already been mentioned. Of their contents nothing is known.

An important work, *The Book on Baptism,* treating mainly, as the title indicates, on baptism, Marpeck published in 1542.[35] A copy of Marpeck's book was sent to Caspar Schwenckfeld, who previously on various occasions had expressed himself favorably regarding the Brethren. Schwenckfeld's attitude toward them, however, had undergone a change, partly, as he frankly stated, because of the danger that he and his friends would be classed as Anabaptists. Having read Marpeck's book, Schwenckfeld wrote a reply to it under the title, *Criticism (Judicium) of the New Book of the Anabaptists.*

In this book Schwenckfeld defended his opinion that under existing conditions the proper thing was to "stand still" as concerned church organization and the observance of the ordinances. He believed that a divinely authorized church did not exist at that time, and that no one was called to organize a true church, hence the observance of the ordinances and other requirements which concern the church were not obligatory. In this book furthermore Schwenckfeld attacked and denounced various teachings of the Swiss Brethren. He asserted that they over-emphasized the importance of the letter of the Scriptures and made an idol of the cross by bearing the cross of persecution. He made such accusations against them because they refused to heed his advice and avoid persecution by outwardly conforming to the practices prescribed by the civil and ecclesiastical authorities of the province or state in which they lived.

Pilgram Marpeck, assisted by his friend Leopold Scharn-schlager,[36] wrote an elaborate reply to this book of Schwenck-feld. Marpeck's reply has the title *Verantwortung* (Vindication). The names of five elders, besides Scharnschlager, are mentioned as co-operating at least in a measure, in the preparation of the book, namely Sigmund Bosch,[37] Martin Blaichner, Valentine Werner, Anton Müller, and Hans Jacob. The book was circulated in manuscript form. Within recent decades three copies of it have been found. It was prepared for the press by Johann Loserth of Graz, Austria, and was printed for the first time in 1929. The book is a thoroughgoing defense of the faith and practice of the Swiss Brethren. The author shows, for example, that to believe one thing and practice another, in order to avoid persecution, is irreconcilable with Christian principles, and that loyalty to Christ includes obedience to Him. Doctrine and practice cannot be separated.

On the question of church organization and the need of obedience Marpeck says in part:

The believers in Christ in the present time have the same right as those of apostolic times to come together in the name of Christ in one body through His Spirit. They all are called to witness to the truth and to admonish. They are under duty to use their gifts for the up-building of the believers. Or, is it not true that faith will cause them to do this? Does not the Holy Spirit urge them to do it? Does not love constrain them? Does not Christ command it? Who, then, can oppose or forbid it? All Christians are priests, and therefore should shew forth His praises (I Peter 2:9).

The church of Christ is standing yet on the same foundation as the apostolic church; it is standing today in its primitive authority and mission which was verified by the miraculous works of Christ and the apostles. How can it be asserted then that at the present time no one has authority and power to assemble a people of Christ, baptize them into one body, and carry out all His commands, such as baptism, communion, laying on of hands, feet washing, teaching, admonishing, reproving, excommunication, and all that is serviceable and salutary for the assembling together and edification of His body which is the Church?

Therefore we would ask Schwenckfeld and all who are of like opinion with him, where, when, and for what reason Christ has repealed or abrogated His commands and institutions, or how it came about that His commands could have been nullified to such extent that their observance in the present time must be authorized again by a special command and a divinely manifested special call. Or where and with what words has Christ commanded, if men for a time through disobedience, apostasy, or seduction, neglect and abolish His commands (as was indeed the case), that in such case one should stand still as concerns these things and should no longer observe them without a special, manifest or miraculous authorization?

Another important work in whose preparation Marpeck evidently had a large part is *Testaments-Erläuterung* (Explanation of the Testaments). It treats on the relation of the New Testament to the Old Testament Scriptures. While the previously mentioned work *"Vindication"* did not appear in print in that age, the *Testaments-Erläuterung* was printed about 1544. Apparently the Brethren had their own printing office somewhere in South Germany.

A point which until recently was under dispute has been settled by the writings of Marpeck, namely, the question of the practice of the ordinance of feetwashing among the Swiss Brethren. Marpeck repeatedly makes mention of feetwashing as one of the ordinances.

CHAPTER 14

CASPAR SCHWENCKFELD

Caspar Schwenckfeld (1489-1561) was in principle a dissenter from all existing churches. On questions of religious observances he took an attitude of complete compromise. In the earliest period of the Reformation movement Schwenckfeld became an adherent of the Lutheran reformation. He was disappointed when Luther consented to a union of the church with the state in consequence of which the whole population, of the states having Protestant rulers, were made members of the church. Schwenckfeld complained bitterly of the absence of discipline in the Protestant state churches. He was disappointed because the Reformation of the state church type failed to result in an advancement of the spiritual and moral condition of the people. "Doctor Luther," he remarked, "has led us through the sea into the wilderness and would now have us believe that we are already in the promised land." He criticised Luther freely on various points. Luther, in his replies to Schwenckfeld, was not sparing in the use of reproachful epithets.

Schwenckfeld found himself differing from all religious parties. He failed to find a party or church whose doctrine and practice were in his opinion scripturally satisfactory. He did not believe himself called to become the leader or organizer of another church. Naturally therefore he would not be identified with any one of the existing churches. He finally adopted the view that to organize a church, beside the Church of Rome, required a special call, a distinct divine authorization, such as in his opinion neither the reformers of the state church type nor the Anabaptists could claim. The former had, as far as the membership of the church was concerned, not started new churches, they represented a reformation of the Roman Catholic Church. The Anabaptists had, in Schwenckfeld's opinion, acted without divine authorization when they organized a church.

Schwenckfeld looked for the appearance of a leader endued with extraordinary spiritual power who would assemble a true church. He expected that the inception of the church for which he hoped, would mean the cessation of persecution. Meanwhile, to avoid persecution, he advised his friends to remain within the dominant churches, be they Catholic or Protestant. His adherents did not organize distinct congregations but formed circles within the existing state churches. He counseled them to accommodate themselves in practice to the demands of these churches. His adherents in the Roman Church he warned to attend the Mass; for to refuse to do so, he said, would cause too great sensation. He advocated an attitude of *Stillstand,* or suspension of such scriptural practices as were not in vogue in those states in which his adherents might chance to live.

Schwenckfeld became the advocate of general *Stillstand.* He often spoke of the type of teaching which he advocated as "the middle way," for the reason that it was designed to strike a medium, or middle ground, between the various existing churches, thus offering a way of escape from religious contention, as well as from persecution. It was an easy way out of immediate difficulties, in contrast to "the way of the cross," that is, the way of enduring persecution. Schwenckfeld became the apostle of the so-called "middle way" type of the Reformation movement.

The reformer Ambrosius Blauer, of Constance, in a letter, written in 1536, expressed the fear that the Schwenckfeldians would yet become a new sect which would be even "worse" than the Anabaptists. This fear proved groundless. Schwenckfeld never organized a congregation or church. In certain South German cities the authorities apparently had an understanding with him that they would refrain from persecution of him and his friends so long as his activity would not result in a hindrance to their work.

Schwenckfeld reached a goodly age. He died at Ulm in Germany, in 1561. Almost to the end he was haunted by the fear of being sought for martyrdom. More than a century after his death the Schwenckfeldians began to approve more definitely of withdrawal from the state churches, and were consequently subjected to serious persecution. In 1734 they emigrated in a body to Pennsylvania, being financially assisted by the Mennonites of Hamburg and the Netherlands. At the present time their membership numbers about 1,800.

Caspar Schwenckfeld was a voluminous writer. His writings not infrequently make mention of the Anabaptists and their principles and doctrine. In his book, *Criticism (Judicium) of the New Book of the Anabaptists,* written in 1542, as noted in chapter 13 above, was a reply to Marpeck in which he attempted a refutation of the evangelical Anabaptists' position. In this book Schwenckfeld defended his opinion that under existing conditions the proper thing was to "stand still" as concerned church organization and the observance of the ordinances. He believed that a divinely authorized church did not exist at that time, and that no one was called to organize a true church, hence the observance of the ordinances and other requirements which concern the church were not obligatory. In this book Schwenckfeld attacked and denounced various teachings of the Swiss Brethren. He asserted that they overemphasized the importance of the letter of Scripture and made an idol of the cross by bearing the cross of persecution. He made such accusations against them because they refused to heed his advice and avoid persecution by outwardly conforming to the practices prescribed by the civil and ecclesiastical authorities of the province or state in which they lived.

Examination of an Applicant for Membership in the Mennonite Church

The original is a painting, with the title (translated): "Agreement and
decision of the ministers and elders in a meeting at
Strasburg, Anno 1568 and 1607."

Strasbourg — Rabenbrücke. — Pont du Corbeau

View of Strasburg, Important Center of the Swiss Brethren Movement After 1560

(From Vedder: "Balthasar Huebmaier")

Balthasar Hubmaier, 1482 (?)—1528

An early leader among the Swiss Anabaptists.

(From "Mennonitische Geschichtsblaetter," 1940)

Hans Hut, ?—1527

A traveling preacher who did much to spread Anabaptism
in South Germany and Upper Austria.

Dirck Philips, 1504—1568

Early Mennonite bishop and writer in Holland and North Germany.

Menno Simons, 1496—1561

A portrait made in 1683.

The Menno Simons Memorial Shaft at Witmarsum
Erected in 1879.

Gerhard Roosen, 1612—1711

Leading Mennonite bishop and writer in northwestern Germany.

Hans de Ries, 1553—1638

Mennonite bishop and writer of Holland.

CHAPTER 15

EVANGELICAL ANABAPTISTS IN SOUTH GERMANY

In South Germany the city of Strasburg in Alsace was the main Anabaptist center. The city of Augsburg in Bavaria also is to be noted as a central point of the early Anabaptist movement.

Hans Denck was apparently the first Anabaptist leader to labor and baptize at Augsburg. In the month of May, 1526, Hans Hut, during a sojourn of only three days at Augsburg became acquainted with Denck and was baptized by him. After that Hans Hut labored with eminent success as an evangelist in South Germany and Austria. In February, 1527, he returned to Augsburg where he baptized many persons, among them the former priest Jacob Dachser and the monk Sigmund Salminger. Both were chosen as ministers of the Anabaptist congregation. Eitelhans Langenmantel, of the nobility, another of Hut's converts, later wrote a little work defending evangelical Anabaptist doctrine.[38] He died a martyr in April, 1528, at Weissenhorn.

On Easter Sunday of the following year an Anabaptist meeting of about eighty-six men and women was taken by surprise and imprisoned. The minister Hans Leopold Schneider[39] suffered martyrdom on April 15, 1528. The rest of the prisoners were banished from the city, most of them after being subjected to cruel torture. Five persons had their cheeks burned through with red hot irons, because they had permitted Anabaptist meetings to be held in their houses. A woman had her tongue cut out. In consequence most of the Anabaptists of Augsburg fled the city. Many refugees from Augsburg went to other South German cities, about one hundred of them to Strasburg. Those who remained repeatedly had meetings for worship in a forest not far from the city, also in a deep gravel pit near the village of Goeggingen.

Before the persecution of the year 1528 Hans Hut had again returned to Augsburg, having labored with great success as an evangelist in Upper Austria and various other German and

Austrian states. Toward the end of the year 1526 he had an important public debate with Balthasar Hubmaier at Bergen near Nikolsburg in Moravia, defending against him the principle of nonresistance. Somewhat later another disputation was held in the castle at Nikolsburg between these two Anabaptist leaders. Hut labored subsequently in Vienna and many other places, and then, as stated above, returned to Augsburg where he was imprisoned on September 16, 1527. He died in prison and his body was burned at the stake on December 7, 1527.

Shortly before Hans Hut's imprisonment, namely on August 20, 1527, an Anabaptist conference was held in the city of Augsburg, with Hans Denck presiding. This meeting was attended by many who had come from different places of South Germany and Austria. Since within a short time a large number of those who were here in attendance suffered martyrdom at various places, this synod is known as the Martyrs' Synod. There is scarcely any definite information about this meeting, however. Evidently some of the Anabaptist leaders who are believed to have been in attendance differed widely on important points from others who were present. As for Hans Denck, he went from Augsburg to Basel, where about two months after the date of this synod he renounced the Anabaptist teaching of the need of believers' baptism.

In a later period (1544-56) Pilgram Marpeck, as noted in chapter 13 above, labored in Augsburg. In many South German cities, at Regensburg, Ulm, Memmingen, Worms, and others there were Anabaptist congregations.

At Alzey in the Palatinate many Anabaptists were imprisoned and threatened with execution in 1528. Since this was previous to the enactment of the imperial law demanding the execution of the Anabaptists, the authorities of Alzey hesitated to pronounce the sentence of death. A minister of the Protestant state church, Johann Odenbach, in a pamphlet warned the judges of the terrible responsibility of putting Anabaptists to death. He wrote:

You should diligently and earnestly cry unto God, the true Judge, for His divine assistance, wisdom and grace. If you do so, you will abstain from polluting your hands with innocent blood.—Thieves and murderers you have treated more mercifully in prison, than these poor people who have committed neither theft nor murder nor any other crime, but with good, sincere intention have been re-baptized. You should give heed to the fact that they only ask to be taught from Holy Scripture and declare that they are ready to yield if shown to be in error. People will say concerning them: "With what great patience, love, and devotion have these poor people died. How valiantly have they resisted the world." They could not be overcome except by violence. They are holy martyrs of the Lord.

The judges of the court at Alzey refused to pass the sentence of death, since there was no definite transgression of law, yet the imperial officer of the place finally had the prisoners executed without a formal sentence. The men were beheaded, and the women drowned.

Under Elector Palatine Frederick II, who began to rule in 1544, the Lutheran Church was made the state church. As an attempt to win the evangelical Anabaptists for Lutheranism a debate between state church theologians and Anabaptists was held at Pfeddersheim near Worms in 1557. This disputation was without success. Elector Frederick III of the Palatinate whose reign began in 1559, abolished Lutheranism and made the church of John Calvin the state church. He arranged for a great debate for the purpose of winning the Anabaptists for the Calvinist creed. The debate was held for nineteen days from May 28 to June 19, 1571, at Frankenthal in the Palatinate. The Elector guaranteed safe-conduct for two weeks before and after the debate to all Anabaptists who would attend. Prisoners also were permitted to attend the debate on condition that they abstained from teaching and baptizing during this period. This new effort to win the Anabaptists, like the one made at Pfeddersheim, proved unavailing. The Anabaptists refused to approve of the creed of their opponents, and were threatened with severer measures of persecution.

CHAPTER 16

EVANGELICAL ANABAPTISTS IN AUSTRIA

In no other European state or province, perhaps, did the evangelical Anabaptist movement show greater strength than in the Austrian province of the Tyrol.

In the spring of the year 1526 we find traces of the labors of evangelical Anabaptists in the valley of the Inn river in the Tyrol. The government of this province published a strict edict against the Brethren in November, 1527. Leonhard Schiemer, a learned man and a distinguished evangelist, fell into the hands of the authorities at Rattenburg in the Tyrol. He did not deny that he had baptized many persons at various places in Austria and Bavaria. On January 14, 1528, he suffered martyrdom by being beheaded. A few weeks later Hans Schlaffer, another zealous preacher and evangelist, was burned at the stake at Schwatz in the same province. Pilgram Marpeck was baptized about the same time at Rattenberg.

On April 1, 1528, the government of the Tyrol published a decree offering grace and pardon to all Anabaptists who would recant before April 28 of the same year. After the latter date even those who recanted should be put to death but should be granted a milder form of execution. Instead of being burned alive at the stake they should be beheaded and their bodies burned. On February 5, 1529, it was decreed, however, that this favor was to be no longer extended to those who recanted.

At the same date the government published a severe mandate against the Brethren. "Since in our principality," it is stated in this document, "more Anabaptists are found than in any other land, we decree that any and all persons, men or women, who have been rebaptized shall be imprisoned and put to death." It was furthermore ordained by this mandate that houses in which Anabaptists met or had been given lodging or hiding places, should be destroyed by fire, or otherwise if other buildings would be endangered. A special police force, called "Anabaptist hunters" was provided, similarly as in the canton

Bern, Switzerland, to track down and arrest the Anabaptists. The authorities persuaded certain men to pretend to be desirous of uniting with them, and thus to obtain information from them in order to betray them and deliver them up into their hands. For delivering up an Anabaptist minister they were offered a reward of forty guilders. Many brethren and sisters, among them Jacob Hutter, were arrested through the assistance of such "children of Judas," as they were designated in the chronicles.

Hans Hut, previously mentioned, was one of the most successful Anabaptist missionaries in various Austrian provinces. Great numbers of converts were baptized by him. As already stated he was the notable defender of nonresistance against Balthasar Hubmaier. Hans Hut made the mistake of setting the approximate time (not the date) of the coming of the Lord. When the persecution of the Anabaptists became more and more severe with no end in sight to the outrage, he came to the conclusion that this condition of things could not continue long. It was an almost general belief at that time, shared also by Martin Luther, that there would be an invasion by the Turks previous to the Lord's coming. From certain statements in Daniel's prophecy Hans Hut calculated that this punishment of nominal Christendom by the Turks would take place in 1528, and this would be followed by the coming of the Lord. Hans Hut, as stated elsewhere, died in prison at Augsburg in 1527.

George Blaurock's martyrdom took place in the Tyrol. After a few years of labor in the Swiss Cantons of Bern and Appenzell he was active with great success as an evangelist in various parts of this province. In August, 1529, he was, with his fellow minister Hans Langegger, arrested at Guffidaun near Clausen in the Tyrol. The two men were subjected to the most cruel torture and were burned at the stake on September 6 of the same year at Clausen. Blaurock was one of the leaders among the first Brethren at Zurich, one of the organizers of the first congregation. He had been apparently the first to urge the need of separation from the state church through the act of baptism, a man of Christian zeal and consecration, of lucid sincerity of conviction. Among those who witnessed his death and heard his testimony for evangelical truth was Peter Walpot, then a boy of eight years, who from 1565 to 1578 was head pastor of

the Hutterian Brethren in Moravia.[40] In a hymn he wrote
Blaurock says, "Blessed are they who in all tribulation will cling
to Christ to the end," and he adds:

> "As He Himself our sufferings bore,
>   When hanging on the accursed tree,
> So there is suffering still in store,
>   O pious heart, for you and me."

The persecution in the Tyrol was one of indescribable severity. A very great number suffered martyrdom. On February
9, 1530, the government of the Tyrol reported to the Austrian
authorities at Vienna that more than seven hundred persons,
men and women, had been executed as Anabaptists in the province, and a greater number had fled the country (to Moravia).
Furthermore, the report stated, such was the "obstinacy" of
the Anabaptists in general that the most cruel punishment, and
even death itself failed to strike terror into their hearts, and
when they were seized and arrested, they were willing and
ready to confess their faith, though they knew it meant death.

Since the death penalty for Anabaptists failed to check the
movement in the Tyrol, a General Mandate was published on
May 12, 1532, decreeing that not only the Anabaptists but also
those who would give them shelter or lodging, or show them
favors in any way, should be put to death. The reward for
delivering up an Anabaptist to the authorities was gradually
raised to one hundred guilders for prominent persons, such as
ministers.

It is of interest to note that the government evidently
shared the almost generally accepted opinion that the Anabaptists were through witchcraft blinded by their leaders who,
so it was supposed, gave them to drink of a little flask, after
which they would give their lives for their alleged heresies.
Leonhard Schiemer, already mentioned, wrote a booklet entitled, *An Answer to those who say we drink something out of
a little flask, the devil knows what it contains.* On May 31,
1533, the authorities at Innsbruck, the capital of the Tyrol,
advised the magistrates at Guffidaun to have the food for imprisoned Anabaptists cooked in holy water. This should be
done for a number of days and they should be watched to see
whether it would break the spell of witchery.

On June 17, 1538, the heads of the Catholic Church at the town of Brixen reported to the government at Innsbruck that in the Puster valley a great increase of Anabaptists was in evidence. The judge of Schöneck had informed them that in his political district there was no one in whom confidence could be placed; all were favorably inclined toward the Anabaptist cause. The judge of Michaelsburg gave a similar report concerning his district.

In a royal decree dated April 22, 1543, and addressed to certain Tyrolean magistrates, the complaint is made that the judges to whose lot it falls to sentence Anabaptists "decide the cases according to their own consciences, and not in accordance with the edicts"—a striking proof that the judges had conscientious scruples against sentencing Anabaptists to death. In another mandate it is demanded that the judges and jurors, before beginning an Anabaptist trial, must swear a solemn oath to God and the saints that they will pronounce sentence as prescribed by the mandates. King Ferdinand I of Austria himself, who had insisted on the utmost stringency, declared in 1543 that he was "terrified" by the many executions. The judges and jurors became progressively more reluctant to pronounce the death sentence over Anabaptists. The mandates demanded that the officials do all in their power to prevent the escape of any Anabaptists to Moravia, where they were tolerated; indeed there is evidence that many Tyrolean magistrates favored their flight. The last martyr of the evangelical Anabaptists in Austria was Jost Wilhelm who was beheaded in the village of Bregenz in Voralberg.

Evangelists of the Hutterian Brethren in Moravia found the Tyrol one of their most responsive and fruitful fields of labor. After the year 1533 the Tyrolean Anabaptists were, with few exceptions, of the Hutterian group. While establishing a Hutterian colony, or *Bruderhof,* in the Tyrol was not possible, nevertheless the brotherhood here was not disorganized. They met for worship in out-of-the-way places and rendered each other such assistance and aid as was found possible. As just indicated, those who escaped the sword of the executioner in the Tyrol fled to Moravia. Many of the refugees fell into the hands of the officers while en route to Moravia, were arrested and executed. Also many of the evangelists from Moravia died a martyr's death in the Tyrol.

In the year 1592 a serious oppression of the Anabaptists in Moravia began. In consequence the migration of Tyrolese Anabaptists to Moravia naturally diminished. In the Thirty Years' War (1618-1648) Moravia ceased to offer a refuge to the Anabaptists. After the victory of the Catholic army near Prague in 1620 all Anabaptists were mercilessly driven from this province. This marked the end of the Anabaptists' migration from other states to Moravia.

CHAPTER 17

THE HUTTERIAN BRETHREN

The Hutterian Brotherhood is named after Jacob Hutter who suffered martyrdom by being burned at the stake on February 26, 1536, at Innsbruck in the Tyrol. This brotherhood descended from the Swiss Brethren and differed from them principally by their practice of "having all things common."

The Hutterian brotherhood originated in Moravia. One of the first Anabaptists to labor in Moravia was Balthasar Hubmaier. He organized an Anabaptist congregation at Nikolsburg in Moravia under the protection of the lord Leonhard von Liechtenstein, in 1526. In the course of about a year thousands united with this congregation by baptism, among them lord Leonhard von Liechtenstein. According to the testimony of Hans Schlaffer, an eye-witness, baptism was administered at Nikolsburg in this way: "A sermon was preached and then all who came forward and desired it were baptized; not every one was examined and questioned in particular."

There were at Nikolsburg many Swiss Brethren refugees who differed from Balthasar Hubmaier on the principle of non-resistance and other points. They held meetings of their own and refused to comply with Leonhard von Liechtenstein's desire that they unite with the larger Anabaptist congregation. Consequently they were informed by von Liechtenstein that they could not remain at Nikolsburg. In the spring of the year 1528 between 200 and 300 persons, among them many penniless refugees, departed from Nikolsburg in a body under the leadership of Jacob Widemann. On the same day these exiles encamped in a village named Bogenitz. Here they chose "ministers of temporal needs." "The chosen men spread a cloak before the people," says a chronicler of the Brethren, "and every one laid down on it his earthly possessions, unconstrained and with a willing mind."

This was the beginning of "having all things common" in this brotherhood. A partial community of goods, however, had been practiced by this congregation before their departure from Nikolsburg. One of the complaints made by their leaders concerning the large Anabaptist congregation at that place was that "they did not open their homes to the pilgrims and refugees from other countries," many of whom arrived destitute. From Bogenitz the exiles proceeded to Austerlitz upon the invitation of the civil authorities of that place, the lords of Kaunitz, who sent them word that, if there were a thousand of them, they would be welcome to come. Here they built their first community houses. The Lords von Kaunitz had for some time granted toleration to dissenters. In 1511 Ulrich von Kaunitz had permitted Picards (Hussites) to settle in his territory.

In the following year (1529) Jacob Hutter of the Tyrol, minister of an Anabaptist group in that province, was sent to Austerlitz for information about the church in that town. He united with this congregation in the name of his flock in the Tyrol, which now migrated to Moravia. After his return to his home land a division took place in the congregation at Austerlitz. The stricter party, under George Zaunring, about 150 persons, in January, 1531, moved to Auspitz, another village in the territory of the Lords von Kaunitz. In great poverty they established here a common household (*Bruderhof*). Jacob Hutter, having returned from the Tyrol, was in 1533 chosen the head pastor of the church at Auspitz. Through the efforts of Hutter and his assistants strict discipline and a rigorous order of community of goods were established. Within a few years Moravia had a number of Hutterite *Bruderhofs* under the protection of the Moravian nobles. In the years 1529 to 1535 Jacob Hutter led many hundreds of Brethren from Tyrol to Moravia.

The royal authorities in Vienna objected persistently to the toleration of Anabaptists by the Moravian nobles. In the year 1535 the nobles found themselves unable to prevent the expulsion of the Brethren from their homes. Ruthlessly they were driven from their dwellings. Jacob Hutter wrote in a letter to the Moravian authorities:

At the present time we find ourselves camping on the wide, wide heath; if God will, without disadvantage to any one. We will not do a wrong or injury to any man, yea, not to our greatest enemy, neither to Ferdinandus [King of Austria] nor any one else, great or small. All our actions and conduct, word and work, life and walk, are open before the world; there is no secret about it all. Rather than knowingly to rob a man of a penny we would willingly give up a hundred guilders. And before we would give our greatest enemy a blow with the hand, to say nothing of spear, sword or halberd as is the manner of the world, we would be willing to lose our lives. We have no weapons of defense, such as spears or guns, as every one sees and knows. In short, in our preaching and speaking and our whole walk of life our object is to live in peace and unity according to the truth and will of God, as the true followers of Christ.

Within a few months, however, the Brethren returned. Again in 1547 there was a great persecution in Moravia. By this time the Brethren had twenty-six communities in this province. The Moravian nobles wrote to King Ferdinand of Austria that the required banishment of the Brethren would entail a great loss to the country, depriving it of its best workers. They were nevertheless forced to obey the orders of the king and expel them. The whole brotherhood was driven from Moravia. They fled to Hungary but within a short time were driven back to Moravia. Again they were compelled by the Moravian authorities to return to Hungary.

This persecution continued for over four years. Much of the time many of the Brethren saw themselves compelled to live with their families in forests, cliffs, and caverns. Toward the end of this period some of the men found employment with the Moravian nobles who greatly valued their faithful service. Finally they were permitted again to form settlements at various places in Moravia. After 1552 persecution ceased almost entirely in this province. There began in 1553 a period to which the chronicles of the Brethren refer as "the favorable time for the Church." This was followed by "the ideal period," 1563 to 1592, in which the Hutterian Brotherhood enjoyed great prosperity and growth. By the end of this period they had in Moravia and at a few points in Hungary about fifty communities (*Bruderhofs*) numbering twelve to fifteen thousand souls.

Of the Hutterian congregations in Moravia it can be said that they were centers of true Christian life and activity. Dr. J. H. Kurtz, a Lutheran church historian, characterized their religious life as follows: "They were noted for their sincere piety, exemplary discipline, moral fervor, strict industry, conscientiously fair business dealing, unparalleled patience in suffering, but above all for their wonderful martyr-courage and martyr-joy." Dr. Josef Beck, a Roman Catholic historian, wrote of them: "To die to the world, to manifest humility, meekness and patience in all conditions of life, to hold death for the sake of the truth as gain and poverty as riches, and diligently to strive to live a life void of offense was to them a sacred duty."

In no other section or country did the Anabaptists enjoy such freedom as in Moravia. Thither they fled from all parts of Austria, Switzerland, and Germany. Many of these refugees were apprehended while en route to Moravia, to be imprisoned and executed. The Moravian lords, or nobles, found it eminently to their own interest to tolerate and protect the Brethren. The economic benefits derived from the Hutterite communities were very great. Their industries reached a high degree of development. Masons, blacksmiths, coppersmiths, coopers, watchmakers, cutlers, tanners, shoemakers, saddlers, harness-makers, wagoners, joiners, turners, hatters, tailors, potters were found in large numbers in their communities.

In reply to the demands of the royal government in Vienna for the suppression of this sect, the nobles insisted that their banishment of these people would involve irreparable loss to the country. Such demands from Vienna were from time to time repeated, but for a long period without success. The nobility of the land saw their business that was entrusted to Hutterites well cared for, and were absolutely sure that they would not be imposed upon or defrauded by them. In their own interest they energetically opposed the expulsion of the Brethren.

The most relentless literary antagonist of the Hutterian Brethren, Christopher Andreas Fischer, a Catholic priest, in his book,[41] *Fifty-four Weighty Reasons why the Anabaptists Should not be Tolerated in the Land,* printed in 1607, gives an interesting description of their life. He insists that they should be persecuted and banished as heretics, but at the same time makes decidedly favorable statements about them. He protests that the lords, or barons, not only tolerated them but preferred them to the Christians (Catholics) for positions of responsibility such as managers of estates, stewards, and the like, as well as for workers and servants, and paid them better wages. Many of the Brethren were in the employ of the lords; the earnings of the Brethren were not considered by them as their own property, but were turned over to the brotherhood of which they were members. They had famous physicians in their midst. In the case of a serious malady which had befallen Emperor Rudolf in 1581, George Zobel, a physician of the Brethren, was called to the imperial court at Prague to prescribe treatment. Their schools were well organized, but they had no institutions of higher learning.

In a war between Turkey and Austria which began in 1593, the Hutterian Brethren had to endure great tribulation. In the twelfth year of this war not less than sixteen *Bruderhofs* were destroyed by the Turks and Tartars and their allies. Many members of their communities were murdered or carried off into slavery. During this time of tribulation, and in their later history, the Brethren stood true to the principle of nonresistance. The first war tax was laid upon them, as upon all others, in 1579. In keeping with their profession of nonresistance they refused to pay it. The lords in consequence seized and confiscated some of their property, such as cattle or sheep, to cover the sum asked for war taxes. "We suffer the spoiling of our goods" (Hebrews 10:34), wrote a chronicler of the Brethren, "rather than do that which would be a stain and burden on our consciences." The seizure of property for this purpose was repeated in 1584 and 1589. During the wars beginning in 1596 property to cover the demanded war taxes was taken annually in this way by the authorities.

The terrible Thirty Years' War (1618-1648), a religious war between Catholicism and state church Protestantism, brought the Brethren indescribable suffering. Moravia was on the whole a poor country. The peasants lived for the most part in small houses or cabins, while the Brethren had large community houses and were supposed to have considerable wealth. The plundering soldiers expected to find in their houses money and valuables. The most inhuman torture of all sorts was used to force them to surrender their supposed treasures. All this seemed to the soldiery to be a mild punishment for a people who, according to the verdict of the dominant church, deserved death as heretics. Many of the houses of the brotherhood were totally destroyed; others were repeatedly plundered. In one night, in the year 1620, fifty-six persons were murdered in the

Bruderhof at Pribitz in Moravia by a Polish army, and sixty others were wounded of whom many soon died. In the wake of the war came devastating plagues to which many of the members of the Hutterian community fell victims.

In the summer of the year 1622 Cardinal Franz von Dietrichstein, the governor of Moravia, obtained from King Ferdinand of Austria, full power to expel the Hutterian brotherhood from this province. They were now compelled to abandon their twenty-four remaining communities and leave Moravia. They fled for the most part into Hungary where in a previous period they had established two or three *Bruderhofs*. A large group of the refugees went to Alwintz in Transylvania where a *Bruderhof* had been established in 1621 upon the invitation of Prince Bethlen Gabor. In Hungary the Brethren suffered much from the armies that passed through this province. In a period of general decline small groups of Brethren returned to Moravia. Thereupon Cardinal von Dietrichstein issued a decree in the name of the Emperor, in March, 1624, demanding that "within fourteen days from date all who are of the Hutterian persuasion must leave Moravia on pain of death. Should, after the expiration of this time, any one of them be found in Moravia, he shall be put to death without further formality, by being hanged to the nearest tree or burned at the stake."

By the year 1631 the brotherhood of the Hutterians numbered only about a half dozen communities in Hungary and Transylvania, having not over two thousand members. Successive Turkish wars and persecution again brought the brotherhood in Hungary very great tribulation. They were reduced to great poverty. In 1665 they sent two brethren to the Netherlands to lay the needs of the brotherhood before the Mennonite congregations there. The delegates visited the churches in Holland, Zealand, Flanders, and Friesland and obtained large contributions.

After again enduring persecutions the Brethren of Transylvania, together with a few persons from the former Hutterian communities in Hungary, fled in 1767 into Wallachia in modern Roumania, a little band of sixty-seven souls. Here they prospered for a time but later suffered severely in the Russian-Turkish war. From here they migrated to Russia where Catharine the Great offered exemption from military service to conscientious objectors to war. In 1874 and successive years all the Hutterians emigrated from Russia to the United States, settling in Dakota. After the World War they, with the exception of a few communities, migrated to Manitoba and Alberta, where they have today fifty communities.

The organization of the *Bruderhofs* today is the same as it was appointed four centuries ago by Jacob Hutter. Each *Bruderhof* has a minister and a "householder" or supervisor who has charge of economic and industrial affairs. As assistants to these men there is a body of elders numbering four or five. These men are in every respect responsible to the congregations and remain in office only as long as they render satisfactory service. The householder is the business manager of the community. The foremen of the various industries are responsible to him. He alone handles the money of the community. No money is in circulation within the community. There is no ownership of any property by individuals. All land, buildings, in fact all material things are owned by the *Bruderhof*. Even articles of furniture and clothing are, strictly speaking, not the property of the individuals who use them. Community of goods does not exist between the various communities but only between the members of the same community. Today each *Bruderhof* consists of from fifteen to twenty families. Their clothing and manner of life are very plain. Illiteracy is not found among them.

The foundation principle and ideal of the Hutterian life is mutual aid and service; in other words, true Christian brotherliness. Their communism has nothing in common with political communism.

CHAPTER 18

HANS DENCK

Hans Denck was a mystic who believed that "the inner word," or the voice of God within the heart, is the highest source of divine revelation, exceeding the Scriptures in authority. He was an Anabaptist for a short time but was never identified with the Swiss Brethren. Various writers have supposed that in his teachings he represented the Swiss Brethren. That inference is not correct. He differed from them fundamentally in doctrine, and finally renounced the Anabaptist views of the need of baptism on the confession of personal faith.

Hans Denck was a highly educated man. For a number of years he was a student in the University of Ingolstadt in Bavaria. He obtained the Master's degree from the University of Basel. In 1524 he became rector of St. Sebaldus classical school at Nuremberg. Being suspected of heretical teaching he, upon orders from the Council of that city, submitted a confession of faith in which he set forth, among other points, his mystical views on "the inner word." This confession was found unsatisfactory from the viewpoint of Lutheranism, and Denck was consequently banished from Nuremberg in January, 1525. In the summer of the same year he sojourned for some time in the city of St. Gall in eastern Switzerland, where there was a large congregation of the Swiss Brethren, and apparently attended their meetings only occasionally.

From St. Gall, Denck went to Augsburg in Swabia, South Germany. Here he was baptized in the early spring of 1526, by Balthasar Hubmaier. In the autumn of the same year he left Augsburg to go to Strasburg in Alsace, a city having a strong congregation of the Swiss Brethren. Here again, as formerly in St. Gall, Hans Denck held himself aloof from the Brethren. For various reasons a union of his party with the Brethren could not take place.

Banished from the Protestant city of Strasburg in December, 1526, Hans Denck went to Landau, then to Worms on the Rhine, where he with Ludwig Hätzer published a translation

of the Old Testament Prophets in German.[42] In the autumn of
1527 Denck returned to Augsburg where there was a large Anabaptist church, but attended their meetings only a few times.
He found himself in failing health and decided to seek a retreat
in Basel, having written a conciliatory letter to Oekolampad,
the Zwinglian reformer in Basel. Denck died in the same year
after a brief sojourn in that city.

As correctly stated by the chronicler Sebastian Franck, and
other contemporary writers, Hans Denck was the head of a
particular group or party, among the Anabaptists. Shortly
before his death, he, as already intimated, renounced his former view of the need of believers' baptism. He expressed regret that he had ever repudiated infant baptism and become a
dissenter. Even before abandoning believers' baptism he had
always materially differed in doctrine from the Swiss Brethren.
The opinion that he ever was of one and the same party with
them is quite erroneous.

Hans Denck is the author of a number of books setting
forth his teachings. His religious views were largely rationalistic. He did not accept the Scriptures as final authority, but
held "the inner word" to be the last authority in matters of
faith. The doctrine of "the inner word" is the belief that God
reveals Himself directly to the individual, independently of the
Scriptures or any other medium. The Swiss Brethren, on the
contrary, were believers in the Bible as the very word of God.

Hans Denck denied the depravity of human nature, and consequently held certain views on the atonement and redemption
which are not satisfactory from the viewpoint of the Scriptures.
Moreover he defended the doctrine of unconditional universal
salvation, believing that all men will finally be saved. And yet
he stressed the importance of strict Christian living. In agreement with the Swiss Brethren and all other Anabaptists he rejected the denial of free will and repudiated the doctrine of
predestination, as held by Zwingli and Calvin.

In the brief period of Hans Denck's labors as an Anabaptist
leader the number of his followers was not large. The last
booklet which he wrote and which was published after his death
under the title *Recantation,* is not a recantation of his mystical
and rationalistic teachings but a repudiation of his distinctly
Anabaptist views. He confessed regret for having ever under-

taken to collect congregations of believers separate from the national churches, by the practice of the baptism of believers. He further expressed his determination "to stand forever still" as concerns baptism.

After Denck's death there were a small number of his friends who, following his advice, constituted a circle within the state church, as did the followers of Caspar Schwenckfeld. Like the Schwenckfeldians they advocated the general policy of "the middle way," or of "standing still," as regards religious observances and ceremonies. Friedolin Meyer, one of the few followers of Denck in Strasburg, referred to this policy as follows: "I have found, as it were, a middle way between popery and Lutheranism, by which I have avoided all separation, and am striving alone for a good, upright Christian life." The expression "middle way" then referred to an attitude of outward accommodation to the practices of the dominant state church. It indicated an attitude of "standing still" as to any practices that were not approved by that church. Those taking such an attitude were, as a rule, granted a measure of tolerance by the state and the state church.

On the principle of liberty of conscience Hans Denck agreed with the Swiss Brethren in their demand for the separation of church and state and for religious liberty. He condemned all persecution of those who erred in faith. Denck seems to have believed, however, that in so far as religious doctrine is concerned, the church should take a similar attitude as the state. In other words, the church should not have a definite doctrinal standard but should permit any sort of teaching within its own bounds. At least, this liberalistic view has been ascribed to Denck by certain writers, though the pertinent evidence adduced from his writings is not altogether convincing. If this was Denck's view, he differed in this regard from the Swiss Brethren, who plainly denied the liberty to propagate any sort of teaching, whether scriptural or not, within the church.

The Swiss Brethren believed that a true Christian church will necessarily stand for definite Christian doctrine and will insist on the profession of the Bible faith. A number of contemporary writers, for example, Urbanus Rhegius, Johannes Kessler, Sebastian Franck, and others (the two first named having been personally acquainted with him) stated that Hans Denck believed, that even Satan will finally be saved. He probably held this view, though it is not expressly stated in his writings. His biographer, Ludwig Keller, was of the opinion that Denck denied even the existence of Satan.

The supposition that Hans Denck was ever identified with the Swiss Brethren, as has been held even by Mennonite historians, is based on the assumption that all the early Anabaptists of Switzerland and South Germany were substantially a unit in faith—an obvious error. In all probability the "false brethren" mentioned in the Schleitheim Confession, were those who advocated "standing still" as concerned the Christian ordinances.

A word about Ludwig Hätzer who was mentioned as collaborator with Denck in translating the Prophets. He was born about 1500 near St. Gall in Switzerland, and in 1523 as a priest in a village near Zurich, became an enthusiastic follower of Zwingli. In the second disputation of Zurich, held October 26-28, 1523, he acted as secretary. In 1526 he expressed himself definitely against the Anabaptists. In the same year he met Michael Sattler at Strasburg and expressed himself very unfavorably about this distinguished leader of the evangelical Anabaptists. There is no support for the supposition that he later united with them.

While Hätzer was of a religious turn, as his hymns and other writings indicate, his life was far from exemplary. On February 3, 1529, after a long imprisonment he was condemned to death for adultery, and was executed on the following day. He died as a sincerely repentant sinner, not by any means as a martyr, as has been supposed. Not a word of protest of his innocence fell from his lips, although he was given full liberty to speak, and freely addressed the bystanders, declaring among other things that he deserved death.

CHAPTER 19

BALTHASAR HUBMAIER

Balthasar Hubmaier was a distinguished Anabaptist leader who differed in doctrine from the Swiss Brethren on one important point: he did not teach the principle of nonresistance.

Balthasar Hubmaier was born in the town of Friedberg near Augsburg in Swabia, South Germany, and was educated in the universities of Freiburg and Ingolstadt in Bavaria. In 1515 he became prorector (dean) of the last named university, the degree of Doctor of Divinity having been previously conferred on him. As the head priest of the town of Waldshut (välds-hoot) on the Rhine in Austrian territory, South Germany, he began, in 1522, to study the writings of the reformers, in particular of Ulrich Zwingli whose follower and friend he became. In the following year he met Zwingli personally at Zurich to confer with him on infant baptism and other points. Zwingli at that time agreed with Hubmaier in the opinion that the baptism of infants is unscriptural.[43]

Hubmaier participated in the disputation held at Zurich concerning Mass and the images in October, 1523. With the approval of the population and the authorities of Waldshut he discarded the Latin language in the public services; he removed the pictures and statues from the churches and entered the state of matrimony. Waldshut was located within Austrian territory and the Austrian government was bitterly opposed to these innovations.

When word reached Hubmaier, in the autumn of 1524, that Zwingli had become a defender of infant baptism, he was bewildered. Upon Hubmaier's urgent request Zwingli promised to write him, giving him his reasons for favoring the baptism of infants; however his promised letter never appeared. Hubmaier was sorely disappointed. He wrote in a letter to Zwingli: "Write me for God's sake about baptism," but he again failed to receive a reply. Early in January, 1525 (i. e., shortly before the government of Zurich decided in favor of the practice of infant baptism), Hubmaier in Waldshut discontinued the baptism of infants, except in instances where parents were yet weak and desired to have their babies baptized. In such cases he took a compromising attitude and "was weak with the weak," as he stated in a letter to Johannes Oekolampad. If parents were willing to dispense with infant baptism, he substituted for it a special act of infant consecration. This, in passing, was the first instance in that period of the practice of the consecration of infants as a special public act.

About a fortnight after the debate on infant baptism which was held in Zurich on January 16, 1525, Hubmaier had a leaflet printed, indicating that he disapproved of the decision of Zwingli and the Zurich Council favoring infant baptism. While he evidently hesitated to contradict Zwingli in a publication, he offered to show to any one requesting it that infant baptism is "an act without any foundation in the divine Word."

On Easter, 1525, Hubmaier, with about sixty of his parishioners at Waldshut, was baptized by Wilhelm Reublin who had been banished from Zurich a few months previously. On the following days more than three hundred persons were baptized by Hubmaier, including a number of town councilors. For the administration of this ordinance a pail filled with water was set upon the baptismal font before the place of the altar which had been removed. Hubmaier formally resigned his office as a priest, together with the salary and benefices connected with it. The newly formed congregation elected him as their minister. Waldshut virtually became an Anabaptist town.

When Zwingli's defense of infant baptism (*Book on Baptism*) appeared, in June, 1525, Hubmaier felt that a reply was urgently called for, yet it was doubtful that a printer could be found for it. He did not give up the hope that Zwingli would yet reconsider his teaching in regard to baptism, and would revert to his former position. On July 10, 1525, Hubmaier wrote a letter to the Council of Zurich presenting an urgent petition that he be permitted to go to Zurich under a safe-conduct to discuss the question of baptism with Zwingli. He stated that he had read Zwingli's recent book and that he had nearly completed a book taking the opposite position. "Such discord," he said further, "is very regrettable. All that is possible should be done to overcome it." He expressed the hope that his desire to meet Zwingli would be granted him. "If it then be found with God's Word that I err," he says further, "I shall from my heart gladly recant." He concludes his letter with this touching appeal:

We are all fallible men. If one err today, the other may stumble tomorrow. Gracious, dear lords, I ask and entreat and beg you again for God's sake to permit me to meet Master Ulrich. If we may have a personal discussion, I hope to God that we shall soon come to an agreement in this matter, for I am ready to submit fully to the clear and plain Word of God, giving God the honor, and I believe my dear brother Ulrich Zwingli is of the same mind. Farewell in the Lord, and grant me, for God's sake, a gracious answer.

Hubmaier's urgent appeal fell on deaf ears. Zwingli and the Council of Zurich had definitely decided for a state church in which the population as a whole were compelled by force of civil law to be members. They saw clearly that for such a church the practice of infant baptism was indispensable. Zwingli seems to have found it difficult to take Hubmaier's statement seriously that he had in preparation a book in opposition to his own teaching. "I had expected," he wrote somewhat later with reference to Hubmaier, "that if others would oppose me in writing, or if I were sick or dead, he would defend me." Failing to receive a reply to the above petition for a discussion with Zwingli, Hubmaier completed his book on baptism.

To Zwingli's keen disappointment, Hubmaier found it possible to have his book printed, not in Switzerland however. The book was printed in Strasburg and is entitled, *The Christian Baptism of Believers*.[44] This book is undoubtedly one of the best written and most lucid books issued in the Reformation period, proving decisively, as has been admitted even by Zwinglian church historians, that there is no scriptural proof for infant baptism. In reply to it Zwingli published a book in the autumn of 1525. He censured Hubmaier severely for daring to defend Anabaptism through the printing press. "If you were willing to be instructed from the Scripture," Zwingli wrote, "why did you embrace Anabaptism before you had received such instruction?" Zwingli ignored the outstanding fact of Hubmaier's appeals for instruction from Scripture on the point in question.

Hubmaier never taught the principle of nonresistance, but opposed this principle by word and pen. He wrote a book against the Swiss Brethren, attempting a refutation of the principle of nonresistance.

The government of Austria, being strictly Roman Catholic, made preparations to take possession of the town and extirpate Anabaptism. With Hubmaier's advice and his active co-operation Waldshut took the sword of war against its rightful government. Hubmaier personally girded himself with a sword to take an active part in the struggle. The armed uprising of the town of Waldshut against the Austrian government was a foolhardy undertaking, even if it would not have been contrary to Christian principles.

Neither Hubmaier nor the people of Waldshut had any complaint against their government, except religious intolerance. So this was a purely religious war, motivated solely by the desire for religious liberty. And yet, unbelievable as it may seem, the people of Waldshut refused such liberty to others who differed from them. Hubmaier had taught the principle of liberty of conscience, but when Jacob Gross, a citizen of Waldshut, refused to take the sword upon the command of the magistrates, he was banished from the town. In all probability it was within Hubmaier's power to prevent this banishment. If he consented to it (concerning this there is not full certainty), it was a clear instance of compromise on his part.

The war of Waldshut with the Austrian government was of brief duration. The town was conquered by a contingent of the Austrian army, and all religious dissent from Romanism was suppressed. The town again became Roman Catholic throughout. It is a remarkable fact that the people of the town, apparently to a man, re-accepted the Roman Catholic faith upon the command of the authorities. They had made use of the carnal sword in defense of their faith, but showed themselves unwilling to bear persecution for it.

Waldshut was occupied by Austrian troops on December 5, 1525. With difficulty Hubmaier succeeded in making his escape. He went to Zurich, where he was arrested and cast into prison. His desire to confer with Zwingli on the question of baptism was now granted him, though only in a limited way. Instead of being given the opportunity to defend his teaching from the Scriptures, he was permitted only to answer certain questions put to him by Zwingli, who manifested an attitude of such haughtiness toward his unfortunate former friend that Hubmaier requested that Judae, Myconius, and Hofmeister, Zwingli's colleagues, instead of Zwingli, should confer with him. In a letter to Peter Gynoräus, Zwingli admitted that he treated Hubmaier uncivilly in this discussion. The latter was subsequently subjected to torture. In one of his later books he made the remark that Zwingli undertook to teach him another faith through the hangman.

After enduring an imprisonment of nearly four months Hubmaier was, through the torment of the rack, prevailed upon to recant. Before his recantation however he wrote a booklet which he published later at Nikolsburg in Moravia, containing a brief confession of his faith for which he suffered persecution. In conclusion he added the following sentences: "This is my faith which I confess with heart and tongue and which I have publicly confessed when I was baptized. And if I, because of the fear of man and weakness, through tyranny, torture, sword, fire, or water am forced from this faith, I pray Thee, merciful Father, raise me up again and let me not depart from this life without this faith." After his recantation Hubmaier was released from prison.

Departing from Zurich Hubmaier visited various cities, laboring for the Anabaptist cause. He finally fled to Nikolsburg in Moravia. He arrived at Nikolsburg in July, 1526, and found here an evangelical congregation. Nikolsburg was the center of a political district ruled by "lord" Leonhard von Liechtenstein who protected those dissenting from Romanism. Hubmaier labored here with great success. Within a year the number of those baptized by him, including lord Leonhard himself, was estimated at over 10,000. He preached and administered baptism in the large parish church of the town.

It is of interest to observe that this congregation at Nikolsburg was not without some similarity to the Protestant state churches. The civil ruler of the district, being a member of this congregation, yielded to the temptation of using, or misusing, his authority by interfering with the principle of liberty of conscience, which Hubmaier had formerly taught. Hans Hut, who in December, 1526, had a disputation with Hubmaier in the castle of Nikolsburg and had among other points defended the principle of nonresistance, was against his will held in the castle after the debate. In consequence there arose great murmuring among some of Hubmaier's congregation. Hans Hut was assisted by a friend to escape at night by the use of a rope.

Upon learning that Anabaptists were tolerated at Nikolsburg, many Swiss Brethren refugees sought shelter there. They disapproved in various respects of conditions prevailing in Hubmaier's congregation. As stated in an earlier chapter, they would not unite with this congregation because of the neglect of church discipline and the principle of nonresistance. Instead of attending the worship services in the churches of the town they held their own separate meetings. Consequently they were informed by von Liechtenstein that they must either attend the divine services held by the recognized pastors of the place, or leave the city. As a result between two and three hundred persons under their minister, Jacob Widemann, departed from Nikolsburg in the spring of 1528.

At Nikolsburg, within about a year's time after his arrival in this town, Hubmaier wrote and published no less than eighteen books and tracts. His publisher was Simprecht Sorg, called Froschower, formerly of Zurich, who had been called by the Liechtensteins from Styria to Nikolsburg, and had brought with him his printery. Hubmaier's writings, treating on nearly the whole body of Christian doctrine, deserve the attention of the serious student of Christian doctrine and of church history. His refutation of the denial of free will and of the doctrine of predestination is particularly noteworthy. In his writings he insisted on the imperative need of church discipline, though in the large congregation at Nikolsburg he apparently found the practice of scriptural discipline a very difficult problem. Hubmaier's vindication of believers' baptism has never been equalled. "In point of scholarship and concentrativeness," says Professor Johann Loserth, "Hubmaier surpassed his opponents, such as Zwingli, by far." Professor Alfred Hegler, of Tübingen, stated that "in Scripture proof, and partly also in formal argument, Hubmaier was Zwingli's superior." And Professor Carl Sachsse, in his work on Hubmaier's theology, says that Zwingli, in the defense of infant baptism, saw himself compelled to resort to various sophistical arguments. The Reformed theologian Usteri says:

Hubmaier's book *Of the Christian Baptism of Believers* demonstrated clearly that a direct scriptural proof for infant baptism can not be given. In contrast with Zwingli's sophistry it affords a peculiar satisfaction to see how clearly, transcendently, and harmoniously Hubmaier arranges the abundant Scripture proof-texts (*Beweismaterial*) around his definition of baptism. The true scriptural order, he points out, is none other than this: (1) preaching; (2) hearing; (3) faith; (4) baptism; (5) works. The scientific exegesis of later times has in the main taken Hubmaier's part, while Güder was of the opinion that Zwingli saw himself compelled to resort to, we should not like to say knowingly sophistical, but certainly violent exegesis.

Other Reformed historians also say that Zwingli failed to establish infant baptism as scriptural. Zwingli, in his reply to the said book of Hubmaier, says derisively:

Your almanac in which you set the saints in this order: preaching, hearing, faith, baptism, works, will not avail you.—And therefore I shall make for you another almanac for the present year in which, if God will, your goose-washing shall cease, namely [this is the order of the saints in my almanac]: (1) The rich, almighty God, (2) Will be Abraham's God, (3) Who shall walk uprightly before him; (4) He is also the God of his seed; (5) He has promised the Saviour in the covenant; (6) In the covenant infants and adults were circumcised.

Of course Zwingli's "almanac for the present year" was not sufficient to convince the Anabaptists of the validity of infant baptism. Even a few of Zwingli's friends and co-workers, besides those who identified themselves with the Anabaptists, found it impossible to accept his arguments as convincing. Leo Judae, Zwingli's principal assistant in Zurich, for a considerable time made no secret of the grave doubts which he entertained concerning the validity of infant baptism. And the Zwinglian reformer Wolfgang Capito of Strasburg for a time openly favored its abolition. It is therefore not surprising that Zwingli's arguments made no impression on the Anabaptists. His assertion that he had overcome the Anabaptists in debate was so much more strange, as they were not permitted to present their arguments in print.

Disquieted by reports of the rapid spread of Anabaptism in Moravia and other Austrian provinces, King Ferdinand I of Austria called the lords of Liechtenstein to Vienna and demanded the extradition of Hubmaier, which was granted. Hubmaier was transported to Vienna, and somewhat later incarcerated in a dungeon of the castle Kreuzenstein. He refused the demanded recantation of all his teachings that were not in accord with Romanism. Having been brought back to Vienna, he was burned at the stake on March 10, 1528. His last words were, "O Jesus! Jesus!" His wife was executed by drowning in the Danube three days later.

During his last imprisonment Hubmaier took a decidedly yielding attitude toward Romanism, though he refused an outright recantation. On nearly every point of faith and practice he expressed himself in a way that was calculated to be satisfactory from the Roman Catholic point of view. Regarding baptism and the Lord's Supper he did not formally recant his former teaching, and yet he showed himself vacillating and weak. He offered, if he were released from imprisonment, he would "stand still" as concerned the teaching and practice of these ordinances and all other disputed points until some future time when a general council was to be held to give pertinent decisions. "Then I will submit myself to the holy Christian church," he said, "and will accept its instruction from divine Scripture." In a petition to king Ferdinand he stated that he believed it would be possible for him, if he were released, to persuade the Anabaptists in general to take a similar attitude of "standing still."

While this offer of Hubmaier was not a proposal to submit outright to the decisions of a general council, the plan of "standing still" regarding the points indicated must have had a strong appeal to Catholic authorities. His participation in the armed conflict at Waldshut stood against him, however.

A General Council, in passing, is a council of the Roman Catholic bishops and archbishops of all lands. Such a council had long been contemplated. It was hoped by Protestants that state church Protestantism would be granted some representation in it, and that it would result in a reformation of the Catholic Church. As concerned Anabaptist representation in the council, it should be recalled that the Anabaptists were considered outlaws. In the year after Hubmaier's death (1529) the Anabaptists in the German empire, as stated elsewhere, were summarily condemned to death. They were to be executed without trial or sentence. The thought of Anabaptist representation in such a council would have been preposterous.

In 1545 the General Council became a reality, but the expectation that Protestant representatives would be admitted proved vain. Even if some Protestants had been admitted, they would at best have been a very small minority whose vote, even if they were permitted to give it, would not have made any appreciable difference in the final decisions. But the very thought of Protestant representation in the Council was fantastic. It seems impossible that in Hubmaier's expectation a general council of this sort might render decisions favorable to any distinctively Anabaptist teachings.

Balthasar Hubmaier was a man of outstanding talents. In ability as a public speaker and theological author he stood in the first ranks among his contemporaries. Ulrich Zwingli, his principal opponent, said of him that in his ability as a writer, he (Hubmaier) surpassed himself by far. Hubmaier's masterful refutation of infant baptism was never surpassed. As concerns his relationship to the Swiss Brethren, his congregation was of quite a different character. Not only did he radically reject the principle of nonresistance, and engage in warfare but, as indicated, he became one of the principal figures in a war waged against the rightful government, a war that was essentially of a religious character.

The immediate effect on Hubmaier's followers of his failure in point of doctrinal loyalty is significant. The concessions which he made to the Roman Catholic government were apparently taken by his followers to imply that he expected them to take a similar attitude. His large congregation at Nikolsburg, although not subjected to persecution at the time, ceased to exist within a comparatively short period. A number of the Anabaptists at Waldshut and Nikolsburg returned to the Roman Catholic Church. The Anabaptists in these cities dispersed almost as rapidly as they had been gathered. A remnant of this congregation finally united with the Sabbatarians. In fact, they could be followers of Hubmaier only by "standing still" as regards evangelical practice.

CHAPTER 20

MELCHIOR HOFMANN

Melchior Hofmann (1493-1544), an Anabaptist enthusiast who differed fundamentally from Mennonite teaching, demands our attention for the reason that Obbe Philips and his brother Dirck, who later became the founders of the Mennonite Church in Holland, were for a time followers of Hofmann.

Melchior Hofmann was born at Hall in Swabia, South Germany. He was a furrier by trade, had a good common school education, and was a born orator. Through Luther's writings he was won for Lutheranism at an early date, and traveled in countries along the Baltic Sea laboring for the spread of the Reformation movement. In a booklet on the twelfth chapter of Daniel he expressed the opinion that the end of the world would come in 1533. He went to Strasburg in Alsace in 1529, having meanwhile become a follower of Ulrich Zwingli on the doctrine of the Lord's Supper.

In Strasburg Hofmann made the acquaintance of a few persons who believed themselves to be prophets, receiving direct divine revelations. Outstanding among them were Ursula Jost and her husband Lienhard. Melchior Hofmann made the mistake of accepting the visions of these prophets as divinely inspired and infallible, and published some of them. The first of these visions dated back to the year 1524, that is, before the beginning of the Anabaptist movement. Hofmann personally entered the ranks of the prophets and published a few tracts of a prophetic nature. Through these prophecies and through a strangely fantastic interpretation of certain passages of the Bible, particularly of the book of Revelation, he was led to accept various fanciful views concerning the end-time. The personal coming of Christ was to be preceded by a time of wonderful victory for the kingdom of God, when all persecution would cease.

One of the prophets proclaimed Hofmann to be Elijah whose coming was to precede the second advent of Christ. Hofmann, after some hesitation, accepted this revelation and claimed to be Elijah. He named himself an "apostolic herald" and believed as foretold by the new prophets, that 144,000 heralds of the faith[45] would rise to preach the true gospel. They would be endowed with such spiritual gifts and power to work miracles that no one would be able to withstand them. Proceeding from Strasburg, they would without the use of force win the nations for the new teaching. Their labors would result in world regeneration. Hofmann, as one of the two witnesses of Revelation 11:3, would be put to death but would be raised to life again. The second witness was supposed by some to be Cornelius Polterman, of Middelburg in Holland.

Melchior Hofmann recognized infant baptism as unscriptural, and yet believed it should be practiced until the predicted time of general toleration. The organization of churches, he held, should be postponed until the beginning of that time of religious liberty.

But the prophets of Strasburg, as well as Hofmann's personal revelations, had left him in the dark as to the exact point of time for the beginning of the new era of liberty. Very eagerly he looked forward to that time. In the month of May, 1530, he went from Strasburg to the city of Emden in East Friesland which he had visited also in the previous year. Here he had a remarkable experience. He was given opportunity to preach in the largest church of the city. His success was such that he came to the conclusion that the expected time of wonderful expansion of the kingdom of God was at hand, and that baptism could now be practiced without persecution. He found it possible to baptize about 300 persons in the large vestry of this church at Emden. Previous to that time Anabaptism was unknown in northern Germany and in Holland.

No sooner had Hofmann performed this act of baptism at Emden than he was banished from the city. He left a certain Jan Volkerts in charge of the work at Emden, but in the course of a few weeks Volkerts also was banished. This evidently convinced Hofmann that the expected time of liberty was still in the future. At any rate, for the following year and a half he traveled in South Germany and Holland without apparently baptizing any one. Jan Volkerts, on the other hand, went to Holland, and at Amsterdam baptized many persons.

In November of the same year (1531) the magistrates of Amsterdam received orders from the state authorities to sup-

press Anabaptism. Bailiffs were then sent to arrest Jan Volkerts, but did not find him. On the following day he voluntarily
went to the residence of the mayor of the city to surrender himself, believing evidently that no harm would befall him, since
the power of the persecutors was supposed to be broken. If
this was his expectation, he was sorely disappointed. With eight
other men, who had been baptized, he was sent to the Hague
to be sentenced. The nine men were executed by decapitation
at the Hague on December 5, 1531. Their heads were sent to
Amsterdam to be set upon poles in a prominent place "for an
example and terror to others."

Naturally the martyrdom of the nine men at the Hague fully
convinced Hofmann and his followers of the fact that the persecution had not abated. However, in their perplexity Melchiorite prophecy apparently came again to their rescue. One
of the prophets declared that, as the work of building the second temple in Jerusalem was interrupted for a space of two
years,[46] so the building of the new spiritual temple was to be
put off for the same length of time. From Strasburg, whither
Hofmann had returned from Amsterdam, he wrote to his followers in the Netherlands, ordering them to "stand still," sus-
pending baptism and the organization of churches for two
years, during which period those who were won for Hofmann's
doctrine should form secret circles without separating from
the dominant church (which in the Netherlands was yet Roman
Catholic).

Again, one of the prophets predicted that before the expiration of the two years of "standing still" Hofmann would be
arrested and imprisoned at Strasburg, and that his release
from prison six months later would mark the beginning of the
predicted time of liberty and wonderful expansion of the kingdom of God. He then, without any use of force, would lead
his followers to victory over all the world. Accepting this
prophecy at its face value, Hofmann, who had meanwhile returned to Holland, went again to Strasburg in May, 1533, and
surrendered himself to the authorities. He was promptly imprisoned, as he had expected. Obbe Philips related that Hofmann, when he was arrested in Strasburg, lifted up his hand to
heaven and swore a solemn oath by the living God that he would
take no other food or drink than bread and water until the time

when he could point with his hand to the Person of the one who had sent him. Hofmann had never made efforts to spread his doctine at Strasburg, since he expected the conversion of this city in a miraculous way. Strasburg was to become the center of the kingdom of God.

However, the part of the prophecy relating to Hofmann's release from prison was never fulfilled. Hofmann was not released, though after about six years of imprisonment he handed the authorities of Strasburg a formal recantation in which he in particular expressed regret for his former rejection of infant baptism. "If I myself had children," he declared, "I would have them baptized in their infancy." He died a prisoner in Strasburg in 1543 or 1544.

Melchior Hofmann, as already indicated, differed radically on various points from the Swiss Brethren and other evangelical Anabaptists. His fantastic interpretation of certain Scripture passages was offensive to them, as was also his acceptance of alleged new revelations which he held to be of equal value and authority with the Scriptures. Furthermore he held the strange view that all transgression committed after conversion is sin against the Holy Ghost for which there is no forgiveness. The evangelical Anabaptists, on the contrary, emphasized the duty of making efforts to lead backslidden church members to repentance. Again Hofmann differed with them also in his expectation of world regeneration through evangelization. He held fanciful views regarding the millennium. He believed that the millennium had even then become a matter of history, and that the angel who bound Satan for a thousand years was the apostle Paul. After the expiration of that period, he believed Satan was loosed again, and the result was the sad spiritual and moral conditions prevailing.

In common with all enthusiastic Anabaptist sects Hofmann advocated the idea of "standing still" and postponing the observance of Christ's commands until a time when to observe them would not result in persecution. As noted before the idea of "standing still" was defended also by Hans Denck in the last period of his life, and by Caspar Schwenckfeld. Hofmann's followers in Strasburg, after the prophecies had failed, continued in an attitude of "standing still." According to a statement made in 1534 by Hans Frisch, an Anabaptist in Strasburg, the Melchiorites and the followers of Denck in this city were "somewhat amalgamated" (*ein wenig mit einander vermischet*). Neither of these two parties approved of separation from the state church, and neither gave the Scriptures the same place of authority as did the Swiss Brethren. In 1546 the magistrates of the city received information that only five persons were present in a meeting of the Melchiorites while about one hundred had come together in a meeting held by the Swiss Brethren. The magistrates of Strasburg always distinguished between the Melchiorites and the Swiss Brethren.

Melchior Hofmann, even before his recantation, spoke of the Swiss Brethren in terms of disapproval and reproach. He sided with their opponents by holding them responsible for the well-known fratricide of Thomas Schugger in St. Gall, a man who was not an Anabaptist at all. Hofmann made the assertion that before the beginning of his labors no one had proclaimed the true gospel. From his prison he sent word to the Swiss Brethren in Strasburg, admonishing them to "stand still," and not to come together for worship without the consent of the authorities. As for the attitude of the Swiss Brethren toward Hofmann, they declared in the debate held in Bern in 1538 not only that he was not of their brotherhood but that his teaching was resisted by them "with all earnestness."

The supposition that Hofmann had been baptized by Swiss Brethren in Strasburg is clearly erroneous. It is improbable that he was baptized at all, except in infancy. He believed he had divine authority to introduce or suspend the observance of baptism.

CHAPTER 21

OBBE PHILIPS AS A MELCHIORITE

Obbe Philips, at the time of the rise of Melchiorism in the Netherlands, lived in the city of Leeuwarden in Friesland, Holland. He was a surgeon by calling, while his brother Dirck Philips was a Franciscan monk living in a near-by cloister.

In Leeuwarden the martyrdom of Sicke Freerks Snyder, a Melchiorite, had taken place in March of 1531. Sicke Freerks Snyder had been baptized by Jan Trijpmaker, a Melchiorite evangelist, before the observance of baptism was suspended by the Melchiorites. The Philips brothers may have been eye witnesses of Snyder's death. Certain it is that not long after this event they joined the circle of Melchiorites in Leeuwarden.

It should be borne in mind that these people had shortly before come out of the Roman Catholic Church. It was through Melchiorite influence that they had obtained enlightenment concerning the unscriptural doctrines and practices of Romanism. Since the Melchiorites were the only non-Romanist group in the Netherlands at that time, it was but natural that Obbe Philips and others who had been under Melchiorite influence became followers of Melchior Hofmann. The Christian ordinances were not practiced among them but they waited eagerly for the time of liberty, predicted by Hofmann, when baptism could be practiced without persecution. At a later time, looking back to this period, Obbe Philips says that he and his friends were but children in understanding. Their knowledge of the Scriptures was very meager. When Hofmann's predictions and fantastic teachings concerning the end-time proved deceptive, Obbe Philips with a number of his friends renounced Melchiorism. Through independent study of the Scriptures Obbe and others obtained true enlightenment. He became the founder of the Holland group of the Mennonite Church. They were named Obbenites before the name "Mennonites" came into use.

But we turn back to the period when Obbe Philips and his friends were still Melchiorites. He gives the following description of conditions in the circle of Melchiorites at the time when they looked for the end of the persecution and for orders from

174

Hofmann to renounce Romanism and begin the observance of baptism: "There was among us great and joyous expectation," says Obbe Philips. "We supposed that all the predictions would prove true and be fulfilled. For we were inexperienced, simple, naive, without craftiness, and as yet we knew of no deception through visions, prophecies, or supposed revelations. In our simplicity we believed that if we guarded ourselves from Romanist, Lutheran, and Zwinglian errors, all was well and there was no need for further concern."

The determination to avoid persecution by postponing to a more convenient season the observance of the commands of Christ, proved fatal to the Melchiorite cause. Such an extremely compromising attitude on practical church reformation naturally attracted to their ranks an undesirable element which would have kept aloof from their group, had the Melchiorites been willing to be "a church under the cross of persecution." On the contrary, they in their thought life dwelt on the expectation of the predicted political and social changes. This created among them a tendency to shift from a religious basis to a political one. The Melchiorite compromises and political expectations appealed forcefully to a class which had little in common with the circle at Leeuwarden, as described by Obbe Philips.

After Hofmann's imprisonment in Strasburg in 1533 there arose among the Melchiorites in the Netherlands a prophet, Jan Matthys, a baker of the town of Haarlem, in Holland, who bade fair to outdo the prophecies and visions which Hofmann had published. In the autumn of 1533 Matthys' friend John of Leiden visited the city of Münster in Westphalia, northwestern Germany, and returned to Jan Matthys with reports concerning conditions in that city. He had made the trip to Münster, having received information, as he later confessed, that there were fearless radical preachers there. He returned to Holland with an almost incredible story. Persecution had actually ceased in Münster. This was taken as a token of the general fulfillment of the prophecies. General toleration prevailed in the city at that time. Catholics, Lutherans, Zwinglians, and Melchiorites lived side by side without persecution, though this condition of things was of short duration. Bernt Rothmann, the leading preacher of the city, until recently a Lutheran, taught openly that infant baptism is unscriptural, though he hesitated to become an Anabaptist by introducing the baptism of adults. Other preachers of the city and many of the citizens approved of the rejection of infant baptism. All attempts to silence Rothmann and his associates failed, since the politically powerful guilds (trades unions) took his part and protected him contrary to the orders of the higher authorities. It is improbable that at any other place the trade unions had the constitutional rights and privileges which were theirs at Münster. The Roman Catholic bishop and the provincial government found themselves powerless to maintain control of the city.

The imagination of Jan Matthys ran riot in consequence of the report which his friend John of Leiden brought him from Münster. He began to consider the question whether Münster, instead of Strasburg, was not to be the center of God's kingdom. Melchior Hofmann had consistently warned his followers of sedition and rebellion, but had not held the principle of separation of church and state. The Melchiorites accepted neither this principle nor that of nonresistance. Was there any reason then why they should not assume political control, if opportunity presented? Was not the work of Luther and Zwingli, the leading reformers of the state church type of Protestantism, closely allied with the state?

For two weeks Jan Matthys conferred with John of Leiden concerning the burning questions of the day. He began to see visions and dream dreams, caused by his own unholy desires and ambitions. The two years of "standing still," prescribed by Hofmann, had not yet expired, but Matthys finally made himself believe that he had divine revelations to the effect that the expected time of liberty and of the termination of the persecution had actually begun. True, there was as yet in the Netherlands no indication of such a change, but had not the marvellous turn of affairs at Münster taken place suddenly? The two men finally believed that Münster, instead of Strasburg (where persecution continued) was destined to become the center from which the new order of things would spread over the earth.

In November, 1533, Jan Matthys came to the Melchiorites of Amsterdam and announced, on the ground of new revelations which he, as "the second witness," had received, that the great change for which they were waiting was at hand. The

time to resume the practice of baptism had come. The wicked
had henceforth no power over the faithful to torture and slay
them. Matthys admonished them to fear no longer the great
tyranny, for no blood of Christians would further be shed on
earth. On the contrary, he said, this was the beginning of the
time when the judgments of God would come upon the ungodly.
Withal, Matthys admonished the believers that, awaiting further orders, they should "remain in Babel," in outward ap-
pearances. They should not openly separate themselves from
the Roman Church; there should be no noticeable change in
their outward attitude toward that church. They were to be
baptized secretly in evidence of their belief that the expected
new dispensation was here.

The new prophet had a cool reception by the Melchiorites of
Amsterdam. As just stated, the two years of "standing still"
had not fully passed, and some of them had supposed that Cornelius Polterman was to be the second witness. "They were
perplexed and knew not what to do," says Obbe Philips. "But
Matthys came to them," Obbe states further, "with great
threatenings and frightened them with the announcement of
great and terrible judgments over those who resisted the Holy
Ghost." For a time the Melchiorites of Amsterdam stood their
ground against Matthys, but finally a number of them accepted
his message and were baptized. "For we were at that time un-
suspecting," Obbe Philips goes on to say, "and had no thought
that false prophets could rise among our own brethren."

Jan Matthys sent his "apostles" to the Melchiorites everywhere with the same message. "They were to proclaim peace
and general toleration and to announce that nevermore would
the tyrants persecute them, and that henceforth there would
be no blood-shed, but the dawn of a new world in holiness and
righteousness was at hand," Obbe wrote further.

Two of the messengers of Jan Matthys came to Leeuwarden,
where they met the men who were destined to become a little
later, the principal opponents of the new prophet, namely Obbe
and Dirck Philips. We let Obbe himself tell the story (as related in his *Confessions*) of the reception and the work of these
men among the Melchiorites of Leeuwarden:[47]

Then there came to us at Leeuwarden two of those messengers,
namely Bartholomew Bookbinder and Dirck Cooper. And when some

of us had come together, about fourteen or fifteen persons, men and
women, they declared to us the authority of their mission, namely that
Jan Matthys had come to them with such signs, wonder-working, and
power of the Spirit that words failed them to describe it to us. They
said we should not doubt that they were endowed with power and mir-
acle-working no less than the apostles at the day of Pentecost.

They also comforted us and said, we should not be in anxiety nor
fear, as we had indeed long feared the great tyranny; for henceforth
no blood of Christians should be shed on earth, but within a short
time God would destroy all the tyrants and godless from the earth.

This assertion I heard with suspicion, although I dared not contradict them, for at that time no one had the courage to contradict
much, and whoever spoke against their message was denounced as one
who resisted the Spirit and blasphemed. In this manner, and by their
threatenings of damnation they terrorized the hearts in such measure
that no one had the courage to contradict them. Everyone feared that
he would in some way transgress and speak against the mission and
work of God. For we were all inexperienced, like children, and had
no thought that we would be deceived by our own brethren who every
day were with us in like danger of persecution and death. At that day
we nearly all accepted baptism at their hands. Then after eight days
came Peter Woodsawer with the same message.

Having thus become Anabaptists Obbe Philips and his friends
were at once made to realize by bitter experience that in no way
was there a greater measure of toleration for Anabaptists now,
than there had been before the rise of the new prophet. We
shall again give the word of Obbe Philips and record his very
interesting narration of immediate developments at Leeuwarden. He wrote:

No sooner had this Peter Woodsawer come outside of the city walls
of Leeuwarden, when all prophecy and lofty assertion proved vain;
for he was immediately sought and pursued by the authorities, at first
in the city and then in the villages of the country, and had a very narrow escape, for the authorities used every means to pursue him.

Meanwhile I returned upon a Sunday with my brother Hans Scher-
der to Leeuwarden, and when we came near the city gate, about noon,
we noticed that the keeper was about to close the gate. But he saw us
coming and called to us, saying, if we desired to enter, we must make
haste. When we heard this, we were frightened and asked the reason
why the gates were closed. He said, "There are Anabaptists in the
city; they are all to be seized." Then we were much more frightened
and remembered the prophecies. But, [realizing the impossibility of
turning back without arousing suspicion] we recovered courage and
went into the city about noon.

Having arrived home, I found my wife in great anxiety, and she
told me of the visit of Peter Woodsawer a short time before, and that

some of the Melchiorites had boldly contradicted his word and his authority, and this resulted in great rumor and persecution. Some had already been apprehended and others were very earnestly sought. She entreated me to go by all means away into another house until darkness would set in [hoping for an opportunity to leave the city unnoticed].

If after these experiences, Obbe Philips had not fully discarded the belief that the predicted time of religious liberty had come, he was soon to be completely disillusioned. Some of the men sent as apostles by Jan Matthys, apparently in order to show that they believed their own message, ventured to preach publicly. They were promptly arrested. Obbe says: "These three men who, having come to them from Amsterdam, had boasted of their mission as apostles and had announced the end of the persecution, were themselves imprisoned as disturbers and Anabaptists. With a number of others, sixteen or seventeen persons in all, they were taken to Haarlem and were all put to death."

Seven of these men, among them Peter Woodsawer and Bartholomew Bookbinder, were executed and broken upon the wheel at Haarlem on March 26, 1534. After this terrible sentence had been carried out, Obbe Philips himself, with a few of his friends, went to the place of their execution. "I desired to ascertain," says Obbe, "which of them were the three who had baptized us and had announced to us such mission and promise of religious liberty, but we were not able to recognize them."

The utter consternation prevailing among these people in consequence of the failure of the prophecies and the realization that they had been deceived, is further described by Obbe Philips:

Now every one may consider for himself how we felt when we remembered the haughty and beautiful words, which I perchance had not read out of a book nor received or heard in a round-about way, but I had heard these words from their own lips. What actually took place was the very contrary of what they had announced to us. All that they had said would come upon the world, upon the tyrants and the godless, came rather upon us, and first of all upon these messengers themselves. Alas, who can describe our great grief. By the world we were terrorized and severely persecuted, and by our own brethren we were daily misled and deceived.

Thus the fact that they had been led into great error was brought home forcibly to Obbe Philips and some of his friends. Not only did they realize that they had been deceived by Jan Matthys and his messengers, but it became clear to them also that the leading teachings to which the Melchiorites had adhered from the beginning were unsound and erroneous. Melchior Hofmann, by his extravagant notions, had prepared the way for further error and deception through Matthys. And now Jan Matthys, who besides John of Leiden had gone to Münster to take charge of affairs, demanded that those who would not accept his message, should eventually be put to death by his own followers. Especially was his heart filled with revengefulness against the persecutors of his followers.

According to Obbe Philips' testimony the first apostles who came to them at Leeuwarden, announced, as we have noticed, the impending judgment of God upon the wicked. Obbe says, he heard this with misgivings. The belief that severe judgment would befall those that opposed and persecuted the gospel, was at that time widely held also within the Protestant state churches, and seemed to be in keeping with certain passages of the Scripture which treat on divine judgment upon the wicked. However the idea of the destruction of the wicked with the sword was foreign to state church Protestantism; it was of distinctly Münsterite origin. There is no evidence to show that Matthys preached the destruction of the wicked with the sword by the righteous before his arrival in Münster.

CHAPTER 22

THE OBBENITES

Obbe Philips gives a vivid description of conditions after he, with others of the Melchiorites, came to realize that they had been misled and deceived by their leaders. He wrote:

Oh how often were some of us in sadness unto death. We knew not whither to turn or what to do. The whole world persecuted us to death for our faith with fire, water, sword, and all bloody tyranny; the prophecies of our leaders had deceived us; the Scripture did not give us liberty to agree to a compromise; the false brethren whom we reproved and rebuked, swore to take our lives; and the love of so many hearts who despite their good intentions were deceived moved us to heartfelt compassion. Ofttimes my soul was sorrowful unto death.

Thus Obbe Philips saw himself confronted by the momentous question of what was to be done under these bewildering and disheartening experiences. He realized clearly, not only that Jan Matthys was a rank fanatic and deceiver, but that much of the teaching of Melchior Hofmann was likewise unscriptural and untenable. Under these circumstances the temptation to resume anew the former Melchiorite attitude of "standing still" and outwardly conforming to Romanism was very real. But even if he would follow such a policy, it would be unsafe for him to remain at Leeuwarden. However, he could go to a place where he was unknown. But he saw that to take such a course of compromise with Romanism would have been to act contrary to his better knowledge.

Moreover, as stated in the above quotation, Obbe Philips felt that he had a duty toward those who, like himself, had been misled and deceived notwithstanding their earnest desire to lead a true Christian life. The former Melchiorites now had to face the danger of following further an unsafe leadership, even though they recognized Jan Matthys to be a false prophet. Obbe says further: "Had it not been for the love and pity I felt toward so many upright hearts who were daily seduced by the false brethren, I should certainly have left them and with a few others withdrawn from all who were acquainted with me. For among all the teachers there was for a time no one but Dirck Philips to stand with me against the false brethren."

Thus, after severe struggles of conscience, Obbe Philips decided to abide by his convictions, even though to do so meant enduring the severest persecution. The disciples of Jan Matthys made strenuous efforts to win him back. These fanatics were able to present a plausible argument against the position of Obbe and his friends, especially so since polygamy and other obnoxious practices had not yet been introduced at Münster. Among the former Melchiorites there were yet those who were weak and easily influenced, and were halting between two opinions. Were not present conditions in Münster a pledge for the further fulfillment of the prophecies and for the beginning of the predicted new era of toleration? The disciples of Jan Matthys came to the Obbenites claiming to be their brethren, since they had been baptized by the same men. Obbe Philips to the contrary insisted that they were false brethren, deceivers, and must be "shunned."

It is of interest to notice that Obbe Philips was the first Mennonite leader to teach strict avoidance or shunning. He took an extreme attitude regarding this point, such as Menno Simons would not approve, though it is clear from the latter's writings that some Mennonites of a later period inclined toward such an extreme view. Obbe did not approve of his followers having anything whatever to do with the adherents of Jan Matthys. Only in case of the most extreme need could church members contact them. There is a case on record of the Obbenites excommunicating a person because he intended to go to Münster.

The Obbenites then incurred the fierce opposition of the followers of Jan Matthys. As Obbe Philips relates, the latter took oath to kill them. There are various evidences of the correctness of this statement. After the rise of the sect of the Batenburgers, who adhered to Münsterite teaching, Gerhard Eilkeman said in Münster (in 1544) : "All who were baptized by the said Obbe Philips are called Obbenites and are opponents of the sect of Batenburg. The latter have persecuted them to compel them to renounce the sect of the Obbenites."

The main sources of information concerning the origin and teachings of the Obbenites are Obbe Philips' book titled *Confessions* which has been already mentioned, and the early writings of Menno Simons. The Obbenites had existed about two years at the time of Menno Simons' conversion and baptism.

Menno testifies that they were unblamable in doctrine and life when he united with them.

It is a fact deserving particular notice in this connection that between the Obbenites and the Swiss Brethren there was substantial agreement in faith and practice, though there had been no contact between the two bodies. The Swiss Brethren (in Switzerland and South Germany) did not find it possible to put forth extensive efforts to spread their doctrine through the printed page. Evidently neither Obbe Philips nor Menno Simons at the time of his conversion and baptism was acquainted with the few booklets published by Swiss Brethren, nor with the writings of Balthasar Hubmaier. As late as the middle of the next century, when Thieleman van Braght published the *Martyrs' Mirror,* the Mennonites of the Netherlands had only very meager knowledge of the Brethren in the southern lands.

It was evidently through the study of the Scriptures, not through Swiss Brethren influence, that Obbe Philips was led to accept what were substantially the same teachings as those of the Swiss Brethren. When later representatives of the two groups met "to compare notes," there was found a substantial accord in faith and practice, and they recognized each other as members of the same brotherhood. The independent study of the Scriptures led both groups to the same conclusions as concerned faith and practice. Yet there were some minor differences, on avoidance and on the theory of the incarnation of Christ, as will be pointed out elsewhere.

Among the most vital points on which Obbe and Dirck Philips differed from Melchior Hofmann's teaching was the all-sufficiency of the Scriptures as the revelation of God, of His plan and will. As for Obbe Philips, he felt a veritable terror of alleged new revelations. Menno Simons also said occasionally that he did not desire new revelations because of the danger of being deceived. Both groups of the early Mennonites—Obbenites and the Swiss Brethren—stressed the need of abiding by the teachings of God's Word under persecution. They held that the opposition of the world is to be expected. They hoped for a time of religious liberty, but did not believe that the end of open persecution would mean the friendship of the world. Menno Simons, in his *Foundation Book*[48] (1539) says that there never will be a time when the true Christian life can be lived without cross-bearing. He says further: "If the God of all mercy will give us a measure of tranquility, peace and liberty, we shall receive it from His gracious hand with thanksgiving; if not, His gracious name is nevertheless to be praised." Both the Obbenites and the Swiss Brethren rejected Hofmann's idea of a world to be converted through their labors.

There is good evidence that at the time of the rise of Jan Matthys not all Melchiorites in Holland gave ear to this false prophet. Again, many Melchiorites who had been led further astray through Matthys' influence, were, like Obbe Philips, disillusioned when the prophecies failed and it became apparent that Matthys' aspirations were largely of a political nature and that he believed the saints should draw the sword against the wicked. But those who had never become followers of Jan Matthys as well as others who had accepted his message and had afterward realized that they were deceived, did not all join the ranks of the Obbenites. There were at that time at least three parties, or sects, among the Anabaptists of the Netherlands.

At Amsterdam the Anabaptists were very numerous. The most notable preacher among them in this city was Jacob van Kampen who, like Obbe Philips, is known to have been an opponent of the Münsterites and probably was of the Obbenite brotherhood. He suffered martyrdom at Amsterdam on July 10, 1535. The Anabaptists and Melchiorites of Amsterdam had six meeting places in and near the city, and their adherents were numbered by thousands. That the party of Jan Matthys was in this city not numerically strong became evident through the uprising undertaken by his followers. Jan van Geelen, a Münsterite emissary, organized a rebellion to overthrow the government of the city of Amsterdam. In a remarkable way he succeeded in deceiving the authorities as to his own identity and aims. But he was able to bring together only between forty and fifty men to take part in the uprising on May 11, 1535. They surprised the authorities and took possession of the city house, but were quickly overpowered. Jan van Geelen lost his life in the struggle, and his accomplices were seized and executed.

CHAPTER 23

MENNO SIMONS

Menno Simons was born in the year 1496 in the village of Witmarsum near Bolsward, West Friesland, in the Netherlands. (The Dutch province of Friesland, with the city of Leeuwarden as capital, was generally named West Friesland in distinction from the German province of East Friesland.) Of his parents nothing certain is known. His father's name was Simon. Like all Netherlanders of that period Menno's parents were Roman Catholics. The fact that as a young man he could go through the educational preparation required for the priesthood makes it probable that the family was in easy circumstances. Menno must have spent a number of years preparing for his chosen calling. There is evidence that he was well educated. He learned to read Latin, an indispensable requisite for a priest. Menno acquired a thorough knowledge of this language, a result of years of study. Some of his books contain paragraphs of considerable length, written in a good Latin style. He also had some knowledge of the Greek language.

In all probability Menno was educated at the school of the Franciscan monastery at Bolsward. This does not mean, however, that he ever took upon himself the vows of the Franciscan monastic order. He never was a monk. The thorough knowledge of the Scriptures, which his writings indicate, was an attainment of later years of private study, as was also his acquaintance with the writings of some of the early church fathers.

In the twenty-eighth year of his life, namely in 1524, Menno Simons was consecrated a priest by the bishop of Utrecht, the date being probably March 26, and was installed as a vicar or priest's assistant in the village of Pingjum, a few miles from Witmarsum. As a priest he led an easy-going life, indulging freely, as he later confessed, in "card playing, drinking, and all manner of frivolous diversions." He was a loyal Romanist and as such held the view that to read the Scriptures is dangerous. Indeed the study of the Scriptures had often led to the acceptance of views which from the Romish viewpoint were considered heretical. Menno abstained from reading them, fearing that he might be misled; "such a stupid preacher was I for about two years," he wrote in a later period.

In one of his larger books, his defense against Gellius Faber, Menno Simons gives a graphic account of his gradual enlightenment, leading to his conversion, and of his call to the ministry. In another of his books, namely his *Meditations on the Twenty-fifth Psalm,* written within a few years after his renunciation of Romanism, he likewise gives valuable information concerning the nature of his earlier life and of his conversion.

Within a year after his installation as a priest at Pingjum Menno began to entertain doubts concerning the daily Mass service. The claim of the efficacy of the Mass for salvation is based on the doctrine that, when the priest pronounces the words of consecration over the host (bread) and wine, these emblems are actually changed into the body and blood of Christ (transubstantiation). The Mass is called an offering, since through it the body and blood of the Lord are supposed to be offered up again, and thus the sacrifice, which was really offered once for all on Calvary, is supposed to be repeated by the priest to atone for sin.

Menno's doubt concerning the Mass was a serious matter, since this doctrine is a chief cornerstone of Romanism. He confessed his doubts to God and to another priest who absolved him of this imagined sin, and yet such thoughts continued to disturb him. He found himself unable to overcome this difficulty. After giving these questions prolonged consideration, he arrived at the conclusion that, since the Bible is God's Word, the study of it, even if it be not altogether justifiable, cannot be a grievous transgression. He had read a certain book of Luther which had convinced him that breaking a commandment which is not based on the Scripture "could never lead to eternal death." Finally Menno Simons began to read the New Testament, having probably not the opportunity at the time to use a complete Bible. Through the study of the New Testament he was eventually led to recognize some of the doctrines of Romanism, among them transubstantiation, as errors. In consequence the nature of his preaching underwent a change. He kept certain Romish teachings more in the background and emphasized that which he found to be based on Scripture. He

says that he was therefore regarded by some, although unde-
servedly, as an evangelical preacher.

In Menno Simons' fatherland, the Netherlands, the hope
for a reformation of the church was widely entertained. The
regent of the Netherlands, Mary of Burgundy, had the reputation of being a secret admirer of Luther, and the pope himself
accused her of anti-Catholic leanings. There were at that time
in the Netherlands, besides Menno Simons, other priests who
favored a reformation, and yet were not taken to account by
the authorities. For example, in the same period, Gellius Faber,
the priest of Jelsum near Leeuwarden, preached certain features of Lutheranism for years without molestation. And yet,
actual deviation from Roman Catholic religious forms and
practices would not have been tolerated by the government.
Both Gellius Faber and Menno Simons knew that swift punishment would overtake them if they dared to discard well-known
Roman Catholic practices, such as the Mass.

Meanwhile the Anabaptist movement had spread from Germany into the Netherlands. The first Anabaptist martyr to die
in the Netherlands was Sicke Freerks Snyder, a Melchiorite
Anabaptist who had been baptized at Emden in Germany. His
martyrdom took place on March 20, 1531, at Leeuwarden, the
capital city of the province of West Friesland. Until this time
Menno Simons had never questioned the Roman Catholic doctrine of baptism, namely that baptism is the instrument of regeneration, and hence all baptized persons are of the number
of the regenerated. He now heard for the first time of Anabaptists and their rejection of infant baptism. "It sounded
strange in my ears," he says, "to hear a second baptism spoken
of." The martyrdom of Sicke Frerichs Snyder made a profound impression upon Menno. Having been previously led to
realize that the official Romish theology was in certain points
not scripturally orthodox, he now gave himself to a more diligent study of the New Testament Scriptures, seeking light on
the question of baptism. He frequently conversed on this question with another priest of higher rank who finally admitted
that infant baptism is not taught in Scripture. Then Menno
consulted the writings of some of the church fathers of the
early Catholic Church. They taught that the infants are
cleansed from original sin through baptism. He found this to

be contrary to the Scriptures which teach, he says, that the blood of Christ is the means of cleansing from sin.

Seeking light on infant baptism, Menno Simons naturally gave thought to the question, What may be the reason that the Protestant state churches, the Lutheran in Germany and the Reformed in Switzerland, had not abandoned this practice? He read the writings of Luther and other Protestant leaders on this question and came to the conclusion that their reasons for taking over from Romanism the practice of infant baptism were inadequate. Concerning Luther's opinion he says this reformer taught that infants are believers and should therefore be baptized. Thus Menno eventually became convinced that the Scriptures teach the baptism of believers, and that the contrary opinion is an error. "I was led to see," he said, "that we were deceived as concerns infant baptism."

This was an important discovery. It meant that the Roman Catholic doctrine regarding the condition required for church membership was erroneous, and that only believers, who take upon themselves the obligations of membership, should be baptized and become members of the church. Furthermore, it meant also that the Protestant reformers were unorthodox on these points. The leading reformers, Luther, Zwingli, and Calvin, never questioned the validity of Roman Catholic baptism and ordination.

Shortly after this, Menno Simons, having served as a priest at Pingjum for a period of seven years, was promoted to the office of parish priest in his native village of Witmarsum. This meant for him an enhanced income and increased prestige. He had by this time made marked progress in the knowledge of evangelical truth, but had failed to act on this knowledge, except on minor points. The reason for his failure to step out and take a positive evangelical position is obvious. As yet he lacked definite conversion and consecration to the Lord's service. He tells us later that he in reality sought a good income, ease of life, and the favor of men. Later, after his conversion he looked with deep regret upon the inconsistencies of his attitude and life in this period when, against better knowledge, he delayed laying down his office and stepping out of the Roman Church. In this connection, it is worthy of note, that at that time there was in the Netherlands no religious party or church which could

rightfully claim the evangelical name; indeed there was no religious body that was truly separated from the Roman Catholic
Church. The Melchiorites, some time after Sicke Snyder's
martyrdom, decided again upon compromise in religious conformity with the Roman Church. And even if the Melchiorites
would have remained a separate body, Menno could hardly
have united with them. However an evangelical Anabaptist
church was organized in West Friesland by Obbe Philips shortly before Menno Simons' renunciation of Romanism.

Menno relates further that about a year after his removal
to Witmarsum a few men came into that vicinity who taught
the baptism of believers—evidently followers of Melchior
Hofmann, who for a short period practiced baptism upon confession of faith but, because of the persecution, soon decided to
conform to the practice of the Roman Church and to postpone
the observance of the ordinances to a more convenient season.
Then, in the autumn of the year 1533, the sect of the fanatical
and revolutionary Münsterite Anabaptists arose in the Netherlands. The founder of this sect was Jan Matthys of Haarlem,
mentioned in an earlier chapter.

Menno Simons realized keenly the grievously destructive
errors of "this perverted sect," as he speaks of the Münsterites.
He did his best to counteract their influence. Twice he conferred with one of their leaders, once privately and then in
public. "The report spread abroad that I could readily stop
their mouths," he said somewhat later, but he adds that his
testimony took little effect because he himself failed to forsake
that which he confessed to be unscriptural. Menno at that time
in his labors avoided mentioning certain doctrines and practices
of Romanism. He was still within the Roman Church and
therefore his efforts to refute the Münsterite teaching appeared to be made in the interests of the Church of Rome. He
says he realized with regret that thus he became the champion
of those who had no intention of an amendment of life. The
adherents of the Münsterite sect, despite their errors, were
radical opponents of Romanism. Menno's temporizing attitude weakened his witness against their errors, and he could
not prevent that, as he stated later, many people of his village
were misled by them.

When the expectations of both the Melchiorites and the Münsterites of an immediâte cessation of the persecution proved false, some of these deluded people, in the relentless persecution, sought refuge in a monastery called the Old Cloister near Bolsward. They took possession of this place, but did the monks no bodily harm. They defended themselves with the sword against the troops sent against them by the authorities. "Contrary to the spirit, word, and example of Christ," says Menno, "they took the sword to defend themselves, which the Lord commanded Peter to put up in the sheath." Nevertheless, it is clear from Menno Simons' writings that these people did not approve of all the offensive teachings and practices of the Münsterites. The Old Cloister was taken by the troops in March, 1535, and many of these misguided people were put to death.

This occurrence made a deep impression upon Menno Simons. For some time previous to this event he had been subjected to severe remorse of conscience because of his failure to act on the evangelical light which had come to him, and to order his life accordingly. Menno had already ceased actually to observe the Mass service. He followed Martin Luther's advice as concerns the observance of the Mass. Luther had given the counsel that in territory where people would take offense in the abolition of the Mass while the government yet demanded its observance, the most essential part of the Mass service (which refers to the Mass as a sacrifice) should be omitted. Since the Latin language was used in the Mass service, and the words in question were always uttered by the priest in a low, inaudible voice, the people would not notice the omission. Thus Menno, as he himself said, observed Mass "only in appearance."

Speaking of the event at the Old Cloister, Menno says that after this tragedy had transpired, "the blood of these people, although they were misled, burned as it were on my heart in such a manner that I could not endure it longer nor find rest in my soul." Comparing his own general religious attitude at this time with that of the people who had lost their lives at the Old Cloister, among whom was his own brother, Menno keenly realized that though they had been in lamentable error, yet they could scarcely be said to have erred against better knowledge.

They had indicated, by stepping out of the Church of Rome, that they had the courage to act on their convictions. Menno saw clearly that his own attitude and conduct was less excusable than theirs. He had pangs of conscience because of his failure to do all within his power by word and example to lead these people in the way of truth.

Reflecting upon these things Menno Simons says further, his burden of conscience became such that he could no longer endure it. He became truly penitent. "My heart trembled in my body," he says. "With grief of soul, and tears I prayed to God to give me, an anxious sinner, the gift of His grace and to create a clean heart within me, to graciously forgive, through the merits of the crimson blood of Christ, my unclean walk and ease-seeking life, and bestow upon me wisdom, candor, and courage, that I might preach His exalted and adorable name and holy Word unadulterated and make manifest His truth to His praise." He began to preach openly the need of true repentance and a change of life in conformity to God's Word, to the extent that he had obtained enlightenment.

Apparently not long after the episode at the Old Cloister Menno Simons learned of the existence of the evangelical Anabaptist brotherhood, the Obbenites, which had shortly before been organized by Obbe Philips. He thoroughly examined their doctrine and became convinced that they had the truth of the Word of God. And yet there was a point that gave Menno difficulty. While the Obbenites emphatically taught the true deity and the true humanity of Christ, they held a peculiar view concerning Jesus' human body. Menno Simons says, when the Brethren first stated this doctrine to him, he was much disturbed and had difficulty to acknowledge it as sound. Eventually he was persuaded that it is scriptural, and yet he states that he did not consider this particular view of sufficient importance to preach it. Evidently this proved for some time a hindrance to his uniting with the brotherhood.

Apparently the opportunity to unite with the Obbenites aided Menno Simons to resolve upon withdrawal from the Roman Church. He laid down his office and publicly renounced Romanism on Sunday, January 30, 1536. He says:

The gracious Lord granted me His fatherly Spirit, aid, power, and help, that I voluntarily forsook my good name, honor and reputation which I had among men, and renounced all the abominations of Anti-christ, Mass, infant baptism, and my unprofitable life, and willingly submitted to homelessness and poverty under the cross of my Lord Jesus Christ.—Behold, my reader, thus the God of mercy, through His abounding grace which He bestowed upon me, a miserable sinner, has first touched my heart, given me a new mind, humbled me in His fear, taught me in part to know myself, turned me from the way of death and graciously called me into the narrow path of life, into the communion of His saints. To Him be praise forevermore. Amen.

Shortly after his renunciation of Romanism Menno Simons was baptized by Obbe Philips. He took this step in the face of the fact that to unite with the evangelical Anabaptists would make him an outcast and a fugitive.[49] From sincere and com-pelling conviction Menno united with a people who had been summarily outlawed and condemned to death. A life of ease, comfort, and worldly honor he, for conscience' sake, exchanged for a life of homelessness, poverty, and continuous danger of violent death.

The supposition that Menno Simons was baptized by Obbe Philips at an earlier date, namely before his public renunciation of Romanism, is without foundation, as is clear from certain statements of Menno himself. In various places in his writings he says that the brotherhood with which he united did not avoid the cross of persecution. Certain Anabaptist sects, such as the Melchiorites, on the contrary, avoided persecution by outward-ly conforming to the religious requirements made by the civil authorities. They followed a course based on expediency, not on principle. The observance of the ordinances was postponed by them to "a more convenient season."

The evangelical Anabaptists (Obbenites), on the contrary, believed it an absolute requirement to follow the teachings of the Word of God and to observe Christ's commands despite the persecution. Menno says of them that they were irre-proachable in doctrine and practice, and that they held the principle of separation from the world according to the teach-ings of the Scripture. That Obbe Philips would baptize a per-son who had not renounced Romanism was out of the question, and it is furthermore unlikely that Menno would have asked it of him. The very fact that Menno presented himself for bap-tism indicated that he did not desire to escape persecution by outward conformity to the state church.

Immediately after his renunciation of Romanism Menno Simons seems to have left Witmarsum. At the place where he was so well known and where his leaving the Roman Church must have caused not a little stir he probably felt the least secure. For a number of months after his conversion and baptism he apparently busied himself in all quietness with writing and study, particularly the study of the Scriptures. He sojourned at this time at various places in the Netherland province of Groningen, due east of West Friesland, where he enjoyed the hospitality of those of like faith. At the same time he apparently served the brotherhood as an "admonisher." In the account of his renunciation of Romanism he describes his call to the ministerial office, which took place in Groningen. He relates that about a year after his conversion (perhaps not a full year) a group of the Brethren, probably including Obbe Philips, came to him urging him to consent to ordination as a minister.

The need for laborers for the Lord's vineyard was particularly urgent in that time of religious commotion. The fields were white unto harvest, and the faithful laborers were few. Men were needed who had a vital grasp of the Christian message, who had the courage of their convictions, and the consecration to labor under the greatest hardships, privations, and dangers. Menno's outstanding talents were recognized, and he had given evidence of his consecration by laying down his position of honor and influence in the world, to follow the dictates of Scripture and conscience.

Menno Simons relates that he was aware, if he accepted this call, that the personal dangers to be encountered by him would be multiplied, "the indescribably heavy cross of persecution" would become the more felt. In this connection it may not be out of place to make a comparison of the circumstances under which Menno consented to ordination as an Anabaptist minister with conditions under which the more prominent reformers did their work. Both Martin Luther and Ulrich Zwingli, in the task of church reformation, had the co-operation of the civil governments of the states in which they lived and labored. Not only were these reformers given the protection of the law, but they were granted special favors by the civil authorities. The latter were entirely in sympathy with their reformatory endeavors, and were fully willing and able to give them every

desirable protection. The price which these reformers had
to pay, however, to procure so favorable an attitude of the
rulers was great indeed. The price was the reformers' consent
to a union of church and state, which meant the organization
of churches comprising by force of the law the whole population. This involved important modifications of the New Testament message; it also implied serious deviations from the
earlier message of these reformers. Among the most fundamental of these deviations was their consent to the persecution
of dissenters and the omission of church discipline. There were
not a few state church people who saw the unscripturalness of
the union of church and the state with all its implications, but
who did not have courage sufficient to stand against it.

Naturally Menno Simons gave thought to the increased
dangers that would beset his way as a minister of the evangelical Anabaptists. Yet he says that he could not overlook
the great need for Christian workers, and the sad condition of
those who were going astray like sheep having no shepherd.
He knew that among them were many sincere souls who were
desirous of being shown the way. He placed himself unreservedly on the altar of service, and asked with one of old:
"Lord, what wilt thou have me do?" Menno requested of the
brotherhood that they unite with him for a time in fervent
prayer for divine direction. When this suggestion had been
complied with, he consented to ordination. "I consecrated myself, soul and body," he says, "to the Lord, and committed myself to His gracious leading."

At a later date, in answer to the accusation of having united
with a seditious sect and being ordained a minister by them,
Menno Simons wrote: "I have been called unworthily to this
office by a people who were willing to obey Christ and His
word, who in the fear of God led devoted lives, served their
neighbors in love, bore the cross of persecution, sought the welfare and salvation of all men, loved righteousness and truth
and abhorred wickedness and unrighteousness."

From the time of his baptism and particularly from his ordination as a minister of the Word, until he left his native land
toward the end of 1543, Menno Simons led the life of "a fugitive upon earth," being compelled to live as an outlaw. The
difficulties, hardships, and dangers under which he labored

were of such a nature that they beggar description. He observes correctly that "nowhere has so fierce persecution prevailed in apostolic times."[50] In 1544 he says that to date he had found it impossible to live for any length of time at any given place. To give him food or lodging was declared a criminal act, punishable by death.

There are evidences of Menno Simons' labors in this period in a number of provinces of the Netherlands and also in northwest Germany. Before the end of the year 1536 he was, at least for a short time, in the German province of East Friesland, as indicated by a statement of one of the martyrs. Peter Janz of Bla kenheim, who was beheaded for his faith at Kampen in June, 1540, testified that he was baptized by Menno in 1536 at Oldersum in East Friesland. Presumably Menno returned soon from East Friesland to Groningen or West Friesland. Toward the end of the year 1538 he was in the latter province, in a village called Kimswerd. Here Tjard Reynders, "a very pious and God-fearing man," as Menno speaks of him, was arrested because he had shown Christian hospitality to Menno Simons, receiving him into his house. In a hearing given him, Tjard Reynders freely confessed that he had been baptized upon the confession of his faith. He was therefore condemned to death. On January 8, 1539, he was executed by breaking upon the wheel. He died "as a valiant soldier in Christ."[51]

Important information concerning Menno Simons' early labors in Friesland is contained in a document preserved in the royal archives at Brussels, in modern Belgium. This document was written in May, 1541, by the imperial counsellors of the province of Friesland to Queen Mary, the regent of the Netherlands. The letter describes Menno Simons as "one of the principal leaders of the accursed sect of the Anabaptists." This sect, the writers say, would by that time doubtlessly have been extirpated in Friesland, had it not been for his labors. They complained further that for a number of years Menno had "wandered about" in this province, had led many people astray, and that despite the offer of a large sum of money for his arrest he was still at liberty. The imperial counsellors asked the permission of the Queen to extend grace and pardon to a few Anabaptists and to spare their lives, if they would recant their errors and be instrumental in bringing about the imprisonment of the said Menno Simons. In the reply of the Queen to this letter, the imperial counsellors were authorized to pardon and release one or at most two Anabaptists who recanted their faith, but this grace was to be granted only on the condition that the authorities must make sure of their being sincere in their recantation, and in addition must exact from them the promise "to report to the magistrates any Anabaptists whom they might find at any later time in Friesland." It was assumed that those who had once been Anabaptists would not find it difficult to aid in bringing about the arrest of others of that persuasion.

Notwithstanding such extraordinary measures for the arrest of Menno Simons, he continued his labors in Friesland for some time. A document dated November 14, 1542, in the Criminal Sentence Book of Leeuwarden, contains the statement made by a brother named Sjouck Hayes, that Menno in the same year had preached in a field not far from the city of Leeuwarden.

Emperor Charles V of Germany and the Netherlands published a severe edict of death against Menno Simons on December 7, 1542. This document shows vividly the extreme difficulties and dangers under which Menno labored. The document also indicates the severity of the persecution to which his brethren and associates were subjected. In this edict a reward of one hundred gold guilders (a few hundred dollars in our money, but in purchasing power representing a far greater sum) was offered for his arrest. Grace and pardon were promised to any Anabaptist or anyone who was guilty of any crime, if he brought about Menno's arrest by the authorities. All magistrates and officers of the law who failed to put forth their utmost diligence in the efforts to arrest him were threatened with "the most grievous penalties." Anyone who received Menno Simons into his house, or gave him food and shelter, was to be punished with death, and the same punishment should be meted out to those who conversed with him, or in whose possession any book written by him would be found.

There is good evidence that, notwithstanding this edict, Menno Simons labored extensively in Friesland and other provinces in that period. Nevertheless, in the first years after his ordination the principal field of his ministerial labors was apparently the province of Groningen including the city of the same name. This province is located between the Netherland province of Friesland and East Friesland. In Groningen he baptized, in 1539, Quirinus Peters, who later went to Amsterdam and in this city was, with five others, burned at the stake on April 16, 1545, about six years after his baptism. Of those who were baptized by Menno in Groningen—their number was presumably large—this martyr is the only one whose name has come down to us.

From 1541 to 1543 Menno Simons seems to have sojourned mostly in Amsterdam and the surrounding territory. The names of two men are known whom he baptized in Amsterdam, namely the aged Lukas Lamberts and the book-seller, Jan Claes. Both suffered death on January 19, 1544.[52] Claes was a minister of the gospel. The meetings of the congregation in Amsterdam were held in his house. In a printery at Antwerp he had some of Menno Simons' books printed, and had made it his business to sell and circulate them. The martyr, Claes Gerbrands, who was burned at the stake at Wormer, August 6, 1552, stated that he had heard Menno Simons preach in Amsterdam (probably previous to 1543).

During the first seven years of his labors in the Netherlands Menno wrote a number of important books and pamphlets, as will be further duly indicated.

In the Netherlands, as already indicated, very extraordinary efforts were put forth by the authorities toward the apprehension of Menno Simons. Not only was his own life in great danger, but his presence endangered those as well who showed him kindness and hospitality, giving him food and shelter. Even members of the Catholic Church who knew of his whereabouts without informing the authorities, were threatened with death. In the autumn of the year 1536 two men, Herman and Gerrit Janz, were arrested in West Friesland on the charge that they "had given lodging to the former priest, Menno Simons, who has now been received into the covenant of the Anabaptists." Queen Mary, the regent of the Netherlands, expressed herself on October 24, 1536, to the effect that the sentence of death should be passed on these two men, although they were not Anabaptists. But since it was ascertained that

Menno Simons himself had not yet been baptized at the time they had showed him hospitality, it was finally decided that they should be set free.

It was apparently not long after his ordination that Menno Simons entered the state of matrimony. His wife—her name was Gertrude—was of Witmarsum. He repeatedly speaks of her consecration and full willingness to share with him the severe hardships of homelessness and untold dangers. They had three children, a son—John—who died young, and two daughters. Gertrude's sister, Margaret, was married to Reyn Edes, a co-worker with Menno, who later served the church in the capacity of an elder (bishop).

It was, at least in part, on account of these extraordinary dangers to himself and those who befriended him, that Menno Simons, in the autumn of 1543 left his fatherland to go to northwest Germany. His principal fields of labor during the following three years were the German provinces of East Friesland and the Electorate of Cologne. However, he also traveled frequently in the interest of the work in the Netherlands and in various German provinces.

The empire of Germany was in that era divided into many states, each of which had its own ruler. The relation of the rulers of the various states to the emperor was somewhat similar to that of the governors of our states to the president of the United States. Besides, there were many "Free Cities" whose magistrates were not responsible to the princes of the territories in which they were located, but to the emperor direct. The reigning emperor, Charles V, was a strict Catholic and desired the suppression of all other creeds, but, despite his efforts to that end, some of the German rulers and of the Free Cities supported the Reformation movement and espoused the Lutheran cause. The emperor did not have the power needed to prevent it.

As concerns the persecution of the Anabaptists in Germany, the representatives of the empire in 1529, passed as it were the death sentence upon all Anabaptists. This decree was not carried out however with equal severity in all the states of Germany. After the first decades of Anabaptist history there were in Germany a number of states in which the persecution was less severe than in the Netherlands.

(From Schijn-Maatschoen: "Geschiedenis")

Thieleman Janz van Braght, 1625—1664

Dutch Mennonite leader, compiler of the **Martyrs' Mirror** in its
present form.

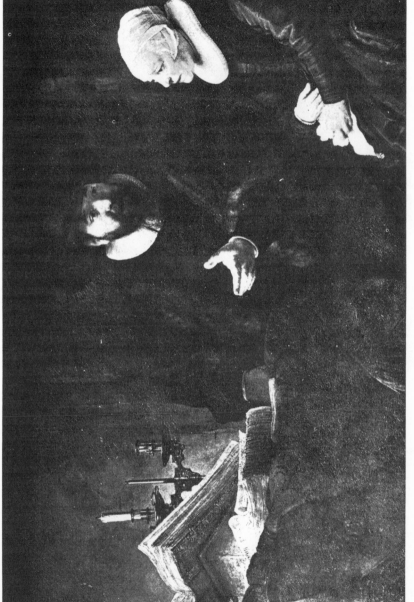

"The Mennonite Preacher C. C. Anslo and a Widow"

Administering Christian Baptism

In the Mennonite Church, "At the Lamb," Amsterdam. (A drawing made by S. Fokke in 1743).

Passing the Bread at the Communion Service

In the Mennonite Church, "The Sun," Amsterdam. (Drawing by A. v. Buisen, jr.).

Passing the Cup at the Communion Service

In the Mennonite Church, "Ark of Noah," Amsterdam. (Drawing by F. de Bakker).

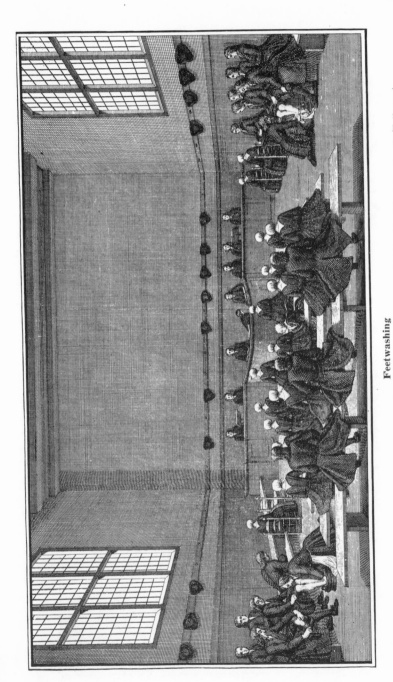

Feetwashing

As it was observed by the Old Flemish Mennonites at Groningen, Holland. (Drawing by J. Folkema).

It was probably about the beginning of winter of 1543, that Menno Simons with his family came to East Friesland in Germany. In this province the Roman Catholic faith had been widely discredited, but a new church was not yet established. In this transitional period the Anabaptists for a short time enjoyed a measure of toleration under the mild reign of Countess Anna of Oldenburg who, after the death of her husband, Count Enno, had become the ruler of this province. In the same year that Menno came to East Friesland, Countess Anna called John a'Lasco, a Zwinglian reformer of a mild type, and a native of Poland, to the office of superintendent of the proposed new state church. At Emden, the capital city of East Friesland, a'Lasco met a number of Mennonite refugees who referred him to Menno Simons. Consequently Menno was given an invitation by a'Lasco to come to Emden for an interview. In the presence of a number of ministers and others, a three-day discussion between Menno Simons and a'Lasco was held in the chapel of the Franciscan monastery at Emden from January 28 to 31, 1544.

The subjects discussed between Menno Simons and John a'Lasco were: the incarnation of Christ, baptism, original sin, sanctification, and the calling of the ministers. On the questions of original sin and sanctification the two men found themselves of one mind, not however on the other points discussed. After the close of the discussions a'Lasco and his associates permitted Menno, as he himself states, to depart in peace, but desired that he should within three weeks send them a written statement of his faith which they might present to the civil authorities, to give them information concerning the principles held by Menno and his friends. A greater measure of publicity was given these discussions than to any other discussions, or debates, in which Menno Simons ever had a part, and yet it was not a debate at which the public was present. At no time had Menno Simons the opportunity to defend his doctrine, according to the custom of the time, in a public debate, yet he often expressed the desire to meet for a public discussion with those who differed from him in doctrine, and to compare the points of difference in the light of Scripture.

Not long after this discussion the provincial government of East Friesland received strict orders from the higher authorities at Brussels to banish all Anabaptists from the province. In 1545 the authorities of this province banished the flagrantly unorthodox Davidian and Batenburger Anabaptists. The Mennonites were threatened with banishment unless they would accept instruction from John a'Lasco and his associates.

Among those present at the discussion between Menno Simons and John a'Lasco was Jelle Smit (the Latinized form of his name was Gellius Faber). Later, as a Lutheran preacher in Saxony, Gellius Faber published a book against the evangelical Anabaptists. To this book Menno Simons wrote a reply which is one of his most important books, the largest work he wrote.

A number of months after the discussion at Emden we find Menno Simons in the province known as the Electorate of Cologne, in northwest Germany. "I know," wrote a'Lasco on July 26, 1544, to his friend Hardenberg, "that Menno just now is sojourning mostly in the bishopric of Cologne"; he adds that Menno's teaching was spread widely in those parts. In this province Menno found a great field of labor. A number of small congregations of evangelical Anabaptists existed here before his coming. The archbishop of Cologne, Herman von Wied, "of praiseworthy memory," as Menno speaks of him, was at the same time the ruler of the bishopric of Cologne which comprised the whole province. Herman von Wied realized the need of a reformation of the church. He decided upon the renunciation of Romish popery but was slow to have another church organized. Meanwhile he tolerated not only Lutherans and Zwinglians in his territory, but Anabaptists also found it possible to sojourn here without severe persecution.

Menno Simons lived in this province about two years. Traces of his labors in this period are found in the confessions of various martyrs. Metken Vrancken, a martyr, said in her examination by the inquisitors that Menno Simons was at Fischerswert in 1545 and she with others was taught by him. Teunis van Hastenrath who was burned at the stake on July 30, 1551, in Linnich stated that "Menno Simons was at Fischerswert five years ago" and that he had read his books. The martyr Lyske Snyer had heard Menno preach in a meadow near Illekhoven, about 1545, where Menno lodged in the house of Lemke, a deacon. Jan Neulen confessed in 1550 that Menno Simons, five or six years before preached at Fischerswert in a field. He had not heard the sermon, but early next morning Menno with two men came into his house and asked him to take him in a boat down the Meuse river to Roermond. This he did and received his hire. His house was confiscated by the authorities for the reason that Menno had entered it without his protest. Menno Simons relates another case of confiscation. In 1546 a house of four rooms was confiscated by the authorities for the reason that the owner had leased it for a short time to Menno's wife, who was sick at the time, with their children.[53] These places were within the territory of the Electorate of Cologne.

Upon Menno Simons' suggestion certain members of the theological faculty of the University of Bonn in the same province gave some consideration to the question of a discussion with Menno, to be held before twenty or thirty witnesses with the understanding of personal safety being accorded Menno. However, John a'Lasco, whose opinion they asked, advised against such a discussion, and the theologians of Bonn accepted his advice. From the town of Wesel Menno Simons received a suggestion to come for a debate. He declared himself ready to go to Wesel to meet the Protestant preachers, but received from them the reply that "the executioner should deal with him."

The mild reign of Elector Herman von Wied came to a sudden end in 1546. He was deposed, and Romanism fully reestablished throughout the province. Early in 1546 Menno Simons saw himself compelled again to flee. He states that his wife was sick at the time. With their small children they turned northward. In the same year he attended a conference of the Mennonite bishops at Lübeck in North Germany and somewhat later another conference at Emden. In the following years he traveled extensively in various provinces of Germany and the Netherlands. In 1547 he was at Goch in the lower Rhine country, where again a conference of the bishops was held, and in the early spring of 1549 he traveled in West Friesland. In April of that year he was entertained in the home of Klaas Janz somewhere in West Friesland. Klaas Janz, apparently was not a Mennonite, but yet was sentenced to death because he had given lodging to Menno Simons, and was executed at Leeuwarden on June 1 of the same year. To the congregations in Prussia Menno Simons wrote an important letter on October 7, 1549, which gives evidence that in the preceding summer he had for a few weeks labored among these churches. In 1552 he attended a bishops' conference at Lübeck. There is evidence also of his visits in cities of the North Sea and Baltic Sea territories. Traces of his labors have been found in Lithuania and Livonia and as far north as Esthonia.

In 1553 we find Menno Simons in the city of Wismar in the province of Mecklenburg, North Germany. A small congregation of the evangelical Anabaptists had existed here for some time. Wismar was one of the cities of the Hanseatic League, a confederation of cities in the Baltic region. The Lutheran reformation had been introduced at Wismar in 1542. The Mennonites and other dissenters were not tolerated. The Hanseatic League, in 1553, published a strict edict against the Anabaptists, forbidding their sojourn in this territory and demanding that the presence of any of these people must be promptly reported to the authorities. These orders were not carried out with equal severity, however, in all these cities.

During Menno Simons' stay at Wismar, a group of Reformed refugees came to this city, having been driven out of England by Queen Mary ("Bloody Mary"). A boatload of these people arrived off Wismar on December 21, 1553. Their ship froze fast in the ice some distance from the shore; and they sorely needed help, which was not readily given them on account of the existing difference in creed, Wismar being a Lutheran city. When Menno and his friends learned of the arrival of these refugees and their needs, they did what was in their power to assist them to effect a landing, and also supplied them with needed food.

The minister of this group of refugees, who came with them to Wismar, was Herman Bakereel. With him Menno Simons had a discussion on various points of doctrine, on December 26, 1553. In consequence the friends of Backereel sent word to a minister of their persuasion at Emden asking him to come to their assistance in their debate with Menno. This minister was Martin de Cleyne who had Grecized his name, calling himself Martin Micron.

Micron arrived at Wismar on January 25, 1554 and had two private discussions with Menno Simons. Naturally a public debate between an Anabaptist and a Zwinglian in a Lutheran city was entirely out of the question, though the magistrates were evidently inclined to leniency toward the Mennonites. The authorities of the city would have exposed themselves to grave danger had they permitted Menno Simons to speak in public. If Menno had preached in public, or if the authorities had received information that he was to speak anywhere, they would have felt obliged to prevent such a meeting. In all probability Menno would have been seized and banished. He says expressly that the magistrates knew nothing of his abode. In fact there was in that period no opportunity in any country for Menno Simons to speak in a meeting that was publicly announced. He and his friends informed both Backereel and Micron that the discussions must be of a strictly private character. He debated with Martin Micron on February 6 and again on February 15, 1554, mostly, upon Micron's suggestion, on the question of the incarnation of Christ.

Martin Micron published later an account of a part of his discussions with Menno Simons, who in turn defended himself against certain charges made by Micron. In a letter to Heinrich Bullinger in Zurich, dated April 12, 1556, Micron stated that Menno Simons' *Reply* had been published about two weeks ago, and, unless a strong answer to it was forthcoming, there was danger that "many may be led astray by Menno's book," an evidence that Micron recognized the notable influence of Menno's writings.

A few weeks after the discussions held at Wismar, namely on February 23, 1554, after the arrival of the refugees from England had become more generally known in adjoining regions, they were banished from Wismar. They went to the city of Lübeck. The Mennonites had not attracted public attention to the same extent, and apparently were not compelled to leave Wismar at this time. But a severe edict was published on August 1, 1555, by six cities of the Hanseatic League, namely Lübeck, Hamburg, Rostok, Stralsund, Wismar, and Lüneburg against both the Anabaptists and the Zwinglians. Menno Simons had in all probability previously gone to Holstein.

In Wismar the Mennonite bishops held a conference in 1554, and adopted a number of rules and resolutions having reference to Christian practice and church discipline. These *Wismar De-*

cisions have come down to us, but evidently not in their original form. Some of the articles, in the form in which they are available are of doubtful authority; the text is in part corrupt and unreliable.

Soon after Menno Simons left Wismar he found a place of refuge at Wüstenfelde near Oldesloe in Holstein, Denmark, on the large estate called Fresenburg. This estate was owned by the nobleman Bartholomew von Ahlefeldt. The estate Fresenburg war located in South Holstein between the cities Hamburg and Lübeck. Von Ahlefeldt was a friend and patron of the Mennonites. He had been an officer in the Netherland army and had witnessed the death of some of the Mennonite martyrs. By their steadfast devotion to their Christian convictions they had favorably impressed him. He was convinced that they were of an entirely harmless character, and their persecution was unnecessary.

The southern part of Holstein constituted at that time a province of the kingdom of Denmark. Here the cruel laws against the Anabaptists, which had been enacted in Germany and the Netherlands, were not in force, and yet the Danish government did not tolerate them. King Christian III of Denma.k, ʲ 1554, protested to von Ahlefeldt against permitting Mennonites to settle in Fresenburg, but this nobleman apparently found it possible to continue his policy of toleration toward them. He permitted Menno Simons to settle at Wüstenfelde. Notwithstanding the dangers to which von Ahlefeldt exposed himself by tolerating the Mennonites, he remained their friend and did all in his power to shield them against the threatening danger of persecution by the state authorities.

An old chronicler relates that at a time when rumors had reached the higher authorities that von Ahlefeldt tolerated Anabaptists on his estate, he gave them orders to leave, but at the same time advised them to absent themselves only for a short time. Meanwhile he succeeded in dispelling the threatening clouds of serious difficulty. Soon after this occurrence Mennonite refugees from persecution came from every side.

Menno Simons lived at Wüstenfelde to the end of his life. His family could remain at this place in safety while he was absent much of the time traveling and laboring in Germany and in Holland. There the persecution continued unabated.

Even aside from the constant danger of falling into the hands of the persecuting authorities, his travels in those times were beset with great inconveniences and hardships. Apparently it was in 1557 that Menno Simons undertook for the last time a journey to Holland where special efforts were made to apprehend him, a great prize having been set on his head, as previously noted.

At Wismar Menno Simons had incurred a severe injury to one of his lower limbs; thereafter he at times used a crutch. In order not to expose himself to unnecessary danger, he signed some of his letters, "Your brother, the cripple."

Very little is known of Menno Simons' family. As previously stated, two daughters and a son—John—are mentioned. His wife and son died before him. One of the daughters who survived him gave some information about his life to the chronicler Peter Janz Twisck.

Menno Simons died at Wüstenfelde on Friday, January 31, 1561. "His last exhortation," says a trustworthy writer, "he gave on his death bed, when his end seemed near, an evidence of his unquenchable zeal. He, however, improved somewhat and was better for several days. But on the day of the anniversary of his renunciation of the Roman Catholic Church he had a relapse and on the day following, in the sixty-sixth year of his life he feel asleep in Jesus."

The exact place where his body was laid to rest is today unknown. The settlement, or village, of Wüstenfelde was completely destroyed in the Thirty-Years' War (1618-1648). A number of the members of the congregation fled to Hamburg. In 1902 an unpretentious monument in memory of Menno Simons was set at the site of the former village of Wüstenfelde.

Menno Simons was the outstanding leader of the Mennonite brotherhood of his time in the Netherlands and North Germany. As an author and exponent of the faith, as a defender of the church against the calumnies of the opponents and persecutors he outranked by far all other writers. His writings have not yet been given the attention and study by church historians in general which they deserve. While not all of his books are of equal importance, some are of intrinsic value for all times. Sometimes he is severe, over-severe in fact, in his criticism of the persecuting state churches, but his writings are singularly free from abusive epithets. This is the more noteworthy since Roman Catholic authors as well as the leaders of the state church type of Protestantism often spoke of the evangelical Anabaptists in almost unbelievably abusive terms.

In Menno Simons' life and character the outstanding characteristic was the determination to serve the Lord conscientiously and consistently without regard to the cost. He had experienced a thorough conversion and for conscience' sake had laid down his position of honor among men to become an outcast, "choosing rather to suffer affliction with the people of God." With his associates he devoted his life to the realization of a truly Christian church conforming strictly to the scriptural standard in doctrine, principle, and practice. Menno fully recognized the compromise of the state church type of the Reformation movement whose leaders consented to a union of church and state, and thus avoided persecution. In many places in his writings he mentions endurance of persecution from the world as one of the characteristics of a true Christian church.

Naturally in his writings Menno Simons often makes mention of the persecution, the dangers that beset his way on every hand. When Gellius Faber accused him of seeking selfish ends in his labors, Menno replied:

With my wife and our children I have borne great and various anxieties, sufferings, griefs, afflictions, miseries, and persecutions for these eighteen years, and have at all times been in danger of my life. While the ministers of the established churches are reclining on their soft beds and downy pillows, we often spend the night in secluded corners. While some of them are celebrating the nuptials or natal days of their children with feasts and musical instruments, we are looking anxiously about, fearing the barking of the dogs, lest persecutors should be suddenly at the door. While they are saluted by every one as doctors, lords, and masters, we must hear that we are Anabaptists, hedge-preachers, seducers and heretics, and must be saluted in the devil's name. In short, whilst they for their ministry are remunerated with large stipends and prosperous days, our recompense and portion must be the fire, the sword, and death.[54]

When Menno Simons was upbraided by Gellius Faber for preaching at night, his reply was that he had taught far more in daytime than at night, and that the apostles also at times preached at night. Menno added: "We are prepared at all times to render an account of our faith to every one, and to defend publicly the truth whenever it is desired in good faith, without deception and secret intent at risk of our lives." Again, he made this pertinent statement: "Although we do not teach in meetings which are publicly announced and for which a general invitation is given, nevertheless the truth is not kept by us as a secret but is preached here and there, both by day and at night, in cities and country places, by mouth and through the printed page, by living example and by martyrdom. Judges, officers, dungeons, water, the sword, and the stake must add their testimony to it. Yea, people must confess that the Word was preached to them in great power, for innocent blood was shed like water for the sake of the truth."

In one of his later books Menno Simons answered as follows to certain charges made against him:

The great and mighty God has made known the word of His grace and power through our humble service, preaching and writing, and the work and help of our faithful brethren, in many cities and countries to such extent that many proud hearts have become humble, many unclean pure, many drunken sober, many avaricious benevolent, many ungodly pious. For the sake of their Christian testimony they have willingly given their earthly possessions and their blood, bodies and lives, as even now may be witnessed daily. They should not be able to endure steadfast under so heavy a cross of cruel persecution, were it not the power and word of the Lord which sustains them.

Notwithstanding the indescribable dangers besetting Menno Simons' way, he showed courage and fortitude in the pursuit of his arduous duties. About the year 1600 Peter Janz Twisck wrote:

From a reliable source I have learned that Menno Simons at Eenighenburg, a village in North Holland, at one time went into a church after the priest had completed the observance of the Mass for the day, and with great courage, readiness of speech and learning he conversed with him in Latin about various papistic superstitions. The priest was greatly surprised, and later, after he had renounced Romanism, related at length his conversation with Menno. Not infrequently Menno conversed with priests, disregarding the danger that they might betray him and cause his arrest. He entered a certain cloister without disclosing his identity and spoke to the prior with great boldness, admonishing him earnestly and pointing out their great errors. Although a decree containing his name, and a description of his person and his clothing, was nailed to the church doors, with the promise of hundred guilders' reward to any one who would cause his arrest, yet God preserved him from all the designs and cunning devices of the persecutors.

Various writers both in America and Europe have expressed the opinion that Menno Simons united with the evangelical Anabaptists at a time when the very existence of the brotherhood was in jeopardy, and that the fact of its further existence is to be ascribed to his labors and influence.

It need scarcely be repeated here that the services which Menno rendered the cause of the evangelical Anabaptists were of the greatest importance. Nevertheless the assumption that without his labors the brotherhood would have become extinct has every probability against itself; it is in fact evidently without foundation.

We may notice first that at the time of Menno Simons' conversion in 1536 the brotherhood in Switzerland was surely not in any danger of extinction. A number of years previously, namely in 1532, the civil authorities of the canton Bern complained of a great numerical increase of the *Taüfer* (Swiss Brethren). Extreme measures of persecution had failed to stop their spread. Two great public debates were held in the Canton Bern in 1532 and 1538, which failed to check the movement by persuasion. Severe persecution continued in Switzerland for a century and a half, but without the results sought by the authorities.

Likewise in Holland the efforts of the persecutors to eradicate the Anabaptists had proved failures even at the time of Menno Simons' conversion. There is convincing evidence that the brotherhood with which Menno Simons united was not by any means discouraged by the persecution. Menno speaks of their willingness to bear the cross of persecution. Such willingness they considered in fact as an essential characteristic of a true church. The members had united with the Brethren, knowing full well what this step involved in the way of self-denial and braving the greatest dangers. A life terminating in martyrdom for Christ they believed to be an eminently successful life. The rapid growth of the church in Holland, not long after Menno's conversion, is remarkable. In all probability it indicates that even previous to his conversion a considerable portion of the population were sympathetic to the cause which the Brethren represented. And there was, besides Menno Simons, also Dirck Philips as a noteworthy leader.

In the southern states of the Netherlands, particularly in Flanders, the Brethren were very numerous, although Menno Simons had never visited these parts. Here ruthless persecution continued during Menno's lifetime, and later. In these regions the French language was widely in vogue. For the benefit of the Brethren in these parts Dirck Philips' *Handbook of Christian Doctrine* was published in a French translation. If there had been only the Mennonite congregations formed by refugees from Flanders in the northern provinces of Holland, Mennonitism would have been very far from extinction in that region. The earliest Mennonite congregations in the Rhineland, in Mecklenburg and Prussia, were organized before Menno Simons visited these parts.

Nevertheless, the fact remains that Menno Simons was the most influential leader in the church in the Netherlands, northern Germany, and Denmark, and the ablest writer in defense of the church and its doctrine.

CHAPTER 24

THE WRITINGS OF MENNO SIMONS

Menno Simons was the most notable religious writer of his time in the Netherlands and North Germany. His writings comprise twenty-four books and pamphlets. His first book, a refutation of Münsterite errors, he wrote before his renunciation of the Church of Rome.

Within five years after his conversion and baptism Menno Simons wrote the following books and booklets:

> *The Spiritual Resurrection*
> *The New Birth or Regeneration*
> *Meditation on the Twenty-fifth Psalm*
> *The Reason Why I Do Not Cease Teaching and Writing*
> *The True Christian Faith*
> *The Foundation (Fundamentals of Christian Doctrine)*
> *Christian Baptism*

The general contents of the first two books mentioned here, and of *The True Christian Faith,* are indicated by the titles. The *Meditation on the Twenty-fifth Psalm* is written in the form of a prayer of penitence. It is largely a contrite confession of his sin in the period of his life when he, in order to avoid persecution, hesitated to take a definite stand for the evangelical truth. In point of general interest this book takes a prominent place among Menno's writings.

One of the most important of Menno Simons' earlier books is *The Foundation,* a treatise on the fundamentals of Christian doctrine and life. It was written probably in 1538 and printed in the following year. In the preface of this book Menno in all humility entreats the authorities that he and his brethren be given at least the same consideration as they gave thieves and murderers whose cases, he says, are thoroughly investigated before sentence is pronounced upon them. He urges upon the magistrates the need of making themselves acquainted with the teaching and practice of the Anabaptists, and to compare them with the Scriptures.

In 1544 his *Defense against John a'Lasco* appeared. From the time of the publication of this book until the year 1554 there appeared only smaller booklets and tracts from Menno Simons' pen. Probably this was partly due to his extensive travels during this period, as well as to the fact that printing his writings was exceedingly hazardous, involving very great risks.

In the last eight years of his life, while he lived with his family at Wüstenfelde, on the estate called Fresenburg, Menno Simons found time and opportunity for writing books and pamphlets. His books of the earlier period were written in the Dutch language. His later books he wrote in the language which in the Netherlands was known as the *Ostersch,* that is the Eastern dialect, being the vernacular in the states east of the Netherlands, particularly in the lands along the North Sea and the Baltic Sea. This language was readily understood in Holland as well. At Wüstenfelde Menno Simons translated his earlier books into the "Eastern" language and re-issued them in print. While translating these books he at the same time revised some of them. The books which he issued at Fresenburg were printed in a shop owned by a member of the Mennonite brotherhood.

Menno Simons' largest book was written in this period. It is his reply to the accusations of Gellius Faber who earlier was an assistant of John a'Lasco in his reformatory labors in East Friesland and took part in a'Lasco's disputation with Menno at Emden in 1544. Menno's well-known account of his earlier life, of his conversion and call to the ministry of the Word, which has often been printed separately under the title, *Menno Simons' Renunciation of the Church of Rome,* is a chapter from this book. It is a defense against Faber's charge that Menno was teaching the errors of the Anabaptists of Münster and that he had been called to the ministry by those who were virtually of the same persuasion with the Münsterites. Menno Simons' comprehensive reply to Martin Micron, with whom he had a debate at Wismar, was printed at Fresenburg in 1556. Among his later books his *Confession of the Triune God,* the booklet on *The Cross of Christ,* also a tract on the training of children and various books on church discipline deserve special mention.

The early editions of the books of Menno Simons and other writers of the evangelical Anabaptists do not bear the name of the printer nor the place of publication. The reason is evident. Printing such literature was exceedingly hazardous; in the Netherlands (including modern Belgium) and Germany it was punishable by death.

One of the first Mennonites to take a practical interest in the printing of religious books was Jan Claes of Alkmaar in Holland who suffered martyrdom in 1544 at Amsterdam. As stated in his death sentence, he had printed six hundred books of Menno Simons at Antwerp, and sold two hundred of them in Holland. In all probability these books were produced in a printery not owned by Jan Claes himself. He was a minister of the Mennonite church in Amsterdam; the meetings of the congregation in this city were held in his house.

Within less than a decade after this martyr's death there was a Mennonite printing shop in the city of Lübeck in northern Germany. In the year 1553 a printery in this city, from which some of Menno Simons' writings were issued, was owned by a Mennonite. Apparently this was the first Mennonite printing establishment.

In the summer or autumn of the following year the owner of this establishment—his name is not disclosed in the records —saw himself compelled to leave Lübeck. Nothing is known of the circumstances under which he departed. It is not improbable that in the face of threatening difficulty he escaped before the approaching storm broke. At any rate he evidently succeeded in moving the establishment to another place. He set up the printery in the town of Oldesloe in Holstein, Denmark, not a great distance from Lübeck.

At Oldesloe this Mennonite's printing plant soon attracted the attention of the authorities. Not less than ten casks of books were found and confiscated by the magistrates, and it was ascertained that fourteen casks of books had been sent to Amsterdam. Most of these books were Bibles. If they were printed at Lübeck, or in part possibly at Oldesloe, the printery must have been one of considerable capacity.

The local authorities of the district gave an official hearing to "those who had printed Anabaptist books at Oldesloe," and a report of this hearing was made on November 28, 1554, and sent to King Christian III of Denmark. Strange as it may seem, not any names of the persons called to account in this hearing are given in the report. Evidently the local authorities desired to shield the accused persons as far as possible. The report indicates that the owner of the printery, who is referred to as "the printer" and "the Anabaptist," had "journeymen" (assistants) in his work.

So it was for a very short time only—a few months—that this printer found it possible to carry on his work at Oldesloe. Again he was forced to move, but this time with the prospect of going to a place of safety. He went to Fresenburg, located a short distance from Oldesloe on the large estate of the nobleman Bartholomew von Ahlefeldt. This nobleman was a patron of the Mennonite people, as mentioned above. Von Ahlefeldt not only permitted the Mennonite printer to settle on his estate but apparently aided him to the extent of having a house built for him. At a time when the printer was waylaid and arrested by a neighboring nobleman, he was subsequently released through the efforts of von Ahlefeldt. At least ten of Menno's books were printed in the printing office at Oldesloe and Fresenburg.

The first larger collection of Menno Simons' writings appeared in 1600, and another more complete edition in 1646. His complete works were first printed in the Dutch language in 1681, at Amsterdam. The title page of this edition has the statement, "translated into our Netherland tongue" (i. e., from the "Eastern" language). The English translation of his Works (Elkhart, Indiana, 1871) and the German translation (1876/81) are based on the edition of 1681. An autograph letter of Menno Simons is preserved in the library of the Mennonite Church in Amsterdam. His book entitled *Foundation* was the first of his writings to be translated into German (in 1575), and later in America into the English language. Not less than ten editions of the *Foundation* in the English and German languages have appeared in Pennsylvania alone.

It is improbable that there exists an authentic picture of Menno Simons. Portraits were often made in those times, but to patronize a painter for a portrait was relatively even more expensive than today. The cost was prohibitive for a man of Menno's circumstances, even if he would have had no scruples about spending so much for something unnecessary.[55]

CHAPTER 25

THE CO-LABORERS OF MENNO SIMONS

In his account of his conversion and call to the ministry Menno Simons does not make mention of his ordination nor of Obbe Philips who ordained him. The reason is obvious. At the time when Menno wrote this account Obbe Philips had forsaken the church with which he had been so prominently connected. To Menno Simons this was a bitter experience, but he did not permit it to discourage him. Obbe Philips' later book, *Confessions,* indicates that at the time of his withdrawal he deviated on various points from the doctrine of the evangelical Anabaptists. He rejected the doctrine of justification by faith, as held by Menno and the Swiss Brethren, and made light of the observance of the ordinances and of all church organization. Before Obbe's withdrawal from the brotherhood Menno Simons had evidently outdistanced him as a leader. The fact also that his withdrawal caused the brotherhood only the loss of a few members points in the direction of an earlier loss of influence. Menno Simons stated in 1554 that not ten persons shared the opinions of Obbe Philips. That he returned into the Roman church, as has been generally supposed, is an error.

The most prominent co-workers with Menno Simons in Holland and North Germany were the bishops, Dirck Philips and Leonard Bouwens. Dirck Philips was born in 1504 at Leeuwarden. He was evidently educated for the Catholic clergy. As a young man he became a Franciscan monk, and was an inmate of a monastery near this city. He was among the first to unite with the brotherhood of evangelical Anabaptists, organized by his brother Obbe. Eventually he was ordained an elder by him. Dirck Philips accompanied Menno Simons on some of his travels and in later years was bishop of the Mennonite congregations in a large territory including the cities of Danzig and Elbing and the town of Montau near Graudenz in Prussia. He lived at Danzig, or more correctly in Schottland, a suburb of this city, where the Mennonites enjoyed a measure of toleration. Apparently the congregation at Danzig was organized by Menno Simons.

Dirck Philips was the author of various books and booklets which later were collected and printed in one volume under the title *Handbook of the Christian Doctrine and Religion.* This book is the most important early Mennonite doctrinal work besides Menno Simons' writings. It has been translated into French, German and English. Three German editions were printed in America.[56] Menno Simons, in his writings, refers repeatedly to the full agreement as to doctrine and practice existing between Dirck Philips and himself. After Menno's death Dirck was the most influential bishop in the Mennonite Church of Holland and North Germany. He died in 1568.

Leonard Bouwens was born at Sommelsdyk, in Holland, in 1515. Before his conversion he had been a member of a society of literary and general educational aims, called "Rederijkers" which flourished in some of the cities of the Netherlands. When the Reformation movement reached the Netherlands, many of the Rederijkers gave it a friendly reception. After serving the evangelical Anabaptists for some time as a minister, Leonard Bouwens was ordained a bishop by Menno Simons, at Emden in 1551. In the same year he undertook a journey to visit congregations in East Friesland, Groningen, West Friesland and some of the islands of the North Sea, administering baptism and the communion.

This work involved great personal dangers. Bouwens decided to brave these dangers; his wife however objected, being not entirely resigned to having her husband expose himself to such great risks. Apparently Bouwens and others suggested to Menno Simons that he attempt to persuade her, if possible, to give her husband her wholehearted support in fulfilling the duties of his calling. Menno Simons wrote her a letter in 1553, in which he enlarged upon the subject of full consecration to the service of the Lord, and urged the need of trust in Him and submission to His will.

Leonard Bouwens was one of the most active Mennonite elders in this early period. He lived at Emden but traveled a great deal, not only in the northern provinces of the Netherlands, but also in Flanders and other parts of modern Belgium where the persecution was particularly severe. He kept a record of baptisms which he administered at every place he visited. This record shows that between the years 1551 and 1554 he baptized 869 persons; in the years 1554-1556, 693 persons; in 1557-1561, 808 persons; in 1563-1565, 4499; and in 1568-1582, 3509, making a total of 10,378 persons, in 142 places within about twenty-five years.

It should be observed that these great numbers of accessions to the church were by no means solely the fruit of Bouwens' labors. These converts were won mainly through the efforts and influence of the congregations existing in these places. In those days every church member was active as a missionary. Those in the congregations who were candidates for baptism and were ready for it were baptized by Bouwens. And he was not the only bishop active in those parts. The above account of accessions to the church in the Netherlands is by no means all-inclusive. Leonard Bouwens died in 1582 at Hoorn in the Netherlands.

Another co-laborer with Menno Simons, though only for a brief period, was Adam Pastor, of Dorpen in Westphalia, northwest Germany. About the year 1530 he was a priest at Aschendorf. The date when he cast his lot with the Mennonites is not exactly known. He served the church as a minister and was ordained elder by Menno Simons and Dirck Philips probably in 1542. About five years later he took an unorthodox position regarding the doctrine of Christ's deity. He and his adherents were excommunicated by a conference of Mennonite bishops. From all appearance the followers of Adam Pastor never had an organized congregation anywhere.[57] For nearly three centuries both Pastor and his writings were forgotten. About a century ago a copy of a book by him was found in Amsterdam. It later appeared in print.

Adam Pastor died in Münster, at that time a strictly Roman Catholic city. He was buried, if we may accept the statement of the contemporary writer, Hamelmann, in the public *Überwasser* cemetery of that city. This would indicate that he was believed to be a Roman Catholic, since no Protestant, much less an Anabaptist, would have been permitted to be buried in this cemetery. Whether Pastor had returned into the Roman Church, or had given any occasion for the supposition that he had again become a Romanist, it is impossible to determine. On the development of the Mennonite Church or, for that matter, on any other church, Adam Pastor did not have any influence.

Gillis of Aachen (Aix-la-Chapelle) was another collaborator with Menno Simons. He was born about 1500. In 1525
he was a Catholic priest, and at an early date united with the
evangelical Anabaptists. He was ordained a bishop by Menno
Simons in 1542. Gillis of Aachen traveled extensively in Holland and parts of Germany, and took part in important conferences, but his career ended in great disappointment to his
friends. In 1557 he was taken prisoner near Antwerp while
preaching in a field. In prison at Antwerp he was prevailed
upon to recant his faith. He was beheaded and his body broken
upon the wheel on May 10, 1557, at Antwerp. Had he remained steadfast, he would have been burned alive at the stake.
Some of the chroniclers say that he was visited after his recantation by a minister of the Brethren, and upon confession
was reinstated into fellowship. His last words, it is said, were,
"It is too much to lose both body and soul." His death was
not recorded by van Braght in the *Martyrs' Mirror*.

CHAPTER 26

MUENSTERITES, BATENBURGERS, DAVIDIANS

A sketch of the rise of the Münsterite sect was given in chapter 21 above. The city of Münster in Westphalia, Northwest Germany, with an extensive adjacent territory, was ruled by a bishop of the Roman Catholic Church. Through a remarkable chain of circumstances a sect of radical fanatics succeeded in usurping the government of the city by the aid of the powerful guilds (trades unions). They drove out all who would not make common cause with them. Early in 1534 the self-styled prophet Jan Matthys, an extreme fanatic, became the ruler of Münster. The city was soon besieged, and Matthys was slain in battle. Thereupon John of Leiden, a man of talent but a worthless character, took charge of the government of the new "Zion," and eventually had himself crowned king. Like Jan Matthys he claimed to be favored with special divine revelations.

John of Leiden introduced polygamy in "the new Israel," as the Münsterites called themselves. The people realized then what sort of character their leader was. They made an attempt to overthrow his reign of indecency and terror. Their revolt within the walls of the besieged city, was crushed with a bloody hand. Famine prevailed at Münster toward the end of 1534. John of Leiden, to make the people forget their misery arranged for amusements in the market place, such as dancing, in which he personally took part till late at night. Theatrical plays were also given. But these diversions failed to satisfy the starving people. Their sufferings became unbearable. On June 24, 1535, the city was conquered with terrible slaughter. John of Leiden and two of his principal accomplices were, after lengthy imprisonment, tortured to death. The bodies of the three culprits were placed in iron cages, suspended from the tower of St. Lambert's Church. For about four centuries these cages remained upon the tower. The Roman Catholic creed was restored in the city by the bishop.

John of Leiden, in the first period of his imprisonment, made bold to defend Münsterite doctrine and practice, but before his

death he confessed to his great guilt incurred by teaching appalling errors, particularly as concerned polygamy and divine
kingship. He also admitted freely that he never had divine
revelations. He manifested deep and sincere repentance for all
the evil he had done, and confessed that if he could be made to
suffer death ten times over, he had deserved it.

After the Münster kingdom had come to an end, Münsterite
principles were advocated for a short time by Johann von Batenburg (1495-1538) who attempted to organize some of those
who had escaped from Münster, and their sympathizers. The
Batenburgians, as his followers were called, defended polygamy and held that those who refused to unite with them would
finally be destroyed with the sword. As concerns baptism, and
in fact all external things, they conformed to the practices of
the dominant churches in order to avoid persecution. Batenburg was finally seized and executed in 1538 at Volvorden in
Brabant (modern Belgium).

Besides the Batenburgians the sect of the Davidians also,
to an extent, followed in the footsteps of the Münsterites. They
were the adherents of David Joris (1501-1556) who taught
extremely unorthodox views which branded him as one of the
most outstanding fanatics in the history of Christendom.

David Joris, after his renunciation of Romanism, was for a
time a Lutheran, then a Melchiorite, and about 1535 he became
an Obbenite. He was baptized and ordained by Obbe Philips.
Within a few years he began to deviate widely from the teachings of the evangelical Anabaptists. After the fall of the Münster kingdom he conceived of a visionary plan for bringing
about a union of all Anabaptists. A meeting with this purpose
in view, held at Bocholt in Westphalia in August, 1536, was not
attended by any Obbenites at all.

Within a few years David Joris caused further offense by
advancing the most serious errors. He had what he believed
to be wonderful divine revelations endowing him with super-
lative wisdom and calling him to be the head of the kingdom of
God on earth. His divine calling, he asserted, marked the end
of the dispensation of the letter and the beginning of a new dispensation. The first and second covenants were imperfect.
Christ Himself, he asserted, had not brought the world the full
light of truth. The true kingdom of God did not exist previous

to David Joris' calling. He held that the evangelical Anabaptists erred fundamentally by basing their doctrine on the letter of the Scriptures. Joris taught that the inner, spiritual man is not affected by outward evil works. Since the outward behavior of man was in his opinion spiritually indifferent, he advised his followers to profess the creed prescribed by the government of the state or country in which they happened to live, thus preventing all persecution. He believed such deception to be perfectly admissible. It has been generally supposed that David Joris was an Anabaptist. He held baptism to be quite unnecessary, however, and was a fierce opponent of the evangelical Anabaptists. His followers practiced infant baptism for the reason that it served a purpose in their general policy of deception. At the same time he was zealous in spreading his teachings. He wrote a surprisingly large number of books and tracts, but was careful not to spread his writings in the territory in which he lived.

In the year 1544 David Joris under an assumed name came with his family to Basel in northern Switzerland. He pretended to be a refugee from persecution, a member of the Reformed Church which was the established creed in this city. His name he gave as John von Bruges, and asked for permission to live in the city. This was freely granted him. He bought a valuable property and lived in opulent style. Soon he became a prominent figure in the state church of Basel. For twelve years, namely to the time of his death in 1556, he succeeded in thus deceiving the people and magistrates of Basel. He was considered one of the most dependable members of the state church. About three years after his death it was discovered through a family quarrel that John of Bruges was none other than the arch-heretic David Joris who defended the most obnoxious errors in his many tracts which had been distributed in northern Germany and the Netherlands. His body was exhumed and, with such of his books as were obtainable, burned at the stake outside the city, in 1559.

Among Menno Simons' extant writings there is a letter to David Joris (not contained in his *Works*) in which the errors of this prince of fanatics are unsparingly exposed and denounced.

The sects of the Münsterites, Batenburgians, and Davidians, because of their extreme fanaticism and moral corruption, were commonly designated by Menno Simons as "the corrupt sects."[58]

Menno Simons has ofttimes been unjustly accused of being of the same persuasion as the Münsterites and other fanatical sects. Even the latest Dutch biographer of Menno asserted that in the period immediately after his conversion he held the Münsterites as brethren. The truth is that even before his renunciation of Romanism Menno Simons wrote a book against the Münsterites in which he speaks of their teaching as an abomination, and refers to John of Leiden as an antichrist and a blasphemer. In his *Meditation on the Twenty-fifth Psalm*, written within a year after his conversion he said:

Through the false, misguided teachers, Satan has perverted the spiritual sense of the Scriptures into carnality. He has preached the use of the sword and weapons of destruction, and thereby has engendered a spirit of revenge against all the world. He has moreover, without any scriptural foundation, cloaked and palliated shameful adultery [by the practice of polygamy] with the example of the Jewish patriarchs, also a literal kingdom and king and other ungodly errors at which a true Christian is stricken with terror.

In the same booklet, as well as in various other places, Menno stated that the errors of "the corrupt sects" were more offensive and grievous than those of Romanism, since the Roman Church did not defend "the abominable works of the flesh." In the first edition of his *Foundation*, written before 1539, he addressed the corrupt sects:

You have been so miserably led astray by the false prophets from the true path of Jesus Christ that the last error has become much worse than the first, for with you it has come to this that you defend as right and good the abominable works of the flesh.

Again, in the revision of the same work, made probably in 1554, he writes under the caption, "To the Corrupt Sects":

Is it not a grievous mistake that ye suffer yourselves to be so wretchedly bewitched by such worthless men, and so lamentably misled from one unclean sect into another; first Münsterite, then of Batenburg, now Davidians, and thus from Beelzebub to Lucifer and from Belial to Behemoth, ever learning and never able to come to the knowledge of the truth (II Tim. 3:7), suffering yourselves to be led about by every wind of false doctrine?

A comparison of Mennonite with Münsterite principles reveals the most radical differences and contrasts. There was a fundamental difference on the point of the authoritative sources of Christian truth. The Münsterites held the new revelations which came to them through their prophets, to be of equal if not greater authority than the Scriptures, and besides, they taught that the Old Testament Scriptures surpass the New Testament in authority and importance. Rothmann wrote on the point in question:

> We presume that everyone now knows what is the principal, indubitable Scripture, according to which all Scripture must be interpreted, namely Moses and the Prophets. These are the authoritative Scriptures. There are also other praiseworthy books which may be called Holy Scriptures . . . especially the Scriptures or books of the New Testament whose truth is founded on the principal Scriptures.

It is seen then that the New Israel of Münster held the Old Testament Scriptures to be the most important and authoritative part of the Bible. In this regard they differed fundamentally from the evangelical Anabaptists. (Menno Simons taught that the Old Testament, although a part of God's Word, was, as concerns many of its commands and practices, intended for pre-messianic times alone. It was not authoritative for Christian life and practice.) All the Old Testament, says Menno, pointed forward to Christ the Redeemer and Inaugurator of the New Covenant who brought the world the full light of truth. Certain points of Old Testament law were expressly abrogated in the Sermon on the Mount. Divorce, the swearing of oaths, retaliation, and war were permitted in the Old Testament law, but forbidden by Christ. "All Scripture must be interpreted according to the spirit, teaching, walk, and example of Christ and the apostles," says Menno.

The Münsterite conception of the relation of the Old Testament to the New differs more radically from Menno's conception than from that of the leading reformers. Luther, Zwingli and Calvin did not make the distinction between the Old and New Testament Scriptures on which the evangelical Anabaptists insisted, but held both parts of the Scriptures to be authoritative as the rule of life and practice for the Christian church. Their defense of infant baptism, state church policy, and other points on which they differed from the Mennonites, was based pre-eminently on the Scriptures of the Old Testament. The evangelical Anabaptists on the other hand held, on the ground of such passages as Hebrews chapters 7 to 10, and Matthew 5:31-48 that the Old Covenant was imperfect in its law, priesthood, and worship.

The Lutheran church historian, Paul Tschackert, says correctly that Luther's approval of the bigamy of Philip of Hesse had its basis in his wrong conception of the relation of the Old Testament to the New. Plurality of wives, the darkest and one of the most characteristic points of Münsteritism, was more radically and consistently opposed by the Mennonites than by the Protestant state churches. Among the Swiss Brethren, Hutterites, and Mennonites transgressors against the seventh commandment were more severely dealt with than in the state churches.

The state church policy of the Münsterites led to the same intolerance and persecution as was in vogue in the Lutheran and Zwinglian state churches. Liberty of conscience was openly repudiated in Münster. The Swiss Brethren and Mennonites excluded false teachers from the church; the Münsterites persecuted them, threatening them with banishment or the death sentence. Capital punishment even for criminals was believed by Menno to be inconsistent with Christian principles. The Münsterites on the contrary undertook to kill all "the wicked." The Mennonites held that "the powers that be are ordained of God;" the Münsterites held that the governments which opposed them were not of God but of the evil one.

Menno Simons repudiated the thought that either the members of the church individually, or the church as such, is perfect. He did not by any means believe that membership in the church assures salvation. The Münsterites, on the contrary, taught that "all Israel will be saved." They held their "Zion" to be in the absolute sense "without spot or wrinkle," and at the same time they countenanced the most glaring transgression and worldliness. Theoretically communism existed in Münster, but the idea of the church as a brotherhood was trampled under feet by John of Leiden. Famine reigned in the city, but the king of "Zion," like Dives of old, "clothed himself in purple and fine linen and fared sumptuously every day." The Münsterites were Sabbatarians, keeping Saturday as the day of rest. And why not, if the Old Testament is the principal rule for Christian doctrine and practice?

Not all who were baptized in Münster or who fled to the city from other places were one in doctrine with John of Leiden. More than fifty persons were executed in Münster for the reason that they refused to consent to polygamy, and it is well-known that those who were put to death were only a minority of the number who were of one mind with them and never became guilty of bigamy or polygamy. And we do not know to what extent the troops of men and women who attempted to go to Münster and aid the Münsterite cause were acquainted with the principles advocated in the city. Nevertheless they have been generally spoken of as Münsterites, and a Münsterite is supposed to be one who approves of polygamy. To what extremes this idea has been carried is well illustrated by the following example. Gillis of Aachen, later a prominent Mennonite elder, was erroneously believed to have been among a band which in February, 1534, was arrested near Düsseldorf for the reason that they intended to go to Münster. On this ground Gillis von Aachen has been represented by a biographer of Menno as a believer in polygamy. But the Münsterites did not defend this offensive institution at this time. It was in June of the same year (1534) that John of Leiden for the first time proposed the introduction of polygamy.

It is worthy of note that the Münsterites did not consider themselves to be the spiritual descendants of the earlier evangelical Anabaptists. In their opinion the latter erred radically on the most important points. The beginnings of the Münsterite movement were traced back by them to the reformation movement of the state church type, not to the evangelical Anabaptist movement. Bernt Rothmann, the theologian of the Münsterites, said that Luther and Zwingli have begun the work which Melchior Hofmann, Jan Matthys, and John of Leiden have completed.

The principle that the Scriptures are the only authority in matters of faith was accepted by the evangelical Anabaptists far more unreservedly than by the Lutherans and Zwinglians, and this principle also made Münsteritism impossible. On the points of the union of the church and state, absence of church discipline, and persecution of false teachers the Münsterites followed not the early Anabaptists but the new state churches. Hofmann was at first a disciple of Luther; the idea that he was ever connected with the Swiss or South German Anabaptists is contrary to fact. Rothmann also was originally a Lutheran. And both Luther and Zwingli had originally been Roman Catholics. To lay the offenses of the Münsterites to the charge of the Mennonites, on the ground that both practiced adult baptism, is, as Menno Simons points out, as unreasonable as to accuse the Lutherans of the crimes of which some of the popes became guilty, on the ground that both were pedobaptists.

CHAPTER 27

THE MENNONITES IN NORTH GERMANY
AND POLAND

In northwestern Germany there are today Mennonite congregations in the cities of Emden, Crefeld, Hamburg, and a few other places. Emden in East Friesland is one of the places of Menno Simons' and Hans de Ries' labors. In Crefeld north of Cologne, in northwestern Germany, a Mennonite church existed as early as 1615. Among those finding a refuge here were Mennonite craftsmen, particularly weavers, from various regions, whose coming to Crefeld marked a turning point in the industrial development of the place. The first minister of the Mennonite Church in Crefeld was Herman op den Graeff (1585-1642), one of the original signers of the Dortrecht Confession in 1632. Three of his grandsons, the brothers Herman, Abram, and Dirk op den Graeff, were among the thirteen families who came to America on the ship Concord in 1683 and settled at Germantown.

In the city of Hamburg on the Elbe River there was a Mennonite congregation as early as 1575. By the year 1605 about 130 Mennonite families, mostly refugees from the Netherlands, had come to this city. In 1672 Emperor Leopold of Germany, in a message to the city authorities, complained that from 300 to 400 Mennonites were living in Hamburg. The magistrates, in their reply to the emperor, said the Mennonites were a peaceable people who had nothing in common with the Anabaptists of Münster; they included the government in their church prayers. Many members of the congregation lived in the neighboring city of Altona where the Mennonite meetinghouse was located.

An influential bishop of this congregation was Gerhard Roosen (1612-1711), the author of a catechism entitled, *Spiritual Conversation on Saving Faith*,[59] which was translated into English and often reprinted in America. He also wrote an important book on the history of the Mennonite Church. From 1649 to 1663 Gerhard Roosen served the church as deacon and was then ordained bishop. The difficulties which caused the division between the parties headed by Galenus Abrahams and Samuel Apostool in Amsterdam disturbed also for a time the peace of the church in Hamburg and Altona. Galenus, the leader of the more liberal party, visited the congregation at Hamburg personally but failed to win them for his views. Somewhat later the Mennonites of Hamburg and Altona declared their agreement with Samuel Apostool. Gerhard Roosen's labors were not confined to pastoral work at Altona and Hamburg; he often traveled extensively in Germany, the Netherlands, and Poland to visit the congregations in the interest of the faith.

After the year 1684 Gerhard Roosen was assisted in his ministerial labors by Jacob Denner (1659-1746), a man of extraordinary gifts for edifying exposition of the Scriptures. In 1708 he became the pastor of a newly organized church in which immersion was practiced. This congregation became extinct at the time of his death.[60] Missionaries of the English Quakers came to Hamburg about 1655 to visit the Mennonites. In the course of a few years the Mennonite congregation lost ten members, among them their deacon, Berend Roelofs, to the Quakers. Gerhard Roosen wrote a booklet in defense of the Mennonite position on the Christian ordinances and other points. In the same century a few members of the congregation were owners of mercantile establishments. In 1673, when a new church building was to be erected, the Mennonite merchants sending boats to Greenland for whale fishing promised to give five per cent of the profit for this purpose. The profits in that year were so great as to nearly cover the cost of the building. In 1711, the congregation in Hamburg contributed the sum of 1470 guilders for the Swiss Mennonite refugees in Holland.

In times of war the general usage in those days was for mercantile vessels to carry arms for defence. This was inconsistent for nonresistant shipowners, and was not permitted by the Mennonites even if the ships were manned by those who were not members of the church. During the siege of Hamburg by the Danish army, in 1686, the Mennonites were exempted from military service on condition that they stand watch upon a certain tower to discover and to extinguish any outbreaking of fire during the bombardment, a service which they could con-

scientiously perform.[61]   The religious services of the congregation in Hamburg were conducted in the Dutch language until
1786. Since the year 1839 the preaching has been in German
only. There is today a strong Mennonite congregation at Hamburg.

In the period of the Reformation Prussia was under the
sovereignty of the kings of Poland. Mennonite congregations
were founded here in various places during Menno Simons' lifetime. Menno visited the congregations in Prussia in the summer of 1549 and addressed to them an important letter in
October of the same year. By the year 1600 Mennonite churches had been organized in various places on the Vistula River,
also in the cities of Danzig and Elbing, in the lowlands between
these cities, and in the eastern part of Prussia. The Mennonite
families in those regions were families of Dutch origin, being
refugees from the Netherlands.

It was apparently after the year 1548 that Menno Simons,
accompanied by Dirck Philips, visited the city of Danzig on
the Baltic Sea. After Menno's death Dirck Philips came again
to Danzig. Since Mennonites were not tolerated in the city,
Dirck Philips lived in the near-by village of Schottland, and
labored here with the minister Hans Sicken until 1568. Numerous Mennonite refugees from Holland found it possible to take
up residence near there and later also in the city. George Han-
sen, the author of a number of theological works, written from
the conservative point of view, was a minister at Danzig after
1655, and elder after 1690. Today the Mennonite congregation in this city has upwards of 1200 members.

In the region of the lowlands between Danzig and Elbing,
under the sovereignty of the kings of Poland, the Mennonites
were tolerated at an early date. The kings of Poland in 1642
and again in 1660 and 1694 granted them "letters of protection." By these documents they were given state recognition.
The letters stated at length that by their work of building dikes
and dams in sections along the Vistula and Nogat rivers, and
by their expert methods of cultivating these lowlands, they had
rendered the country inestimable services.

In the year 1737 King August II of Poland published a manifesto stating that the Mennonites had been called into the
country to clear and bring into cultivation the swampy waste-

lands of those regions, and that they had given proof of their expert knowledge of the most practical methods for accomplishing this task. For this reason, the manifesto stated further, they were granted the privilege of freely practicing their religion, of holding religious services in private houses and other places (not in special church buildings), of having their own schools with teachers of their communion, of instructing and baptizing their own youth, and so forth. Until about 1750 the religious services of these churches were conducted in the Dutch language.

In 1772 the region between the cities of Danzig and Elbing and other eastern districts, in which Mennonite churches of Dutch descent were located, was incorporated into the Kingdom of Prussia under King Frederick the Great. At that time the Mennonite congregations sent two of their men to Potsdam, the residence of the king, to submit a petition for the recognition of the privileges permitted them by the former government. King Frederick guaranteed them "for all times" exemption from military service on the condition of the payment of an extra assessment of 5000 thalers annually for the cadet school at Kulm. They agreed to this compromise, though on the whole these churches represented conservative Mennonitism.

The Mennonites of the country districts of Prussia during the eighteenth century enjoyed great material prosperity. About the year 1785 they owned a land area of 2000 *Hufen*, (more than 80,000 acres). A decree designed to make it difficult for Mennonites to acquire more land was published in 1789. Somewhat later the government prohibited their further acquisition of land. Steps were taken also, looking for a reduction of their actual land possessions, and persons born of non-Mennonite parents who had in recent years united with the church, were not eligible for military exemption.

At the time when such measures of oppression were enacted in Prussia, Czarina Catherine II addressed a number of decrees to the Mennonite people. She invited them to colonize the wide steppes (prairie lands) of South Russia, granting them favorable conditions. The Mennonites of Prussia recognized in this a gracious divine providence, and largely availed themselves of the invitation. Though the Prussian government looked with disfavor upon this exodus of the Mennonites, many hundreds of families migrated to Russia.

During the period of the Napoleonic wars (1806-1814) the Mennonites of Prussia succeeded under great difficulties in maintaining their position of refusing military service. But later, in the period of political unrest, beginning in 1848, when military preparedness was given special emphasis by political leaders, some of the Mennonites of Prussia and other German states, decided to abandon their testimony against service in the army. A member of the Frankfurt Parliament, Herman von Beckerath, a member of the Mennonite Church at Crefeld, urged the Mennonite people to discard their opposition to military service. The majority of the Mennonites of Prussia, however, maintained their former position. New migrations to Russia took place from 1853 to 1859.

In 1867 a new Prussian military law was passed by the legislature annulling the privilege of exemption for the Mennonites, but in the following year King William decreed that, while service in the army was obligatory for all, Mennonites of the older families would be permitted to serve as sick-attendants, secretaries, and drivers of provision wagons. With the exception of a comparatively small number who refused to abandon the principle of nonresistance and emigrated to America (Nebraska and Kansas) the Mennonites of Prussia and other parts of Germany have since then accepted so-called "noncombatant" service; while during the World War many did not even avail themselves of this privilege but chose the regular service.

A few decades before the beginning of the migration of Mennonites from Prussia to South Russia a Mennonite settlement was formed at Kazun in the territory which at that time was known as Russian Poland. Somewhat later another group of Mennonite emigrants from Prussia organized a church at Wymysle in the same region. Both these churches are located in a district which after 1918 became a part of Poland.

Previous to the World War of 1914-1918 the most numerous groups of Mennonite churches in Germany were located in the northeastern parts of that country, principally between the cities of Danzig and Elbing. Through the treaty of Versailles, some of this territory was included in Poland, while another part, with the city of Danzig as the commercial center, was also severed from Germany and declared an independent state to form the so-called "corridor" between Germany and Poland. Thus Germany had lost more than half of the Mennonite population of the northeastern region.

Again, a notable migration of Swiss Mennonites from the Palatinate and Alsace to Austrian Poland took place between 1780 and 1790, under Emperor Joseph II, of Austria. They settled in the region of Lemberg in the province of Galicia which in 1919 was incorporated in the Republic of Poland. A considerable number of these Mennonite families, in 1796, moved on from Galicia to Russia, settling in the region of Tschernikow, and later in the Russian province of Volhynia. From the settlement near Lemberg in Galicia about 75 families came to America between 1874 and 1883. The congregation near Lemberg in 1939 numbered about 400 members. In 1940 the entire Mennonite settlement in Lemberg was transferred by German government order from Galicia to northern Prussia.

As a result of the Russian invasion and conquest of eastern Germany, the entire Mennonite population of East and West Prussia and Danzig Free State, as well as those Mennonites living in Poland proper, including the resettled Lemberg group, was forced out of their ancient homeland in 1945, partly by evacuation of the German army, partly by flight as refugees, and partly by forcible expulsion by the Polish government which took over the former German lands in the east. Out of about 12,000 souls, probably at least 3,000 perished during the bitter tribulations of this time. A small number, who had been for several years interned in Denmark, together with their close relatives in Germany, and the bulk of the surviving Lemberg group, were resettled in Uruguay in 1948 by the Mennonite Central Committee, some 750 souls being in this group. The remainder are largely refugees in Western Germany, mostly in the British Zone, hoping for resettlement elsewhere.

The German Mennonites of Northwest Germany and South Germany, did not suffer so severely, although the church in Emden was destroyed and the ones in Gronau and Ludwigshafen were severely damaged. The Mennonite Central Committee has succeeded in removing from Germany to Canada and Paraguay almost all of the 12,000 Russian Mennonite refugees who were brought into Germany in 1943 by the retreating German army.

CHAPTER 28

THE MENNONITES IN HOLLAND

During Menno Simons' lifetime the Mennonite Church was practically the only non-Romish church in the Netherlands. Protestantism of the state church type was not represented in Holland until a later date when the Calvinistic reformation was introduced.

In regard to general conditions in the Mennonite congregations in the Netherlands about the time of the death of Menno Simons, there is evidence that the church in that period proved to be truly the light of the world. Menno Simons, in many places in his writings, gives testimony to the power of the gospel in individual lives, pointing his readers to the fact that many thousands had been saved from a life of sin, and were leading an exemplary Christian life in the power of the Spirit. Brotherly love, spiritual fervor and Christian zeal were generally in evidence. Concerning the spiritual condition of the brotherhood in that period, Hans de Ries, publisher of an earlier edition of a Book of Martyrs, wrote:

In that time of cross-bearing, when we could come together only under danger of life, the zeal for the cause of the Lord was such that we nevertheless often came together. Frequently we met at nighttime and under adverse weather conditions, in corners and nooks, in fields and woods. How precious was at that time the opportunity to spend an hour for mutual edification, strengthening each other in the most holy faith! How thirsty and hungry were the souls for the bread of life! How pleasing and satisfying was its taste!

On the same subject, namely the general conditions in the Mennonite churches of the Netherlands, we have another testimony in a letter written by Dirck Philips. A few years after Menno Simons' death Dirck Philips visited the churches in the Netherlands. After his return to Germany he addressed to them a letter containing valuable information on the point under consideration. In this letter to the congregations in the Netherlands Dirck Philips said:

While I was with you I had great joy and my soul was refreshed in the Lord as I saw your fervency and constancy in the faith, your love to God and His truth, your Christlike peace, your brotherly unity and

233

the good rules of discipline observed among you, and that God's Word is so fruitful, and so many are added to the churches of the Lord, so that it seems to me that a particular blessing from God has come upon my fatherland.

I thank Almighty God for you, my beloved in the Lord, and rejoice over His work in my fatherland. I praise God from the depth of my heart for the abundant blessings of God in heavenly riches, the precious fruits of righteousness which are in evidence among you, that the vineyard of the Lord is blossoming and emitting a fragrant odor (Sol. Song 2:13). The plants of all manner of fruits of the Spirit are in evidence, and not only in the Netherlands but also in the adjacent countries. Oh, what a great change and difference, that such a barren waste has become so fruitful a land, yea a garden of the Lord!

In Friesland and other northern provinces of the Nether-lands the Mennonite Church had a remarkable growth, though the persecution had not entirely ceased here; in Flanders (Bel-gium) it continued to be far more severe. During the period when the persecution was in full sway faithful Anabaptists were in Flanders as a rule burned alive at the stake within a week after the sentence had been pronounced; in Friesland they were commonly strangled and their bodies burned. The magistrates in Flanders used all diligence for the apprehension of Mennon-ites, while in Friesland by the middle of the century there was in evidence a general attitude of leniency toward Anabaptists. Nowhere in the Netherlands had the laws demanding the ex-tirpation of the Anabaptists been abrogated, but in Friesland the authorities had obviously become tired of using the sword against them. "The Friesian government," said a contempo-rary chronicler, "although it continued to adhere to the Papacy, was far more tolerant and reasonable in its attitude toward the Anabaptists than many other governments."

About the time Dirck Philips wrote the letter quoted above there were in the northern Netherlands many Mennonite con-gregations, some of them with a very numerous membership. In 1567, for example, the congregaton at Harlingen in Fries-land numbered 1700 and the one of Franeker, in the same prov-ince 1300 members. And yet severe edicts were from time to time issued by the higher authorities of the land, requiring the death penalty for adherence to the Mennonite creed. These edicts were published apparently upon the demand of King Philip II of Spain, a fanatical Roman Catholic, of whose domain the Netherlands were a part. Personally he was absent from the Netherlands and may not have been well informed about existing conditions. In consequence of the leniency of local authorities who had been led to see the injustice of this persecution, the bloody edicts became more and more a dead letter. The last martyr to be executed in the northern Netherlands was Reitse Ayses, who suffered death by being burned at the stake in 1574 at Leeuwarden. In the southern Netherlands the last execution took place near Brussels in Brabant in 1597, when Anna Uttenhove was buried alive. From the year 1530 to 1597 about 2,000 persons were sentenced to death in the courts of law in the Netherlands, and executed. About 1,500 of these were Mennonites, nearly one third of them women.

As a result of the severe persecution in Flanders there was an extensive exodus of Flemish Mennonite refugees to Friesland and other northern provinces. Among the refugees were Hans de Ries and other men who later became outstanding leaders among the brotherhood. Many came destitute and penniless, and were dependent upon the charity of the church, which was freely extended to them. The refugees were welcomed into the existing Mennonite congregations. In a few places of the northern provinces congregations of Flemish refugees were organized. This may have been partly for the reason that the Flemish language differs considerably from the Friesian. Notwithstanding minor differences between the Flemish and Friesian Mennonites, unity and harmony prevailed among them.

The churches of the area called Waterland, a small district between Amsterdam and Purmerend in Holland, differed somewhat in the practice of discipline from the general usage of the Mennonite Church. The difference concerned the treatment of those who became guilty of some heinous offense. The Waterlandian churches held that every expulsion is to be preceded by at least three admonitions. Originally this had been the general Mennonite usage, as is clear from Menno Simons' writings. He said in the latter period of his life (1558) that he had changed his mind on this question. Earlier he had held to the view that there must be no expulsion without three preceding admonitions, according to Matthew 18:15-17. In a booklet written in 1558 he stated that he was now of another opinion, believing that immediate excommunication should fol-low heinous transgression. His former opinion he said, had been due to his inexperience, for he had supposed that among those "who have once entered upon the path of righteousness, immediate repentance would follow the transgression without fail."

This departure from the former practice resulted, in 1555, in the separation of the congregations in the Waterland from the main body of the Mennonites, the Waterlandians continu-ing the older usage. If in a Waterlandian congregation a member who fell into gross sin, repented and made confession, he was not excommunicated. Expulsion took place only if after three admonitions, he refused to confess and repent. In the larger body of the Mennonite Church with which Menno Simons was identified, grievous sin was followed by immediate expulsion. In the case of other transgressions expulsion took place only after three fruitless admonitions. Clearly then the points of difference between the main body of the Mennonites and the Waterlandians were entirely secondary. There was some controversy with the Waterlandians on this question, but finally it was decided that the hand of brotherly fellowship was not to be withheld from the Waterlandian congregations. All indications are that peace prevailed despite this difference in the practice of church discipline.

The first actual division in the Mennonite Church in the Netherlands and North Germany took place in 1567, about six years after Menno Simons' death. The causes of this schism are not altogether apparent. Difficulties began with the ordina-tion of a certain brother to the ministry at Franeker in Fries-land. The newly ordained minister, with the approval of a part of the congregation in Franeker, began to hold separate meet-ings. Those supporting him in this venture seem to have been of the Flemish refugees. The disharmony soon spread to other congregations.

After earnest efforts to adjust the difficulties had failed, Dirck Philips (who lived near Danzig, Germany) was invited to visit the church in Holland as an arbiter. His orthodoxy was recognized by both parties. Evidently he failed to exercise the tact which existing needs required. On his way to Holland he was met and interviewed by a number of brethren of one of the groups, and he made the mistake of virtually deciding in their favor before giving both parties a hearing. In consequence there were regrettable misunderstandings on the part of a few ministers. The membership became disunited, taking sides with the one group or the other. The final outcome was an actual disruption, a division of the church involving most of the Mennonite congregations of Holland and northern Germany, with the exception of the Waterlandians and other congregations which refrained from taking sides.

The majority of one of the groups involved in the division were of the Flemish refugees, therefore this group became known as the Flemish, while the other group were named Friesians because most of their churches were located in Friesland. In the course of a few years certain congregations that had not taken sides united with the Flemish. Dirck Philips was identified with this group. Among the Friesians the most outstanding leader was Peter Janz Twisck, the author of the larger Friesian confession consisting of thirty-three articles. This division was the more deplorable since both the Flemish and the Friesians held strictly to the tenets of the conservative Mennonite faith. Both adhered to the doctrines and principles of the church as laid down in the writings of Menno Simons and Dirck Philips. This is clearly indicated by their confessions of faith and the writings of their leaders. Efforts for reunion were put forth at an early date. Among those working for reunion Hendrik Roosevelt, a Flemish elder, deserves mention.

Thus that which Menno Simons had so greatly feared and which he had put forth every effort to prevent, namely a division of the brotherhood, became a reality. Yet the causes of the division had nothing to do with matters of faith and practice. In passing we may notice that this division occurred after the persecution had practically ceased in the Netherlands, except in the southern provinces. And within a quarter of a century various other divisions took place. We may add that the causes of some of the later divisions were such that Menno Simons would undoubtedly have approved of a separation.

An indirect evidence of the interest of the early Mennonites of northern Germany and Holland in Bible reading is afforded by the history of what is known as the Biestkens Bible, a Dutch version translated and printed by Mennonites. Until the year

1555 both a Netherlands version and Luther's translation of the Bible were in use in non-Romish circles in these countries. In 1556 a new version of the New Testament into the Dutch language was issued by Reformed translators. This translation differed considerably from earlier versions of the Scriptures. The Mennonites believed that the renderings of certain passages in the new translation favored the teaching of the Reformed state church. They consequently issued a new translation of the New Testament in 1557, and three years later a translation of the whole Bible. Among the translators of this Bible, Gerrit Brixius, a Mennonite bishop of Groningen in Holland, seems to have been most prominent. According to the testimony of a contemporary Reformed scholar Ubbo Emmius (1547-1625), Brixius was a man of excellent scholarship, well versed in the Greek, Latin, and Hebrew languages.

This Bible was known as the Biestkens Bible because it was published by Nicholas Biestkens, a Mennonite printer at Emden in East Friesland. It was for a long period in general use among the Mennonites of the Netherlands and North Germany. It was many times reprinted in various cities of Holland. From 1562 till 1600 there appeared thirty-one editions of this Bible, and from 1602 to 1650 twenty-four editions. Until the year 1725 the whole Bible in this version was printed at least ninety times. Sixteen editions were issued in folio, ten in quarto, and one in octavo. Moreover, not less than sixty-four editions of the Biestkens New Testament were printed in quarto, octavo, duodecimo, and 16mo. These facts are a testimony to the zeal of the early Mennonites for the use and spreading of the Word of God.

Under the noble Prince William of Orange the government of Holland took a decidedly tolerant attitude toward the Mennonites. In 1572, after he had been elected stadtholder or governor of two provinces of the northern Netherlands, two Mennonite ministers, Jacob Frederiks and Dirk Jans Cortenbosch, on their return trip from a visit to their brethren in the Rhine country, called upon him at his castle in Dillenburg to ask him if they could be of any service to him after their return to Holland. The prince replied that some of their people might be willing to raise a special contribution in money for his government.

On May 5, 1572 the Prince wrote a letter to the Mennonite minister Peter William Bogaert who at that time was at Emden, making a similar request. Bogaert and Cortenbosch consequently visited some of the Mennonite people in this interest. The two men acted on the request and collected 1060 carolus guilders for this purpose. At the time when they met the prince to hand him the money, they informed him that it was a gift for the support of the government and was not to be returned. They added that it was given as an indication of their loyalty and that they "desired only his friendship if God would confer upon him the government of the Netherlands." In the receipt given them by the prince it was stated that this money was given "for the advancement of the common cause"—an intimation that it was not to be used for purposes of war.

By that time the Mennonites, as already indicated, had become numerous in Holland. Even some of those who took an antagonistic attitude toward them admitted that they were useful citizens. The theory that a state tolerating various creeds could not prosper had become untenable in view of the presence of the numerous Mennonites. Under existing conditions it was small wonder that William of Orange granted the Mennonites toleration. He knew them too well to consent to their persecution. In 1577 he gave the magistrates of the city of Middelburg orders not to burden the conscience of the Mennonites by requiring of them the oath and military service. In regard to religious toleration the government of Holland differed from the Lutheran and Zwinglian governments of certain German and Swiss states, in which membership in the state church was compulsory to all. By the year 1581 toleration for the Mennonites had become the general usage in Holland. About a century later, namely in 1672, they were formally recognized as a sect that was to be protected in the free exercise of their religion.

Holland was the first country whose government recognized the principle of general religious toleration. As we have seen, this principle was defended by the Swiss Brethren and Mennonites from the beginning. The Brethren held that it is not in the province of the state or the civil authorities to intermeddle in questions of creed. This does not mean that they would have the church take a similar attitude of neutrality on ques-

tions of faith and practice, as in modern religious liberalism.
Though the Mennonite people took no active part in politics, it
was partly through their influence that toleration was granted
in Holland. In this connection it may be recalled that the Pilgrim Fathers, before their coming to America on the May-
flower in 1620, had sought and found a refuge in Holland. In
the southern Netherlands the Roman Catholic Church continued in power. By the year 1625 the last Mennonites of the
south had fled to Holland. There is no Mennonite congregation in Belgium today.

During the first half century of the existence of the Mennonite Church in Holland many prints and reprints of the various books and tracts of Menno Simons and Dirck Philips were
published. Collections of some of the writings of these prominent leaders also appeared at an early date. The first Mennonite Book of Martyrs, entitled *Het Offer des Heeren* (the
Offering of the Lord) was published in 1561. In the following
period, namely from the time open persecution in Holland
ceased (1576) to the close of the following century, a great
number of books and pamphlets were published by the Mennonites of Holland. These books treat mainly on Christian
doctrine and practical Christian living, partly also on the history of the church, and there were several large volumes of
sermons.

In the period from the death of Dirck Philips (1568) to the
end of the following century the Mennonite Church in Holland
had a number of talented leaders, some of them men of outstanding ability. Foremost among them, probably, was bishop
Hans de Ries. He was born in December, 1553, at Antwerp
in Flanders and was brought up in the Roman Catholic faith.
As a youth he shunned gay society and interested himself in religious things. Having been led to recognize some of the teachings of the Church of Rome to be errors, he was particularly
offended by her cruel persecution of those who did not accept
her doctrine. He first turned to the Reformed Church, whose
members had become somewhat numerous in Antwerp, but it
proved disappointing to him to see some of them "attend their
places of worship with weapons in their hands to defend themselves in case of an attack." He was of the opinion that this

"was not a sign of a New Testament church." Eventually he became acquainted with the doctrine of the Mennonites. Their determination to bear for Christ's sake the bitterest persecution without the least resistance made a deep impression on him. He believed them to manifest the evidences of true followers of Christ and decided to unite with them.

Hans de Ries' intimate friend Hans Bret was a member of the Mennonite Church, and was arrested by the magistrates of Antwerp in 1576. After terrible tortures which he endured with true Christian heroism he was burned at the stake in the year 1577. Hans de Ries was baptized and ordained a minister in the same year by the bishop Simon Michaels of the Waterlandian Mennonites. De Ries was employed as the cashier of an Italian mercantile house at Antwerp. His employer, although a Catholic, was well disposed toward him on account of his faithfulness. Shortly after the martyrdom of Hans Bret, de Ries came near being seized by the officers. He had a narrow escape, but succeeded in getting out of the city. The merchant who had employed him heard of his flight and, desiring to aid him, through extraordinary efforts supplied him with a considerable sum of money in recognition of his faithful services. In a village not far from Antwerp Hans de Ries, with his wife and other refugees, was arrested and arraigned before the magistrates. He gave a candid confession of his faith, and said in conclusion: "Know ye, my lords, that we did not flee because we would refuse to shed our blood for the name of Jesus, for we have long ago surrendered our lives to God, but because we would not give our persecutors an occasion to commit a sin against us. But if you so choose, and if a handful of blood be of such value to you—behold we are here. Do unto us what you may find best in your consciences to do. As concerns us, we are ready to meet death." Such candid language made an impression and the prisoners were freed or given an opportunity to escape.

After his escape from Flanders Hans de Ries labored in various places of Holland and northwestern Germany. At Middelburg in Holland he was imprisoned in 1580 upon complaint made by a minister of the Reformed Church, but was soon released. From 1593 to 1598 he was the minister of the Waterlandian Mennonite Church at Emden in East Friesland. Again, for many years he served the church at Alkmaar in Holland as pastor and elder. He was a gifted preacher and spoke with warmth and conviction, and gave much attention to pastoral work. His sermons proved attractive to many outsiders. The marked growth of this congregation was, under the blessing of God, due largely to his faithful labors. By a prolonged study of medicine he became a proficient medical adviser and took delight in serving the poor without remuneration. His wife aided him wholeheartedly in his religious and benevolent work.

As a writer in defense of evangelical doctrine and practice Hans de Ries held a prominent place. Among his most important books is a defense of the deity of Christ against the Socinians (Unitarians) of Poland. The Socinians sent a few of their ministers, among them Christopher Osterot, to Holland to visit the Waterlandian Mennonites, urging a union with them. They met de Ries who pointed out to them the impossibility of such a union. They were greatly disappointed and addressed to him a letter in offensive language. De Ries replied in a book entitled, *Clear Proof of the Eternity and Deity of Jesus Christ.* In the preface he stated that he would refrain from using calumnious language, for he "had not learned such a thing from his loving and meek Lord," but he would answer with the Word of God.

Together with Lubbert Gerrits Hans de Ries wrote a confession of faith consisting of forty articles. This confession was published about 1581, and was again published in 1610 upon the request of one, John Smyth, who with a number of English refugees had (like the Pilgrim Fathers) fled to Holland from persecution in England. These people had been subjected to persecution because they disapproved of the union of church and state. They finally united with the Waterlandian Mennonites in Amsterdam in 1614.

De Ries had a part in the publication of one of the earliest Mennonite books of martyrs, and published one of the first Mennonite hymnbooks in the Dutch language. At Emden he made successful efforts toward a union of Waterlandian, Friesian, and the High German Mennonites. The latter name was applied to the Mennonites of South (Upper or Higher) Germany and of Switzerland in contradistinction to the churches of the Lower Countries (Netherlands). Hans de Ries died in 1638.

The most prominent Mennonite writer of that period was Peter Janz Twisck, bishop of the Friesian Mennonite Church at Hoorn in Holland. He was born at Hoorn in 1565 and married a granddaughter of Menno Simons. He was the outstanding leader in the group of churches with which he was identified, and made many journeys to visit the various congregations. The books and pamphlets published by him numbered at least twenty-five, among them various large volumes on doctrines and on historical subjects.

Among his more noteworthy books is a defense of the deity of Christ and a treatise on the atonement, also a comprehensive history of the principle of liberty of conscience. He published a "Bible-Concordance" which is in fact a Bible dictionary containing over 1,000 folio pages. Peter Janz Twisck is the author of what is known as the larger Mennonite Confession of Faith, consisting of thirty-three articles.[62] Peter Janz Twisck died at Hoorn in 1636.

Another eminent bishop of the same period was Tieleman Janz van Braght, the compiler of the *Martyrs' Mirror* in its present form. He was born January 6, 1625, in Dortrecht. His father was a cloth merchant. He united with the Flemish Mennonite Church at Dortrecht and was ordained an elder in 1648. He was an able defender of Mennonite principles. In 1657 he published a catechism which was reprinted at least seventeen times. His most important work is the *Martyrs' Mirror,* mentioned above. As a book on the history of the early Mennonite Church this work holds a unique place. Van Braght's reliability as a historian, though assailed by some writers, was convincingly established by the late Professor Samuel Cramer of Amsterdam. Van Braght died in 1664. A volume of sermons written by him was published after his death by his brother.

From about the year 1560 to near the close of the following century (the time of the first Mennonite immigration to America) the Mennonite Church of Holland had a period of notable expansion and growth. By the year 1700 the Mennonites in Holland numbered about 160,000 church members, constituting about five per cent of the population of that little country.

As already stated, the Mennonites of Holland enjoyed toleration since the beginning of the reign of Prince William of Orange as sole ruler, though oppression and at times even persecution by local authorities were not entirely absent. Prince William was their friend and protector. The synods of the state church often protested to the civil authorities against the liberties granted the Mennonites. These protests urged the need of various obstacles to the spread of the Mennonite Church, such as forbidding any increase in the number of their ministers and of their places of worship, and permitting ministers to preach only in their home congregations. Synods of the state church even petitioned the authorities that Mennonite meetings be forbidden. A curtailment of Mennonite liberties was demanded in fifty-three different sessions of the synods. The ministers of the state church were salaried by the state from funds raised by general taxation, hence the Mennonites' share in providing the salaries of these ministers was as great as that of the members of that church. The preachers of the state church had the right to interrupt sermons of Mennonite preachers at any time by questions and contradictions.

In the town of Sneek in Friesland a persecution took place in the year 1600. Two men of the state church clergy of this town, with the express permission of the magistrates, entered the Mennonite meeting to give the congregation instruction, as they said. The congregation refused to hear them. Shortly afterwards the ministers of this congregation were forbidden to preach, hence they refrained from attending the meetings, though the congregation met as usual. The two state church clergymen had supposed this would be for them the opportunity to win the shepherdless congregation for the state church creed and, with this in mind, went to the meeting place of the congregation to preach. Their efforts were fruitless.

In the year 1601 the same ministers translated into the Dutch language a part of a Latin work by Theodore Beza (1519-1605), the successor of John Calvin in Geneva, in which the severest punishment of heretics by the magistrates of the land was advocated. In this booklet, which appeared in print in the same year, the contemporary Anabaptists (Mennonites) were charged with scandalous errors and misdeeds. The ministers who published the booklet wrote a preface for it in which they defended the view that only one creed should be tolerated by the state. To take such an attitude toward those who taught heresies, they said, would be not to rule over consciences but only to carry out God's command. To exile the heretics, they said further, may mean a loss to the prosperity of the town, but "it were better to have a desolate, uninhabited town, than a place full of heretics." A copy of this booklet was presented to the magistrates of the town of Sneek who immediately issued an order forbidding all meetings of the Mennonites.

In a few other places, also, Mennonite meetings were forbidden. Preachers were sentenced to pay heavy fines, and a few were even exiled, as was the case at Leeuwarden. These outbreaks on the part of local magistrates were of short duration, however. For a time marriages among the Mennonite membership had to be solemnized by state church ministers, but this restriction was withdrawn in 1672. Somewhat later the central government of Holland intervened in behalf of the persecuted Mennonites in Switzerland, addressing a letter to the authorities of the canton Bern in which they had only praise for these persecuted people.

A great debate between representatives of the Mennonite Church and the Reformed state church took place in Emden in East Friesland in 1578. In this city a number of edicts had been published against the Mennonites, some of them demanding their banishment while others merely forbade their meetings. In 1577 a Mennonite minister was imprisoned because he had held religious services. He addressed the magistrates saying that it did not appear altogether just to forbid him and his friends to teach without having examined their doctrine, and an investigation might lead the authorities to take a more lenient attitude. He offered to meet the ministers of the state church and give them an account of his faith. He was released.

In the following year a number of Flemish, Friesian, and Waterlandian Mennonite preachers met in Emden for the purpose of conferring on the question of a union of these branches or groups of Mennonites. The Reformed preachers of the city, together with the magistrates, having been informed of their presence in the city, suggested a public debate between ministers of the Mennonite Church and of the state church. The Friesian and Waterlandian Mennonite ministers expressed doubt regarding the expediency of a debate. They declined the offer, while the Flemish Mennonite ministers accepted it. The debate began on February 27, 1578. One hundred and twenty-four sessions were held between this date and May 17. The leading speakers on the Mennonite side were the bishops Peter van Cologne, Hans Buschert, and Gerrit Brixius, who proved themselves able defenders of the doctrine. While the greater number of their opponents surpassed them in scholarship, Gerrit Brixius apparently was the equal of any of his opponents in this regard. And Peter van Cologne was a man of wide information and extraordinary mental vigor and penetration. One of the moderators of this debate addressed him, "If you had the learning, which we have, you would prevail over us to leave the church." The report of this debate was printed and was valued by both parties, since it defended the position of each. A disputation of similar nature was held at Leeuwarden in 1596. Ruardus Acronius, a prominent Reformed minister, debated here with Peter van Cologne. Like the former debate it passed off without noticeable results.

The first Confession of Faith drawn up by Mennonites in Holland is the Waterlandian Confession of 1577. Two years later a number of Articles of Agreement were drawn up at Emden, probably by Hans de Ries, and were subscribed by ministers of various congregations. These articles would scarcely deserve the designation of a confession of faith. The confession called "The Concept of Cologne," of the year 1591, was the result of an effort for a union of Friesian and Flemish with High German Mennonites (Swiss Brethren). It was signed by representatives of congregations in the Rhine country, Alsace, Strasburg, Württemberg, and Holland. The Friesian Confession, consisting of thirty-three articles,[63] drawn up by Peter Janz Twisck, was printed about 1600, and the second Waterlandian Confession of forty articles by Hans de Ries and Lubbert Geritts about 1582. The confession of 1627, named "Olive Branch," was written with a view of bringing about a union between the Friesian and Flemish churches. The confession of a group of United Friesian and High German churches was prepared by Jan Centsen in 1630. It was published after its adoption by fourteen representatives of Mennonite congregations.[64]

The Dortrecht Confession of Faith of 1632, the confession generally recognized and used by conservative Mennonites in America, was drawn up by Adrian Cornelis, a bishop of the

Flemish Mennonite Church at Dortrecht in Holland. The brotherhood at Dortrecht and many other places, deploring the existing divisions between congregations which did not differ from one another in faith and practice, decided to put forth efforts toward union. Adrian Cornelis wrote the first draft for a confession in the hope that it would prove an instrument for restoring peace. Upon his invitation many Mennonite elders and ministers gathered about the middle of April, 1632, at Dortrecht, despite the protests of the state church clergy of the city who demanded of the authorities, not to permit "this extraordinary gathering of Anabaptists from all provinces."

The archives of the Mennonite Church in Dortrecht contain the following account of the results of the work of this gathering:

On April 21, 1632, a general union was brought about in the holy name of the Lord among those who had gathered here in Dortrecht through the efforts of the beloved bishop Adrian Cornelis and others. The deliberations were concluded by extending the right hand of fellowship and the kiss of peace, and by the observance of the communion. Thus they recognized each other as a united brotherhood to the great joy and delight of many.

Of the fifty-two Flemish and Friesian ministers who signed this confession on this date or soon after, two were of Crefeld in Germany and two of "the upper country" (central or south Germany). This Confession was translated into the German language and printed in 1658 at Rotterdam. On February 4, 1660, it was approved and signed by the ministers of the congregations in Alsace, France, assembled at Ohnenheim. It is worthy of note that this took place previous to the division of 1693 in which Jacob Ammann figured most prominently. This, among other evidences, indicates that in the Swiss Brethren congregations in Alsace the ordinance of foot washing, which is taught in this confession, was observed before Ammann's time.[65] The Dortrecht Confession is doubtless the best written and most concise of the Mennonite Confessions. It was published in the English language for the first time in 1712.

These various confessions differ from each other principally on the matter of avoidance of the excommunicated. On the strength of such Scriptures as I Corinthians 5:11 and II Thessalonians 3:14 it was held that the excommunicated should be shunned and their company avoided except for the purpose of spiritual address and admonition. While all the early Mennonite confessions teach avoidance in a general way, only one, namely the Friesian Confession of thirty-three articles, mentions and demands avoidance in the case of children and parents and between husband and wife (marital avoidance). The "Concept of Cologne," and the Waterlandian Confession of 1582, and the "Olive Branch" (1627) expressly disapprove of avoidance between husband and wife. The Confession of Jan Centsen (1630) contains a warning against contentions and disputings in case of differences of opinion in this regard among church members. This confession demands mutual forbearance in case of differences on this point. As concerns the peculiar opinion on the Incarnation of Christ, this opinion is taught only in the Friesian Confession just mentioned. Of the confession by John Centsen (1630) there is a version containing an approving sentence on this opinion. The same confession, as contained in the *Martyrs' Mirror,* does not have the sentence in question. In most of the Mennonite Confessions this peculiar opinion on the Incarnation is declared to be nonessential, and in one or two instances warnings are expressed against controversy on this point.

The particular value of the Waterlandian confessions consists in the fact that they disprove the view that the Waterlandians were less conservative in theology than the other Mennonite bodies. The confessions of the Waterlandian Mennonite churches indicate clearly that on all theological points they were conservatively orthodox. In truth, on a number of points, the larger Waterlandian Confession (1582), being very full and explicit, is from the conservative point of view more satisfactory than most other Mennonite confessions. This Waterlandian confession, while teaching excommunication and avoidance, disapproves avoidance in the case of partners in the marriage bond when one is excommunicated. Within a brief period avoidance was discarded by the Waterlandians.

John Philip Schabalje, bishop of the Mennonite Church at Alkmaar in Holland, was the author of a work which has had a larger circulation than any other book ever published by a Mennonite writer. The title is, *The Wandering Soul . . . con-*

taining a *Succinct Epitome of Leading Historical Facts From the Creation of the World to the Year A.D. 109.* It is a well-written résumé of Bible history together with gripping observations on the occurrences recorded. The first edition appeared in 1635.[66]

Among the leading Mennonite ministers in Holland previous to the eighteenth century, Galenus Abrahams and Samuel Apostool deserve mention. Galenus Abrahams was born in 1622 at Zierikzee in Holland. He was a practicing physician and a minister of the large Flemish Mennonite congregations in Amsterdam, a man noted for his learning and vigor of expression. From the beginning of his ministry he sustained a close relationship with the Collegiants, a party which had originated in the Reformed state church. The Collegiants did not constitute an organized church or sect and had no ordained ministry. They practiced baptism by immersion, when desired by the applicant, but neither Galenus nor any other Dutch Mennonites followed them in this regard. In 1657 Galenus with another minister, David Spruzt, wrote a booklet defending some of the peculiarities of the Collegiants, such as the disapproval of all confessions of faith besides the Scriptures.

The great majority of the members of the congregation with which Galenus was connected did not approve of such views. After the publication of the booklet just mentioned, a division became inevitable. The more conservative wing of the congregation was led by the bishop Samuel Apostool (1638-1699). With the minister Tobias Goverts (one of the signers of the Dortrecht Confession in 1632) and about 700 members he withdrew from this congregation. This division spread to many congregations in other places. The great majority of the churches involved in this controversy sided with the conservative wing under Samuel Apostool. About one hundred ministers and deacons met in September, 1664 at Utrecht, and again in October of the same year at Leiden, and adopted a declaration of their assent to the generally recognized Mennonite confessions of faith. Five of these confessions, among them the Confession of Dortrecht, they reissued in print. In the preface to this book of confessions they defended the need of definite confessions, though their authority is derived from their agreement with the Scriptures.

Galenus was repeatedly visited by prominent Quakers, among them George Fox and William Penn. These Friends came to him in the capacity of missionaries. For a time his attitude toward them was such that they entertained strong hopes of winning him for their society. The consistory of the Reformed state church accused Galenus of denying the deity of Christ, but the civil authorities, after a thorough investigation, acquitted him of this charge. He died in 1706 at Amsterdam.

The successor of Galenus Abrahams as leader of the same congregation in Amsterdam, was John Deknatel whose general attitude, however, was decidedly more conservative than that of Galenus. He was born on November 1, 1698, at Norden in the German province of Hannover. In 1725 he was chosen a minister of the congregation in Amsterdam just mentioned, and preached his first sermon on the text First Timothy 4:16. In October, 1735, he with other preachers founded a seminary for the training of ministers, under Tjerk Nieuwenhuis as teacher. John Deknatel manifested a fatherly interest in the welfare of the students. In his diary John Wesley relates that he visited Deknatel in his home at Amsterdam and was very kindly received by him. Wesley heard a sermon preached by Deknatel in his church which made a deep impression on him. He considered the sermon of such importance that he took notes while Deknatel was preaching. For many years (until about 1750) Deknatel also was a personal friend of Count Zinzendorf.

John Deknatel was the author of many books and tracts, among them a catechism which was translated into German and was very often reprinted in both the Dutch and German languages. In 1753 he published an important volume of selections from Menno Simons' writings. This book also was translated into German and printed in several editions. A volume of his sermons was published in Dutch and German.[67] Deknatel was a man of deep spirituality whose life and labors wielded a vast influence for Biblical Christianity. He died January 22, 1759.

Herman Schijn, the author of the first history of the Mennonites, was born in 1662 at Amsterdam. He studied medicine at Leiden and Utrecht and followed the calling of a physician in Rotterdam and later in Amsterdam. In both places he was the bishop of Mennonite congregations. He wrote a number of books in defense of the conservative viewpoint, insisting on loyalty to the faith laid down in the Mennonite confessions as well as in the Scripture. The practice of open communion, where each person participates entirely on his own responsibility, he, with most of the Mennonite groups of his time, did not approve. In his writings he pointed out the inconsistency of observing the communion with those who do not accept the doctrine of the atonement, of believers' baptism, or of nonresistance.

Herman Schijn published two works on the history of the Mennonite Church. Both were printed in the Dutch and also in the Latin language, Latin being then the language of scholarship. Schijn believed, and rightfully, that a Latin work would attract the attention of scholars to a greater extent than one in the vernacular. And in foreign countries Latin was familiar to far greater numbers than the Dutch language. Some time after Schijn's death (in 1727) his second work on Mennonite history was re-issued with many important additions, by Gerard Maatschoen, a Mennonite minister at Amsterdam, who held the same conservative point of view.

Concerning the life of the Mennonites of Holland, a statement made by John a'Lasco is noteworthy. After he had met Menno Simons in a debate, he wrote in a letter to H. Lenth that he knew many Mennonites to be good and virtuous people. Another opponent, Heinrich Ludolf Bentheim, a Lutheran theologian, in 1698 gave the following interesting description of the life and characteristics of the Mennonites of Holland:

> Although there is need of guarding against the errors of these people, yet as concerns their life, one can learn from them much that is good, namely humility, contentment, sobriety, and especially charity toward the needy. For although the Reformed people of the Netherlands in general deserve commendation for their liberality toward the poor, yet the people of this sect excel other sects in this regard. Above all, they insist on modesty in respect to clothing, although in Amsterdam there are some who are attracting attention by using periwigs and other indications of worldliness. However, in Friesland and in Groningen one will see them in plain dress, although they also as a class are well-informed and well-to-do.

Christian Joachim Jehring, a Lutheran clergyman in East Friesland, wrote in 1720:

It is a matter of common knowledge that their outward life and walk are highly praised by many; and it is indeed true that they, by their commendable life, attract the attention of people in general. They are toward every one very friendly and unassuming. One does not hear of them that they indulge in profanity or swearing. They show a zeal against all forms of sin.

The following is a part of a letter of intercession sent in 1710 by the government of the Netherlands to the authorities of the canton Bern in behalf of the persecuted Mennonite people:

We have tolerated the Mennonites for many years, and have found by experience that they are loyal subjects who live in quietness and simplicity and concern themselves strictly with their own matters. . . . As concerns undertaking anything that would result in disadvantage to the country, we are of the opinion that there is less ground for fearing anything of that nature from the Mennonites than from other churches, for they are subject and obedient to the government in all things which in their view are not contrary to the Word of God.

Again, in 1671 the Mennonites of Holland contributed 12,-000 guilders for the Mennonite refugees in the Palatinate who had arrived there penniless from Switzerland, having been compelled to leave all their possessions behind.

In 1672 the Mennonites of Holland also sent aid to their brethren in Switzerland, and in 1674 and 1678 in the Palatinate. They also extended help to the persecuted brotherhood in Jülich (northwestern Germany) and in Lithuania. And their work of benevolence was not limited to those of their own faith. The civil authorities of Amsterdam who were of the Reformed state church, in a letter written in 1660 to certain state authorities in Switzerland who professed the same creed, made mention of the benevolence extended by the Dutch Mennonites to persecuted people of the Reformed communion. The magistrates of Amsterdam gave this as a reason for their disapproval of the persecution of the Mennonites by Swiss Reformed governments.

The authorities of the capital city of Holland said in the letter just mentioned:

The Mennonites are a people which at no opportunity have failed to extend noteworthy charity toward the people of the Reformed faith. Only recently, when our brethren, the Waldenses, were so cruelly driven from their homes (by the duke of Savoy), they have in this city, simply upon our recommendation, contributed the sum of about 7,000 pounds in Holland money for the support of the afore-mentioned Waldenses.

Evidently this relief was given by the Mennonites of Holland through the authorities of the state church. As pointed out elsewhere, the Waldenses of that time adhered to the Reformed creed. Again, after the revocation of the Edict of Nantes (1685) when the persecution of the people of the Reformed Church in France (Huguenots) began afresh, the Mennonites extended relief to them.

About 240 Swiss Mennonite families in the Palatinate found themselves in direst need, when the country was laid waste by an invading French army in 1689. The Mennonites of Holland rendered them substantial aid. Within a few years they contrib-uted about 100,000 guilders for their afflicted brethren in the Palatinate.

When information about a renewed outbreak of severe per-secution of the Mennonite brotherhood in Switzerland had reached the Mennonites of Holland, a meeting of representa-tives of many Mennonite churches was held at Amsterdam on February 24, 1710, to consider ways and means of extending aid. Shortly afterwards the "Funds for Foreign Needs," a Mennonite relief organization, was founded, which for about a century was active in relief work. 50,000 guilders were con-tributed through this organization during the same year for the persecuted Swiss Brethren, of whom many in consequence fled to Holland. Four ships with about 400 Swiss Mennonite refugees landed, on August 2, 1711, in the Dutch city of U-trecht. They were followed by another numerous group of refugees in 1713. The majority of these fugitives apparently remained in Holland. At various times substantial aid was rendered to refugees, from Switzerland and the Palatinate, who decided to migrate to Pennsylvania. Between the years 1709 and 1736 over 270,000 guilders were given by the Men-nonites of Holland for relief work in foreign countries and for refugees that had fled to Holland.

Many Swiss Mennonite refugees migrated to Pennsylvania by way of Holland, while others settled in Holland. As a rule the Swiss Mennonites remaining in Holland formed their own congregations. Such congregations were organized at Groningen, Sappemeer, Kampen, and other places. For a considerable period they kept in close touch with some of the Swiss refugee congregations in the Palatinate and Alsace, and were sometimes visited by ministers from these provinces. In general these Swiss Mennonites in Holland were more conservative than the great majority of Dutch Mennonite congregations of that time. A booklet printed in 1713, at Haarlem in Holland, has the title, *Complaint of the Swiss about the Tainted Practices of the Holland Mennonites.*

Notwithstanding the additional Swiss immigrant congregations, and other decidedly favorable circumstances, the Mennonite Church in Holland in the period beginning about 1690 found itself in a state of steady decline. Neither the salutary influences proceeding from a small number of men, such as John Deknatel and Herman Schijn, nor the efforts for the training of young ministers put forth in the theological seminary at Amsterdam (existing since 1735) could stay the sad decline and decadence. In the year 1700 the number of Mennonites in Holland was about 160,000; by the year 1809 it had dwindled to less than 28,000. In this period over one hundred Mennonite congregations in Holland became extinct, among them the one at Dortrecht.

As to the causes of this unparalleled decline, opinions may differ. At the present day most Mennonites of Holland hold to a liberal (modernistic) position in theology. Their answer to the question of the causes of the decline may be expected to differ, at least to some extent, from an opinion given from the conservative viewpoint. We prefer to listen in this regard first to Mennonite writers of Holland, and note what they have to say on the subject under consideration.

Two booklets entitled *De Doopsgezinden* (The Mennonites), both written by Mennonite ministers in Holland, have been published since the beginning of the present century.[68] In both books the opinion is expressed that one of the causes of the decline was worldliness. The author of the first pamphlet quotes from a book of an earlier century: "Formerly the Mennists were in the world, but now the world is in their own midst."

The writer of the second booklet says: "Marked progress in social attainments [on the part of the Mennonites as a whole] resulted in a change of their attitude toward the world. Originally the ideal was 'in the world but not of the world'; later it was 'free in and of the world.' " The same writer says in this connection: "For such freedom of activity, as was desired, material prosperity was necessary. Now, riches are not always a blessing. Many, after they have become rich, have both in a literal and figurative sense bade farewell to the church which had kept them separated from the world."

Various writers of that period, among them the church historian Mosheim, have observed that the great material possessions of many Mennonites, particularly in Amsterdam and a few other cities, proved the reverse of a blessing. S. F. Rues, a German writer who traveled in the Netherlands and became acquainted with the Mennonites, wrote in 1743 that there were in Holland Mennonites who, as concerns love of the pomp and vanity of the world, were not exceeded by any other class in that country, and that they had the means to indulge in these things. He adds however that there also were congregations in Holland which held to the former Mennonite position regarding their attitude toward the world.

In this period the Mennonite people of Holland enjoyed full liberty of conscience; nevertheless the profession of the Mennonite creed still carried with it a stigma of social unpopularity. Worldliness manifested itself in the endeavor to avoid unpopularity. The attainment of recognized standing in the social world was possible only to those included in the membership of the state church of Holland. All others were also ineligible for government offices. Many Mennonites, aspiring to such offices, withdrew from the church.

The so-called "enlightenment," a type of extreme rationalism, which spread over parts of Europe from France in the eighteenth century, had a telling effect also on Holland and on some of its Mennonite circles. It is to the credit of those who yielded to such influences, that they did not retain the Mennonite name.

An indication of spiritual decline is seen in the fact that many who were called to the ministry by the congregations refused to consent to ordination. Many congregations were without ministers. Only a small number of these vacancies could be supplied with ministers from the graduates of the seminary in Amsterdam. The usage of an unsalaried ministry, to which the church had held for two hundred years, was abandoned.

In this period the practice of church discipline was generally neglected and finally discarded. Disowning infant baptism was no longer a characteristic of all the congregations. In 1760 a member of the Reformed Church (who had been baptized in his infancy only) was received into the Mennonite congregation at Utrecht without baptism. Cornelis Ris, the author of a Mennonite confession of faith, proposed in 1776 a union between the Mennonite and Reformed churches. The Mennonite congregation at Utrecht installed an organ into their church in 1765. Other congregations soon followed their example.

The principle of the entire separation of the church from the state was first set aside in 1809 by one of the Mennonite congregations in Holland, when in that year they accepted an augmentation from the state to the salary paid their minister. Recently about forty Mennonite congregations received such a subsidy from the Holland government. In case a full separation of church and state were practiced in Holland, these subsidies would cease.

The principle of nonresistance was also discarded by the Dutch Mennonites. A group of Old Flemish Mennonites, 52 persons, under the leadership of R. J. Smit and N. J. Symensma emigrated from the village of Balk in Holland to America, in 1853, to escape military service. They settled near the village of New Paris in Elkhart county, Indiana. They were the last of the Mennonites of Holland to uphold this principle. At the time of this migration a few members of the Mennonite Church in Holland had gone to such an extreme in the rejection of this principle as to choose military service as officers in the army of Holland for their profession. Long before that date the ruling that officers of the government must be members of the state church had been rescinded. In the first decade of the present century a deacon of the Mennonite congregation at the Hague, by the name of Cool, held the office of secretary of war in the Holland government.

The first Mennonite conference (called "sociëteit") was organized in Holland about 1638. It consisted of congregations of the Friesian group in which Peter Janz Twisck was at that time the outstanding leader. This conference, and all other Mennonite conferences of that period, were of a character similar to our conferences of today. Beginning with the period of decline the Mennonite conferences lost the character of organizations giving authoritative advice to the congregations. In 1811 the "Allgemeene Doopsgezinde Sociëteit" (General Mennonite Conference) was organized, with which eventually all Mennonite congregations of Holland and four congregations of northwestern Germany have united. Since 1887 the Mennonite churches of Holland have an official church paper in "De Zondagsbode."

The *Gemeentedag* (an untranslatable term) movement among the Mennonites of Holland dates from the year 1917. It owes its existence to the influence of the Woodbrookers, an English Quaker organization. The organization of this movement among the Mennonites grew out of a recognition of the need of more aggressive church activity and of counteracting the extreme theological liberalism in Mennonite circles which would substitute "ethical culture" for religious faith. Interest in foreign missions has been stimulated and improved through this movement, and in other ways also there have been gratifying results. Committees were created for the advancement of Bible study, foreign missions, temperance, and pacifism. To counteract the efforts of the last mentioned committee (for opposition to military service) some of the members of the Mennonite Church who are officers in the army of Holland have, with a few others, organized another committee under the somewhat voluminous name: "Mennonite Committee to Warn against Propaganda for Refusal to do Military Service and against One-Sided Disarmament."

While the great majority of the Mennonites of Holland frankly profess unitarianism, a few ministers have in recent years come forward with a defense of the deity of Christ, at the same time declaring, however, that they do not disapprove of fellowshiping with the extreme liberals. With the exception of a very few congregations, the Mennonites of Holland look upon Christian doctrine as a secondary matter regarding which no definite position should be required by the church.

The beginnings of this general attitude of "neutrality" on all doctrinal questions date back to about 1860, when modernism first came into evidence and was tolerated in the Mennonite theological seminary in Amsterdam. Within a short period the attitude of the seminary became largely modernistic. Practically all Mennonite ministers of Holland are graduates of the seminary. Today the number of baptized Mennonites in Holland is about 45,000. Because of the late age of baptism which often comes in the age scope of eighteen to twenty-one or even later, this probably represents a total body above fourteen years, the common age of baptism in America, of at least 50,000.

The general trend of continental European theology away from modernism and back toward a more evangelical faith, in addition to the impact of the trials of World War II, have combined to bring about a distinct reorientation of the Dutch Mennonite leadership toward a more conservative theology. The old-fashioned liberalism is no longer taught at the seminary, and many of the newer pastors are evangelical. A strong peace movement has also sprung up, organized in the *Vredesgroep* (Peace Group) which is working for a return to Biblical nonresistance as well as a more Biblical church life in general, centered around Christ. There is also a trend toward a more closely knit church organization, with the Algemene Doopsgezind Societeit holding a central leading position. The three totally destroyed churches, among which Rotterdam was the chief, are being rebuilt.

CHAPTER 29

THE MENNONITES IN FRANCE

The history of the Mennonites of Strasburg, the capital city of Alsace, has already been considered in chapter XII above. The imperial mandate of Speier of the year 1529, demanding the execution of all Anabaptists, was published in Alsace in May of the same year, and its publication was repeated in 1535 and 1544. Four times a year, and in particular on certain holidays, this law was to be read from all pulpits. In addition it was decreed that all who did not approve of infant baptism were to be considered Anabaptists and were to be dealt with accordingly.

The pertinent sources contain various records of evangelical Anabaptists in towns and villages of Alsace in the Reformation period. In 1538 twenty-five Anabaptists were arrested in a grove near Epfig, and about the same time a large Anabaptist meeting gathered in the same vicinity. Sixty-nine Anabaptists were arrested near Illkirch in one day. At Ensisheim, the seat of the Austrian government located in this region about six hundred Anabaptists suffered martyrdom.

During the Thirty Years' War (1618-1648) Swiss Anabaptists began to settle in the Vosges mountains in Alsace. They were refugees coming from the cantons of Bern and Zurich. Landowners in Alsace gave them preference as renters, since they were reliable and willing to pay increased rentals. Toward the end of that century sixty-two Anabaptist families were reported living in sixteen villages of the bishopric of Strasburg. Upward of 2,400 Mennonites, mostly of the Swiss Brethren, were believed to live in Alsace at this time. On February 4, 1660, at a conference of bishops and ministers held at Ohnenheim, they subscribed to the Dortrecht confession of faith. Some time after the Thirty Years' War the province of Alsace was allotted to France, and protest was made to King Louis XIV against tolerating the Mennonites. The king, on September 9, 1712, gave strict orders to the officers of the districts in which Mennonites lived, to drive them all out; and that they should not be permitted to settle in any province under French rule. This decree must have caused great consternation among the Mennonites of Alsace. Many emigrated to the principality of Montbeliard, and to the Palatinate. On October 23, 1727, the French government asked for a complete list of all Mennonites living in Alsace. This information was gathered and sent in October, 1727, to the royal court at Versailles. A petition for toleration was handed in at the same time. The reply came on June 7, 1728, granting toleration, provided that there would be no increase in their number. It was further decreed that their children must emigrate, when they reached the age of responsibility, or the parents must leave France. Their patrons had interceded for them, pointing out their skill and diligence as tillers of the soil.

Two "letters" of considerable length containing rules of discipline drawn up by Mennonite conferences held in Alsace have come down to us. The earliest is dated April 28, 1752, and was adopted by a conference of bishops and ministers "of sundry lands," held at Steinselz in Alsace. This "letter" contains various rules of conduct, among them the prohibition of the use of tobacco, of shaving the beard, and of immodesty in dress. The second discipline of the Mennonites in Alsace was approved by a conference held on January 21, 1779, at Essingen near Landau in the Palatinate.[69] It treats on various points of doctrine and practice. The above-mentioned points in particular, from the discipline of 1752, were again stated and confirmed.

In France proper the early Anabaptists seem not to have gained a firm footing. When in 1712 the magistrates of Alsace received orders to drive out the Mennonites, some fled to the Palatinate and a greater number to the principality of Montbeliard. This principality, though almost surrounded by French territory, was independent of France in that period. Prince Leopold Eberhard of Montbeliard about the year 1705 permitted Swiss Mennonite refugees to settle in his land. Later on the Mennonites spread from here over some of the territory of France. Montbeliard lost its independence in 1796 to France. In the following century universal military service was introduced which caused extensive emigration of Mennonites to America.

The original Mennonite settlers in what is today the republic of France were either natives of Switzerland, or of Swiss descent. Originally they all spoke the German language but today, except in Alsace, the German tongue has given way to French, both in the homes and in public worship. As was the case also in certain sections of America, the Mennonites of France in general insisted too long for their own good on the use of the German tongue in worship. In Alsace, which from 1871 to 1918 was a province of the German empire, the Mennonites have retained to this day the use of German in public worship. All the French speaking congregations are of Amish Mennonite descent. The number of the Mennonites of France is about 2,600. They are organized in two conferences. Their church organ, *Christ Seul,* is published monthly with a German supplement.

CHAPTER 30

THE AMISH DIVISION

This was the first division among the Swiss Brethren (Mennonites of Switzerland and South Germany). It took place in 1693, or about ten years after the first Mennonite emigration to America. This division has been practically obliterated in Europe, partly also in America; yet large Amish groups in the United States and Canada are still distinct from other Mennonite branches.

It may be recalled here that, as Menno Simons' writings indicate, there was in some of the churches of Holland and northern Germany a controversy regarding the practice of the avoidance of excommunicated church members. Menno expressed his misgivings concerning the danger of a disruption of the church because of this dispute. While this apprehension proved needless, about a century and a half later the division here under consideration took place in Switzerland and Alsace, caused mainly by disagreement on this point. In this disruption Jacob Ammann, a bishop in Switzerland (or Alsace) figured most prominently. In the group that did not side with Ammann the bishop Hans Reist of Obertal near Zaeziwill in the Emmental, Switzerland, was a prominent leader.

Concerning Jacob Ammann's life nothing definite is known. In 1693 he, with his brother Ulrich and a few others, visited all the Mennonite churches in Switzerland and Alsace and asked every minister in particular about avoidance. Ammann held this practice to be strictly necessary. Furthermore he stated there were reports that some of the ministers were of the opinion that the "treuherzigen" (truehearted) persons were to be considered as saved people.

For the exact meaning of the latter expression we turn to a letter written by a brother in Switzerland in 1784. The letter contains a reply to an inquiry from Alsace for information how the expression "truehearted people," as used by Jacob Ammann was to be understood. In reply to this question the letter stated that this expression referred to persons who in the persecution of the Mennonite people had rendered them every possible service by giving them food and lodging, and warning them of approaching danger from their pursuers, contrary to the orders of the authorities. These people approved of the teaching of the Brethren but on account of the persecution failed to make a public confession of their faith by being baptized. This class of people was numerous in the canton Bern. In the edicts of the authorities they were designated as *Halbtäufer* (Halfway-Anabaptists).

As for the practice of avoidance apparently a mild form of it had been introduced in some of the congregations of Alsace and Switzerland shortly before the time of Ammann. Probably it was generally known that in the churches of the lower countries it was the common practice. Menno Simons in his writings defended avoidance, and his *Foundation Book* had been published in 1575 in a German translation for the benefit of the Swiss Brethren in South Germany and Switzerland. Menno taught a mild form of this observance. He did not believe that avoidance should be enforced as a rigorous rule. His books contain warnings against disciplining those church members who may not be convinced of the necessity of this practice and may decline to observe it. Again, the Dortrecht Confession which teaches avoidance had become known in South Germany and Switzerland at an early date. In 1660 this confession was subscribed to by thirteen ministers of Alsace, and about the same time the congregations in Switzerland, when asked by the authorities for a statement of their doctrine, handed them this confession. In this connection it may be noted that the Mennonites of Pennsylvania at an early date (1725) adopted the same confession, though the practice of avoidance was not general among them.

On a tour of visitation among the Mennonite churches Jacob Ammann met Hans Reist who contradicted him regarding the need of a strict observance of avoidance. Somewhat later a meeting was held at Friedersmatt near Bowill in the Emmental, to which Reist was invited. Apparently offended at the spirit manifested by Ammann, Hans Reist failed to appear at this meeting. At a second conference of ministers and others in the Emmental, which likewise was not attended by Reist, Jacob Ammann declared Reist and six other ministers to be excommunicated, notwithstanding the earnest pleas of a number of persons present to have patience and not act rashly. Thus the threatening disruption became a fact.

Word about what had taken place naturally spread throughout the congregations. The division of the church caused marked anxiety and gave occasion for writing many letters of inquiry and information. Many of these letters have been preserved and have in consequence often been copied. In a more recent period they have been printed in various pamphlets and yearbooks.[70]

Some of the Brethren in the Palatinate wrote to Ammann and to those who sided with him, imploring them to modify their severe attitude toward the other group. The Palatinate Brethren asked that another meeting for reconciliation be appointed. The meeting was held at Ohnenheim in Alsace and was attended by both parties but was without tangible results.

Further attempts at reconciliation were made. In 1698 the party of Ammann confessed that they had acted too rashly in pronouncing the ban without the consent of their congregations, consequently they declared that they considered themselves as in fact excommunicated. They did this probably in the expectation that the Brethren of the other group would also confess to mistakes, and that this would lead to a reconciliation. The other group, however, were not unanimous in their reaction to this proposal. Again, the followers of Ammann, somewhat later, expressed the desire to be received as brethren by the other group, but on the condition that the others agreed with them on avoidance. In 1700 again some leaders of the Amish group decided to consider themselves excommunicated. This attempt for peace and unity also proved unsuccessful.

In the source material pertaining to this division there is reference to other points of controversy, but it was the disagreement regarding avoidance that caused the disruption. The question of the "truehearted persons," who were not willing to be baptized, has been mentioned above. Other points of controversy were the attendance at services of the state church, and the question whether persons telling a wilful untruth should be excommunicated. On these points the issues were not sharply drawn. Regarding feet washing there was no controversy but there is evidence that this rite was observed in all the Amish congregations. In general the Ammann party held out for a stricter enforcement of discipline.

The Alsatian churches as a unit followed Ammann, although practically none of the Palatinate group did so, and very few of the Swiss who remained in Switzerland. The following modern European churches are of original Amish background, although they have almost without exception ceased to have any Amish distinctiveness: All the churches in present-day France, the small group in Luxembourg, one small church in the western part of the Palatinate, the majority of the membership of the churches of Munich and Regensburg in Bavaria. The churches in Volhynia, who later emigrated to Kansas, were originally Amish. Large groups of Amish immigrants settled in eastern Pennsylvania, northwestern New York, west of the Mennonite settlement in Waterloo County, Ontario, and in various places in Ohio and Indiana. Most of the original settlers in central Illinois, eastern Iowa, and eastern Nebraska were Amish. About half of the membership of the (Old) Mennonite Church in the United States is of Amish background, in addition to the large Old Order Amish group and the Conservative Amish group. One of the major points of distinction of the Amish, the practice of foot-washing, has almost died out among the former Amish churches in Europe, except for one congregation, that of Birkenhof in Alsace near Altkirch.

CHAPTER 31

THE MENNONITES IN THE PALATINATE

The Mennonites of the Palatinate after the Thirty Years' War (1618-1648) will claim our attention in particular for the reason that they were the lineal ancestors of the early Mennonites in America. Before the beginning of the Thirty Years' War there had been for various reasons a marked decrease in Mennonite membership in the Palatinate and, in fact, in South Germany in general; many had fled to Moravia. Then in this long, cruel war the population was decimated by the sword, epidemics, and famine, and thus the number of Mennonites was further reduced. In fact it is doubtful that any of the original Palatinate Mennonite families survived.

In passing we may notice that the Palatinate (*Kurpfalz*) was one of the largest provinces of Germany, located on both sides of the Rhine in South Germany, with Heidelberg as the capital. The Palatinate was an electorate.[71]

The Thirty Years' War was primarily a religious war between Roman Catholic and Protestant states, but the religious issue was often overshadowed by purely political considerations. The armies of certain Protestant rulers used to take sides with the Catholics when to do so served their political ambitions. The conclusion of this war left the Palatinate in a state of almost unbelievable devastation. Workers were sorely needed to reclaim and cultivate the wasted land. The ruler of the Palatinate, Elector Karl Ludwig, decided in 1664 to permit the immigration of a limited number of Mennonite families from Switzerland. He gave this permission with a number of stipulations, however. The Mennonites were allowed to have meetings for worship, but not in public church houses, and in no case could any such meeting be attended by more than twenty persons. The practice of baptism was forbidden the Mennonites. They were informed that they must furnish the authorities lists of the names of all members of their congregations, and these lists must be revised as newcomers arrived. Every Mennonite family was under obligation to give three florins "protection money" the first year, and six florins annually thereafter to the authorities. These and various other restrictions imposed upon Mennonites show that they had not the recognized rights of citizenship; they were merely tolerated on certain conditions.

There is evidence that even previous to the year 1664 a number of Swiss Mennonite families had settled in the Palatinate. In 1657 small Mennonite and Quaker groups existed at Kriegsheim near the city of Worms. Some of these people had Swiss names, such as Strohm, Meyer, Herstein, Becker.

A great Swiss immigration took place in the year 1671. In that year about seven hundred Bernese Mennonite refugees came to the Palatinate. They arrived in a pitifully destitute condition. Valuable information concerning the continued persecution in Switzerland and the needy condition of the refugees is contained in a number of letters written by Jacob Everling, a Swiss Mennonite elder, to the Mennonites in Holland. He reported that among them were cripples and old people, and that they had large families. They arrived destitute, some carrying their bundles on their backs and infants on their arms.

The refugees in the Palatinate were visited by Thieleman Janz van Braght, of Dortrecht, Holland, who found that conditions had been correctly described in the letters of Jacob Everling. Again, a letter dated January 1, 1672, written by Valentine Huetwol from Kriegsheim in the Palatinate to the brotherhood at Crefeld contains a touching appeal for help for the newly arrived Swiss Brethren. The Brethren in Holland undertook a great work of relief for the refugees in the Palatinate. Funds amounting to above 11,000 guilders were spent for this purpose. Great assistance and help was no doubt extended to the refugees also by the earlier Mennonite settlers in the Palatinate.

The Mennonite refugees coming to the Palatinate were mostly from the Swiss cantons of Bern and Zurich. Among them were the ancestors of Heinrich Funck, later bishop in the Franconia district in Pennsylvania. In Switzerland persecution continued. One of the above-mentioned letters of Jacob Everling, written at Obersülzen in the Palatinate to friends in Amsterdam, states that in the canton Bern the Mennonites were daily hunted by constables, and all they could lay hands on were taken prisoners to Bern, so that four weeks before about forty men and women were imprisoned there.

In 1726 under Elector Karl Philip the law known as the "Right of Retraction" was imposed upon the Mennonites in the Palatinate. This right gave Catholic and Protestant citizens permission to buy back at any time any real estate which Mennonites had bought of them. In particular was it stipulated that the price of such real estate, when bought back by former owners, was to be the same as had been paid for it by the Mennonite purchaser. This meant that if Mennonites had bought devastated farms at a low price and had made them productive by years, often many years of hard work, these farms could be bought back by the former owners at the original small purchase price. After many urgent petitions and protests this "Right of Retraction" was in 1737 limited to three years from the time when the real estate had been bought by a Mennonite.

For a time it appeared that Mennonites would be deprived even of the right of owning property at all. In a consequent petition to the government they said pointedly:

We have done more than any other subjects in building up bare and destitute farm lands, and in bringing them back to a high state of productivity. . . . It will be especially hard for our poor wives and children if we must now give up our homes in which some of us have lived [as renters] for eighty years; many of us also have owned our farms for ten, twenty, and thirty years, and have brought them to a high state of productivity.

Oppression of the Mennonite people continued in the Palatinate, though some of the above-mentioned restrictions imposed on the Mennonites by Elector Karl Ludwig in 1664 were revoked by his successors. At times the government of the Palatinate exacted from the Mennonites special taxes. In 1686 a special levy of one thousand thalers, and in 1717 a contribution of fifteen hundred florins was demanded of them. An enumeration taken in 1739 revealed that there were three hundred and forty Mennonite families in the Palatinate. The government decided that the number must be reduced to two hundred families. Various new measures of oppression were enacted and the annual "protection money" was raised from six to twelve florins per family. About five years later it was again reduced to six florins. The question of increasing the amount

(From Wenger: "Glimpses of Mennonite History")

Interior of a Dutch Mennonite Church
Located at 452 Singel Street, Amsterdam.

Mennonite Church in Danzig
Built in 1819.

(From "Mennonitisches Lexikon," Vol. II)

Mennonite Church in Elbing, Germany
Built in 1900.

Mennonite Church, Belfort, France

Mennonite Girls' School, Halbstadt, Russia

(Courtesy of Bethel College Historical Library)

Mennonite Church at Ohrloff, Russia

(From "Mennonitisches Lexikon," Vol. III)

Pictures from the Molotschna Mennonite Colony in Russia

School for the Deaf, in Tiege   Central School in Ohrloff
Village Street in Ohrloff   A Mennonite Farmstead

Mennonite Hospital in Ohrloff. Russia

Kirche, Nikolaifeld, Sagradofka.

Mennonite Church at Nikolaifeld, Sagradofka, Russia

of the "protection money" was again considered in 1763. At this time a noteworthy "Opinion" was rendered by an official of the government. He wrote about the Mennonites:

This sect is generally detested, and unquestionably should be exterminated. And yet daily experience indicates that better, more industrious, more efficient people cannot be found. Notwithstanding their heretical religion they should be taken as examples to be followed by people in general. One will never hear concerning them that they are guilty of any profanity, swearing, or of any misdeeds. Never are they accused before the courts of law of any misdemeanor, while some of those who are not of their persuasion and who should show indications of Christian character, are guilty of transgression of all kinds, such as must be punished by the courts.

The author of the "Opinion" warned the authorities against making the burden laid upon the Mennonites so heavy as to become unbearable. The "Right of Retraction" was in force until the year 1801.

In all probability some of the Mennonite refugees were of the class called *Halbtäufer* (Halfway-Anabaptists). They were friends of the Mennonites but, on account of the persecution in Switzerland, they refused to unite with them.

There was continuous emigration of Mennonite refugees from Switzerland to the Palatinate. The great majority of the Swiss Mennonite refugees in the Palatinate were desirous of going on across the Atlantic to the land of religious liberty. A letter dated April 16, 1717, written by the ministers of the Mennonite congregation at Rotterdam, indicates that 300 Mennonites had arrived at this city en route for America. Within fifteen years from that date about three thousand Mennonites from the Palatinate emigrated to Pennsylvania.[72] A majority of them were natives of Switzerland, while many had been born in the Palatinate, their parents or forebears having been Swiss refugees. The Mennonites of the Palatinate were practically all of Swiss descent. The same is true of present-day Mennonites in the Palatinate and of the Mennonites of the South German states in general, as well as of the great majority of Mennonites in Alsace and of eastern France.

The Palatinate Mennonites brought with them to Pennsylvania the dialect of the Palatinate to which however in America many English expressions have been assimilated. In America this dialect is known as Pennsylvania German. The Mennonites were by no means the only Palatines to settle in eastern Pennsylvania. In consequence, partly, of a new devastation of large sections of the Palatinate by the armies of Louis XIV of France, many of the Reformed and Lutheran people of that province became interested in emigration. Among the Palatines settling in Pennsylvania the Mennonites constituted in fact but a small minority. And within a brief period some of the oppressed sects in Germany, the Dunkers of Westphalia, the Moravians of Saxony, the Schwenckfelders of Silesia also found refuge in Pennsylvania. The immigrants from these parts of Germany were, however, far outnumbered by the Palatinate immigrants. Some of the Mennonite settlers spoke a Swiss German dialect. Within a few generations the Palatinate dialect became the language of the Germans of Pennsylvania.

In the course of time Palatinate Mennonites emigrated into the territory of Germany east of the Rhine, establishing small and scattered congregations in the provinces of Baden, Württemberg, and Bavaria. About 1785 a group emigrated to the region of Lemberg, Galicia, then Austrian, later Polish, where they continued until the end of World War II. Those who settled in southeastern Germany were mostly renters of larger estates, whereas most of those who remained in the Palatinate west of the Rhine were owners of smaller farms.

These two regions of South German Mennonite settlement gradually diverged in church organization, polity, and practice. Those in the Palatinate for the most part adopted the system of trained and salaried ministers, while those east of the Rhine retained the lay ministry, largely untrained and completely unsalaried. Each group organized into a conference during the 19th century, The Palatinate-Hesse Conference, and the Baden-Wurttemberg-Bavaria Conference. The South German Conference was later organized as an over-all body. An outstanding leader in the Palatinate was Elder Christian Neff, for more than fifty years (1885-1940) pastor of the congregation at the Weierhof and leading historian as well as conference moderator. He and Christian Hege initiated and carried to partial completion the *Mennonitisches Lexikon,* a great historical encyclopædia. An East Rhine leader of the past generation was Elder Michael Horsch of Hellmannsberg near Ingolstadt (1870-1949).

CHAPTER 32

THE MENNONITES IN RUSSIA

Czarina Catherine II of Russia in 1763 published a manifesto offering various inducements to attract foreign settlers to her vast domains. The traveling expenses to their new homes were to be partly refunded them and they were to be permitted to settle in closed colonies. Those who accepted the invitation had the right of taking the civil administration of such colonies largely into their own hands. They were promised exemption from taxation for a considerable period, and were guaranteed perfect religious liberty. Under no circumstances, however, would they be allowed to make converts among the membership of the Russian state church which comprised practically all the native Russian population.

The Russian government held favorable opinions about the Mennonites. Czar Peter the Great, during his sojourn at Zaandam in Holland in 1698, had come in contact with some of the Mennonite people; his own physician was a Mennonite. Czarina Catherine II in the summer of 1786 sent an officer, George von Trappe, to Danzig in Prussia to visit the Mennonites of that region for the purpose of creating among them an interest in her colonization project. Under the conditions prevailing in Prussia he found this an easy task. In the same year two Mennonites, Johann Bartsch and Jacob Höppner, made a trip of investigation to South Russia at the expense of the Russian government. They selected a region on the Dnieper River suitable for colonization, and before their return were received in audience by the Czarina as well as by grand duke Paul, the heir to the throne.[73]

The Russian government offered every Mennonite family 65 hectares (about 162 acres) of land free, and ten years exemption from taxation. Every family was promised a loan of 500 rubles. George von Trappe, who was named director of the prospective colony, accompanied the delegates back to Danzig. Within a few months about 230 families started for South Russia. Because of a threatening war with Turkey, they were detained for almost a year at Dubrovna at the expense of the Russian government. Finally they settled at the river Chortitsa in the province of Jekaterinoslav, somewhat north of the region first selected for the colony.

This group of settlers reached the place of their new homes in July, 1789. The difficulties confronting the pioneers on these treeless prairie lands surpassed their expectations by far. The sod huts which they built proved inadequate in various respects. During the following winter many of the families were given shelter and provisions in the fortress of Alexandrowsk about twelve miles from the settlement. In the spring of the following year a beginning was made in building more substantial houses and in cultivating the land. This settlement, called Chortitsa Colony or Old Colony, comprised at first eight villages.

Czar Paul I, the successor of Catherine II, in 1800 confirmed "for all times" the privileges granted the Mennonites "and their children and descendants," including complete exemption from military service, and these privileges were again confirmed by Czar Nicholas I, in 1838. From 1804 to 1806 a colony, consisting of eighteen villages, was organized on the Molotschna River in the province of Tauridia. News of the evident success of this colony brought from Prussia new groups, which settled in the same region on the Molotschna. By 1830 this colony had grown to forty-six Mennonite villages, incorporating a total population of about 10,000, with the towns of Halbstadt and Gnadenfeld as centers. The coming of Mennonite families in groups from Prussia ceased almost entirely before the middle of the same century.

The available land in these regions was inadequate to afford homes for the natural increase of the population of the Mennonite colonies. The farms in the colonies were to be "model" farms, hence a ruling was in force against dividing them. Therefore only one of the sons in a family could become a landowner. In the course of the years the number of landless families became very large. By 1860 about 2,000 families in the Molotschna Colony did not own land. Some found opportunity for renting farm land; many followed trades and handicrafts for a living. The landless class appealed to the government for aid, presenting their need. The government replied that while the state had given free homes to the first settlers, their children and descendants could not expect any special favors. However, dividing the farms was finally permitted.

From the mother colonies of Chortitsa and Molotschna new colonies were formed by the landless class. As time passed colonies were established in several other Russian provinces east of the older colonies, also in the Black Sea peninsula, Crimea, and in western Siberia. In various instances the older colonies rendered substantial assistance in the establishment of later settlements. Such aid was given by the landowners in the Molotschna Colony toward establishing colonies in the provinces of Sagradowka, Memrik, Orenburg, and in Siberia. In at least two smaller new colonies the settlers came directly from Prussia.

The Mennonite colonies of Russia were granted a large measure of self-government. In fact they constituted a separate state within the state. The colonists were farmers but, in German fashion, lived in villages comprising twenty-five to fifty families each. A group of villages—as a rule about twenty —formed a political district called *Wollost*. Before the Bolshevist revolution the Molotschna region, where the Mennonites were more numerous than in any other province, comprised about fifty-four Mennonite villages. The whole Mennonite population of Russia was about 100,000 in 1914.

During the first half century the schools of the colonies were inadequate. A humble beginning in the way of training teachers was made in 1820 at Orloff on the Molotschna. An institution for this purpose, as well as for general education, was established at Chortitsa under the name of Central School, in 1840, and another in 1858 at Gnadenfeld. This resulted in a gradual improvement of the village schools. Two other central schools were established later as well as a normal school for training teachers. Teachers' conferences helped to raise the schools to a higher standard. Religious instruction always held a prominent place in all Mennonite schools. The schools were conducted principally in the German language, though Russian was also taught and, in later periods, the Russian language was used in some of the classes.

As concerns material prosperity the Mennonite colonies in Russia were eminently successful. The Russian Mennonite colonists who in the seventies of the last century immigrated to America were quite prosperous as farmers here. It is questionable, however, whether they on the whole attained to the degree of material success which had been theirs in Russia. Under the rule of the Czars the Mennonite colonies were the pride of the Russian government. In cleanliness, order, culture, and prosperity the native Russian villages could not be compared with the Mennonite villages; in fact, in these respects the Mennonite colonies surpassed the colonies of the other German religious sects which had migrated to Russia about the same time as the Mennonites.

The man who did more than any other for the external success of the Mennonite colonies in Russia was Johann Cornies. As a youth of sixteen he came with his parents from Prussia in 1805. He was a man of eminent organizing and executive talent. For many years he was the chairman of the "Agricultural Society" in the Molotschna colony. The wollost authorities as well as the higher officials of the government co-operated with him in his endeavors for improvements along various lines. Some of the improved methods of farming which he recommended were made obligatory for a few years, until their unquestioned superiority made compulsion unnecessary. Unfortunately it must be said that at times he used his authority to meddle with things which concerned the government of the church and not the secular authorities or the civil government. Cornies died in 1848.

It may be said that the prosperity of the Mennonite colonies aroused the envy of some of the native Russians. The Mennonite farmers often employed native Russian servants or farm hands and on the whole did not treat them as their social equals. Nevertheless they were treated better than those working on estates of the Russian nobility. The air of superiority in the attitude of some of the "foreign" employers caused bitter resentment on the part of some of the native Russians, but was never questioned or criticized by the Russian government.

Their attitude toward the government is illustrated by the following incident. Czar Nicholas I, in 1818, was making a tour through Molotschna, the Mennonite colony. There was no good hotel within reach, and he decided to stop for dinner with a Mennonite family. When the meal was ready he asked the woman of the house to sit down with him at the table. Her reply was: "Far be from your majesty's handmaiden to sit down at the same table with the anointed of the Lord." The Emperor then took her by the hand and leading her to a chair insisted that she sit down.

We have stated that the Mennonite colonies in Russia formed virtually a state within the Russian state. They were given a free hand in matters of civil administration. It was an interesting experiment, though it was easy to foresee that this arrangement would not prove satisfactory from the viewpoint of principle. In consequence of this arrangement the Mennonite Church in Russia in the earlier period of its history exhibited certain features of a state church. While, as a matter of fact, no one was compelled to unite with the Mennonites against his will, the force of precedent was so strong that all the children of Mennonite parents united with the church. Baptism in many instances resembled a civil rather than religious ceremony, being required for those who would enter the state of matrimony. So it came about that to a large extent the civil population was identical with the membership of the church, though among the members there were those who showed by the lives they lived that they failed to take their Christian profession seriously. Church discipline was sadly neglected in many of the congregations. Many a church member had an evil reputation without being called to account by the church. In many of the villages there were drinking houses; though at Gnadenfeld and some other villages drinking houses were not tolerated.

In various respects, then, the Mennonite colonies as such fell short of exemplifying the characteristics of true Christianity. At a time when the landless class in the colonies had become very numerous, some of the more well-to-do class refused to give them the benefit of the use of those lands which were held in common ownership by the colonies. The ensuing contentions about the use of such lands form a dark chapter in the history of these colonies.

The civil administration of the colonies was committed to the colonists themselves. They elected the village authorities who in turn elected the *Oberschultz* for the *Wollost*, a political district consisting of a group of villages. In the large Molotschna Colony the heads of the wollosts were responsible to the commission located in the city of Odessa who were named by the Secretary of State in St. Petersburg. Though the civil officers of the villages were Mennonites, it fell to their lot at times to administer corporal punishment, consisting sometimes in giving a whipping to a member of the church.

The most regrettable consequence of this arrangement as concerns the civil administration was, that in various cases Mennonite officers of the government rendered decisions regarding things that were outside the province of the civil administration, things which concerned the church and its officers, and such decisions were then enforced. In a number of instances the officers became guilty of persecution, and such guilt was sometimes shared by church officials who yielded to the temptation of advising the use of force to advance what they believed to be the best interests of the church.

About 1855 a Mennonite elder, Heinrich Wiens of Gnadenheim, was called upon to report to one of the Commissioners at Odessa, because he had spoken disapprovingly of the punishment by whipping administered to an offending member of the church by an officer who also was a church member. Wiens was told by the Commissioner that upon his command even he, a minister, must give a beating of this sort to a church member. In reply Wiens stated emphatically that he would not comply with such an order. In consequence he was immediately banished from the Mennonite colonies. In this case the sentence was pronounced by an official who was not a Mennonite but in other instances Mennonite officials, both civil and ecclesiastical, transgressed in somewhat similar ways.

The first instance in which the use of force was threatened in the settlement of church matters occurred in connection with the movement which resulted in the inception of what is known as the *Kleine Gemeinde*. Klaas Reimer, the leader in this movement, had been ordained a minister in Prussia in 1801 and a few years later had emigrated to Russia. He was a diligent student of the Scriptures and of Menno Simons' writings, a man of strong convictions who saw with sincere regret the spiritual decline and the almost general neglect of scriptural discipline. With a few associates he suggested to the bishops of the church that there should be a stricter attitude toward transgressors. When such suggestions proved fruitless, Reimer, after years of waiting, began to hold separate meetings, though he and his associates never withdrew from the old church. He was finally ordained as elder by one of his associate ministers. The name "Kleine Gemeinde" was due to the fact that the membership of these congregations was not numerous.

The Kleine Gemeinde emphasized the need of repentance and newness of life, and took a strict attitude in regard to discipline. This group of churches disapproved the holding of civil offices which necessitated the use of force. They were outspoken in their testimony against worldliness, including the use of tobacco. After Reimer's death the congregation chose a bishop and requested the bishop of the congregation of Halbstadt to ordain him, but the request was not granted. For a time the Kleine Gemeinde was threatened by the village and wollost authorities with banishment to Siberia, but in 1843 this group was formally recognized by the higher authorities as a Mennonite church. Somewhat later a congregation was organized in the Black Sea peninsula Crimea (Krim), consisting of members of this communion who had moved there from the Molotschna Colony.

A number of the members of the Kleine Gemeinde in the Crimea with preacher Jacob A. Wiebe (1836-1921) as their leader, withdrew from this church in 1869 and organized themselves as an independent congregation under the name *Krimmer Mennoniten Brüdergemeinde*. Somewhat later Wiebe was chosen as their elder. They held strictly to conservative Mennonite principles. They accepted the view that Menno Simons baptized by immersion—an evident error—and practiced this mode of baptism.

Other divisions among the Mennonites in Russia were caused through influences proceeding partly from a colony of Lutheran Pietists who had come from Württemberg in 1822.[74] They constituted the colony Neu-Hoffnung which was located near the Molotschna Mennonite Colony. In 1845 and in following years the minister of the Neu-Hoffnung Colony was Edward Wüst, a man of great earnestness and extraordinary gifts as a preacher. His influence extended far beyond the colony of which he was the pastor. From the Lutheran and Mennonite villages of the Molotschna district many flocked to hear him. On special occasions he was invited to preach in the large Mennonite church at Gnadenfeld. His emphasis on the need of the personal experience of free grace and the resulting peace and joy made deep impressions. There followed a religious awakening, manifesting itself in various villages in the closing of drinking houses and by other indications. And yet, as Wüst later confessed with regret, he neglected to duly stress the need of consistent holy living.

It was through the influence of Edward Wüst and the reading of the book of sermons by Ludwig Hofacker of Germany that in Kronsweide, one of the villages of the Chortitsa Mennonite colony, there was a religious awakening under the leadership of Johann Löwen, who was not an ordained minister. He held meetings in private houses and stressed the importance of Christian experience. Private meetings for prayer and Bible study had been in vogue for some time at Gnadenfeld and other places. Unfortunately the movement in Kronsweide was opposed by measures of persecution. It was soon disclosed, however, that Johann Löwen held various antinomian errors. In consequence this movement ended in failure. The meetings held in private houses ceased, but after a few years permission was again given for such meetings.

In the Molotschna Colony the influence of Edward Wüst was stronger than in the Old Colony. Partly as a result of Wüst's influence, meetings for edification, led by unordained men, were held in various villages, and Menno Simons' writings were studied by some of the leaders. Since in many of the congregations various failings in regard to the enforcement of discipline were in evidence, sentiments favoring separation developed. In the village of Gnadenfeld, one of the centers of this movement, a group of church members asked the elder in charge to officiate in a communion service for themselves exclusively. Naturally this request was not granted. On January 6, 1860, at this place, eighteen persons of this group (there was no minister among them) handed the bishop a written declaration of their withdrawal from the church. At the same time they declared their determination of adhering to Mennonite teaching and principles. In the same year they organized themselves as a congregation under the name of *Mennoniten Brüdergemeinde,* and chose ministers who assumed their office upon the request of the group, without formal ordination. The movement, in its early stages, was marked by extravagant practices. In their gatherings they sometimes became very loud. Descriptions of their meetings correspond strikingly with those of the American Methodist camp meetings of about the first quarter of the last century. Shouting, jumping, and other extravagances were considered in order as expressions of the joy of salvation. These questionable practices originated in the Pietist colony at Neu-Hoffnung, despite the protests of Edward Wüst who died in 1859.

The authorities of the old church, with the notable exception of Johann Harder, elder of the church at Orloff, made the serious mistake of complaining to the civil authorities (the wollost officers who also were Mennonites). These officers, instead of declining to act, since the matter in fact did not concern them, threatened the seceders with arrest and attempted to apply to them the law against secret societies. In some cases the threats were followed by arrests and actual punishment.

In the difficulties arising from the withdrawal of the Brüdergemeinde from the old church the wollost officers at first favored the expulsion of the seceders from the colonies. The latter appealed to the higher authorities. A representative of the Brüdergemeinde, Johann Klassen, was given the opportunity to present a petition to the Czar. They were finally recognized by the government as a Mennonite church having the same privileges as the Old Mennonite Church.

As already intimated, not all Mennonites of Russia had departed so far from one of the outstanding principles of the Mennonite Church, as to approve of the measures suggested and partly used against the Brüdergemeinde. The above-named bishop, Johann Harder, personally interviewed the leaders in the new movement to obtain firsthand information. While he pointed out to them that they had offended against scriptural church regulations, he at the same time recognized the fact that because of their withdrawal from the old church, the church had no authority in the case, and the interference of the civil authorities was out of place. Such was also the attitude of the Kleine Gemeinde toward the new movement. Both Johann Harder and the bishop of the Kleine Gemeinde addressed the wollost authorities protesting against the course taken for some time against the new organization.

As already intimated, a religious awakening was in progress in the old Mennonite Church in Russia at the time of the rise of the new church. Among the prominent spiritual leaders were the previously mentioned bishop Johann Harder of Orloff (1811-1875), the minister Lenzmann of Gnadenfeld, Leonhard Sudermann of Berdjansk (later of Kansas), the distinguished evangelist and gifted poet Bernhard Harder (1832-1888), and others. The first foreign missionary of the old church was Heinrich Dirks who began his work in Sumatra in the Dutch East Indies in 1871 under the Holland Mennonite Mission Society. His home was at Gnadenfeld, where great annual mission meetings had been held for many years. The first foreign mission work of the new church dated from the year 1889.

In 1870 the news reached the colonies that a new law was about to be enacted, making military service compulsory for all. Naturally this report caused great anxiety in the Mennonite colonies. In February, 1871, a Mennonite deputation was sent to St. Petersburg to petition the government for the continuance of military exemption in accordance with repeated solemn promises made by the Czars. The high officers who gave them audience did not hold out to them any hope for having their petition granted. Greatly disappointed with the results of their mission the delegates returned home. The more conservative Mennonite leaders now felt that emigration was the only choice left them. It was largely through Cornelius Jansen of Berdjansk in South Russia (later of Beatrice, Nebraska) that the colonists' attention was directed to America as a land granting liberty of conscience to the Mennonites. Jansen had carried on a prolonged correspondence with John F. Funk of Elkhart, Indiana, and had received through him valuable information regarding inducements offered Mennonite colonists in this country.

In the summer of 1873 a delegation chosen by various Mennonite groups and the small Hutterite group in Russia, as well as representatives from Poland and Prussia, visited America in a search for land suitable for colonization. They were accompanied in their travels in America by John F. Funk, and Jacob Y. Schantz of Berlin (Kitchener), Ontario. The delegates of the Hutterite group soon after their arrival in this country, had an audience with President Grant on July 27, 1873. They were received by the president in a most friendly manner. The delegates returned home with favorable reports. In the following winter hundreds of families made preparations for emigration. They disposed of their farms at prices representing half their value, and less.

The Russian government observed these developments with alarm. These colonists were Russia's best agriculturists who had made the Ukraine "the granary of Europe." Their departure would mean a great shock to the country's economic prosperity. The authorities decided to place every hindrance possible in the way of prospective emigrants. Selling their land was made difficult and obtaining the needed passports very expensive. Cornelius Jansen, who was regarded as the first agitator, was expelled from Russia. When all such measures proved fruitless to halt the movement, the government decided to offer concessions.

General von Todtleben, a man of genial nature and humble demeanor who spoke German fluently, was sent into the colonies to dissuade the people from emigration and to ascertain on what conditions they would be willing to remain. At first he offered exemption from "combative" military service, but finally, on behalf of the Czar, he promised full exemption. In lieu of military service the young men of military age were to serve the state in forestry work under an administration that had no connection with the military organization. An arrangement of such nature was somewhat later actually effected and was placed largely under Mennonite management. This arrangement was to them unobjectionable from the viewpoint of the principle of nonresistance.

Upon the promise of such an arrangement the majority of the Mennonites decided to stay in Russia. Many had already disposed of their property, however, and had made arrangements to leave the country. In particular the more conservative groups had made ready to emigrate after their petition for the prolongation of military exemption had been refused by the authorities. The whole constituency of nearly all the more conservative groups, such as the Kleine Gemeinde, the Krimmer Mennoniten Brüdergemeinde, the Alexanderwohl and the Bergthal congregations, the congregation organized by Isaac Peters,[75] and the Hutterian Brethren emigrated to America.

The first group of emigrants, thirteen families, left Russia in the autumn of 1873. Many groups followed them the next summer and fall. From 1873 onward until 1880 about 15,000 Mennonites, or about one third of the Mennonites of Russia, emigrated from South Russia, the Volga region, Volhynia and Russian Poland to America, settling chiefly in Kansas, Nebraska, Minnesota, Dakota, and Manitoba.

Before there was among the Mennonites of Russia any thought of emigration to America the curious idea of a migration in the opposite direction, namely to Central Asia, was entertained in a few small Russian Mennonite circles. The originators of this idea were two Protestant religious writers, Heinrich Jung-Stilling and Christoph Clöter, editor of "Der Brüderbote" (published in Germany). These men were of the opinion that according to prophecy[76] a definite place of refuge would be prepared for the true church in the time of tribulation which was to precede the coming of the Lord. Furthermore they entertained the fanciful view that this place of refuge was to be somewhere in Central Asia.

In a few Mennonite circles in South Russia, where the writings of these men were read, the thought of a migration to the East rather than westward was entertained. It was hoped that exemption from military service was obtainable in the distant East. A delegation of those interested in this project met at St. Petersburg with the governor-general of Turkestan, von Kauffmann. He invited them to come to Turkestan, a Russian dominion in Central Asia, where they would be granted fifteen years of complete freedom from all state service. In consequence, a caravan under Abraham Peters, an elder, started from the Molotschna Colony in the autumn of 1880. They traveled by wagon and, having braved great hardships, reached Tashkent, the capital of Turkestan, in about three and a half months. A second caravan, led by Claas Epp, came somewhat later to join the first group, but it soon developed that Epp held extravagant opinions concerning his own mission and calling, claiming to be a divinely commissioned prophet. The great majority of the group, under Abraham Peters finally settled on a tract of land about 45 miles from the city of Aulie Ata, while Claas Epp insisted that the Lord had revealed to him that they should go to Khiva as the land of refuge. Thither he led the way. This group occupies a very small tract of land; they follow gardening and a few industries for a livelihood. Epp died in 1913. The majority of this group have come to their senses and renounced their former peculiar views. In 1936 the colony in Khiva numbered about twenty families. Some of them joined the colony at Aulie Ata.

The colony at Aulie Ata, in 1918, consisted of two hundred families, while a report of the year 1934 states that the population of the five Mennonite villages was about 1500. A correspondent of this group wrote in 1936 that since Christmas of the preceding year public worship had ceased, and conditions among the young people were sad indeed, indicating that under Soviet rule these people are not faring better than the churches of South Russia.

The Mennonite Church in Russia in the period immediately preceding the World War experienced marked growth and prosperity. Missionary interest was on a steady increase. The support of the Mennonite Missionary Society in Amsterdam, both as regards workers and material means, came mainly from the congregations of Russia. The Brüdergemeinde carried on a successful mission work at Nalgonda in India. Educational facilities were well developed and there were a number of benevolent institutions and hospitals.

The Mennonite colonies in this period enjoyed great material prosperity, as indeed they had for about half a century. Agriculture remained the principal occupation of the colonists, but there also were important industries of various kinds. Many mills and not a few large factories were established. The expense of housing and keeping about 500 Mennonite men in the state forestry service, amounting to about 700,000 rubles ($375,000) annually, was met by the colonists. The Mennonite population of Russia at the beginning of the Great War was about 100,000 (inclusive of children). The land owned by the

Mennonites in Russia equalled the area of the former kingdom of Saxony, or the combined area of the states of Connecticut and Rhode Island.

At the beginning of the World War nationalistic feeling was at high tide in Russia, not excepting the German colonies. Nevertheless the colonists were soon suspected and accused of disloyalty.

Agitation against the German colonists in Russia began in the second year of the war. In the same year the infamous "liquidation laws" were passed and published, which deprived the German colonists of the right of ownership of their land. In fact, they were ordered to leave the country. The Mennonite colonies presented to the government a petition pointing out that they were in reality of Netherland, or Dutch, extraction, but the government insisted that they were Germans, and refused to grant their petition.

After the revolution of 1917 which marked the end of the Czar's government, Russia made peace with Germany and disbanded its army. The decrees demanding the banishment of the Germans and the liquidation of their property were now invalid. The Ukraine, comprising the largest Mennonite colonies, was declared independent of the Russian government, and was occupied by German and Austrian troops. While the Czarist government had in recent years persecuted the Mennonites, the latter were now given special protection.

Before the end of the World War the German-Austrian army of occupation was compelled to withdraw from the Ukraine. Some time before the departure of the army weapons and ammunition were distributed among the German colonists. The Mennonite colonists, with some praiseworthy exceptions, made the mistake of accepting these means of armed defense and warfare. The protests of the nonresistant minority were ignored.

Even before the departure of the last remnants of the German army, bandits began to rove through the land in groups. Some of these groups consisted of anarchists and had the anarchist Machno for their leader. Through the dangers threatening the colonies from these bands the principle of nonresistance was put to a real test.

The presence of the army of occupation in the colonies, and the distribution and acceptance of weapons of war had created a military spirit among many of the Mennonite young men. When the army withdrew a number of officers remained for some time longer to drill young men in the use of arms and effect a military organization. This organization was called *Selbstschutz* (self-protection). Sad to say, the great majority of the Mennonite young men became identified with this movement.

The first fight between the Selbstschutz and one of these bands took place on December 10, 1918, in the Russian peasant village of Tschernigowka, located in the Molotschna region, some distance from any Mennonite village. The Selbstschutz organizations of various Mennonite villages marched on this peasant village to attack a band of Machno anarchists. A battle ensued. The anarchists soon attempted to flee but found themselves surrounded. Many made their escape nevertheless, and many were killed. Two men of the Selbstschutz also lost their lives. This occurrence indicates to what extent the military spirit had taken possession of the Selbstschutz.

For about four months the Selbstschutz easily held its own against the roaming bands which outnumbered them by far. A large number of the bandits fell in the encounters, while very few men of the Selbstschutz lost their lives. But these bands became too numerous and were finally re-enforced by regular Red (Bolshevik) troops against whom the Selbstschutz would not and could not offer armed resistance.

Untold ill feeling was created against the Mennonites by the Selbstschutz activities. The deplorable mistake of throwing the principle of nonresistance overboard (though a small minority never did so) gave the greatest offense. The native Russians reminded the Mennonite colonists that they had held fighting to be contrary to their principles when the country was in trouble, but that they now took the sword to defend their property.

The cessation of the Selbstschutz activities left the Mennonite colonists in great fear. When on March 3, 1919, in the Molotschna Colony, the largest of the Mennonite colonies, the Selbstschutz abandoned their last position, the colonists left their homes in wild flight. Many were robbed while fleeing.

A small number escaped to the Crimea. Most of the fugitives were compelled to return to their farms and dwellings which had meanwhile been looted by the bandits who were particularly desirous of getting weapons, and also by Russian peasants. Thus the colonists fared far worse than they would have, had there been no Selbstschutz. And the punishment overtaking the colonies for accepting and using weapons did by no means end at that time.

A number of months later two bandits were shot at Blumenort by colonists. Various groups of bandits vowed revenge. They cruelly put to death fifteen Mennonite men in the same village. Then the claim was made that the killing of the two bandits was an indication of an uprising of the colonists. An organization of anarchists which styled itself "the Asiatic (Siberian) regiment" burned down the buildings of fifteen of the twenty-one farms in Blumenort and murdered six more men. By a hair's breadth the town of Halbstadt escaped the same fate. At Orloff, also, a number were killed. Here and in Altonau the bandits committed unnamable crimes.

Against the Red and Anarchist Army, approaching from the north, General Denikin organized in 1919 a White Army in Caucasia. The region of the Chortitsa Colony ("Old Colony") was eventually occupied by this army. The officers persuaded many Mennonite young men to volunteer for military service. But when Denikin met with serious reverses and was compelled by the Red and Anarchist army to retreat southward, the Mennonite colonists, having supported Denikin, were severely punished. A number of the villages of the colony were destroyed by fire. The colonists were robbed not only of their food but also of their clothing. Indescribable terror prevailed in the colony. A severe epidemic of spotted fever broke out and raged for weeks. In the fifteen remaining villages of the colony schoolhouses and some of the residences were occupied by sick anarchists to whom the inhabitants were supposed to minister. Some of the colonists here showed a truly Christian attitude toward their oppressors; they did the best they possibly could for them.

Soon many of the colonists themselves came down with the fever. There was no medicine, and the two physicians of the colony also were seized by the same illness. The mortality was very high. In consequence of the famine those who were well were so enfeebled that to bury all those who had succumbed to the epidemic was found an almost impossible task. These horrible conditions, including extreme famine, prevailed until after the retreat of the anarchists about the middle of December 1919.

The Molotschna Mennonite Colony, as we have seen, had suffered severely, but not to the same extent as the Chortitsa Colony. A relief work for the latter colony was undertaken by the Mennonites of the Molotschna villages. The first transport of flour and lard from the Molotschna arrived in the Old Colony on February 21, 1920, and was received with great joy, though about half of the wagons carrying supplies were confiscated en route. This work of mercy, furnishing food and clothing to the famished colonists in Chortitsa, was continued as long as it was necessary and possible.

The story of the Selbstschutz and other missteps of similar nature presents a sad chapter in the history of the Mennonites. The Selbstschutz was a mistake not only from the Christian but from every other viewpoint as well. For a short time it afforded protection, but after its collapse the punishment meted out to the colonists was all the more severe. The comparatively few villages and districts which refused to depart from the principle of nonresistance suffered far less than those who yielded to the temptation to take the sword.

A conspicuous example is the Mennonite colony of Memrik. Here the colonists had refused to accept the weapons that had been taken from the peasants and offered them by the German-Austrian army of occupation. Machno and his hordes passed through this colony also, but they did not deal out such punishment here as in most of the colonies that had accepted arms.

Many thousands of penniless refugees arrived in Constantinople, the capital of Turkey, after the collapse of Wrangel's army, among them a few hundred Mennonites. The American Mennonite Relief Organization provided a Home in Constantinople for the Mennonites and other refugees. Sixty-two Mennonite young men, with few exceptions former soldiers in the White Army, were entertained here until August 3, 1921, when, through the aid extended by the Mennonite relief organizations, they set sail for America, to make room in the Home for other Mennonite refugees.

In 1919, private letters from the Mennonite colonies in Russia reported conditions of near-famine, and a great need for clothing. M. B. Fast and Wm. P. Neufeld were sent to Siberia by way of China with supplies of clothing and funds. On September 27, 1920, the first American Mennonite Relief unit for Russia, including the brethren Orie O. Miller and Clayton Kratz, arrived at Constantinople, en route for Russia. Supplies of food and clothing were shipped from America. Besides the Mennonite Home for young men which has already been mentioned, a Mennonite Refugee Home for women, and a Children's Shelter were opened in the same city.

The two brethren last named proceeded from Constantinople to Halbstadt, where Clayton Kratz remained for some time, while Miller soon returned to Constantinople. Altogether unexpectedly the Red Army advanced south to Halbstadt and carried Kratz away a prisoner. To all appearance he lost his life at the hands of the Reds. Beginning in the autumn of the following year an extensive relief work was carried on for a few years in famine-stricken Russia, under the American Mennonite Central Committee[77] through a strong staff, with A. J. Miller as director. Over a million dollars were expended in this work.

The extremely militant, atheistic attitude of the Soviet government created unbearable conditions for the Mennonite people in Russia. A delegation consisting of four brethren was sent to America in 1920 to investigate the possibilities for immigration. They reported favorably concerning opportunities for settlement in Canada. The "Canadian Mennonite Board of Colonization" was organized in 1922. An "order in council" which had been passed in the course of the World War, forbidding further immigration of Mennonites into Canada, was repealed. About twenty thousand Mennonite refugees of Russia subsequently came to Canada and a few hundred to the United States, from 1922 to 1927.

In the autumn of 1929 about fifteen thousand colonists rushed to Moscow in the hope of receiving permission to emigrate. Of this number several thousand (3,700) Mennonites, through the efforts of the German ambassador in Moscow, were granted permission to leave the country. They were transported to Germany at the expense of the German government for a temporary sojourn in the old fatherland. The German Reichstag in a special session unanimously assigned a credit of six million marks (one and a half million dollars), and private institutions also made large contributions for the support and further transportation of these refugees.

Not all the refugees, however, found it possible to go to Canada, as had been their intention, although about one thousand of them reached that dominion. About twelve hundred were settled in the state of Santa Catharina in Brazil, while about fifteen hundred migrated to the Gran Chaco in Paraguay under the auspices of the Mennonite Central Committee.

The Mennonites of Russia find themselves today in a sad plight, undergoing, with all other Christians of that unhappy land, an appalling persecution. Not since the days of the great persecutions in the sixteenth century have there been so formidable and persistent efforts made to eradicate completely the Christian faith. Many have lost their lives by execution, and many have perished from hunger and cold in northern regions whither they were deported. The Mennonite meetinghouses are with few exceptions, no longer available for worship, having been closed or confiscated by the government.

From various Mennonite colonies reports have been received announcing the arrest of the last ministers. For example, the last minister in the "Trakt" Colony was arrested early in 1936, and since then no public services were held. The correspondent complains about the spiritual and moral decline in the church. The Mennonite Church of Russia, which before World War I numbered about 100,000, has practically ceased to exist.

During the World War II the German army extended its conquests to the territory in the Ukraine occupied by the old Mennonite colonies of Chortitsa and Molotschna. When they were forced to retreat in 1943, they took with them about 25,000 Mennonites, resettling them in the western part of Poland. With the collapse of the German eastern front, about half of these were recaptured and taken back to Russia where no doubt many of them perished. About 12,000 escaped to western Germany, where they found a temporary haven of refuge. Through the Mennonite Central Committee and the help of the International Refugee Organization (IRO) operating under the United Nations, over ten thousand of these were resettled in Paraguay and Canada, about half in each country.

PART THREE

Life and Faith of the Early Mennonites

CHAPTER 33

CHARACTER OF EVANGELICAL ANABAPTISTS

The contemporary chronicler Sebastian Franck, a reliable historian but an opponent of the Anabaptists, wrote in 1531, scarcely seven years after the rise of the Anabaptists:

The Anabaptists spread so rapidly that their teaching soon covered, as it were, the land. They soon gained a large following, and baptized many thousands, drawing to themselves many sincere souls who had a zeal for God. For they taught nothing but love, faith, and the need of bearing the cross [that is to say, they were not politically motivated]. They showed themselves humble, patient under much suffering; they brake the bread with one another as an evidence of unity and love. They helped each other faithfully and called each other brothers. They increased so rapidly that the world feared an uprising by them, though I have learned that this fear had no justification whatsoever. They were persecuted with great tyranny, being imprisoned, branded, tortured, and executed by fire, water, and the sword. In a few years very many were put to death. Some have estimated the number of those who were put to death in this period to be far above two thousand. They died as martyrs, patiently, and humbly endured all persecution.

"The Anabaptist messengers of the Gospel," says Dr. Carl Adolf Cornelius, one of the profoundest students of Anabaptist history, "came in humble appearance and unassuming attire, much like the apostles. They labored preferably among the poor and lowly. With a greeting of peace they entered the dwellings to read from the Word of God and deliver their message. Their language was simple and straightforward, with no pretense to scholarship. But the message-bearers were confessors and martyrs, and the warmth of their hearts impressed the hearers. Persecuted and fugitive, uncertain of the bare material necessities, their life bore a strong testimony to their words. Therefore, their message, in the full strength of its Biblical content, was edifying and soul-winning, moving, and convincing."

Great numbers of the people became interested in religion. Church reformation was in the air. The Anabaptists were then practically the only missionaries. They especially endeavored to win the common people. The Anabaptist missionary, Claus Felbinger, said:

Some have asked us why we came into the country of the duke of Bavaria. I answered, We go not only into this land but into all lands, as far as our language extends. For wherever God opens a door unto us, shows us zealous hearts who earnestly seek Him and who have an aversion to the ungodly life of the world, and desire to amend their lives, to all such places we aim to go, and for this we have scriptural ground.

About the close of the year 1524 Ulrich Zwingli recognized the intentions of the Anabaptists as good, though they erred in judgment. Later he tried to show that this favorable opinion was erroneous. While even then he freely recognized that their lives were above reproach, he denounced in the severest terms their piety as hypocrisy. He says in his last book against the Swiss Brethren: "If you investigate their life and conduct, it seems at the first contact irreproachable, pious, unassuming, attractive, yea, supermundane. Even those who are inclined to be critical will say that their lives are excellent." And yet he declared it all to be hypocrisy.

Heinrich Bullinger, the successor of Zwingli, in Zurich, who wrote two books against the Anabaptists, says of the early Swiss Brethren:

Those who united with them were by their ministers received into their church by rebaptism unto repentance and newness of life. They henceforth led their lives under a semblance of a quite spiritual conduct. They denounced [in Christian professors] covetousness, pride, profanity, the lewd conversation and immorality of the world, drinking and gluttony.

He states further that they were sedate and slow to speak, thus guarding against idle words and levity. "In short," concludes this bitter opponent, "their hypocrisy was great and manifold."

In his smaller book against the Brethren, written in 1531, Bullinger says that "the people are running after them as though they were the living saints." The latter expression is evidently an allusion to the idea that saints were persons who had departed this life, since only after a man's death could he be canonized, or declared to be a saint. But here, in the opinion of many, were living saints.

Johannes Kessler, the contemporary Zwinglian chronicler, says of them: "Their life and conversation was distinguished for its piety, holiness, and irreproachableness." Again, he wrote: "Oh, what shall I say about these people! My heart is moved with deep compassion for them. They die gladly and heroically for the name of Christ, though they are tainted with some error." Joachim Vadian, the Zwinglian reformer of St. Gall, testified: "None were more favorably inclined toward Anabaptism and more easily entangled with it than those who were of a pious and candid disposition."

Wolfgang Capito, Zwinglian reformer of Strasburg, wrote in 1527 concerning the Swiss Brethren:

I frankly confess that in most Anabaptists there is in evidence piety and consecration and indeed a zeal which is beyond a suspicion of insincerity. For what earthly advantage could they hope to win by enduring exile, torture, and unspeakable punishment of the flesh? I testify before God that I cannot say that on account of a lack of wisdom they are somewhat indifferent toward earthly things, but rather from divine motives. I cannot notice in them any passion or excitement, and they meet death as confessors of the name of Christ, not carelessly or wrathfully but with due consideration and the greatest endurance.

The preachers of the state churches of the canton of Bern in 1532 admitted in a letter to the Council of Bern that "the Anabaptists have a semblance of outward piety to a far greater degree than we and all the churches which unitedly with us confess Christ, and they avoid offensive sins which are very common among us."

Concerning the early Brethren of Augsburg a contemporary writer said: "In their brotherhood there was in evidence the purpose to render each other the greatest possible service on the ground of brotherly love."

Walter Klarer, the Protestant chronicler of Appenzell in Switzerland, wrote in the Reformation period: "Most of the Anabaptists are people who at first had been the best with us in promulgating the Word of God."

A Roman Catholic theologian, Franz Agricola, in a book entitled, *Against the Terrible Errors of the Anabaptists,* written in 1582, says:

Among the existing heretical sects there is none which in appearance leads a more modest, better, or more pious life than the Anabaptists. As concerns their outward public life they are irreproachable. No lying, deception, swearing, strife, harsh language, no intemperate eating and drinking, no outward personal display is found

or discernible among them, but humility, patience, uprightness, meekness, honesty, temperance, straightforwardness in such measure that
one would suppose that they have the Holy Spirit of God.

Another Roman Catholic author, Christopher Andreas
Fischer, wrote concerning the Hutterian Brethren:

They call each other brethren and sisters, they use no profanity nor
harsh speech, they do not swear, they do not use weapons, and in the
beginning they did not even carry knives. They are not intemperate in
eating and drinking, they do not wear apparel which indicates worldly
show. They do not go to law before the magistrates; they bear everything in patience, as they pretend, and in the Holy Ghost.

In the mandate against the Swiss Brethren published in 1585
by the Council of Bern it is stated that both among the preachers
and the membership of the state church offensive sins and vices
are common, "and this is the greatest reason that many pious
God-fearing people who seek Christ from their heart are offended and forsake our church [to unite with the Brethren]."

Concerning the life of the Brethren in the Netherlands, van
Bentheim, a Dutch author, wrote in 1698:

While we should be on our guard to shun the errors of these people,
we may nevertheless learn from them much that is good, namely,
humility, contentment, moderation, and especially mercy toward the
needy. For although the people of the Reformed church of Holland
deserve to be commended for their benevolence toward the poor, yet
this virtue is particularly characteristic of these people. Also, they are
very careful to dress unassumingly.

J. C. Jehring, a Reformed historian of East Friesland, wrote
in 1720 about the Mennonites of the lower countries:

Their external life and walk are, as is generally known, highly
praised by many, and it is verily true that through their good life they
attract much attention. They are very friendly and unassuming toward all people. When others owe them money, they will settle in
some way rather than go to law. One does not hear of them that they
use profanity or swearing, or that they quarrel among themselves.
And whatever occasion demands, they show a zeal against all immorality.

The late Professor Alfred Hegler, of Tübingen, pointed out
the high ideals of the evangelical Anabaptists, such as "liberty
of conscience, rejection of all state-made Christianity, the demand for personal holiness, and a vital personal acceptance of
Christian truth." Professor Karl Bauer says, "Their strength

lay in the earnestness of their striving for holy living." The historian K. W. H. Hochhuth wrote: "Their avowed aim was the restoration of primitive Christianity." Christian Meyer, the author of a work on the Anabaptists in Augsburg, said: "Many were won by them from an inordinate life to seriousness and repentance." Professor August Lang, of the Reformed Church, speaks of their moral energy and sincere devotion to their cause, and states that by the common people they were often considered "holier than the leading reformers themselves."

The Reformed church historian, Prof. Ernst Stähelin of Basel, says: "Anabaptism, by its earnest determination to follow in life and practice the primitive Christian Church, has kept alive the conviction that he who is in Christ is a new creature, and that those who are identified with His cause will necessarily encounter the opposition of the world." Professor Walther Koehler, of Heidelberg, repeatedly referred to the Swiss Brethren as "Bible Christians." The Lutheran historian, Dr. Wilhelm Gussmann, speaks of "their rigorous purity of life, their immovable faithfulness in confessing their faith and suffering for it, and last, not least, the fervent mutual feeling of brotherliness which was in evidence among them." He stated that "they lived and moved in God's Word," and spoke of their earnest endeavor to live holy lives.

Ernst Müller of the Reformed Church, the author of a thorough work on the Bernese Anabaptists, wrote: "They placed the principal emphasis on holiness of life and established themselves firmly among the lower strata of society, imparting to them true religious conviction, while the movements proceeding from Luther and Zwingli involved more particularly the upper classes and only by compulsion comprised the broad masses."

Gottfried Strasser, a theologian of the same church said:

Despairing of the possibility of bringing the purity of the Christian life to realization among the broad masses, they aimed at establishing, within the narrower limits of those who took the Christian life more seriously, a true Christian church of those who were striving for active holiness according to the example of the apostolic church.

Abraham Hulshof, a Dutch Mennonite historian, wrote in a work on the Anabaptists in Strasburg: "The Anabaptists' aim was a church of those who took their Christian profession seriously, who were in real earnest in the endeavor to conform their lives to the requirements of the gospel. They aimed [in contrast to the state church type of Christianity] to form voluntary congregations of those who believed and were truly converted. Their aim was to constitute in the midst of the world a living church of Christ that was separated from the world and was following Him in brotherly unison."

Max Goebel, author of the distinguished work, *A History of the Christian Life in the Rhenish Westphalian* [*Protestant*] *Church,* wrote in 1849:

The essential and distinguishing characteristic of this church is its great emphasis upon the actual personal conversion and regeneration of every Christian through the Holy Spirit. . . . They aimed with special emphasis at carrying out and realizing the Christian doctrine and faith in the heart and life of every Christian and in the whole Christian church. Their aim was the bringing together of all the true believers out of the great degenerated national churches into a true Christian church. That which the Reformation was originally intended to accomplish they aimed to bring into full immediate realization.

Professor Johann Loserth, of Graz in Austria, was an authority on Anabaptist history. He wrote:

More radically than any other party for church reformation the Anabaptists strove to follow the footsteps of the church of the first centuries and to renew the unadulterated original Christianity.

The above are some representative samples of the many testimonials to the high character and pure life of the early Mennonites found in the writings of persons outside their own membership.

CHAPTER 34

PERSECUTION AND SPREAD OF EARLY ANABAPTISTS

The Anabaptists from their beginning spread with surprising rapidity. Sometimes a congregation was founded at a given place within a few hours after the arrival of an Anabaptist preacher. "Anabaptism spread with such speed," says a contemporary writer, "that there was reason to fear that the majority of the common people would unite with this sect." There is abundant evidence that in certain provinces large portions of the population were openly sympathetic toward the Anabaptists. In various sections of Switzerland, Germany, and Austria the evangelical Anabaptist movement easily surpassed in inherent strength the Lutheran and Zwinglian movements in those states whose governments accepted the Reformation of the state church type. In various states the strength of the Anabaptist movement was such that it was found difficult to carry out the bloody decrees against the Anabaptists. We shall directly see that the Reichstag, the House of Parliament of Germany, being the highest legislative and executive authority of the empire, in 1551 passed a decree ordering the removal from office and punishment of judges who had scruples against sentencing Anabaptists to death. To avoid giving offense to the people in general, Anabaptists were often executed secretly. Clearly in these sections the Anabaptist movement, if tolerated by the authorities, would have completely upset the plans for a state-governed church in which the whole population would hold membership by force of civil law.

It need scarcely be said that Roman Catholicism had always taken an attitude of intolerance and persecution toward all dissenters from its creed. On the contrary, the principal leaders in the Reformation movement, Luther and Zwingli, in the first period of their reformatory labors, condemned Romish intolerance. They were in the earlier period defenders of the principle of liberty of conscience. Later they agreed to a thoroughgoing union of the church with the state, which meant the abandonment of the principle of religious liberty. Furthermore, the natural and inevitable consequence was the persecution of the Anabaptists by the established Protestant state churches.

It is a fact recognized by many recent historians that the persecution of the Anabaptists surpassed in severity the persecution of the early Christians by pagan Rome. Persecution began in Zurich soon after the Brethren had organized a congregation. Imprisonment of varying severity, sometimes in dark dungeons, was followed by executions. Felix Manz was the first martyr to die in Zurich, but at least two Brethren had been martyred earlier in other cantons of Switzerland by Roman Catholic governments. Within a short period the leaders of the Brethren lost their lives in the persecution. Among the early leaders of the evangelical Anabaptists who suffered martyrdom were Eberli Bolt, Johannes Krüsi, George Blaurock, Hans Lüdi, Hans Brötli, Thomas Herman, Eitelhans Langenmantel, Leonhard Schiemer, Hans Schlaffer, Hans Leopold Schneider, Wolfgang Uliman, Wolfgang Brandhuber, Georg Zaunring, Jerome Käls, Leonhard Seiler, Jacob Hutter, Offrus Griesinger.

Anabaptism was made a capital crime. Prices were set on the heads of Anabaptists. To give them food and shelter was made a crime. In Roman Catholic states even those who recanted were often executed. Generally, however, those who abjured their faith were pardoned except in Bavaria and, for a time, in Austria and also in the Netherlands. The duke of Bavaria, in 1527, gave orders that the imprisoned Anabaptists should be burned at the stake, unless they recanted, in which case they should be beheaded. King Ferdinand I of Austria issued a number of severe decrees against them, the first general mandate being dated August 28, 1527. In Catholic countries the Anabaptists, as a rule, were executed by burning at the stake, in Lutheran and Zwinglian states generally by beheading or drowning.

Emperor Charles V of Germany issued a general mandate against the Anabaptists on January 4, 1528, which was read from the pulpits of all cities, towns, and villages, decreeing that not only those who had received baptism but all parents who did not have their children baptized in good time were guilty of a criminal offense deserving death. Within a few years a number of imperial decrees followed. Not only were the Anabaptists to be executed by fire, but their dwellings also should be burned, unless they were located in towns or cities in which case they should be razed to the ground. In certain provinces their houses were not destroyed but confiscated. Speaking of northern Germany Menno Simons relates that in 1546 a small house of four rooms was confiscated because the owner had rented it to Menno and his family. In the Tyrol even the houses in which an Anabaptist had been given temporary lodging were to be destroyed.

Thousands sealed their faith with their blood. When all efforts to halt the movement proved vain, the authorities resorted to desperate measures. Armed executioners and mounted soldiers were sent in companies through the land to hunt down the Anabaptists and kill them on the spot without trial or sentence. The old method of pronouncing sentence over each individual dissenter proved inadequate to exterminate this faith.

In the first week of Lent, 1528, while Hubmaier was in prison at Kreuzenstein, King Ferdinand of Austria commissioned a company of executioners to root out the Anabaptist faith in his lands. Those who were overtaken in the highways or fields were killed with the sword, others were dragged out of their houses and hanged on the door posts. Most of them had gone into hiding in the woods and mountains. In a forest near Lengbach seventeen were put to death.

In the province of Swabia, in South Germany, four hundred mounted soldiers were, in 1528, sent out to put to death all Anabaptists on whom they could lay hands. Somewhat later the number of soldiers so commissioned was increased to eight hundred and then to one thousand. In various provinces an imperial provost marshal by the name of Berthold Aichele, with his assistants, put many Anabaptists to death. On Christmas day, 1531, he drove seventeen men and women into a farmhouse near Aalen in Württemberg and burned the building together with the inmates. Three hundred and fifty Anabaptists were executed in the Palatinate before the year 1530. The Count of Alzey, in that province, after having put many to death, was heard to exclaim: "What shall I do? The more I kill, the greater becomes their number." At Ensisheim, "the slaughterhouse of Alsace," as it was called, six hundred were

killed within a few years. Within six weeks thirty-seven were
burned, drowned, or beheaded at Linz, in Austria. In the town
of Kitzbüchl in the Tyrol, sixty-eight were executed in one year.
Two hundred and ten or more were burned in the valley of the
Inn River. The number of Anabaptist martyrs in the Tyrol and
Görz was estimated at one thousand about the end of the year
1531.

It may be recalled here that it was comparatively easy for the
catchpolls to ascertain who was and who was not an Anabaptist.
They simply put the question to suspected persons. A true Anabaptist would disdain saving his life and burdening his conscience by telling an untruth and denying his faith.

In April of the year 1529 the national legislative assembly
(Reichstag) of the German Empire, in session at Speier in the
Palatinate, passed an edict demanding that "every Anabaptist
and rebaptized person of either sex shall be put to death by fire,
sword, or in some other way." Thus the sentence of death was
summarily passed by imperial law upon all Anabaptists. "The
men in authority," says Menno Simons, "do not consider why
one has begun a new life and has received the baptism of Christ.
They only ask whether he was baptized. If the answer is in the
affirmative, the sentence is already pronounced and he must
die."

It was expressly stated in the edict of Speier that any parents
who failed to have their infant children baptized, were to be
considered Anabaptists and were to be punished as such. Only
those who recanted instantly could, according to this edict, be
pardoned. The cruelty of this persecution caused grievous offense even within the Protestant state churches whose representatives, with the exception of the Landgrave of Hesse, had
consented to the adoption and publication of the edict of Speier.
This persecution was all the more inexcusable, since with the
official recognition of the Protestant state churches by the imperial authorities, the religious unity of the empire was broken.
Again it should be recalled that this was in the earliest period
of Anabaptist history, a number of years previous to the rise
of the fanatical, revolutionary Anabaptists. It is therefore impossible to hold revolutionary Anabaptism responsible for the
persecution of the evangelical Anabaptists as has been frequently done.

Two years after the Reichstag of Speier, in 1531, the representatives of the German empire assembled at Frankfurt-on-the-Main, in a new edict against the Anabaptists, admitted that the law to put to death all Anabaptists was passed somewhat hastily. And yet the curious assertion was made that these people were not punished for their faith but for transgressing the imperial laws against the Anabaptists. Hence the severity of the edict of 1529 was not mitigated. In subsequent sessions of the Reichstag also the execution of this edict was insisted upon. The clause was added, in 1544, that those of the clergy who were tardy in their duty of denouncing Anabaptism from the pulpits "should be duly punished." Since it had been learned that in certain sections some of the judges had indicated conscientious scruples against pronouncing the death sentence upon any one on account of matters of faith, the Reichstag of 1551, assembled at Augsburg, passed a decree ordering that judges and jurors who had such scruples, should be removed from office and punished by heavy fines and imprisonment.

It is particularly noteworthy that these edicts and orders were passed with the consent of the Protestant members of the Reichstag. At Speier, in 1529, the Protestant members had protested against a proposed curtailment of certain religious rights claimed by the Lutheran princes. Indeed it was for this reason that they were given the name "Protestants." But both here and in subsequent sessions of the Reichstag the Protestants failed to protest against the tyrannical edicts passed against the Anabaptists. On the contrary, as we shall see anon, the Lutheran ruler of Saxony in later years insisted on the right and duty of the magistrates to execute Anabaptists, as demanded in the edict of Speier.

The most heroic examples of primitive Christian martyrdom were paralleled in the persecution of the evangelical Anabaptists. Their courage, fortitude and patience were admired even by many of their antagonists. A contemporary Catholic writer said concerning the way in which the Anabaptist martyrs met their death: "Such valiant dying has never been seen before, nor heard of except in the legends of the saints." The masses were impressed with the fact that they were in great earnestness in living up to the light they had received. When Michael

Hassel, after much suffering, died in the prison of Hohenwit-
tling in Württemberg, the warden said: "If this man did not
get to heaven, I shall despair of the courage even to knock at
heaven's gate." The hangman of Burghausen, having beheaded
three Anabaptists, exclaimed: "I should rather have executed
seven thieves than these men. God have mercy!" In 1549 a
Mennonite martyr at Leeuwarden in Friesland was burned at
the stake. Many people witnessing the execution exclaimed:
"This was a good man; if he is not a Christian, there is no
Christian in the whole world."

Berthold Aichele, the imperial provost marshal already
mentioned, who put to death a great number of Anabaptists,
finally became greatly troubled and stricken in conscience because of these executions. While putting to death Offrus
Griesinger, at Brixen in the Tyrol, by burning at the stake,
Aichele was filled with terror and dismay. He lifted up his
hand to heaven and swore a solemn oath, never again to put to
death an Anabaptist, and he kept this vow. In many instances
the executioners expressed their regret for being obliged to put
them to death. Often they begged their victims to recant and
save their lives. Instead of following this advice, the martyrs
praised God on the scaffold or stake for giving them grace to
stand by His truth to the end. They died as Christian heroes
in the triumph of the faith.

The fact deserves notice that evidently there was no un-
healthy desire for martyrdom. True, a number of the martyrs
did express themselves in a way which might seem to indicate
a desire of this kind. For instance, Adrian Pan wrote that he
never had a happier day in a dungeon of *Het Steen* prison at
Antwerp than the day when he was sentenced to death. And
Julius Bernarts said: "When the sentence of death was pronounced over me, my joy was full, since my redemption was so
near." Others also have expressed themselves in a similar
way.[78] But such utterances must be considered in the light of
the plain fact that there was absolutely no hope for liberation
from their inhuman imprisonment during which they were, as
a rule, at intervals subjected to the most cruel torture. To be
apprehended and imprisoned meant certain death for them
and it was only natural that they did not desire their time of
dreadful suffering to be prolonged.

Nevertheless, they were fully resigned to the will of the Lord. "My dear friends, thus I am still minded, and I so love my Lord and my God that, if I could save my life by thinking a thought, which I knew would not please the Lord, I would rather die than to think such a thought." An evidence of the absence of an unsound desire for martyrdom is also found in the fact that they were possessed of an ardent love for their kin. Of this there is abundant proof in their letters. In the letters written in the prisons husbands often take a touching farewell from their wives, and wives from their husbands, or fathers and mothers from their children.[79]

Invariably, when the martyrs were taken to the torture chamber to be laid on the rack, their greatest anxiety was that they, in order to have the excruciating pain alleviated, might yield to the demand to betray their brethren. Therefore they sometimes expressed the desire that they might know less about their brethren and their whereabouts. Many of their letters from the prisons contain warnings against too great inquisitiveness concerning the names and dwelling places of those of like faith.

The records contain many testimonies that under the most severe tortures no name came over their lips. They testified that the Lord kept their mouths sealed, while the inquisitors did all in their power "to drive out the dumb devil," as they said.[80]

An Anabaptist chronicler, after recording the death of 2173 brethren and sisters who gave their lives for the sake of the faith continues as follows:

No human being was able to take away out of their hearts what they had experienced, such zealous lovers of God were they. The fire of God burned within them. They would die the bitterest death, yea they would die ten deaths rather than to forsake the divine truth which they had espoused.

They had drunk of the water which is flowing from God's sanctuary, yea of the water of life. They realized that God helped them to bear the cross and to overcome the bitterness of death. The fire of God burned within them. Their tent they had pitched not here upon earth, but in eternity, and of their faith they had a foundation and assurance. Their faith blossomed like a lily, their loyalty as a rose, their piety and candor as the flower of the garden of God. The angel of the Lord battled for them that they could not be deprived of the helmet of salvation. Therefore they have borne all torture and agony without fear. The things of this world they counted in their holy mind only as shadows, having the assurance of greater things. They were thus drawn unto God that they knew nothing, sought nothing, desired nothing, loved nothing but God alone. Therefore they had more patience in their suffering than their enemies in tormenting them.

From the shedding of such innocent blood arose Christians everywhere, brothers all, for all this persecution did not take place without fruit. Many were moved thereby to give thought to these things, and to order their thinking, and doing and living in the light of the future, so many indeed that finally the authorities in many places would no longer execute the martyrs publicly, as for instance in the Tyrol, but condemned and slew them secretly by night so that the people could not know of it.

In some places they literally filled the prisons and dungeons with them, as did the Count Palatine. The persecutors thought they could dampen and extinguish the fire of God. But the prisoners sang in their prisons and rejoiced so that the enemies outside became much more fearful than the prisoners and did not know what to do with them. Many others lay for years in dungeons and prisons and endured all sorts of pain and torture. Others had holes burned through their cheeks and were then let free.

The rest, who escaped all this, were driven from one land to another, from one town to the next. They had to be like owls and bitterns which dare not be seen by daylight. Often they had to hide away in rocks and cliffs, in wild forests, in caves and holes in the earth to save their lives. They were sought by catchpolls and dogs, hunted and were taken down like birds. All were without guilt, without the least wicked deed, since they neither did nor desired to do any one the least harm or injury.

Everywhere they were cursed and slandered and lied about scandalously. It was said of them that they could bring people under their control by giving them to drink from a little flask. Scandalous lies were told about them, such as having their women in common. They were slandered devilishly as Anabaptists, seducers, rioters, fanatics. Everywhere were issued imperial, royal and princely mandates, decrees, and commands against them.

Many were talked to in wonderful ways, often day and night. They were argued with, with great cunning and cleverness, with many sweet and smooth words, by monks and priests, by doctors of theology, with much false testimony, with threats and scolding and mockery, yea, with lies and grievous slanders against the brotherhood, but none of these things moved them or made them falter.

Some sang praises to God while they lay in grievous imprisonment, as though they were in great joy. Some did the same as they were being led to the place of execution and death, singing joyfully with uplifted voice that it rang out loud. Others stepped to the place of death with a smile on their lips, praising God that they were accounted worthy to die the death of the Christian hero, and would not have preferred even to die a natural death.

Menno Simons wrote concerning the persecution in the Netherlands:[81]

Those who fear God must bear great persecution, as we witness with our eyes. How many pious children of God have the magistrates within a few years deprived of their homes and possessions, confiscated their property, and committed the proceeds to the bottomless imperial money chests; how many have they driven out of cities and countries and put to the stocks and torture. The poor orphans were turned destitute into the streets. Some they have executed by hanging, some they have tortured with inhuman tyranny, and afterwards choked with cords at the stake. Some they roasted and burned alive. Some they have killed with the sword and given them to the fowls of the air to devour. Some they have cast to the fishes. Some had their houses destroyed. Some had their feet cut off, one of whom I have seen and conversed with. Others wander about here and there, in want, homelessness, and affliction, in mountains and deserts, in holes and caves of the earth, as Paul says. They must flee with their wives and little children from one country to another, from one city to another. They are hated, abused, slandered and lied about by all men.

While large numbers of Mennonites were put to death in Friesland and other northern provinces of the Netherlands, the persecution was more severe in the southern provinces, particularly in Flanders and Brabant (modern Belgium). In both the northern and southern provinces new "blood-decrees" (as they were sometimes called) were from time to time published, ordering the severest persecution of the Anabaptists, but these decrees were heeded and carried out more stringently in the southern than in the northern provinces. Within a few decades the worst storms of persecution had subsided in the North, while in Flanders and Brabant the persecution continued unabated. The Mennonites in the latter provinces, who escaped the sword of the executioner, fled into the northern provinces.

At no other place in the Netherlands were so large numbers of Mennonite confessors executed as in Antwerp, "that den of murderers" as this city is referred to in one of the martyrs' hymns. The Mennonite church in this city was very strong, being estimated to have numbered at one time about two thousand members. Those who could be apprehended were imprisoned in the dungeons of the castle called *Het Steen.* This castle is located on an elevation close to the Scheldt river. The dungeons under the castle consist of about a dozen low compartments, from about four by seven to sixteen by sixteen feet in size. The light of day does not reach this dreary place and there is, with two exceptions, no opening whatever for ventilation, except in the doors leading from one compartment into another. At the foot of the stairway leading to the dungeons there is a large flat stone covering the opening of a channel about three feet in diameter down into the Scheldt river. A martyr's hymn makes mention of three Mennonite women who, in 1557, were imprisoned in *Het Steen,* and whose bodies, identified by their clothing, were seen floating down the river toward the sea.

Mennonite prisoners in Antwerp and other cities of Flanders were treated with the greatest cruelty. A number of them, in letters written from their prisons, said that telling an untruth would have secured their release. This means that they could have denied that they were ever baptized upon the confession of their faith. Because they had admitted this, they were sure of being condemned to death. Recantation would not prevent their execution, after they had once confessed that they had been baptized. Gillis of Aachen, a Mennonite prisoner at Antwerp, formerly an elder, was sentenced to death by fire. He weakened and recanted his faith. In consequence the sentence was commuted from death by fire to beheading. He was executed on July 10, 1557.

The Anabaptists, as already indicated, were persecuted in Protestant as well as in Roman Catholic provinces and countries. In Saxony and other Lutheran states Anabaptists who refused to recant were put to death. In one extraordinary case an Anabaptist—his name was Frederick Erbe—was imprisoned for life in Saxony. His execution was prevented by peculiar circumstances. In 1531 he was seized and arrested in the county of Hausbreitenbach. This county was not an integral part of Saxony but was under the joint jurisdiction of Saxony and Hesse. A sentence of capital punishment could be pronounced only with the consent of the rulers of both provinces. The Elector of Saxony insisted on passing the death sentence on Frederick Erbe, while Landgrave Philip of Hesse persistently refused to give his consent to so cruel a punishment.

The landgrave had scruples against capital punishment in matters of faith; he did not approve of severer measures against the Anabaptists than imprisonment and banishment. The Elector of Saxony, on the contrary, claimed scruples of conscience against dealing so leniently with Anabaptists, as the ruler of Hesse proposed—a striking evidence that conscience without enlightenment is an unsafe guide. In letters to Landgrave Philip, the Elector pointed out repeatedly that the edict of Speier demanded the greatest severity against the Anabaptists, and that he had given his vote for passing the edict, and it had been ratified in successive sessions of the Reichstag. The Elector of Saxony had asked the opinion of his advisors and of the theologians in Wittenberg who had expressed themselves in favor of capital punishment to root out Anabaptism. Though both Luther and Melanchthon approved of the death sentence against the Anabaptists, Landgrave Philip, himself a Lutheran, stood firm in the disapproval of such cruel severity.

In consequence, Frederick Erbe, after having been subjected to torture by Saxon magistrates, was kept in prison for seventeen years, namely, until his death in 1549. His first prison was a remote tower in the city wall of Eisenach. Here he found it possible, through a window, to converse with and admonish his brethren, some of whom gathered here at times in the quiet of the night. Two of his friends were seized here by officers of the law, and executed, in November, 1535. Erbe was then incarcerated in the dungeon of the rear tower of Wartburg castle, the castle in which Luther, less than a score of years before, had translated the New Testament Scriptures. However, while Luther had been taken to the Wartburg for his personal protection, Frederick Erbe was thrown into a dungeon there for the reason that he could not approve of some of the teachings of the Lutheran state church. Erbe consistently refused to buy his release from prison by the repudiation of his convictions. After his death the warden of the prison gave him the testimony that he had lived a good life and had always been obedient.

At Rotterdam in Holland, in 1558, three Mennonite men were to be burned at the stake. The executioner, who seems to have been intoxicated, caused great suffering to the first of the three, whereupon the people who witnessed the scene, drove him away and liberated the three prisoners.

The severest storms of persecution, as described above, befell the evangelical Anabaptists in South Germany before the rise of the Mennonite Church in the Netherlands. Nevertheless the number of Mennonite martyrs in the Netherlands is likewise very large. Here, as in Switzerland and South Germany, the brotherhood rose and expanded under severe persecution. The number of Mennonite martyrs in the Netherlands is estimated at about 1,500.

Menno Simons wrote concerning the tolerant attitude of some of the rulers and magistrates:[82]

In short, dear reader, if the merciful Lord had not, in His great love, tempered the hearts of some of the rulers and magistrates, but had let them proceed according to the instigations and cruel preaching of their theologians, no pious person would survive. But yet a few magistrates are found who, notwithstanding the words and writings of all theologians, tolerate the fugitives and at times show them mercy, for which we will forever give praise to God, the Most High, and also return our thanks in all love to such kind and discreet rulers.

The first country to grant the Mennonites toleration was Holland. The last martyr in that country was Reitse Ayses who was burned at the stake in the city of Leeuwarden in Friesland, in 1574. At the time when Prince William of Orange came into power the Mennonites had become numerous in Holland. He was a prudent, tolerant ruler who clearly saw the unreasonableness of persecuting the Mennonites. Even some of their antagonists did not deny that they were useful citizens. The very presence of the numerous Mennonites was an unanswerable argument for the refutation of the theory that a state tolerating various religious creeds could not prosper.

While the central governments of the states and provinces, as a rule, still insisted on enforcing and carrying out the edicts against the Anabaptists, some of the minor authorities, such as the magistrates of certain cities in Holland and Northern Germany, began to take a more lenient attitude toward the Mennonites. They had in a measure become acquainted with them and had been led to recognize the cruelty and unreasonableness of the persecution. While such magistrates would not have permitted the Mennonite people to hold public meetings, they were willing to overlook and ignore their presence, so long as they could do so without incurring danger to themselves.

Leonhard Schiemer, an Anabaptist minister who suffered martyrdom on January 14, 1528, at Rattenberg in the Tyrol, describes conditions as follows:[83]

> Thine holy place they have destroyed,
>   Thine altars overthrown,
> And reaching forth their bloody hands,
>   Have foully slain thine own.
> And we alone, thy little flock,
>   The few who still remain,
> Are exiles wandering through the land
>   In sorrow and in pain.
>
> We are, alas, like scattered sheep,
>   The shepherd not in sight,
> Each far away from home and hearth,
>   And, like the birds of night
> That hide away in rocky clefts,
>   We have our rocky hold,
> Yet, near at hand, as for the birds,
>   There waits the hunter bold.
>
> We wander in the forests dark,
>   With dogs upon our track;
> And, like the captive silent lamb,
>   Men bring us, prisoners, back.
> They point to us amid the throng,
>   And with their taunts offend;
> And long to let the sharpened ax
>   On heretics descend.

Caspar Schwenckfeld wrote: "I am being maligned, by both preachers and others, as being an Anabaptist, and indeed all who lead a truly devoted Christian life are now almost everywhere given the reproachful name 'Anabaptist.'" Johann Valentine Andreae (1586-1654), a theologian of a Protestant state church, wrote, "Whoever seeks now to lead an irreproachable life is called a fanatic, a Schwenckfelder, an Anabaptist."

Heinrich Bullinger, in his larger work against the Swiss Brethren, stated clearly that pious members of the state church were called Anabaptists. He says: "There are also those who in reality are not Anabaptists but have a pronounced aversion to the sensuality and frivolity of the world, and reprove sin and vice; they are therefore called or misnamed Anabaptists; such should indeed not be molested [by the authorities] in any way."

Almost from the earliest years of the history of the Mennonite Church leaflets and booklets were published, giving accounts of the martyrdom of persons who gave their lives in testimony of the truth. Some of these booklets also contained the confessions and letters of the martyrs.

The first Mennonite Book of Martyrs has the title, *Het Offer des Heeren* (*The Offering of the Lord*). The title was chosen for the reason that the book treats of the "offered-up children of God." The first edition of this book was printed in 1561. The book contains confessions, letters, and hymns of many whose martyrdom it relates, as well as hymns describing their imprisonment and execution. It is the martyrology of the Dutch and Flemish Mennonite martyrs and the repeated editions of the work are an indication of the esteem in which this book was held by the early Mennonites. No other human book was so highly prized by them.[84]

Renewed efforts for the collection of material pertaining to Mennonite martyrology were made by Jacques Outerman of Haarlem, who in 1599, made a trip to Flanders for this purpose. In consequence Hans de Ries and others published an enlarged work bearing the title, *History of the Martyrs or True Witnesses of Jesus Christ.*[85]

The most important work on Mennonite martyrology is the large volume published in 1660 by Thieleman Janz van Braght, at Dortrecht, Holland, under the title *Martyrs' Mirror.*[86] Van Braght's aim was to record the story of the martyrs of the evangelical Anabaptists of all countries to the extent of the information obtainable. The title of this work is aptly chosen. The book reflects the inner life, the spirit, and the motives of the martyrs. There are, as a matter of fact, the accounts of their martyrdom and in many instances the preceding imprisonment, often in noisome dungeons, frequently also the description of the cruel tortures to which they were subjected. Of particular importance and value are their confessions and the numerous letters written in the prisons, which are contained in this work, and which present a mirror of the inner life of the martyrs. Many of these letters breathe the spirit of deepest piety and consecration, of immovable conviction and glowing certainty, of ardent love to God and the brotherhood. They express the willingness to bear the cross of persecution, to suffer and, if need be, to die for the faith.

CHAPTER 35

MISSIONARY ZEAL AMONG THE ANABAPTISTS

The Mennonite Church at the beginning was pre-eminently a missionary church. This was one of the reasons for its rapid spread. In that period there were no special mission organizations, yet the church was engaged in aggressive evangelistic work. In the earliest years of its history its congregations, like the primitive Christian congregations, consisted of men and women who were noted for their zeal for propagating the gospel. Of the first Christians in Jerusalem it is stated that, when they were scattered abroad by persecution, "they went everywhere preaching the word." This does not mean that all preached in the sense as preaching is generally understood today. They did not all conduct public services. They all considered it their duty to spread the good news of salvation through Jesus Christ.

A certain writer says that as one who has been in a shipwreck will tell the story of how he was rescued, so the early Christians related that they had found personal salvation in Christ. The missionary spirit was very much in evidence. The same may be said of the early Mennonite Church. This was one of the reasons why some of the state church leaders did not approve of exiling and scattering the evangelical Anabaptists. Their antagonists were aware that such measures of persecution would only result in their further spread. The early Brethren insisted that the life of the membership of the church should in all its aspects be of a distinctly Christian character and influence; their whole life should be a distinct testimony for Christ.

In the first period of the history of the Mennonite brotherhood their principal fields of labor were Switzerland, South Germany, and Austria. The work of spreading the gospel was carried on under indescribable difficulties. They were in constant danger of apprehension and death. Their willingness to endure persecution was evidence, however, of their firm conviction that their message was the gospel truth. They endeavored to reach the common people, and their word of testi-

314

mony, being spoken from sincere conviction, made a deep impression on their hearers. Sometimes their efforts resulted in the organization of a congregation within a few days after the arrival of a messenger of the gospel at a given place.

For reasons previously stated the preachers of the Swiss Brethren and Mennonites were practically the only missionaries of that time. The historian C. A. Cornelius says correctly that in Catholic countries, where Protestantism was persecuted, the field was left entirely to the Anabaptists who did not shrink from dangers of torture and death. Pilgram Marpeck, in 1532, said of the preachers of the state church, that they preached only in places to which the protection by the Protestant government extended "and not freely under the cross of Christ"; he gave this as one of the reasons why their gospel did not bring the expected fruit. Again, Menno Simons in his writings says repeatedly that he was constrained in conscience, through love to God and the unsaved, to risk his life in the endeavor to spread the evangelical truth.

A chronicler of the Hutterian Brethren wrote concerning their missionary work:

The witnesses to the truth who were sent forth by the brotherhood, gave testimony earnestly and steadfastly to the Word of the Lord, by their life and work, by word and deed. They spoke with power of the kingdom of God, showing that all men must repent, be converted, and turn to God from the vanity of this world and its unrighteousness, from a sinful, vile, and wanton life. To all such work God gave His blessing, so that it was carried on with joy.

Menno Simons, as well as other evangelical Anabaptist and Mennonite leaders, were in a real sense missionaries. Menno was engaged in the work of spreading the gospel through preaching, teaching, and personal work, as well as through the printed page. On the point of the missionary calling of the church Menno Simons' views differed from those of Luther, Zwingli and Calvin. These reformers held that Christ's commission to preach the gospel to all nations concerned only the apostles. Menno, as is clear from his writings, recognized that the great commission is binding for the Christian church of all periods. It is impossible to estimate in numbers the visible results of Menno's labors. There is no record of the baptisms which he performed. However, his co-worker Leonard Bouwens, who had the oversight of the congregations in a large part of Holland and North Germany, kept a list of persons baptized by him. This list is still preserved. It shows that from 1551 to 1582 Leonard Bouwens baptized 10,252 persons. Obviously the greater number of these were not of Mennonite parentage but were won through special effort put forth by local congregations.

Following are excerpts from Menno Simons' writings on the subject of missionary work:

In the second place we seek and desire with yearning, ardent hearts, yea at the cost of our life and blood that the holy Gospel of Jesus Christ and His apostles, which alone is the true doctrine and will remain until Jesus Christ will come again in the clouds, may be taught and preached throughout all the world, as the Lord Jesus Christ commanded His disciples in His last words which He addressed to them on earth.[87]

This is my only joy and the desire of my heart that I may extend the borders of the kingdom of God, make known the truth, reprove sin, teach righteousness, feed the hungry souls with the Word of the Lord, lead the stray sheep into the right path and win many souls for the Lord through His Spirit, power, and grace.[88] Therefore we seek, to the extent of our opportunity, to make known and proclaim to all mankind the grace of God which has appeared, and His great love toward us, that they may experience with the same joy and renewing of the Spirit, and know and taste with all saints how sweet and good and kind the Lord is to whom we have come. To this end we preach as much as opportunity and possibility affords, both in day time and by night, in houses and in fields, in forests and wildernesses, in this land and abroad, in prison and bonds, in the water, the fire and on the scaffold, on the gallows and upon the wheel, before lords and princes, orally and by writing, at the risk of possessions and life, as we have done these many years without ceasing.[89]

A contemporary chronicler of the early Hutterian Brethren in Moravia wrote concerning their missionary work:

The Christian mission work is carried on among us according to the command of Christ: "As my Father hath sent me, even so send I you," and again: "I have chosen you and ordained you, that ye should go forth and bring fruit." Accordingly, ministers of the Gospel and their assistants are annually sent forth into the various countries to those who desire to amend their lives and are asking for the truth. Such are brought to the brotherhood in Moravia, in spite of hangman and headsman, notwithstanding the fact that many were apprehended while on their way to Moravia and suffered martyrdom.

The oldest extant Christian missionary hymn, containing twenty-three verses of eight lines each, was written about 1563 by a Hutterite brother in Moravia.[90]

An indication of the serious purpose of the early Swiss Brethren to live a life of consecration to the service of God and their neighbor is found in their teaching and practice regarding the use of earthly possessions. The principle of Christian stewardship and Christian brotherhood, as held by them, was more than an abstract theory; they were seriously determined to carry it into practice. It is known from Martin Butzer's writings that the Brethren believed it inconsistent for Christians to live in luxury while there are those who do not have the necessaries of life and to whom help could be given. Butzer criticized the Brethren for holding such views which he believed extreme and unwarranted.

Hans Leopold who suffered martyrdom in 1528 at Augsburg, said of the Brethren that "if they know of any one that is in need, whether or not he is a member of their church, they believe it their duty, out of love to God, to render him help and aid." Heinrich Seiler, who in 1535 was executed by drowning at Bern in Switzerland, said: "I do not believe it wrong that a Christian has property of his own, but yet he is nothing more than a steward." Heinrich Bullinger, in his larger work against the Swiss Brethren, made the charge that they were of the opinion that to be rich is inconsistent with Christian principles ("*rych syn sye böss*"). While this charge cannot be substantiated from the source material, they obviously believed that in the acquisition of material wealth a point may be reached where further accumulation would be a violation of Jesus' teaching on wealth, being contrary to the Christian principle of stewardship.

A testimony to the point under consideration is also found in a book of the early Hutterian Brethren, in which is stated that among the Swiss Brethren one of the questions addressed to applicants for baptism was, "whether they consecrated themselves with all their temporal possessions to the service of God and His people." In 1557 a member of the established Protestant church of Strasburg in Alsace visited a meeting of the Swiss Brethren near that city. A number of persons were received into the Church by baptism on that occasion. Among the questions addressed to the applicants before the ordinance was administered, was this, "Whether they, if necessity required it, would devote all their possessions to the service of the brotherhood, and would not fail any member that is in need, if they were able to render aid."

Heinrich Bullinger's writings contain various corroborations of these statements concerning the position of the Swiss Brethren on the principle of Christian stewardship. He says for example that, according to their teaching, "every good Christian is under duty before God from motives of love to use, if need be, all his possessions to supply the necessaries of life, to any of his brethren who are in need. The Lutheran church historian Paul Tschackert speaks of the evangelical Anabaptists as "a voluntary Christian fellowship for manifesting the Christian spirit in the practice of brotherly love." Again, a contemporary writer of the early Anabaptists says of the Brethren at Augsburg in Swabia: "In their brotherhood there was in evidence the purpose to render each other the greatest possible help from motives of brotherly love."

The first Mennonite foreign mission society was established in the year 1847 at Amsterdam by a small number of Dutch Mennonites. In 1851 this society sent its first missionary, John Peter Jansz, to Java, Dutch East Indies, and in 1871 Heinrich Dirks, of Gnadenfeld, South Russia, began work at Pakanten, island of Sumatra, under this society. At the time of the beginning of the World War these missions were fairly prosperous. Most of the financial support, as well as nearly all the missionaries, came from the Mennonite colonies in South Russia. In recent years a very considerable part of the needed financial support of these missions is supplied by the congregations of Germany, Switzerland, and France. The missionaries—six in number—are of the last named countries, while the three missionary physicians are Netherlanders.

CHAPTER 36

BELIEVERS' BAPTISM

In the period of the Reformation the Anabaptists stood practically alone in the practice of the baptism of believers. The almost universal practice of infant baptism in that period was due in the main to two reasons. The principal reason was that both the Roman Catholic Church and the Protestant churches, as organized by the leading reformers, were state churches. These churches were united with the state and comprised the whole population by force of the civil law. Dissent from the teaching and practice of the state churches was not permitted but was severely persecuted. For such churches the practice of infant baptism was absolutely necessary. The second reason for the general prevalence of infant baptism was that both the Catholic and the Lutheran churches taught baptismal regeneration, the doctrine of salvation through baptism. The import of this doctrine is that all baptized persons are saved. This teaching was often reported in the writings of the Anabaptists.

It is seen then that infant baptism was firmly established in popular Christendom. Questioning it was generally supposed to be an indication of serious doctrinal unsoundness. All opponents of the baptism of infants were considered to be of one and the same party with the fanatical, revolutionary Anabaptist sect of the city of Münster. After the rise of the Münsterites, in 1533, the designation "Anabaptist" was often used as a synonym for "Münsterite." It was commonly supposed that all who disowned infant baptism were in the final analysis Münsterites.

Now, such an adverse attitude toward believers' baptism is the more remarkable in view of the striking weakness of the argumentation advanced for infant baptism. The defenders of the baptism of infants failed to give a worth-while reason for it aside from the argument based on the unscriptural doctrine of baptismal regeneration. The truth is that the leading reformers found themselves unable to give a definition of the meaning of baptism which was satisfactory from their own viewpoint, or which, in other words, would make infant baptism excusable. Both Martin Luther and Ulrich Zwingli, as well as Martin Butzer and others of their associates, defined baptism in a way which in reality called for the baptism of believers.

No other author of the Reformation period wrote so much in the defense of infant baptism as Ulrich Zwingli. Nevertheless, in his controversy with the Anabaptists, Zwingli was forced to admit that infant baptism is not taught in the New Testament Scriptures. As indicated in another place, he publicly confessed, in 1525, that he was formerly of the opinion that "it would be far better" to discontinue the practice of infant baptism. Referring to this confession of Zwingli, Balthasar Hubmaier wrote: "This was your opinion; you have set forth this view in writing and have preached it from the pulpit; many hundreds of people have heard it out of your own mouth."

Zwingli made the statement just quoted regarding his former disapproval of infant baptism in his *Book on Baptism* which is a defense of infant baptism. In the same book he gives a noteworthy definition of the meaning of baptism, a definition which would in reality call for the baptism of believers. He says: "Baptism is a rite which lays definite obligations on those who accept it and indicate that they are determined to mend their lives and follow Christ." In his reply to this definition, Balthasar Hubmaier makes this significant statement; "God be praised; the truth has at last come to the light."

The Reformed church historian Johann Martin Usteri, wrote: "Zwingli, although he defended infant baptism, looked upon baptism as an act of confession and of acceptance of definite duty." Even in his later writings Zwingli defined baptism in agreement with this view, thus leaving no ground for the baptism of infants. Again Usteri says concerning Zwingli's argument for infant baptism: "The attempt to justify infant baptism as altogether scriptural misled Zwingli to various acts of exegetical violence." And furthermore the same author says: "The impulses which led him in this instance were not the result of theological thinking but had their origin in the needs of the church." Zwingli's program called for the establishment of a church that was united with the state and comprised the whole population. For such a church the practice of infant baptism was indispensable.

Professor Walther Koehler says: "In the last analysis Zwingli could maintain infant baptism only as a concession to human weakness and historical development." Professor Johann Loserth made this statement with reference to the Anabaptist controversy: "On the basis of his own premises Zwingli was now opposed by his former associates, and only by carrying the struggle over into the political field was he able to maintain his position." His opponents were silenced through the strong arm of the civil authorities. Since Zwingli did not hold the doctrine of baptismal regeneration, he could not make use of the foremost argument of Catholic and Lutheran theologians for infant baptism. According to his own repeated statements it was through his controversy with the Anabaptists that he was led to discard the doctrine of salvation through baptism.

Martin Luther based his principal argument for infant baptism on the supposition that infants are believers. But since infants are unable to hear the Word of God and accept its message, he found it impossible to say wherein consisted the faith of infants. Luther wrote: "Baptism should be administered to no one except those who personally believe and no one should be baptized except on his own faith." "Now if we can not prove that infants believe for themselves and have faith, then my honest judgment and advice is straightway to cease, the sooner the better, and nevermore baptize an infant."[91]

Philip Melanchthon, Luther's most distinguished assistant as a reformer, was confronted for the first time by the question of the scripturalness of infant baptism, in 1521, at the time of Luther's sojourn at Wartburg castle. The so-called Zwickau Prophets came to Wittenberg at that time. While they never were Anabaptists, they held that infant baptism is unscriptural and that the faith of the church is not an acceptable substitute for the faith of the one to be baptized. On January 1, 1522, Melanchthon wrote to George Spalatin, a Saxon official, informing him that these men advocated the opinions just stated regarding baptism. "These two opinions," Melanchthon said in this letter, "are verily not to be lightly regarded, and will probably cause difficulty to people more learned than I, as well as to the masses. Well, I had expected that the devil would touch us at a weak place. . . . Not without cause, it seems to me, has this question of baptism moved me." Very soon Melanchthon discarded his scruples against infant baptism, however.

Martin Butzer, of Strasburg, confessed freely that "the baptism of believers would be far more in accord with the practice of the early church and also with the Scriptures in general." He defined baptism as "an outward testimony by which those who are baptized testify that they are decided wholly to deny the old man and all the world and to die unto sin." Butzer expressed regret that "at present the usage prevails that people are baptized in their infancy and cannot confess the faith when baptism is administered to them." He consented, however, to the establishment of a state church, and consequently could not dispense with infant baptism.

Professor Paul Tschackert, a Lutheran church historian, says that the greatest uncertainty prevailed among the Lutherans and Zwinglians in the question of the proper defense of infant baptism. "It is now almost unanimously admitted that in 'this controversy the opponents of infant baptism were only apparently silenced, not refuted," says Professor Friedrich Niffold; "both Zwingli and Luther saw themselves compelled, in view of the objections of the Anabaptists, to modify their original position whose implications clearly favored the view of the Anabaptists."

As already intimated, criticism of infant baptism was widespread before the beginning of the Anabaptist movement. As early as the first part of the year 1522 Ulrich Hugwald, of the Swiss city of Basel, who somewhat later was a lecturer at the university of the same city, wrote a number of theses defending baptism upon the confession of faith. There is conclusive evidence that in the early spring of 1523 Balthasar Hubmaier had the abolition of infant baptism under consideration. On July 21, 1523, Benedict Burgauer, the leading minister of St. Gall, stated in a letter that he had encountered those "who would not baptize infants that do not have faith." Other theologians who had expressed doubt as to infant baptism were Wolfgang Capito, Caspar Schwenckfeld, Martin Cellarius, Joachim Vadian, Sebastian Castellio, Michael Servetus, Johann Campanus, Sebastian Franck, William Farel, Andreas Carlstadt, Eberhard Weidensee.

CHAPTER 37

LIBERTY OF CONSCIENCE

Whoever is acquainted with the story of the persecutions of the Anabaptists and Mennonites is aware that the Reformation movement of the sixteenth century, as represented by the leading Protestant reformers, did not result in an advancement of religious toleration. Nevertheless, as has been repeatedly noted, Martin Luther and Ulrich Zwingli, in the earlier years of their reformatory labors, defended the principle of liberty of conscience, and denounced all persecution. Later, they, as well as John Calvin, consented to a close union of church and state. The consummation of this union meant persecution for the dissenters. The state agreed to force the creed of the state church upon the population and make the demands of the church obligatory for all. The evangelical Anabaptists and Mennonites stood alone in the defense of the principle of liberty of conscience.

Liberty of conscience, as interpreted by the Mennonite church fathers, did not mean a general toleration within the church. It did not mean that a religious body, or Christian church, should not exercise the right to stand for a definite creed. The fathers of the Mennonite Church took liberty of conscience to imply the separation of church and state and the rejection of all persecution. They saw clearly that the Christian faith cannot be forced upon any one, and that the use of coercion in this respect is out of place. The early Mennonites believed that it is a mistake for the state to demand doctrinal qualifications for citizenship. They held that the state as such is a secular, not a religious institution, and that a non-Christian may yet be a law-abiding citizen. And yet, since Christianity is decidedly conducive to good citizenship, they held it to be fully consistent for the state to take a favorable attitude toward religion, without however favoring those of a particular creed. At the same time, for membership in the church some doctrinal qualifications must necessarily be demanded if the church is to maintain its true character. An evidence that the early Mennonites did not hold the principle of absolute individualism or doctrinal indifference in matters of faith, is the fact that they endured cruel persecution and many suffered death for their faith. A recent author, though writing from the liberal point of view, speaks of their "immovable conviction of faith." Now, an immovable conviction of faith is the opposite of doctrinal indifference. It implies the acceptance of a definite, positive content of faith. The principle of absolute individualism in matters of faith will never bear such fruit. The Mennonite martyrs had the firm conviction that the definite faith which they unitedly held was the truth of God, as revealed through His Word and confirmed by personal experience.

The assertion that the Mennonites tolerated any and all religious teachings within the church, is incorrect, indeed surprising. It betrays a striking lack of acquaintance with the writings of the Mennonite church fathers. Menno Simons expressed himself frequently concerning the paramount importance of true scriptural doctrine. So far from regarding the fundamentals of the faith as open questions, or as suppositions which the church may accept or reject, he held that the rejection of the fundamentals of the faith meant the repudiation of the Christian religion. He says for example that the denial of the deity of Christ is a terrible blasphemy, a curse, and an abomination. Both Menno Simons and his most prominent collaborator, Dirck Philips, stated in many places in their writings that church discipline is not only to be used to correct moral failing and offensive conduct, but also in cases of persistent heretical teaching. "The true reason why this cutting off or exclusion from the church is so earnestly taught and commanded in the Scripture by Jesus Christ and His holy apostles," says Menno, "is, first, for the sake of false doctrine and secondly for sinful, carnal life." The ministers Adam Pastor, David Joris and others, were expelled by Menno Simons and his brethren on account of persistently defending unscriptural doctrine.

The Socinians (Unitarians) of Poland, in 1592, through Christopher Osterod, one of their ministers, addressed a letter to the Swiss Mennonites expressing the hope that they would consent to a union with them. The Swiss Brethren, in their reply to this letter, emphatically declared the teaching of the Socinians to be unscriptural and unacceptable. The Brethren addressed them as "dear men" and stated that they could not receive them as brothers in case of a visit by them.

The Mennonites of the Netherlands and the Hutterian Brethren of Moravia were also approached by the Socinians with a view of bringing about a union. This was in both instances refused them. Hans de Ries, the spokesman of the Waterlandian Mennonites and principal defender of scriptural orthodoxy among the Mennonites in the Netherlands against the Socinians, wrote a book entitled *Clear Proof of the Preexistence and Deity of Jesus Christ,* and declared that a union with the Socinians was altogether impossible.

The evangelical Anabaptists and early Mennonites accepted the Scriptures as the Word of God. They believed that certain truths (doctrines) and historical facts (such as the Incarnation and Redemption) constitute the fundamentals of the Christian faith; hence it was an impossibility for them to take an attitude of doctrinal indifference and general religious toleration within the church.

Erroneous as is the view that the Mennonites stood for religious individualism and doctrinal liberty within the church, they plainly taught the need of a separation of church and state; they condemned all interference of the state in matters of doctrine and religion. Concerning their position on this point, we have a comprehensive statement of outstanding value, given by Heinrich Bullinger in his larger work against the Swiss Brethren which was published in 1561. Bullinger quotes various pertinent statements made by the Brethren.

According to Bullinger the Swiss Brethren asserted:

One cannot and should not use force to compel any one to accept the faith, for faith is a free gift of God.

It is wrong to compel any one by force or coercion to embrace the faith, or to put to death any one for the sake of his erring faith. It is an error that in the church any sword other than that of the divine Word should be used.

The secular kingdom should be separated from the church, and no secular ruler should exercise authority in the church.

The Lord has commanded simply to preach the Gospel, and not to compel any one by force to accept it.

It is the work of the great Judge to separate the tares from the good seed. This will be done by Christ at the last day only. For when in the parable of the tares among the wheat the servants came to their master saying, "Wilt thou that we go and gather in the tares?" his reply was, "Nay, lest while you gather up the tares, you root up also the wheat with them. Let both grow together until the harvest; then

I will tell the reapers to gather together the tares and bind them in bundles to be burned." And since the field is the world and the tares are the children of the wicked one, or of the evil doctrine, and the Lord has clearly ordered, "Let both grow together," therefore the government should not undertake to destroy the tares by punishment and death.

Paul gives definite instruction as to the attitude which the church should take toward a heretic, and says, "A man that is an heretic after the first and second admonition exclude." So Paul instructs the church to exclude a heretic (Titus 3:10), not to torture, maltreat, or kill him.

The true church of Christ has the characteristic that it suffers or endures persecution but does not inflict persecution upon any one.

To put to death an erring man before he has repented means to destroy his soul. Therefore one should not kill him but wait for his conversion, lest both body and soul be destroyed. Ofttimes a man who is in fatal error, forsakes it and turns to the truth.

Bullinger records these statements of the Swiss Brethren as charges against them. Thereby he has rendered the student of Mennonite history a distinct service by recording the views of the Swiss Brethren on liberty of conscience. He condemns these views as erroneous, and urges the need of severest persecution against those who held such "heretical" views. After quoting the Swiss Brethren, as just stated, he added his refutation point for point to these statements. Furthermore he attempts to justify the persecution. He says:

There are those who say that by approving and defending such punishment [as was meted out to the Brethren], we simply press the sword into the hands of those who have always persecuted and put to death evangelical people, and who will now storm and rage against them the more furiously. But those who assert this are doing us an injustice. For, the fact that some do misuse the sword in such a way [against Bullinger's party] is no valid argument that it should not be used at all.

Bullinger then proceeds to state that to persecute and kill "evangelical people" is "a grievous, great sin which is crying to God for vengeance," but at the same time he insists that to put to death Anabaptists is a necessary, commendable work. "Since we admonish the Christian governments not to tolerate the dissenters," he says further, "the Anabaptists call us men of blood who put to death good people who refuse to believe what we believe and practice." These statements of Bullinger represent the position of virtually all the Protestant reformers of the state church type.

In the debate of Zofingen in the canton Bern, Switzerland, (1532) the Swiss Brethren said:

Clearly the Lord has instituted in His church no severer punishment than excommunication, which was also practiced by Paul. If now you would inflict punishment according to the Law, which is based on justice, the adulterer would have to be put to death without mercy and could not be spared, even if he repented. Thus the Law demands punishment according to strict justice, but the Gospel according to love by excommunication for repentance. . . . Therefore we do not admit nor confess that the church has power to use the sword, or to mete out punishment beyond excommunication.

From Menno Simons' writings many quotations could be given indicating that he consistently defended the same principle of liberty of conscience.

CHAPTER 38

MENNO SIMONS ON AVOIDANCE

The practice of shunning the excommunicated church members was unknown among the early evangelical Anabaptists (Swiss Brethren) before the rise of the Mennonite Church in the Netherlands. This practice was first introduced in the church in the Netherlands by Obbe Philips.

The chief Scripture passages on which this practice is based are: "But now I have written unto you not to keep company, if any man that is called a brother be a fornicator, or covetous, or an idolator, or a railer, or a drunkard, or an extortioner; with such a one no not to eat." "If any man obey not our word by this epistle, note that man, and have no company with him, that he may be ashamed." "Now I beseech you, brethren, mark them which cause divisions and offences contrary to the doctrine which ye have learned; and avoid them."[92] The first of these passages was interpreted differently among the Brethren.

Within about a century after the rise of the evangelical Anabaptists a controversy was carried on regarding the origin of shunning in the Mennonite Church. The Waterlandian Mennonites in Holland had by this time discarded this observance, and a certain writer among them made the assertion that Menno Simons had taught avoidance only in the last period of his life. The same writer made the statement that Leonard Bouwens, who was ordained a bishop in 1551 in Emden, was the first to defend shunning among the Mennonites.

The practice of shunning was introduced among evangelical Anabaptists in the Netherlands before Menno Simons united with it. As stated above, it was defended by Obbe Philips from the beginning. This practice was observed not only against excommunicated church members but also against any one who would make it his business to turn people away from sound doctrine, as taught by the Obbenites. This included in particular the emissaries of certain fanatical sects which claimed to have the true Anabaptist doctrine. Among the Hutterian Brethren shunning was observed in particular also against Roman Catholic priests.

There is an evident indirect connection between the origin of the practice of avoidance and the principle of secret discipleship, as may be directly indicated. The advocacy of the latter principle in the Netherlands was in part responsible for the emphasis laid by the Obbenites on this practice.

The early Obbenites had originally been Melchiorites; that is, followers of the enthusiast Melchior Hofmann. On account of the persecution, Hofmann advocated the principle of secret discipleship. He believed and predicted on the ground of supposed special revelation, that the day of religious liberty was just then about to dawn. He was of the opinion that the actual separation from the Roman Catholic Church should be postponed until the arrival of that day, when the truth could be openly confessed without serious danger. Until the coming of the anxiously looked for time of liberty there should be outward conformity to the practices and prescribed forms of the dominant state church, which in Holland was then the Roman Catholic Church.

Obbe Philips and his followers, on the contrary, were led to see clearly that secret discipleship, such as Hofmann advocated, not only falls far short of scriptural requirements, but the implied deception as to religious profession is in direct conflict with Christian principle. Menno Simons, in the account of his own conversion, says significantly that the church with which he united taught the need of a willingness to bear persecution for the Christian truth.[93]

While it is readily seen that there is no excuse for the idea of secret discipleship, nevertheless it stands to reason that under the then existing circumstances human weakness was prone to seek a way of compromise for avoiding the cross of persecution. As already intimated, it could not be denied that such secret discipleship on the part of the Melchiorites and other enthusiastic sects was at least in part motivated by a desire to deceive. It should be recalled that upon all Anabaptists the death sentence had been summarily passed. What this in reality meant for our ancestors is scarcely comprehensible to us who live today in a land of religious freedom.

Besides the Melchiorites there were in that period a number of other fanatical sects which advocated temporary outward accommodation and conformity to the religious forms of the dominant state church. They were the Münsterites, Batenburgers, and Davidians. The latter went so far as to assert that to deceive the godless persecutors was entirely justifiable. The attitude of these sects in this regard was condemned outright by the Mennonites as deceptive and hypocritical.

Great and fundamental as were the differences between these fanatical sects and the Mennonites, they all agreed in recognizing infant baptism as unscriptural, though the former did not publicly teach their views. Adult baptism was practiced by these sects when it did not result in persecution; as, for example, in Münster. Their representatives came to the Mennonites with the claim of being brethren and defending the Anabaptist doctrine. The Mennonites in turn designated them as false brethren and practiced strict avoidance against them, as is abundantly clear from Menno Simons' writings.

The emissaries of the Münsterite Anabaptists came to the Obbenites with a seemingly marvellous message. They announced that the new day of religious liberty predicted by Melchior Hofmann had actually begun for all who would avail themselves of the refuge which, they asserted, the Lord had provided in Münster. Previous to the destruction of their supposed kingdom of God at Münster (in June, 1535), they could point to the fact that without bloodshed they had come into possession of a great and well fortified city. Was it not blindness to deny that God had in this way put His seal of approval upon their undertaking? And was it not folly on the part of the Obbenites to be in daily and hourly danger of death, instead of seeking refuge in Münster where adult baptism was freely practiced? The Münsterites minimized and partly denied the existing fundamental differences in doctrine and practice between themselves and the Obbenites. In silence they passed over the fact that in Münster, after the first months of their history, only such as adhered to the distinctive Münsterite teaching were tolerated. They hoped that those who would arrive in Münster would accommodate themselves to Münsterite teaching.

After the passing of the Münsterites some of the fanatical sects named above continued the advocacy of secret discipleship, including conformity to the religious rites of the dominant church. As already said, to some of those who were in constant danger of death this idea naturally had an appeal. Weak church members were in danger of yielding to such influences. Avoidance was, as stated before, practiced against the members of these sects. Menno Simons wrote in 1558 that he had personally known not less than three-hundred persons who had been led astray by these sects because those persons did not observe shunning toward them.

The activities of these sects were confined to the lower countries. The Brethren in the upper countries (South Germany and Switzerland) were not exposed to untoward influences from these quarters and did not practice avoidance. The practice of this observance in certain sections of the upper countries began only toward the close of the seventeenth century, after some of the writings of the Brethren of Holland and North Germany, defending this observance, had been spread in those parts.

Concerning the origin of the practice of avoidance, an early Mennonite chronicler in the Netherlands relates that Obbe Philips was the first to teach avoidance, and that he advocated an extreme view of this observance. Obbe Philips, so this trustworthy chronicler says, was of the opinion that a person toward whom avoidance is to be practiced could be given aid only in extreme circumstances; namely, when he was in actual danger of life.[94] In his book, *Confessions,* Obbe makes the interesting remark that the false brethren did, naturally, not take kindly to such an attitude. He says that "the false brethren" made oath to take his life.

It might seem that the said chronicler made an overstatement in recording Obbe's extreme opinion on avoidance. However, it is evident from Menno Simons' writings that such extreme views were held by some of Obbe's followers at a later date.

Menno wrote in 1550:[95]

I hear and see, and have, alas, seen these many years more than too much of it, that on both sides some use no standard or measure in this matter and there is therefore continuously much disputing, trouble and shortcoming concerning avoidance. . . . Therefore some err, to my understanding, not a little who have narrowed down this expression "to have nothing to do with" [I Cor. 5:9, Dutch and German translation] to such extent that they [saying "nothing" means "nothing"], take it similarly as the words, "Thou shalt not steal; thou shalt not commit adultery," of which Paul testifies that those who are guilty thereof shall not inherit the kingdom of heaven. Yea my brethren, if this were the case, who could stand before his God?

Again Menno wrote in the same year:[96]

My brethren, I tell the truth and lie not: such unmerciful, cruel opinion and practice [namely, to refuse needed aid to the excommunicated when they are in need] I hate from all my heart. Nor do I desire to be a brother among so unmerciful, cruel brethren if there should yet be any holding such an opinion, if they do not desist from such abomination and in all discretion follow love and mercy according to the example of God and Christ. For my heart can not consent to such unmerciful treatment which exceeds the cruelty of the common heathen and Turks; but by the grace of God I shall with the sword of the Lord fight against it unto death; for it is contrary to all teaching of the New Testament, and contrary to the Spirit and nature of Christ, according to which all the Scriptures of the New Testament should be judged and understood.

In very many passages of his writings Menno Simons expresses similar sentiments as concerns the attitude to those toward whom avoidance was observed.

There were, then, within the brotherhood differences of opinion regarding avoidance, yet the view of Obbe Philips, as expressed in the above quotation, was apparently never defended in print. Menno Simons mentions it only to give warning regarding it. There was in a few sections of the Low Countries a sharp controversy regarding avoidance between husband and wife when one was excluded from the church (marital avoidance). The question whether every excommunication is to be preceded by three admonitions also gave occasion for differences of opinion. Menno Simons repeatedly gave expression in his writings to apprehension regarding a possible disruption of the church caused by differences of opinion on this point. This anxiety proved needless. The first permanent schism in the Mennonite Church was the division between the Flemish and Friesians which took place a few years after Menno Simons' death. This division was not caused by differ-

(From "Roesehgarte," by the artist Rudolf Muenger, Bern)

The Last Moments of the Martyr Hans Haslibacher

Het Steen (Antwerp) and a View of the Scheldt River

Today a Museum; it was once a place where Dutch Mennonites were imprisoned for their faith.

(From "Martyrs' Mirror," 1938)

Dirk Willems, a Dutch Mennonite, Saves His Captor's Life, 1569

Willems was later burned at the stake.

Two Young Girls Led to Execution, about 1550

(From "Martyrs' Mirror," 1938)

(From "Martyrs' Mirror," 1938)

Martyrdom of Anneken Heyndricks, a Dutch Mennonite Woman, 1571

ences of opinion regarding any point of church discipline. The withdrawal of the Waterlandian Mennonites, in 1555, could not properly be named a church division.

In a much later period there was a controversy regarding Menno Simons' personal attitude on the question of avoidance. The assertion has been made by a certain unnamed writer that only in the latter period of his labors did Menno approve of avoidance between husband and wife. The said writer held that this supposed change in Menno's views was to be ascribed to the influence of Leonard Bouwens. Clearly this view is contrary to fact. Menno Simons taught avoidance in his early writings. In his *Loving Admonition,* 1541, he insisted that the excommunicated are to be shunned, "whether it be father or mother, sister or brother, husband or wife, son or daughter, without any respect of persons." He held that such avoidance is to be observed "with prayer, tears, and a compassionate spirit, out of great love;" its purpose being to bring the erring to repentance.[97] Similar statements are found in various other passages of his writings.

While Menno Simons obviously held this view from the beginning, he nevertheless always counselled an attitude of leniency on the question of avoidance between husband and wife. So far from becoming more stringent on this point, toward the last decade of his life, he placed himself, in 1550, on record as disapproving any attempt to enforce marital avoidance in case the persons directly concerned were not convinced that it should be observed.[98] In 1554, and again in 1558, he repeated the same sentiments on avoidance.[99] The Mennonite elders (bishops) assembled at Wismar in North Germany, including Leonard Bouwens, in 1554, expressed themselves definitely to the same effect.

Menno Simons' attitude on the point under consideration is made clear by a concrete example. In the Mennonite congregation of the city of Emden a sister named Swaen Rutgers objected to avoiding her excommunicated husband. There were those who advised setting a time within which she must decide upon avoiding him, or lose her right to membership. Menno Simons, in a letter written regarding this case to the congregation at Emden, said that when he was informed of this threat, his heart was filled with grief. He warned the church at Emden of the evil reports which such a procedure would cause concerning the church and the word of the Lord. "We have never dared to follow such a practice," he wrote. "I shall never consent to such a course." Swaen Rutgers was not excommunicated. In a letter written in 1558 Menno defended the same views.[100]

The two last books of Menno Simons treat on excommunication and the question of avoidance. One of them is his *Thorough Instruction on Excommunication.* Before writing this book he was visited at Wüstenfelde by two Mennonite ministers from the Rhineland, Sielis and Lemke, who had come to confer with him on this point in the hope of bringing about an agreement. They were of the Swiss Brethren and differed from Menno on the question of avoidance.

Sielis and Lemke, on their visit at Wüstenfelde, were received by Menno Simons as brethren, as is stated specifically by him. For two days they conferred with him on the point in question. Menno did not make the suggestion that the two brethren approve of a rigid rule on this point; he hoped to persuade them that the practice of the Brethren of the Low Countries was not unacceptable. For a time it seemed that the desired adjustment was in sight. After the departure of Sielis and Lemke the discussion was continued in writing. Menno received a letter from the Upperlandians and then in reply wrote his above-named book, *Thorough Instruction on Excommunication.*[101]

When Sielis and Lemke had read this book they made a serious mistake, indicating that they were incompetent for their assumed task of effecting full agreement between the Netherlandians and Upperlandians,[102] and that they were unworthy of the confidence which Menno had placed in them. They decided to address an appeal directly to the congregations of the Low Countries, urging them to withdraw from Menno Simons' leadership and to accept the Upperlandians' attitude, contrary to his advice. Apparently they made another trip to the Low Countries, as seems to be indicated in statements made by Menno. Then they wrote to the brotherhood in those countries, bringing personal charges against Menno Simons. The contents of their letter are in part cited in the last book of Menno, directly to be mentioned. Menno was not fitted for a leader, they urged; he was a fickle man and contradicted himself in his writings. Formerly he had held that three admonitions must precede every exclusion, but later he had discarded this view. They advanced various slanderous accusations against him. Menno himself, they stated, had said regretfully in their hearing that too much was made of the word of Menno Simons.[103] Was it not apparent then that it were better if his word counted for less?

Naturally Menno Simons was grieved over these developments. He wrote a little book, *A Thorough Reply to the Slander, Defamation, Backbiting, Unseasoned, and Bitter Words of Sielis and Lemke Concerning our Position and Doctrine,* the last book from his pen.[104] He rebuked them in no uncertain tones, but withal endeavored to show a Christian spirit of love, addressing them in such terms as "my dear men," "most beloved," "ye dear chosen men."

The oft repeated opinion that Menno Simons in this book declared the Upperlandians to be excommunicated is clearly erroneous.[105] Menno tells them that he and the pious who were with him could recognize them as their brethren only if they took another attitude and made amendments for the wrongs they committed. The book contains clear evidence that this admonition is not directed against the Upperlandians but only against Sielis and Lemke.

Chapter 39

MENNO SIMONS ON THE MODE OF BAPTISM

In not a few books and pamphlets by various writers the statement is found that Menno Simons taught and practiced baptism by immersion. The first author to advance this view was Morgan Edwards, a Baptist writer, who made the statement in 1770. This opinion was later repeated by others, among them J. Newton Brown whose booklet, *The Life and Times of Menno, the Celebrated Dutch Reformer,* passed through various editions in both the English and German languages.

Some of these writers based this opinion on the supposition that the Dutch word for baptism, *doopsel,* as used by Menno, means immersion. Furthermore, in support of the view that Menno defended baptism by immersion they quoted a notoriously false (not to say falsified) translation of a certain passage from his writings. In the original Dutch, as well as in the English edition of his works, the passage in question reads:

For however diligently we may search day and night, we yet find but one baptism in the water, pleasing to God, which is expressed and contained in His Word, namely the baptism on the confession of faith, commanded by Christ Jesus, taught and administered by His holy apostles.

Menno adds at the end of the paragraph: "But of that other baptism, that is infant baptism, we find nothing."[106]

Following is the translation of this passage, as given by some of these writers:

After we have searched ever so diligently, we shall find no other baptism but dipping in water which is acceptable to God and approved in His Word.

The claim has been made that the rendering, as given by these writers, corresponds with the text as found in the earliest edition of Menno Simons' Works. This opinion is erroneous. Various Mennonite authors, as well as a number of Baptist historians, including Ira Chase, Henry Burrage, August Rauschenbusch, William H. Whitsitt, have shown that the assertion is without foundation.

In the Reformation period there was no controversy regarding the mode of baptism. Menno's writings do not contain a defense of a particular mode, but incidentally he made statements which clearly indicate the mode of baptism in use in the church which he represented, namely effusion. He says in his book, *Foundation,* that, compared with such commandments as to love one's enemies, to crucify the flesh, and the like, it is an easy matter to submit to the act of baptism, and he describes this act as "having a handful of water applied."[107] Again in his book, *The True Christian Faith,* he refers to the act of baptism as receiving "a handful of water."[108] The late William H. Whitsitt, president of the Southern Baptist Theological Seminary, said rightfully that these are plain statements indicating the act or mode of baptism. Without question this is correct.

An attempt has been made to annul the force of these passages. The passage from the *Foundation* is a part of a treatise in which Menno pointed out that no rite, or ceremony, can save the soul, and that the whole ocean could not cleanse from sin. This does by no means disprove the fact that in this passage, as well as in the other passage above quoted, he clearly refers to the act of baptism as the application of a handful of water. These passages show beyond the possibility of a doubt how baptism was practiced in the early Mennonite Church.

CHAPTER 40

THE EARLY MENNONITE VIEW OF THE CHURCH

The early Swiss Brethren and Mennonites held that a true Christian church consists of those who by their own choice have accepted Christ and bidden adieu to the world. In the language of the New Testament, the believers are those "called out" from the world, implying the idea that the Christian church is distinct and separate from the world. The Brethren held that the church and the world differ so vitally in their nature that compromise with the world means defection for the church. In the Protestant (as well as Catholic) state churches of Reformation times, on the other hand, the membership consisted of such as in their earliest infancy had been made members of the church by baptism. These churches then did not in principle consist of only believers, or of such as had personally repented and believed.

In the state churches of the Reformation period the church consisted of the whole population of a given state. All were made members without their knowledge and consent; that is, without personally accepting the obligations of church membership. There was no separation between the church and the world. The world was the church, and the church was the world. There was no church discipline. Although every person was a church member by force of the civil law, those "who were in earnest in their Christian profession" (to use an expression of Luther) were often few and far between. It should be observed that the mission field of the state churches was within the church itself. The task of the ministers who took their profession seriously was to labor for the Christianization of the church. For the New Testament type of churches, such as in principle consist of believers, the mission field is the world.

In view of the regrettable imperfections of the church, it is sometimes said that the true church exists invisibly within the professing church, and that this invisible church is in a literal sense "without spot or wrinkle, or any such thing." It is an obvious fact, however, that not even believers who lead a consistent Christian life are faultless in the eyes of the Lord, except in the sense that Christ's righteousness is imputed to them. In other words, even the so-called invisible church cannot lay claim to the predicate of perfection. Martin Luther held that wherever the gospel is preached in its purity and the sacraments are properly administered, there is within the visible church (the state church) an invisible true church.

But "invisibility of the church" is a self-contradictory term. A church necessarily consists of persons. True conversion and walking in newness of life do, as a matter of fact, not result in personal invisibility. No one would question that the apostolic church was a true Christian church, and yet it was not a perfect church. And the apostolic church was of course not invisible. Our Lord, in the Sermon on the Mount, compares His followers to a city that is built upon a hill which cannot be hid. The early Mennonites held that when the church is invisible, it does not exist.

In the great debate held in 1532 at Zofingen, Switzerland, the spokesmen of the Swiss Brethren said:

In the early church only those were received as members who were converted through repentance to newness of life.

The true church is separated from the world and is conformed to the nature of Christ. If the church is yet at one with the world, we cannot recognize it as the true church.

We cannot admit that a true church is united with the worldly government.

Thus the church was established: When the apostles came to any place, they preached the Word and there was a separation from the world [on the part of those who accepted the teaching].

Menno Simons wrote on the same subject:

The true messengers of the gospel who are one with Christ in Spirit, in love and life, teach that which is entrusted to them by Christ, namely repentance and the peaceable gospel of grace which He Himself has received of the Father and taught the world. All who hear, believe, accept, and rightly fulfill the same are the Church of Christ, the true, believing Christian church, the body and bride of Christ, the ark of the Lord. They are ordained to proclaim the power of Him who has called them from darkness unto His marvelous light.[109]

Christ's church consists of the chosen of God, His saints and beloved who have washed their robes in the blood of the Lamb, who are born of God and led by Christ's Spirit, who are in Christ and Christ in them, who hear and believe His word, live in their weakness according to His commandments and in patience and meekness follow in His footsteps, who hate evil and love the good.[110]

On the principle of separation Menno wrote:

The whole evangelical Scriptures teach that Christ's church was and must be a people separated from the world in doctrine, life, and worship. It was likewise so in the Old Testament (II Cor. 6:17; Tit. 2:14; I Pet. 2:9, 10; I Cor. 5:17; Ex. 19:12).

Since the church always was and must be a separated people, as has been said above, and since it is clear as the meridian sun that for many centuries there was [in the Catholic countries] no difference between the church and the world, but all people [all inhabitants of a given state] have been united together in baptism, supper, life, and worship without any separation, (a condition which is so clearly contrary to all the Scripture), therefore we are constrained from sincere motives, by the Spirit and Word of God, to the praise of Christ and for the service and salvation of our neighbor, to gather together a pious, penitent assembly or church which is separated from the world, as the Scriptures teach.[111]

The early Mennonites did not teach that a true church is necessarily free of unworthy members, or that hypocrites may never be found in it. This is clear from many statements of the Brethren themselves, as well as from the testimony of their opponents. Heinrich Bullinger relates that the Brethren protested against the civil authorities' interference in religious and spiritual things. According to Bullinger's testimony they said: "How can the civil authorities judge matters of faith, when in fact faith and unbelief are of an invisible, spiritual nature and are hidden in the human heart, so that even the church cannot judge the true condition of its members?" Again, the spokesmen of the Brethren in the great debates in Switzerland pointed out, as noted before, that discipline would not be needed if the church were perfect. The Reformed theologian, George Thormann, in his polemical work against the Swiss Brethren, makes the following statement: "Since no other church insists so strenuously on the need of discipline as they do, it is evident that their preaching of the Word is not so effective as is commonly supposed." This writer failed to consider that the apostolic church also held the practice of discipline to be essential.

In the discussions at Zofingen and Bern the Brethren made these statements:

It is also true that evil persons, false Christians, may steal into the church and the church may not be aware of it.

No one should be excluded except for actual transgression deserving this act of discipline.

If one was warned once and twice and will not give heed, the matter should be brought before the church and the offending one should be excommunicated.

If the vices which Paul mentions in the sixth chapter of Galatians are known to the church, those who are guilty should be excluded by excommunication.

We do not make haste with excommunication but we warn according to the nature of the case, and use such disciplinary measures only if the guilty one continues in transgression.

Pilgram Marpeck wrote in reply to the charge made by Caspar Schwenckfeld that the Brethren considered their church perfect: "As concerns faults or failings, we are falling far behind the church in apostolic times, and even the apostolic church was not without faults."

Schwenckfeld, in passing, was of the opinion that there existed at that time no organization which was a Christian church in the New Testament sense; hence no one was under obligation to unite with any church. Marpeck, replying to this opinion, says at the same place:

If Schwenckfeld is waiting for a church, such as he thinks the church should be, he will assuredly have to wait long, like the Jews who are yet waiting for the Messiah. They were offended in Him and would not have a carpenter's son. Schwenckfeld would obviously have disapproved even of the apostolic church and would have found fault with it.

The early Mennonites' rejection of perfectionism, indicates that they did not claim sinless perfection for the church. Menno Simons, as already indicated, taught that true Christians are perfect in the sense that Christ's perfect righteousness is accounted to them. He held that the church as an organization should be "unblamable" in the sense that its teachings are founded upon God's Word alone; that it stands for all the truth of the Word and is conducted and maintained throughout in accordance with it. Not infrequently he referred to the fact that among the apostles there was a Judas. He believed the church to be "the communion of the saints" in very deed, but did not ascribe to it perfection in purity in the absolute sense. Menno Simons wrote:[112]

In the fifth place we teach, seek and demand that the Lord's supper be observed as the Lord Jesus Himself has instituted and observed it, namely with a church that is outwardly without spot or blemish, that is without open transgression and wickedness; for the church judges that which is visible. But what is inwardly evil, but does not appear outwardly to the church, such God alone will judge and pass sentence on them; for He alone, and not the church, discerns hearts and reins.

It is worthy of notice in this connection that in Menno's opinion not all grievous sin need be publicly confessed. If a transgression is unknown both to the world and to the church, and the guilty one repents and confesses his sin to a brother, Menno did not believe it proper to make the matter public. He wrote in 1558:[113]

If at any time it would come to pass that any one commit sin against his God in secret in any carnal abomination, from which may He through His power preserve us all, and if the Spirit of Christ who alone must awaken true repentance in us all, again touched his heart and granted him genuine repentance, such a case we are not called to judge, for it is a matter between him and God. For since it is evident that we do not seek our righteousness and salvation, the remission of our sins, divine grace, reconciliation, and eternal life in or through church discipline, but alone in the righteousness, intercession, merit, death and blood of Christ, and since now the two real objects why excommunication is commanded in the Scripture can not be sought in the instance of such an one, because, firstly, his sin is private, hence no offense can follow from it, and secondly, he is contrite at heart and penitent in life, therefore there is no need of putting him to shame in order that he may be brought to repentance. There is no injunction of Christ, no divine command that such an one should be more severely taken to account, or excluded, or brought to shame before the church.

The supposition that the early Mennonites condemned those who were not of their persuasion is incorrect. In the debate of Zofingen, in 1532, the Brethren were asked: "If a man, living in Roman Catholic territory, had been led to recognize the errors of Romanism and was leading a good life but desired to remain with his wife and children and did not move out of such territory, would you consider him your brother?" Their reply, as given by one of their spokesmen, was: "So long as one attended idolatrous worship and swallowed the god consisting of bread and had a part in abominations, I could not hold him a brother or Christian. But if one lived among Romanists and desired to remain with his family, hoping for their enlightenment, and did not defile himself with such usages, I could not repudiate him."

Even one who had been excommunicated they would not condemn. They said: "We are not informed that one who was thus excommunicated and does not turn may be an heir of the kingdom of God."

Pilgram Marpeck wrote in his *Reply* to Schwenckfeld: "He says that we condemn all who are not of one mind with us. This, again, is not the truth. We have no right to condemn any one. But, seeking the salvation of men, we testify to the truth of God. If some one is hit or judged by it, this is not our responsibility."

George Thormann, a clergyman of the Protestant state church, in his polemical work against the Swiss Brethren, said in 1693: "If you ask them whether they are of the opinion that no one among us [the state church] could be saved they say unhesitatingly: No, they do not hold such a view."

In the course of the great debate held in Bern in 1538 the state church theologians asserted that the church of the Brethren could not be a true Christian church, because the Brethren would not condemn one who had renounced their own church, "for," said the state church leaders, "those who renounce the true Christian church are damned."

The members of the early Anabaptist and Mennonite churches had come out of the Roman Catholic Church. In the states in which the authorities had at an early date accepted a Protestant (Lutheran or Reformed) creed, they had been Protestants. In many instances the early Anabaptists' personal testimony of their former religious experiences is yet preserved. The following example to the point is the statement of a spokesman of the Swiss Brethren in the disputation of Bern, in 1538 (his name is not given in the protocol) :

While yet in the national [Reformed] church we obtained much instruction from the writings of Luther, Zwingli, and others concerning the mass and other papal ceremonies, that they are vain. Yet we recognized a great lack as regards repentance, conversion, and the true Christian life. Upon these things my mind was bent. I waited and hoped for a year or two, since the minister had much to say of amendment of life, of giving to the poor, loving one another, and abstaining from evil. But I could not close my eyes to the fact that the doctrine which was preached and which was based on the Word of God, was not carried out. No beginning was made toward true Christian living, and there was no unison in the teaching concerning things that were necessary. And although the mass and the images were finally abolished, true repentance and Christian love were not in evidence. Changes were made only as concerned external things. This gave me occasion to inquire further into these matters. Then God sent His messengers, Conrad Grebel and others, with whom I conferred about the fundamental teachings of the apostles and the Christian life and practice. I found them men who had surrendered themselves to the doctrine of Christ by *Bussfertigkeit* (penitence and contrition). With their assistance we established a congregation in which repentance was in evidence by newness of life in Christ.

Again a spokesman of the Brethren, on the same occasion, after stating that they had found the state church type of the Reformation unsatisfactory, said:

Meanwhile we became acquainted with the Brethren. We found that they had the doctrine of Christ and followed Him in the point of discipline according also to the apostolic command, and that they carried these things into practice. We found that they had truly attained to newness of life, to live no longer in sin. Therefore we gave ear to their message, and since we observed that they walked according to the Apostles' doctrine, we joined ourselves to them.

The fact will bear repetition, for emphasis, that at the time when the first congregation of the Swiss Brethren was organized, the Protestants (Zwinglians) in Zurich constituted as yet merely a party, not a church. The followers of Zwingli favored the intended withdrawal from the Roman church whenever the Council of Zurich would give orders to this effect. But in January, 1525, when the Swiss Brethren first organized themselves as a church, the Catholic Mass was yet observed in all the churches, the Zwinglian church having not yet been called into existence. The church from which the Brethren withdrew was not the Zwinglian but the Roman church.

Now, at first thought, one would naturally suppose that Zwingli and his adherents had no objection to the withdrawal of Grebel and his associates from the Romish church. But, as pointed out repeatedly, this was not by any means the case. Zwingli had decided that the Protestant church should, in its relationship to the state, take the place which hitherto the Roman church had held. By force of the civil law the membership of the new church was to be the same as the membership of the Catholic Church. It should comprise the whole population, just as had been the case beforehand. Hence, separation from the Romish church was not to be permitted before the withdrawal of the people in a body.

In later years, namely after the rise of the Anabaptist movement, both Luther and Zwingli held that the Roman Catholic Church is and always was the true Christian church, though it needed a reformation. After the new Protestant churches had been established, these reformers asserted that they had not forsaken the Roman Church, but had reformed it, or sections of it, and that the Anabaptists, had withdrawn, or separated, from the true church. In the great debate held at Bern in 1538 the state church leaders demanded of the ministers of the Brethren to prove their calling by working miracles, like the apostles, while they themselves needed no such proof, being called by those who were of the true Christian church. Nearly all the ministers of the state church had formerly been priests, and none of them had been reordained.

The Swiss Brethren wrote in a booklet entitled *Vindication* (reprinted in Bullinger's larger work against the Anabaptists) :

They [the leaders of the national Protestant churches] accuse us saying that we despise them, and that we desire to be better, or consider ourselves better than they. They do not take into consideration that we, in turn, could ask them: Why do you think yourselves better than the Romanists?—and indeed the Romanists do address them in such un-Christian fashion. . . . If they, then, would confess that they of themselves are not better than the Romanists, but only in respect to the faith, or because of a better faith and practice; well, now, they should grant to us the same liberty [to hold that our teaching and practice is more scriptural]. Yet it is not of us but of God, to the degree that we desire by the grace of God to be more obedient to the gospel and the commandments of God.

Luther as well as Zwingli, in their earlier reformatory writings, however, had denounced the Roman church in severe terms. Zwingli often stated that he did not recognize "the papal rabble" (to give his own words) as a Christian church. In his book, *The Shepherd,* written in the spring of the year 1524, he said that the church whose head is the pope is the Christian church "no more than Belial is God." As just stated, these reformers in a later period thoroughly modified their views of the Roman Catholic Church. Luther in particular in later years, spoke in terms of highest praise of that church, though he never ceased to denounce the pope as the very Anti-christ, that is to say, the principal representative of the kingdom of darkness on earth.[114] These reformers never undertook to explain how the Roman Catholic Church could be recognized as the true church, while the Mass, one of the main features of the practices of this church, was in their opinion idolatry and blasphemy. They apparently never stopped to consider the inconsistency of how the community of those who held the Antichrist to be the rightful head of the church, could be the true church, or how an ordination performed on his authority could be valid.

The leaders of the Swiss Brethren realized that the Roman church was built upon an unscriptural foundation. The theological and ecclesiastical structure of that church was erected upon the principle of salvation through the sacraments and the mediation of the priesthood. In the disputation held at Bern in 1538 a spokesman of the Swiss Brethren said:

We do not contradict that there may have been those [in the Roman Catholic Church] in whom God had pleasure, though they were in ignorance and darkness; this we leave to God. But since the popish church was founded on error, we cannot admit that it was the true Christian church. . . . A true church must be conformed to the teachings and institutions of Christ.

The Brethren saw clearly that the existing needs did not call for a mere reformation, but for preaching the primitive gospel and for building anew on no other foundation than that of the Scriptures. It may be observed that while Conrad Grebel, who performed the first act of baptism, had not been ordained in the Catholic Church, other leaders of the Brethren had received such ordination. This was not taken into account by the Brethren. They did not recognize Roman Catholic ordinations.

CHAPTER 41

CHURCH DISCIPLINE

The early Mennonites were a unit in the emphasis they placed on the need of scriptural church discipline. Originally the leaders in the Protestant state churches, Luther and Zwingli, were of one mind with them on this point. Within a short period, however, both these reformers, as elsewhere indicated, consented to a close union of the church with the state. In consequence they found scriptural discipline impracticable.

Ulrich Zwingli, in the earlier years of his reformatory labors, taught that discipline, including excommunication, "was instituted by the Lord Himself." As late as April, 1525, Zwingli defended discipline as indispensable. But very soon after the establishment of the Reformed state church in Zurich, Zwingli found that under existing conditions discipline was an impossibility. He began to oppose it and to teach that it is not only unnecessary, but adverse to the best interests of the church. Contrary to his advice, the introduction of discipline was attempted in the Zwinglian churches at Basel, St. Gall, and other places, but was soon abandoned as impracticable.

In a synod of the Reformed state church held at Frauenfeld, in 1529, there was a lengthy discussion on this subject between Zwingli and Dominic Zili, the head pastor of St. Gall, who had obviously been under Swiss Brethren influence. Zili demanded the introduction of discipline, asserting that for a true church it is absolutely necessary. Zwingli, on the contrary, spoke as an opponent of discipline. Replying to Zili, he made the remarkable statement that the practice of excommunication "would cost many preachers," indicating that many ministers were guilty of open transgression. In a synod, held in the following year at St. Gall, Zili again defended the need of discipline, against Zwingli who opposed it on the ground that, as he expressly stated, it would jeopardize the material prosperity of the city of St Gall. Thereupon Dominic Zili, addressing Zwingli, replied, "I believe that all temporal things should be forsaken and counted but loss for the sake of the eternal Word of God, but according to your statement the divine Word must

be abrogated and forsaken in the interests of material prosperity." The well-known Reformed church historian, Emil
Egli says: "Zwingli at first approved of excommunication and
intended to introduce it, but later rejected and opposed it."

Martin Butzer, the Zwinglian reformer of Strasburg admitted that without the practice of discipline there can be no
true Christian church. In other words, he conceded that the
national church, in which he was a prominent leader, could not
claim the prerogative of a true church. John Calvin, in the
earlier period of his reformatory labors, was for a time associated with Butzer at Strasburg, and there is adequate ground
for thinking that Calvin's strict views regarding the need of
discipline are at least partly to be ascribed to the influence of
Butzer. There is furthermore convincing evidence that Butzer
was, in turn, influenced by the Swiss Brethren. Calvin, in his
treatise on the Schleitheim Confession, admitted that the teaching of the Swiss Brethren on church discipline was scriptural.
He remarked that the Brethren had learned and adopted their
views on this point from his writings. And yet they had held
these teachings from their inception as a church and long before
Calvin's renunciation of Romanism.

Butzer, realizing the need of discipline, as indicated above,
did his best to introduce it in the Reformed state church in
Strasburg, but his attempts to this end were in vain. Calvin,
on the other hand, was successful in his efforts toward this end.
He enforced church discipline in the city of Geneva. His method of enacting discipline was by coercion through the civil authorities. To a greater degree than Luther, Zwingli, Butzer,
or any other reformer, John Calvin succeeded in the endeavor
of making the state do the bidding of the state church. Excommunication was practiced in the Geneva state church, and
excommunicated persons were not tolerated within the borders
of the state.

In the debate held at Zofingen in 1532, a spokesman of the
Reformed state church said, that to excommunicate (according
to the usage of the Anabaptists) all who were guilty of transgression, was impracticable, for the reason that the result
would be that "the number of the excommunicated would ex-
ceed that of the pious, and they would exile and drive out the
pious."

The Swiss Brethren, as repeatedly stated, never swerved from the position which Zwingli and other reformers had originally shared with them, as concerns scriptural discipline. In the great disputations which, after Zwingli's death, the Brethren had with the leaders of the Protestant state church, the Brethren showed that discipline is a vital characteristic of a true Christian church. "There is no [true] church where there is no excommunication after the manner and method of the apostles," said one of their spokesmen in the disputation of Bern, in 1538. The theologians of the state church, on the contrary, defended the view that under a [nominally] Christian government, where the civil authorities punish wrongdoing, church discipline is not essential. And yet at the same time they expressed regret that discipline could not be practiced in their church.

Menno Simons wrote on church discipline:[115]

It is evident that a congregation or church cannot continue in the salutary doctrine and in a blameless and pious life without the proper use of discipline. Even as a city without a wall and gates, or a field without an inclosure or fence, or a house without walls and doors, so is also a church without the true apostolic exclusion. For it would be open to all deceiving spirits, all godless scorners and haughty despisers, all idolatrous and insolent transgressors, yes to all lewd debauchers and adulterers, as is the case with all the great sects of the world. In my opinion it is a vital characteristic, an honor and a means of prosperity for a true church to practice with Christian discretion the true apostolic exclusion and to observe it carefully with vigilant love according to the teaching of the holy divine Scriptures.

CHAPTER 42

AUTHORITY OF THE SCRIPTURES

Regarding this question regrettable confusion has been caused by an erroneous view; namely, by the supposition that Hans Denck, the mystic, was of the Swiss Brethren or Mennonite persuasion, and that his teachings represented the Mennonite faith. As indicated elsewhere, Denck taught that not the written Word of God, but "the inner Word," is the final authority. This view of the Scripture is sometimes spoken of as the spiritualistic view. On the contrary the Swiss Brethren and Mennonites invariably stressed the importance of the written Word of God.

The contemporary chronicler, Sebastian Franck, (himself a defender of the "spiritualistic" view of the Scripture), wrote in 1530:

There arose from the letter of Scripture, independently of the state churches, a new sect which was called Anabaptists. . . . By the good appearance of their sect and their appeal to the letter of Scripture, to which they strictly adhered, they drew to themselves many thousand God-fearing hearts who had a zeal for God.

The Protestant church historian, Urban Heberle, gives this testimony to the point:

First of all, we must recognize the outstanding fact that Grebel and his associates held the Scriptures in the highest regard in both their oral testimony and religious practice. Never do they appeal to direct divine revelations; never do they speak of the Scriptures as the dead letter in contrast to new revelations and to the living divine voice. Grebel never complains that the opposite party (the leading theologians of the national church) overemphasize the need of following the letter of the Scripture but, on the contrary, his criticism is that they take this matter too lightly.

Following are a few pertinent statements from the writings of the Brethren:

In a letter, Conrad Grebel wrote, in 1524:

We would ask you to discard the old ordinances of Antichrist and hold to the Word of God alone and be guided by it.

Again Grebel said on another occasion:

You should regard neither the opinion of the civil authorities nor of any man but should do only what God requires of you; and what the mouth of God has spoken, that you should heed.

Michael Sattler wrote:

Let no one cause you to depart from the standard that is laid through the letter of Scripture which is sealed by the blood of Christ and of many witnesses of Jesus.

The Anabaptist preacher, Leonhard Schiemer, who was executed Jan. 14, 1528, at Rattenberg in the Tyrol, proposed to the judges who condemned him to death: Since they regarded his doctrine and faith heretical, they should arrange for learned persons, doctors, priests, and monks to discuss the disputed points with him on scriptural grounds. He suggested further, both orally and in writing, that if they could show from the Scripture that he was in error, and as often as any one of the learned men could do this and show that his teaching was wrong and was not the doctrine of the Scriptures, the executioner should sever one of his limbs from his body, and when deprived of his limbs, tear out the ribs from his body until he expired.

In the great debates of the Swiss Brethren with the representatives of the Zwinglian state church, held at Zofingen in 1532 and at Bern in 1538, they continually appealed to, and demanded that their opponents abide by the Scripture. They said:

We hold that all things should be proven to ascertain what is founded on the holy Word of God, for this will stand when heaven and earth pass away, as Christ Himself said.

Pilgram Marpeck wrote concerning the Scriptures and their authority:

We would sincerely admonish every Christian to be on the alert and personally study the Scriptures, and have a care lest he permit himself to be easily moved and led away from the Scripture and apostolic doctrine by strange teaching and understanding; but let every one, in accordance with the Scripture and apostolic teaching, strive with great diligence to do God's will, seeing that the Word of truth could not fail us nor mislead us.

Concerning the "spiritualists'" opinion that "the inner Word" is the final authority, Marpeck said:

We say again that there are not two, but there is only one Word of God, and the word of divine evangelical preaching (which Schwenckfeld calls the Word of the letter) is truly the Word of the Holy Spirit and of God, for the Holy Spirit, who is God, has spoken through and out of the heart and mouth of the apostles.

The fact is noteworthy that, as already indicated, the Swiss Brethren were not accused by the representatives of the Protestant state churches of teaching the doctrine of the inner Word. On the contrary, the state church theologians asserted that the Brethren laid undue stress on the letter of the Scriptures. A number of impartial Reformed (Zwinglian) church historians have admitted that the position of the state church on the points in dispute was incapable of defense on scriptural ground. The Protestant church historian, Urban Heberle, says concerning Zwingli's conflict with the Brethren:

Zwingli had serious difficulty in defending his position, for he himself had originally defended the principle of the sole authority of the Scriptures in the same radical manner in which it was now applied by his opponents.

Since the Brethren defended the authority of the written Word of God, they were accused by their opponents of emphasizing "the dead letter." In the disputation of Bern in 1538, when the state church theologians had much to say that the Brethren were following "the dead letter," a spokesman of the Brethren asked the question: "Is that which Christ has spoken the dead letter?" Pilgram Marpeck pointed out that according to Christ's own definite statement, His words are "spirit and life." Marpeck showed that the words of Paul, "The letter killeth," refer to "the letter of the Law which had the purpose to kill." Yet they freely admitted that one may have the letter or knowledge of the truth without the Spirit.

In their controversy with the Swiss Brethren, the theologians of the Protestant state churches finally took a position of obvious compromise on the question of the authority of the Word of God. Failing to prove their position from the Scriptures, they made the assertion that, even though the teaching of the Brethren was founded on the Scriptures and was in accord with it, they were, nevertheless, under obligation, from considerations of love and forbearance, to yield to the demands of the state church and unite with it.

Zwingli wrote:

Even if the Anabaptists had the Scripture to support their views, these things should be decided by love.

Johannes Oekolampad, the Zwinglian reformer of Basel, often expressed the same view. After reading Balthasar Hubmaier's book, *The Christian Baptism of Believers*, Oekolampad wrote to Zwingli:

It seems to me the Anabaptists leave love out of consideration, which shows us what is to be observed of external things.

In his discussions with the Swiss Brethren, Oekolampad repeatedly accused them of transgressing against Christian love by their refusal to identify themselves with the state church. "We have taught," he says, "that the abolition of infant baptism is unacceptable, being contrary to Christian love." And again, Oekolampad said on the same occasion: "Your doctrine is in direct opposition to true love."

One of his books against the Swiss Brethren has a chapter bearing the title: "The Abandonment of Infant Baptism is Contrary to Christian Love." In the debate of Zofingen the representatives of the Zwinglian state church expressed the same views, insisting that love and forbearance must be the final arbiter in deciding the disputed points. Wolfgang Capito, a Zwinglian reformer of Strasburg, admitted that infant baptism is unscriptural but held that for love's sake, it should be practiced to maintain ecclesiastical unity.

Menno Simons wrote on the authority of the Scriptures:

My dear brethren, I for myself confess that I would rather die than to believe and teach to my brethren a single word concerning the Father, the Son, and the Holy Ghost, at variance with the express testimony of God's Word, as it is so clearly given through the mouth of the prophets, evangelists, and apostles.[116]

But that Gellius appeals to Tertullian, Cyprian, Origen, and Augustine, my reply is, first, If these writers can support their teachings with the Word and command of God, we will admit that they are right. If not, then it is a doctrine of men and accursed according to the Scriptures.[117]

If any one under the canopy of heaven can show us from the Scripture that Jesus Christ, the Son of the Almighty God, the eternal wisdom and truth, whom alone we acknowledge as the lawgiver and teacher of the New Testament, has commanded one word to that effect, or that His holy apostles have ever taught or practiced the like, then there is no need of an attempt to compel us by tyranny and torture. Only show us God's Word and our matter is settled. For we seek nothing else (God who is omniscient knows) than in our weakness to walk in obedience according to the divine ordinances, word and will, for which we poor persecuted people are shamefully reviled, banished, robbed and slain in many countries.[118]

Regarding the relation of the Old Testament Scriptures to the New Testament the Brethren differed fundamentally from state church Protestantism. They believed indeed that all Scripture was given by inspiration of God and is inerrantly true in all its statements and doctrinal teachings. Nevertheless they recognized the fact that the relation of the Old to the New Testament Scriptures is that of promise to fulfillment, of type and shadow to reality, of the groundwork of a building to the building itself. God's promise under the Old Covenant was that a New Covenant was to be established at the coming of the Redeemer; and the New Testament Scriptures teach that Christ is "the Mediator of a better covenant."

Christ in the Sermon on the Mount literally quotes from the Old Testament and sets over against it His, "But I say unto you." He also declared that some features of the Old Law had their occasion in their "hardness of heart," using the same figure of speech as is found in Ezekiel 11:19 and 36:26 in connection with the promise that in the gospel dispensation "the heart of stone" is to be taken away. A "faultless covenant" was impossible before Christ's coming and His work of redemption. The Old Testament Scriptures were the rule of life for pre-Messianic times. The New Testament obligations ("the law of Christ," Galatians 6:2) are more far-reaching and perfect than the Mosaic Law. Whatever of the Old Law is obligatory for the Christian is repeated and taught in the New Testament Scriptures.

This was the position of the Swiss Brethren and Mennonites concerning the Old Testament. The theologians of the state churches, on the contrary, found themselves compelled to go back to the Old Testament for maintaining the points on which they differed from the Brethren. They believed that in the Old Testament Scriptures they had found ground for defending infant baptism, the union of church and state, the persecution of dissenters, and war, for the followers of Christ. They failed to make the distinction between the Old and New Testament Scriptures on which the Mennonites insisted.

The Swiss Brethren expressed themselves regarding the point in question as follows:

Truly believing Christians use neither the worldly sword nor war, seeing that we are not any more under the old Law.

Hans Pfistermeyer, a minister of the Brethren, in 1531, in a discussion with state church leaders, said:

The New Testament is more perfect than the Old, and the Old was fulfilled and interpreted by Christ.[119] Christ has taught a higher and more perfect doctrine and made with His people a New Covenant. . . . I make a great difference between the Old and New Testament and believe that the New Covenant, which was made with us, is much more perfect than the Old that was made with the Jews.

In the debate of Zofingen (1532) the Brethren said:

Since you demand of us to say what of the shadow is passed and put away, and what is light, we must go back to the foundation than which none other can be laid. We say that the Old is the shadow, and that which is in unison with the words of Christ is light. This is clearly set forth by Christ (Matthew, chapters 20 and 5) when He states the order of the Old Testament and of the world and adds, "But it shall not be so among you."

In the great discussion of Bern, in 1538, the Brethren said:

We confess that the Old Testament is a witness of Christ. We accept it in so far as Christ has not abolished it and as it is in agreement with the New, and in so far as it pertains to faith, love, and a true Christian life.

Following is a quotation from a booklet of the Brethren:

They [the leaders in the state church] have taken measures whereby force is used in matters of faith and conscience through a Mosaic manner of coercion. This is contrary to their first teaching and means that they have reversed themselves and gone back to Moses, that is to say from the light of the sun into the shadow (Hebrews 10:1).

In the great debate of Frankenthal in the Palatinate the Swiss Brethren said:

Since we have been asked concerning the relationship between the two Testaments, we would say that the Old Testament Scriptures offer strong proof that Jesus Christ is the true God and Saviour, the Son of the living God of whom all prophets have testified. . . . Moses points us forward to Christ, our Saviour. . . . We believe that the New Testament surpasses the Old. So much of the Old Testament as is not irreconcilable with the doctrine of Christ, we accept. . . . If anything that is necessary for salvation and a godly life was not taught by Christ and the Apostles but is contained in the Old Testament Scriptures, we desire to be shown.

Menno Simons says on the point in question: "All Scripture must be interpreted according to the spirit, teaching, walk and example of Christ and the Apostles."[120] Dirck Philips, a leader of the Brethren in the Low Countries, wrote:[121]

The false prophets cover and disguise their deceptive doctrines by appealing to the letter of the Old Testament consisting of shadows and types. For whatever they cannot defend by the New Testament Scriptures, they try to establish by the Old Testament, on the letter of the books of the prophets. And this has given rise to many sects and to the many false religious forms. Yea, from this fountain have flowed the sacrilegious ceremonies and pomp of the church of Antichrist and the deplorable errors of the seditious sects [Münsterites and Batenburgers] which in our day, under a semblance of the holy gospel, of the faith and the Christian religion have done great injury and caused much offense.

The citations given from the writings and recorded oral testimony of the early Mennonites indicate that they took the doctrine of the authority of the Scriptures seriously. They condemned the compromising attitude of those who, while defending in theory the sole authority of the Scriptures, made in fact the civil government the authority to be followed on questions of practical reformation. The theory that a principle or practice may be unscriptural and yet needful for safeguarding the best interests of the church was unacceptable to them. They held the New Testament to be the foundation and rule of faith and practice, for the Christians. They believed that God reveals Himself continuously through Christian experience, in accordance with and in confirmation of His Word, though such experience could never take the place of the Scriptures as the foundation of the Christian faith.

CHAPTER 43

PRACTICE OF FEETWASHING

The apostle Paul, in his first letter to Timothy (5:10), refers to feet washing, indicating that it was observed in the apostolic church. Within about a century from the time of the apostles, Tertullian (A. D. 160-220) makes mention of it as an observance in the church. Ambrose (340-397), Augustine (354-430) and others of the church fathers defended it. This practice was far more common in the early church than has been generally supposed.

In the synod of Toledo, in Spain, held in 694, the assembled bishops decided that only those who had participated in feet washing should be permitted to take part in the communion service. Bernard of Clairvaux (1113-1153) defended feet washing as a divine commandment. Some of the dissenting sects of pre-Reformation times also observed it. In the Eastern (Greek) Church and in the Church of England this rite was practiced until a comparatively recent date. It was commonly observed on Thursday of Passion week.

Luther, in his *Greater Catechism,* favorably mentions feet washing as an observance. Caspar Schwenckfeld (1490-1561) taught that feet washing is a commandment of Christ, as well as baptism and the Lord's Supper. He says: "But why do they [the Lutherans] not insist as strongly on feet washing which was commanded of the Lord as well as the communion, and which was also observed in the early church? This is indeed a command of the Lord, as well as the breaking of bread."

The first mention of feet washing among the Anabaptists dates from the year of their first organization (1525), when it was practiced in the congregation of Balthasar Hubmaier at Waldshut in South Germany. The chronicler Sebastian Franck wrote, in 1531, that feet washing was practiced by some of the Swiss Anabaptists, and Heinrich Bullinger, in his larger work against the Swiss Brethren, written in 1560, confirms this statement. Also in central Germany there were Anabaptists who practiced this rite.

The writings of Pilgram Marpeck, who labored at Strasburg, Augsburg, and other places of South Germany, make repeated mention of feet washing, indicating definitely that in these churches it was accepted and practiced as a Christian ordinance. The *Ausbund,* the hymnbook of the early Swiss Brethren, contains two hymns teaching the washing of the saints' feet.

Menno Simons mentions feet washing twice in his writings.[122] Dirck Philips speaks of feet washing as the third ordinance of Christ. The Waterlandian Mennonite Confession of 1577, the "Concept of Cologne," of 1591, the larger Friesian Mennonite Confession of about 1600, consisting of thirty-three articles, the "Olive Branch," of 1627, the confession of Jan Centsen of Amsterdam, 1630, and the Dortrecht Confession of 1632, all teach feet washing. There is good evidence that all Mennonite churches of the Netherlands and northern Germany practiced this ordinance. The Amish Mennonite churches from the beginning observed it. Before the years 1874 and 1875, when the more conservative Mennonite groups of Russia emigrated to America, very many of the Russian Mennonite churches observed feet washing. It seems, however, that the Swiss Brethren and South German Mennonites did not observe the practice.

CHAPTER 44

NONRESISTANCE

The earliest testimony against war by a leader of the Swiss Brethren is that of Andreas Castelberger of Zurich, Switzerland, dating from the year 1523, about two years before the first congregation of the Swiss Brethren was organized by Castelberger and others. Castelberger had held meetings for Bible study which were attended by Lorenz Hochrütiner and others who later united with the Swiss Brethren. Hochrütiner, when asked what Castelberger had taught in these meetings, replied that he among other things "had said a great deal against war and had showed that the evangelical doctrine is radically opposed to it."

Another important testimony to the point was given in September, 1524, by Conrad Grebel, in a letter to Thomas Münzer who had taken the sword in the interest of the cause which he represented. Grebel wrote:

The Gospel and those who accept it are not to be protected with the sword, neither should they thus protect themselves. . . . True believing Christians are as sheep in the midst of wolves. . . . They must be baptized in anxiety and trouble, tribulation, persecution, suffering, and death. They must be tried in the fire and must reach the fatherland of eternal rest, not by overcoming bodily enemies with the sword, but by overcoming spiritual foes. They use neither the worldly sword nor engage in war, since among them taking human life has ceased entirely, for we are no longer under the Old Covenant.

Felix Manz said: "No Christian smites with the sword nor resists evil." In the death sentence pronounced over him on January 5, 1527, it was charged that Manz held that no Christian can carry out the death sentence on any person, nor put to death any one.

The attitude of the evangelical Anabaptists as concerns this question was set forth by Hans Schlaffer who suffered martyrdom on February 4, 1528, at Schwaz in the Tyrol. In his last confession he replied to questions regarding their principles, and in particular whether he knew of any one who was to be their leader in an uproar against the government. He said:

Our faith, life, and baptism is founded on nothing else than the commandment of Christ, and all the days of my life has no uproar or sedition come into my heart. Yes, I have fled from a house whose inhabitants lived in discord. There is no plot or other intention among us except to amend our lives and to abstain from the vicious, unrighteous life of the world. Not the least among our doctrines is that which enjoins subjection and obedience to the government in all that is good. I know of no other leader or beginner of my faith than Jesus Christ, the Son of God alone.

The Schleitheim Confession was drawn up by Michael Sattler and adopted by a conference held February 24, 1527. On the question of peace and nonresistance this confession contains the following articles.

Jesus Christ has made us free from the servitude of the flesh and meet for the service of God through the spirit which He has given us. Therefore we shall surely lay down the unchristian, yea satanic weapons of force, such as sword, armor and the like, together with all their use, whether for the protection of friends or against personal enemies; and this in the strength of the words of Christ, "I say unto you that ye resist not evil."

The government using the sword to punish and put to death the wrongdoers and to guard and protect the good is an appointment of God outside the perfection of Christ. In the law of the Old Covenant the sword is ordained against wrongdoers for punishment and death, and to exercise it the worldly governments are appointed.

In the perfection of Christ, however, church discipline alone is used for the correction and exclusion of those who have sinned, not indeed for the destruction of the flesh but as an admonition and injunction to sin no more.

Here it is asked by many who do not know Christ's will toward us, whether a Christian may or should use the sword against wrongdoers for protecting or defending the good, or for love's sake.

Our unanimous answer is: Christ teaches and commands that we should learn of Him, for He is meek and lowly in heart and we shall find rest to our souls. Now Christ did not say concerning the woman taken in adultery that she should be stoned to death according to the law of His Father, and yet He says: "I do nothing of myself but as my Father has taught me." He spoke to her words of mercy and forgiveness and admonition to sin no more. In such a way we also should act, according to the rule of church discipline.

The Schleitheim Confession and nearly all other Mennonite confessions contain articles on the question whether a Christian may be a magistrate, or an executive of the civil government.

In the discussions held in Zofingen, in July, 1532, the spokesmen of the Swiss Brethren said:

In Matthew, chapter 5, Christ forbids the believers all use of force. He says that rather than go to law they should permit others to defraud them, they should not strive with any one and should give the cloak to him who takes away their coat. The civil government was ordained of God to punish the evildoers and protect the good. . . . We believe the civil government should be separate from the church of Christ and not be established in it. Whatever we owe to the government: interest, tithes, taxes and customs, we give willingly and obediently. We obey the government in everything that may be asked of us that is not contrary to the will of God.

In March of the year 1538 an eight days' discussion was held in the city of Bern. Here the representatives of the Brethren said:

Christ, in teaching the principle of nonresistance, does not desire to abolish the civil government. He recognizes the rightfulness of the government, but teaches that it should be outside the Christian church. This is our position on this question. . . . On this point the Gospel differs from the Mosaic law.

Heinrich Bullinger states that the Brethren considered war "the greatest evil conceivable." Further he says:

They believe that Christians should stand ready to suffer (rather than strike back). No Christian may be a ruler. The government should not undertake to regulate matters of faith and religious practice. Christians do not resist violence and do not take recourse to law. They do not use the law courts. Christians do not kill. The punishment used by them is not imprisonment and the sword but only church discipline. They do not defend themselves, therefore they do not go to war and are not obedient to the government on this point.

Pilgram Marpeck (1495?-1556) wrote:

To say that those of the Old Covenant were Christians . . . , though the earthly, Mosaic sword was used among them, is equivalent to saying that such use of the worldly sword is permitted in the church of Christ today. Through which the true spiritual order, the sword, discipline, ban, power and government of the Holy Spirit, of the true Church of Christ and the spiritual priests, would be broken up and annulled. And through such confusion (*vermischung*) of the two priesthoods and other things of the Old and New Testaments nothing follows but the introduction of a desolation and wasting of the holy city. Dan. 9, Matt. 24, etc.—Today [there is] another King, another Kingdom, another priesthood, another law, which is not a carnal law of ruling, or worldly, earthly judicial procedures as that of yesterday but a spiritual, and a law or commandment of the Spirit,—love and patience, which God "yesterday" promised and "today" for the first time wrote in the hearts, and the Man Christ commanded His priests who were appointed today [in the New Covenant]. Also that they should love all people, not merely their friends or dear ones, but also their enemies, and not to resist evil, as is clearly shown in Matt. 5, Luke 6 and Rom. 12. Also that one should not use carnal weapons against another; nor they against their enemies. Isa. 2, Micah 4, Matt. 5. All bodily, worldly, carnal, earthly fighting, conflicts and wars are annulled and abolished among them through such law. Psalms 4, 5, Hos. 2: Which law of love, Christ . . . then, as the present High Priest, Himself observed and thereby gave His followers a pattern to follow after.—In contrast, the worldly government is not one which shows mercy, but is a revenger (Rom. 13), as the one breaking the law of Moses died without mercy (Heb. 10). And this law today outside of Christ stands unannulled by Christ for vengeance and discipline over the wicked.

Jacob Hutter, after whom the Hutterian Brethren were named, wrote in a letter to the Moravian authorities, in 1535, when the congregation under his care had been driven from their dwellings by a detachment of soldiers upon the command of the authorities:

At the present time we find ourselves on the wide, wide heath; if God will, without disadvantage to any one. We will not do a wrong or an injury to any man, yea, not to our greatest enemy, neither to Ferdinandus (King of Austria) nor any one else, great or small. All our actions and conduct, word and work, life and walk, are open; there is no secret about it all. Rather than knowingly to rob a man of a penny we would willingly give up a hundred guilders. And before we would give our greatest enemy a blow with the hand, to say nothing of spear, sword or halberd as is the manner of the world, we would be willing to lose our lives.

As every one sees and knows, we have no weapons of defense, such as spears or guns. In short, in our preaching and speaking and our whole walk of life our object is to live in peace and unity according to the truth and will of God, as the true followers of Christ.

In Moravia it was in the year 1579 that for the first time a sum of money was demanded from the Hutterian Brethren as a war tax. In accord with their principle of nonresistance and their Confession of Faith which forbids paying war taxes, they refused to give it. The authorities in consequence seized some of their property, such as horses, cattle and sheep, to cover the amount demanded as war taxes. "We suffer the spoiling of our goods" (Heb. 10:34), wrote a chronicler of the Brethren, "rather than do that which would be a stain and burden on our consciences." Confiscation of property for this purpose was repeated in 1584, and again in 1589. Beginning with the year 1596 property to cover the demanded war taxes was for a long period taken annually by the authorities from the Brethren.

The martyr Jan Claes, who had printed and distributed a number of Menno Simons' books, and was executed in 1544 at Amsterdam, wrote:

Christ and those who are His own were in the beginning put to death. In this you may know who are His own. Not those who boast of His name and defend their own cause with the sword, but those who live after the example of the Lord and prove their cause by the divine Word. They are the true witnesses.

Adrian Cornelis, who suffered martyrdom at Leyden, in 1551, wrote:

Woe is you who shed the innocent blood of those who have no desire to defend themselves with material or carnal weapons but only with God's Word. This is our sword, and it is two-edged and sharp.

The martyr Jan Geritz, who was burned at the stake in 1566 at The Hague, wrote:

See, my good friends, here is the weapon and sword of my faith, with this and none other. Not with the sword or spear of iron and steel, I would attack the kingdom of Antichrist. I say with the Apostle that the weapons of our warfare are not carnal but mighty before God.

Jan Pauw, deacon of the first evangelical Anabaptist congregation at Amsterdam, wrote that he would not with material weapons protect himself in the persecution.

Menno Simons' writings contain many expressions on nonresistance. Following are a few selections:[123]

The regenerated do not go to war, nor engage in strife. They are the children of peace who have beaten their swords into plowshares and their spears into pruning hooks, and know of no war. They render unto Caesar the things that are Caesar's and unto God the things that are God's. Their sword is the sword of the Spirit which they wield with a good conscience through the Holy Ghost.

Since we are to be conformed to the image of Christ (Rom. 8:29), how can we then fight our enemies with the sword? Does not the apostle Peter say: "For even hereunto were ye called, because Christ also suffered for us, leaving us an example that ye should follow his steps; who did no sin neither was guile found in his mouth; who, when he was reviled, reviled not again," etc. (I Pet. 2:21-23; Matt. 16:24)?

Again, our fortress is Christ, our defence is patience, our sword is the word of God, and our victory is the sincere, firm, unfeigned faith in Jesus Christ. Spears and swords of iron we leave to those who, alas, consider human blood and swine's blood of well-nigh equal value. He that is wise, let him judge what I mean.

Dirck Philips says:

The people of the Lord arm themselves not with carnal weapons, as, sad to say, some have done for want of understanding, but with the armor of God, with the weapons of righteousness, at the right hand and at the left . . . and with Christian patience, with which to possess their souls and overcome all their enemies.

A conference of Waterlandian Mennonites, held in 1568 at Emden in East Friesland, made the following decision concerning those who had given offense by taking part in drilling for military service:

If a brother has taken part in this, he shall desist from it, confess to sorrow for the offense and ask the forgiveness of God and the church before he may be recognized as in peace with the church.

In the Reformation era the persecutors of the evangelical, nonresistant Anabaptists often advanced the charge that their teaching on nonresistance was but a cloak to hide their evil intentions against the civil governments. Zwingli in particular often made this charge. He wrote:

Anabaptism is practiced for no other purpose but to furnish an excuse for conspiracy against the government. And again: As soon as the number of the baptized is strong enough for effectual armed resistance, they will rise in arms against the government.

Zwingli said further, in June, 1525, that the proof for these assertions is found in their disobedience to the government, since they preached and baptized contrary to the orders of the civil rulers. However, only a few years before Zwingli made these charges he had earnestly admonished his followers to obey God rather than men, even though to do so was interpreted as disloyalty to the government and as insurrection.

It is needless to say that accusations of this sort against the Swiss Brethren and Mennonites were wholly unfounded. Neither Zwingli nor any one else could point to a single instance of tumult or riot, or any other transgression of this sort, caused by any Anabaptist. The rise of the revolutionary Anabaptists —the Münsterites—took place after Zwingli's death. It is of course a fact that they disobeyed some of the religious regulations and orders of the civil authorities, but this does not prove the point. That the charges of disloyalty to the government are unfounded is recognized today by all writers who have studied their history from the sources. Dr. Adolf Fluri, of Bern, Professor Wilhelm Hadorn and other impartial writers, have pointed out that the Swiss Anabaptists always consistently adhered to the principle of nonresistance. The same is true of all the early Mennonites. Dr. G. Uhlhorn said in the great Protestant Encyclopedia, that Swiss Anabaptism was of an absolutely peaceful nature.[124]

There were Anabaptists who differed from the Mennonites on practically only one point, namely nonresistance. The most noteworthy of these were the followers of Balthasar Hubmaier. His booklet *On the Sword* is addressed to the Swiss Brethren. In this booklet he attempted to persuade them by many arguments that their position on nonresistance was unscriptural. At Nikolsburg, under the protection of the Lords of Liechtenstein, Hubmaier, within a short period, won many followers. After persecution arose his large congregation became extinct within a short span of time.

The fact deserves notice that not only the followers of Hubmaier but all Anabaptists who did not teach the principle of nonresistance, had a very brief history. Few of them indicated a willingness to endure persecution. Hubmaier's large congregation in Waldshut, after an Austrian army had taken possession of the city, accepted again their former Roman Catholic creed upon the command of the authorities. His congregation at Nikolsburg also had but a brief history. Of the Anabaptists that did not teach nonresistance, a very small number died a martyr's death, and yet in their history the words of Christ were verified that they who take the sword shall perish with the sword. Within a few years after the conversion of Menno Simons (1536) the Anabaptist sects which did not advocate nonresistance had become extinct. Only the Anabaptists who taught nonresistance—the Mennonites and Hutterian Brethren—survived the persecutions.

During the period of the severest persecution there were scarcely any standing armies. In case of war, armies consisted for the most part of mercenaries. Later, when citizens were called upon for military service, Anabaptists were not considered citizens. So extremely intolerant was the attitude of the governments toward the Anabaptists that they were treated as criminals and were not wanted in the armies.

In the year 1528 the authorities of various German states used detachments of soldiers and police to apprehend and put to death all Anabaptists. They were not given a hearing nor was there a formal sentence passed. The question to be settled was simply whether the one apprehended had been baptized on the confession of his faith and this was, as a rule, easy to decide. If he did not give a negative answer when asked, he was put to death. Many suffered martyrdom at the hands of detachments of soldiers and bands of police.

This explains why, in the earliest period of their history, there is no record of any effort on the part of Mennonites to secure exemption from military service. The fact that there is no such record does not by any means prove that they were not conscientious objectors. There is convincing proof that the Mennonites, from the beginning of their history, held the principle of nonresistance.

It was only after severe persecution had ceased and the Mennonites had been granted a measure of toleration that they were expected to render military service. The first country to tolerate them was Holland. When that country became involved in war, the Mennonites for the first time encountered difficulties on account of their refusal to render such service. In 1577 Prince William of Orange, the ruler of the United Netherlands, granted them exemption, and this exemption was ratified by his son and successor, Prince Maurice.

CHAPTER 45

NONCONFORMITY TO THE WORLD

There is abundant proof in the source material that from its inception the Mennonite Church taught the principle of nonconformity to the world. Heinrich Bullinger wrote two books against the Swiss Brethren. In his first book, published in 1531, he says that they disapproved of dancing and all other forms of worldly amusement. Furthermore he states that they insisted on modest apparel and condemned outward adornment. In his larger work, printed in 1561, Bullinger wrote concerning the early Swiss Brethren: "They led their lives under a semblance of a quite spiritual conduct, and reproved sharply covetousness, pride, profanity, the frivolous talking and inordinate life of the world." In another place he says: "They reproved earnestly all vain display, all intemperance in eating and drinking, all profanity and other sin." He states further that they had regulations in regard to clothing, and that "they rejected all wearing of costly clothing and ornaments." Their walk and conversation, he observes, "were of a serious turn and they were very outspoken in their testimony against the sensuality and unscrupulousness of the world."

Johannes Kessler, the chronicler of St. Gall, describing the origin of the Swiss Brethren church, says: "Their life was irreproachable. They shunned costly clothing. Their walk and conversation were quite humble." The chronicler Sebastian Franck, who lived in South Germany, wrote in 1531 that there were Anabaptists who followed regulations in respect to simplicity of clothing. In the following year, at the disputation held at Zofingen in Switzerland, the spokesmen of the Swiss Brethren stressed their teaching that worldly conformity of any description should not be tolerated in the church. Again, in the great disputation held in 1538 in the city of Bern, the Mennonite representatives emphasized their rejection of worldly conformity.

Berthold Haller, the leading Zwinglian reformer of Bern, wrote in 1532 of the Swiss Brethren: "All their followers earnestly guard themselves against sin. They come together frequently and strictly conform to their rules." The preachers of the Protestant state church, assembled in a synod at Zofingen in 1532, admitted in a letter to the civil authorities, that the Swiss Brethren "have an appearance of outward piety to a far greater degree than we and all the churches which unitedly with us confess Christ." Wolfgang Capito, Zwinglian reformer of Strasburg in Alsace, wrote concerning the Swiss Brethren: "They are determined to shun the evil life of the world . . . and to flee from that which is in conformity with the lust of the flesh and of the world."

August Pfeiffer, an early Lutheran theologian, wrote: "The Mennonites shun immodesty in dress, swearing, insincerity, intemperance, immorality, and discord. Judging from their lives you would suppose that they are all true and holy Christians." Concerning the life of the Brethren in the Netherlands, van Bentheim, a Dutch author, wrote in 1698: "We may learn from these people much that is good, namely humility, contentment, sobriety, and especially charity toward the needy. . . . Above all, they insist on modesty in respect to clothing."

George Thormann, a minister of the Swiss Reformed state church, writing in 1693, says that the Swiss Brethren insisted on simple dress. In a mandate against the Brethren in the canton Bern warning was given against giving aid to Mennonite fugitives; it was stated that they were readily recognizable at first sight; apparently they were known by their simple manner of life. In 1568 a conference of the Swiss Brethren held at Strasburg ruled that church members who were tailors and seamstresses should refrain from making clothing that was unbecoming for a Christian.

Menno Simons addressed the Münsterite sect of fanatic revolutionaries as follows:

The kingdom of the Lord is not a kingdom in which a swaggering show of gold, silver, pearls, silk, velvet, and display has any place, as is the usage of the proud, haughty world and as also your leaders teach and permit under the pretense that it is harmless if the heart is not proud. . . . But in the kingdom of Christ—the kingdom of all humility—the outward adorning of the body has no place, but the inward ornaments of the Spirit are sought and coveted with great zeal and diligence and with a broken, contrite heart.

Again Menno Simons wrote:

They say that they believe, and yet there are no limits nor bounds to their accursed wantonness, foolish pride and pomp with silk, velvet, costly clothes, gold rings, chains, silver belts, pins, and the like. Notwithstanding all this, they still desire to be called the Christian Church.

Regarding nonswearing of oaths the Swiss Brethren took a strict attitude. At times the government of various Swiss states demanded taking oaths of the whole population, in order to ascertain which individuals had conscientious objections against swearing. The objectors were accused of being Mennonites. It may be worth noticing in this connection that Ulrich Zwingli, in his earliest years as a reformer, believed that the New Testament Scriptures forbid the swearing of oaths. Menno Simons, in many places of his writings, testifies against the oath.

In the disputation of Zofingen the Swiss Brethren condemned slavery as a feature of worldliness and contrary to Christian principles. Again, from a statement made by Martin Butzer it is clear that they disapproved of indulgence of luxuries while any of their neighbors were suffering want. The writings of Bullinger and other contemporary authors indicate clearly that the Swiss Brethren took a strict attitude regarding the sin of profanity. Bullinger says: "The Anabaptists should not be censured for their custom of reproving those whom they hear using profanity." He adds with regret, that the ministers of the national church "do little or nothing" against this sin, but that on the contrary some of the clergy themselves were guilty of profanity. It is of interest to notice from the source material that one who was accused of being an Anabaptist could clear himself of this charge by using profanity. Profane swearing was accepted as a proof of being untainted by "the Anabaptist heresy." Again Bullinger, as well as other writers of the state church, stated that the Swiss Brethren shunned the public houses where strong drink was sold. Menno Simons has much to say concerning the evil of "the accursed drink houses," to use his own words.

CHAPTER 46

SIN, SALVATION, SANCTIFICATION

On the doctrine of original sin the early Mennonites agreed with the leading Protestant theologians. They taught that the descendants of Adam inherited a sinful nature, but that through the atoning sacrifice of Christ all infants are within the covenant of divine grace and are saved. Rejecting the view that the act of baptism removes the guilt of original sin, they attributed to the blood of Christ which was shed for all men what in Catholic and Lutheran theology is ascribed to the act of baptism.

"We believe that all children who cannot yet distinguish between good and evil are assuredly saved through the sufferings of Christ, the second Adam," says Conrad Grebel. And again: "As concerns the argument that faith is required of all [for salvation] we hold that infants are excepted, and believe that they are saved without faith." In the disputation of Bern, in 1538, the spokesman of the Brethren said: "The infants are saved and are heirs of eternal life through the death of Christ . . . although they have inherited the sinful nature from Adam. But as they have inherited it without any fault of their own, so also they are saved without faith."

Menno Simons wrote on the salvation of the infants:

And although infants have neither faith nor baptism, think not therefore that they are lost. O no! they are saved, for they have the Lord's own promise of the kingdom of God. They are saved not indeed through any element, ceremony or external rites, but only by grace through Jesus Christ.[125]

Dirck Philips wrote:

Hence we conclude with the apostles and with the entire Holy Scriptures that inherited sin has been atoned for and taken away by Christ to this extent: The infants may not be judged and condemned for the sin of Adam. That the nature of the children is inclined toward evil does not condemn them; it is through the grace of God not accounted as sin to them, but as long as they are childlike and without the knowledge of good and evil, they are pleasing and acceptable to God through Jesus Christ.

The supposition that the Swiss Brethren did not accept the doctrine of justification by faith, or salvation through the blood of Christ, is another unfounded insinuation of their opponents. George Blaurock, in a brief confession of faith which he addressed to the Council of Zurich, wrote:

Christ Jesus came to bring again what was lost through the fall of Adam, through which we all would be dead in sin if God had not sent His Son and given Him all power in heaven and on earth, that every one who would call upon His name and trust in Him should have eternal life. Through His death all who call upon His name shall have forgiveness of sins.

Wolfgang Capito, one of the Zwinglian reformers of Strasburg wrote in 1527 about the Swiss Brethren: "Their most prominent point of teaching is that we should hear Christ, the Son of God, and that whoever believes in Him has everlasting life." Martin Weniger, the principal spokesman of the Brethren in the debate of Zofingen, in 1532, said: "As the people of Israel were delivered from raging Pharaoh by the blood of the Passover lamb, so also we are delivered from the fetters of Satan by the blood of Christ." Again, in the debate of 1538, at Bern, the Brethren said: "Christ is the new and living way. . . . As through one man—Adam—death came into the world, so also through one—Christ—it was taken away. All who believe in Him have eternal life through His blood."

Pilgram Marpeck says on justification by faith:

The apostles have preached the Gospel as they were bidden, namely that Christ died for the sins of the whole world, that He has reconciled the Father, has atoned for unrighteousness by His blood, and saves from eternal death, so that henceforth every believer, being a temple of God the Father, Son, and Holy Spirit, has become partaker of the new, eternal life and is to live blamelessly.

Menno Simons wrote:

There will in eternity be found no other remedy for our sins, neither in heaven nor upon earth, neither works, merits nor ordinances (even though they are observed according to the Scriptures), neither enduring persecution and tribulation, neither the innocent blood of the saints, nor any other means, but alone the immaculate blood of the Lamb which out of pure grace, mercy, and love was shed once for all for the remission of our sins.[126]

Those who trust in their works or ceremonies for salvation deny thereby the grace and merits of Christ. For if our reconciliation consisted in works and ceremonies, grace would come to naught and the merits and virtue of the blood of Christ would all be void. O no! it is grace and will be grace in all eternity, all that the merciful Father through His dear Son and Holy Spirit has done for us grievous sinners.[127]

The Scriptures know of only one remedy, which is Christ with His merits, death and blood. Hence, he who seeks the remission of his sins through baptism, rejects the blood of the Lord and makes water his idol. Therefore let every one have a care, lest he ascribe the honor and glory due to Christ, to the outward ceremonies and visible elements.[128]

The fact that regeneration was ascribed to baptism was a point of offense to the evangelical Anabaptists. Martin Butzer, having had a number of conferences with Michael Sattler, said that "his principal objection to infant baptism was the general belief that man is christened, or saved, through it, when in fact it is faith that saves." Pilgram Marpeck says:

To believe that baptism cleanses the infant from original sin and through it the child is christened, or made a Christian, as is the general belief of the people, is terrible idolatry and an abomination before God; it is, as said above, a derision and mockery of the blood of Christ. For only the blood of the spotless lamb, Jesus Christ, through every one's personal faith and renewing of the heart, cleanses from sin.

It has been generally supposed that among the reformers of the sixteenth century Martin Luther in particular emphasized the doctrine of salvation through faith in Christ and His atoning sacrifice. In plain fact, however, Menno Simons stressed this doctrine as much as any other of the reformers, and he was more consistent than Luther and others in his teaching on this point. As stated above, the Mennonites rejected the doctrines of regeneration through baptism and of forgiveness of sin through partaking of the communion. While they recognized the fact that the Lord, in the institution of the latter ordinance, stated that His blood was to be shed for the remission of sin, they pointed out that the thought of the communion being observed for remission of sin is foreign to Scripture teaching.

The writers of the early Mennonites placed particular emphasis on the imperative need of consistent Christian living. They insisted on recognizing the fact of "the exceeding sinfulness of sin," that the nature of sin is enmity against God. They believed that striving after holiness is the necessary fruit of saving faith. The true Christian life, according to their teaching, is a holy life of separation from sin and the world, a witness to the saving and keeping power of Christ, and such a life alone is consistent with the Christian profession. While they consistently taught the doctrine of salvation by faith, they placed equal emphasis on the truth that saving faith is fruitful of true Christian living. They differed from state church Protestantism by emphasizing the fact that in the Scriptures justification by faith is inseparably connected with conversion and newness of life. They denounced as unscriptural the idea, largely prevailing in state church Protestantism, that one may be a Christian (being justified by faith) without scriptural repentance and without taking the Christian profession seriously and walking in newness of life. The Brethren were of the opinion, according to a statement of Bullinger, that in the national church the preaching of grace was much too *ringfertig* (superficial).

In their booklet *Vindication* the Swiss Brethren protested against the opinion "that it is possible for no one to live according to the gospel and be obedient to the divine commands and to keep them, or to believe in Christ and die to sin according to the requirements and doctrine of the Gospel." "In our time," says Conrad Grebel, "every one hopes to be saved by a faith which consists of outward appearance, without the fruits of faith . . . and while remaining in the old life of sin."

The accusation against the Brethren that they disowned the doctrine of salvation by faith and believed that they would be saved by their own works was made on entirely inadequate grounds. Ulrich Zwingli quotes as evidence of this charge the following sentence from the Schleitheim Confession: "Baptism shall be administered to all who have been instructed, who show repentance and newness of life, and who of a truth believe that their sins were taken away by Christ, and are willing to walk in the resurrection of Jesus Christ." To mention walking in the resurrection of Christ in this connection, says Zwingli, is a veiled denial of justification by faith, since a willingness to walk in newness of life is insisted upon.

The evangelical Anabaptists and Mennonites steadfastly held to this teaching. Menno Simons emphasized the need of a holy life as persistently as the doctrine of salvation by faith. He wrote:

But that we shun carnal works, and desire to conform ourselves in our weakness to His word and commandment, this we do [not because we would be saved by our own works and merit but] because He has thus taught and commanded us. For whosoever does not walk according to His doctrine, testifies by his deeds that he does not believe in Him nor know Him, and that he is not in the communion of the saints. (John 15:7; I John 3:10; 5:10; II John 6).

For the truly regenerated and spiritually minded conform in all things to the word and ordinances of the Lord; not for the reason that they suppose to merit the propitiation of their sins and eternal life; by no means. For this they depend on nothing except the blood and merits of Christ, relying upon the sure promise of the merciful Father which was graciously given to all believers, which blood alone, I say again, is and ever will be the only and eternally valid means of our reconciliation, and not works, baptism or Lord's Supper, as said above.[129]

For this can never fail; where there is true Christian faith, there is also dying to sin, a new creature, true repentance, a sincere, regenerated, unblamable Christian. One does no longer live according to the lusts of sin but according to the will of Him who purchased us with His blood, drew us by His Spirit and regenerated us by His Word, namely Jesus Christ.

True faith which avails before God, is a living and saving power which is, through the preaching of the holy Word, bestowed of God on the heart; moving, changing and regenerating it to newness of mind. It destroys all ungodliness, all pride, unholy ambition and selfishness, and makes us children in malice. Behold, such is the faith which the Scriptures teach us, and not a vain, dead, and unfruitful illusion, as the world dreams.[130]

One of the spokesmen of the Brethren in the disputation at Zofingen said:

From these Scripture passages it is clear that a faith which is without works is no faith and does not avail before God. It is a mouth confession but a denial by the works. . . . The Kingdom of God does not consist in words nor in boasting but in the power of God.

Martin Weniger wrote in 1535 in his *Rechenschaft* (confession):

If Christ's kingdom is truly within us (Luke 17:21), we obtain grace to do the will of God and serve Him acceptably with reverence and godly fear (Heb. 12:28). If we are under grace (Rom. 6:14), sin cannot reign in our mortal bodies (Rom. 6:12), for Christ died for all that they which live should not henceforth live unto themselves but unto Him who died for them and rose again (II Cor. 5:15). . . . John says, If we say we have fellowship with Him and walk in darkness (that is in sin, Eph. 5:11), we lie and do not the truth.

Pilgram Marpeck wrote:

We recognize as true Christian faith only such a faith through which the Holy Spirit and the love of God come into the heart, and which is active, powerful, and operative in all outward obedience and commanded works. We believe that one is made a child of God and free from the law and the bondage of sin only through such a faith by which the Spirit, as the power of God, lives in the heart and does His work. There, then, is liberty. (II Cor. 3:17). . . . To such liberty one comes by abiding in the words of Christ (John 8:31) and through the law of the Spirit of life through which one is made free from the law of sin and death (Rom. 8:2), but not from the law of Christ, or from the obligation of obedience in the things which He has taught and commanded. This is disowned by Schwenckfeld [who denied the need of practicing the Christian ordinances].

In a *Supplication* handed over to the civil authorities by the Brethren in the Canton Zurich, in 1589, they say:

But, dear sirs, as concerns the accusation made by your preachers that we would be saved by our own works and sufferings [namely by enduring persecution], and thus render the redemptive work of Christ vain and useless, in this charge they do us wrong; for all the good that we can do or accomplish is only the fruit of a true living faith.

From a later period we have an important statement to the point from the pen of George Thormann, a minister of high rank in the state church of Bern. He said that the Brethren do not believe that we are saved by our works or merit, "but by grace alone, through the redemption that is in Christ Jesus (Rom. 3:24)." Furthermore Thormann made the statement that an elder (bishop) of the Brethren whom he asked regarding this point assured him that "they ascribe no merit whatever to their works, knowing fully that their own works are quite imperfect before God and do not merit anything before Him."

The Swiss Brethren, as well as the Mennonites of North Germany and the Netherlands, have often been charged with teaching perfectionism, or the doctrine of the entire eradication of sin from the heart of the believer, eliminating the further need of praying, "Forgive us our debts." Past sins being forgiven, the believer's own righteousness is, according to this doctrine, flawless before God. This doctrine of perfectionism has been to this day ascribed to the Swiss Brethren by leading church historians who make such assertions as an evidence of and as a proof that they were the "spiritual children" of Thomthe supposed general doctrinal unsoundness of the Brethren as Münzer, the enthusiast.

The writings and oral testimony of the Swiss Brethren explicitly contradict the charge of teaching perfectionism. Zwingli accused Felix Manz of defending this doctrine but added that he (Manz) would not confess to be entirely sinless. Manz did not admit the charge. In the great disputation held in Bern, in 1538, it was found that there was agreement on the point of perfectionism between the Brethren and the theologians of the Zwinglian state church.

Of the pertinent testimonies that the Brethren did not teach this doctrine we shall quote a few. Heinrich Hottinger of Zollikon, near Zurich, in a letter dated August 19, 1525, petitioned the Council of Zurich "not to believe every liar who slanders me and others. For some time a report has been spread that some of us [the Brethren] teach that one may live without sin, also that we boast of living without sin. And now it has been asserted that I have taught that to commit murder, adultery, or theft is not sin [to the believer]. Thus I am being slandered. . . ." Martin Weniger said in the disputation of Zofingen: "In me personally there is nothing good. I am unable of myself even to think anything that is good, but am, as others, flesh and blood and subject to temptation. But that I should let these reign, I answer, No. Therefore God must give me grace to overcome." In the disputation at Bern, in 1538, the Brethren stated that they "never taught that they could not sin, or were without sin." They said further: "It is quite possible that one may be overtaken, and sin from weakness." Andreas Castelberger, having been accused of trespassing certain ordinances of the Council of Zurich, protested his innocence of the charges made, but added: "Before God I am among the greatest of sinners."

Probably the most frequently quoted statement of Zwingli, in which he asserts that the Swiss Brethren taught perfectionism, is the following: "Those among us who have caused the controversy in regard to baptism had previously often asked us to organize a new church or meeting. They supposed that they could gather a church which was without sin." In making this statement Zwingli failed to take into consideration that, if the church which they desired to establish was to be sinless, he could not be the leader in such a church, for, as the Brethren were fully aware, he did not accept the doctrine of sinless perfection.

The well authenticated fact that the Brethren asked him to accept the leadership in a church that was to be organized in accordance with his former program, shows that his statement concerning a sinless church is unfounded. Such self-contradictory statements regarding the Brethren, as the above, have been uncritically accepted by many writers.

Menno Simons and Dirck Philips, in their writings, often protested against the insinuation of teaching perfectionism. They explained that this accusation was occasioned by the fact that they laid stress on the imperative need of consistent, holy Christian living. Furthermore they complained that they were for this reason accused of hoping to be saved by their own works and merits. Menno Simons wrote, "But they accuse us falsely that we assert to be without sin. They do this because we insist with all the Scripture on the need of a life showing the fruits of repentance."[131] Again, Menno says: "The preachers [of the state churches] tell a falsehood concerning us when they say that we would be saved by our merits and works and that we pretend to be without sin."[132]

Chapter 47

DOCTRINE OF THE TRINITY OF GOD

A number of Dutch historians have defended the view that the early Mennonites were, on the whole, liberal in theology and did not teach the deity of Christ and the Trinity of God. In particular it is supposed by some that the Waterlandian Mennonites in Holland held various liberalistic opinions. In view of such assertions it is worth while to review the teachings of the early Anabaptists on these points.

Heinrich Bullinger, in his larger work against the Brethren, enumerates the points on which the Brethren differed, or were supposed to differ, from the Protestant state churches, but does not mention any disagreement as regards the Trinity or the deity of Christ. Without question he would have made mention of it, had there been the slightest ground for a suspicion of unorthodoxy on these points.

Again, in the great debates between the Brethren and the state church leaders at various places in Switzerland no such charge was advanced against them. This is a truly significant fact. On the contrary, in the disputation held at Bern in 1538 a spokesman of the state church said: "Some have taught that Christ, our dear Lord, was not truly and in very reality God, although I believe that you [the Swiss Brethren] are not by any means of this opinion; I do not think this of you."

Again, in a conference of the Swiss Brethren held at Strasburg in 1555 they confessed the deity of Christ, and, in a large gathering of bishops and ministers from many countries, held in the same city in 1592, they also expressed themselves clearly on this point.

Some of the less conservative Mennonites of the Netherlands were approached by the Socinians with a plea for union with them. The proposal was bluntly refused them. Especially among the Waterlandian Mennonites the Socinians had counted on success for their plan, since the Waterlanders took a somewhat less conservative attitude than the Mennonites in general in regard to discipline. In this expectation the Socinians were wholly disappointed. Hans de Ries, the most prominent bishop among the Waterlandian congregations was personally visited and interviewed by Christopher Osterod and another Socinian minister. In his reply to their proposal Hans de Ries said that "a union is not only undesirable but impossible." He wrote in consequence a strong defense of the deity of Christ, entitled, *Clear Proof of the Pre-existence and Deity of Jesus Christ.* The first Waterlandian Confession (drawn up in 1577), Article VI, says: "We confess Christ Jesus to be truly God and from eternity God's Son, and that He became truly a man, having the divine and the human natures." Could there be clearer disproof of the assertion that the Waterlandian Mennonites were unorthodox as regards the deity of Christ? The outstanding defender of Biblical orthodoxy in Holland was a Waterlandian Mennonite bishop. The Mennonites, including the Waterlanders, then stood solidly for Biblical orthodoxy and conservatism.

On the deity of Christ Dirck Philips wrote: "He who does not confess the eternal Godhead and true humanity of Jesus Christ is an antichrist."[133] Menno Simons taught that Jesus Christ was truly divine and truly human. In his writings he often testifies to his belief in the two natures of Christ.[134]

Menno Simons realized the importance of the doctrine of the deity of Christ and he taught it with consistent emphasis. In the *Confession of the Triune God* Menno made a reply to Adam Pastor who was unorthodox on this point. Adam Pastor of Dorpen in Westphalia, northwest Germany, was about the year 1530 a priest at Aschendorf. The exact time when he cast his lot with the Mennonites is not known. He served the church as a minister, and was ordained as elder by Menno Simons and Dirck Philips probably in 1542. About 1546, or somewhat later, certain doctrinal deviations of Pastor, in particular regarding Christ's deity, became apparent. In 1547 the bishops met at Emden to confer concerning this matter and the needed steps to be taken. Adam Pastor persisted in the denial of the deity of Christ. Since all hopes for his restoration to his former position proved vain, the bishops in the same year held a convention at Goch in the Rhineland which resulted in his excommunication. His adherents were expelled with him from the church. He defended his views in a work which appeared later in print. Menno in his reply to him (the *Confession of the Triune God*) speaks of the denial of Christ's deity as "a blasphemy, a curse, and abomination."[135]

According to statements made by a number of Dutch historians Adam Pastor was excommunicated by Dirck Philips without Menno's consent or against his counsel. These writers have expressed the opinion that excommunication on account of false doctrine was in every instance out of place. The fact is that in various places Menno stated that excommunication is to be used in case of persistent false teaching as well as of unrepented transgression. Besides, there is clear indication that Pastor held Menno, with others, personally responsible for his expulsion.[136]

PART FOUR

Appendices

THE EDICT OF EMPEROR CHARLES V AGAINST MENNO SIMONS OF 1542

By the Emperor

To our worthy, beloved Mayors, Boards, and Counsellors, etc., of our city of Leeuwarden, Greeting:—

Whereas, it has come to our knowledge and we have fully ascertained that a [former] priest, Menno Symonss, formerly pastor at Witmarsum in our land of Friesland being polluted with Anabaptism and other false teachings, had departed out of the said land, and we have now obtained trustworthy information, that he has again secretly returned into our aforesaid land where he is now sojourning, endeavoring at night and other unseasonable times and in diverse places, to seduce by his false teachings and sermons the simple people, our subjects, and to lead them away from the faith and unity of the Holy Church; and that he also has undertaken to make a few books treating on his aforesaid erroneous teachings, and to circulate and scatter the same among our aforesaid subjects, which he has no right to do and we can not tolerate the same;

Therefore, to take appropriate steps in this matter, we ordain and command herewith, that ye everywhere in your jurisdiction, do publish, cry out and proclaim in the places where such matters are usually brought to the knowledge of the public, that every one in our aforesaid land, of whatever station he may be, should be on his guard, not to receive the same Minne Symonss into his house or on his property, or to give him shelter, or food, or drink, or to accord him any favor or help, or to speak or converse with him, in whatever manner or place it may be, or to accept or keep in possession any of the aforesaid books published by the same Minne, or any other books that he may publish at any future time—all on penalty of punishment on life and property, as heretics, as may be found due according to the law and our previous placards;

And further that we have permitted and authorized every one of our subjects, whoever he may be, and permit and authorize through decree, that they may apprehend the same Minne wherever they may be able to find him, no place or jurisdiction excepted, and send him captive to our court in Friesland; for which they, in case they accomplish this, shall receive for a recompense besides the expense they may have incurred in this matter, the sum of one hundred golden Karolus gulden, which shall be paid them by our General Treasurer of Friesland without any hesitancy.

To him who may undertake and accomplish this work, we decree and promise grace and pardon regarding that which he may have committed against us in the matter of Anabaptism or other heresy, or in lesser crimes, on condition, in case he was polluted by Anabaptism or other heresies, that he repent of the same and come again to the unity of the holy Church.

In the same manner we most earnestly command, on pain of the most grievous penalties, that ye do the utmost diligence to investigate and inquire concerning the said Minne among his followers and adherents who may be apprehended anywhere within your jurisdiction and, together with such information as ye may obtain, to send them as prisoners to our aforesaid court, that they may be dealt with according to their deserts.

We hereby also give authority and special command to you and all our subjects, in whatever jurisdiction it may be found possible to apprehend him, to be guided by the instructions above given; we bid and command every person as regards the above said capture [of Menno] to put forth their united efforts and render all help and assistance that may be asked of them toward that end. In doing this, they will incur our pleasure.

Given in our city of Leeuwarden under our secret seal, published as a placard, on the seventh day of December of the year 1542.

By the Emperor to his Majesty's Stadtholder, President and Counsellors in Friesland.   (Signed) Boeymer.

Received on December thirteenth and published on the fourteenth of the same month.

PALATINATE MENNONITE FAMILY NAMES

*Names of Swiss Mennonite Refugees in the Palatinate after 1664 who later came to Pennsylvania.**

A
Allenbach
Augsberger
Aberfold
Aschberger
Auer (Oyer)
Althaus

B
Bechtel
Bauman
Bieri
Beutler
Brenneman
Borcholder
Bachman
Baumgartner
Bühler
Brubacher
Biehn
Becker
Burkhart
Bossert
Berg
Brand
Beer
Bähr
Blickensdörfer
Binggele
Berger
Blaser
Blank
Beery
Brechbühl
Bixler

Bornträger
Bitschi
Bauer
Bichsel
Brunk
Baltzer
Buller
Bergthold

C
Clemens
Crayenbühl
Cassel
Cressman
Christophel

D
Dallem
Dester
Dierstein
Danner
Detweiler

E
Erb
Engel
Eymann
Ebersole
Eicher
Egli
Ellenberger
Eschelmann
Eschbacher
Enger
Eberly
Everling

F
Frick
Funk
Forni
Fried
Frey
Frantz
Fellman
Finger
Fretz
Fischer
Freienberger

G
Gram
Geiger
Guth
Gochnaur
Gerber
Gäuman
Glücki
Galli
Gross
Göbel
Garber
Güngerich
Gascho
Grunewalt
Groff
Gerig
Gindelsberger
Grimm

H
Hüthwohl
Herstein

* "Palatinate Mennonite Census Lists," *The Mennonite Quarterly Review,* Vol. XIV, pp. 5-40, 67-89, 170-186, 224-248; Vol. XV, pp. 46-63; Kauffman, D., *Mennonite Cyclopedic Dictionary;* Müller, E., *Geschichte der Bernischen Täufer,* Frauenfeld, 1895.

Hirschy
Holl
Hackman
Heer
Hiestand
Hirschler
Hirschberger
Hagman
Huber
Hochstetler
Hoffman
Hofstetter
Herr
Hauser
Hess
Hauri
Hiernli
Habegger
Harnish
Haldeman
Hallman
Holley
Heller
Hunsinger
Hertzler
Hege

I

Imhof
Ingold

J

Jansen
Jodter
Jorde
Johnson

K

Kaegy
Kolb
Kreybül
Kauffman
Kindig
König
Kreiter
Kropf
Kennel
Kurtz
Kraybill
Kintzi

L

Lescher
Lichti
Lehman
Lentz
Löscher
Longinegger
Landes
Leisy
Lüthi
Litmiller
Lang
Leatherman
Lapp
Latscha
Leuti

M

Mayer
Müller
Moselman
Möllinger
Meili
Moser
Mosimann
Mast
Mumaw
Metzler
Mininger
Moyer
Marten

N

Neuwkomet
Neff
Norri
Noldt
Neuenswander
Neuhauser
Nussbaum
Nüssli
Nafziger

O

Oberholzer
Oswald
Oberli
Oesch

P

Pletcher
Peters

R

Rediger
Rutt
Rychener
Richard
Rosenberger
Roth
Rupp
Reuser
Rink
Reber
Rocki
Rasy
Ramseier
Reist
Rugibill
Rediger

S

Seiler
Schertz
Schultz
Schelly
Stähly
Stutzman
Suter
Schlatter
Schnegg
Schrag
Schwartzentraub
Schlabach
Stoltzfus
Schmucker
Strickler
Schuhmacher
Schmidt
Schneider
Strahm
Stauffer
Schenk
Schwartz
Steiner
Schaub
Showalter
Schmutzer

Schantz

Schauman

Schmutz

Schellenberger

Stettler

Steinmann

Sommer

Stoll

T

Thut

Treyer

Tauscher

U

Umel

Uebi (Eby)

W

Wideman

Weiney

Witmer

Wenger

Würtz

Wagner

Weber

Welti

Weyss

Widman

Wahli

Wisler

Wedel

Z

Zehr

Zurflüh

Zimmerman

Zerger

Zug

Ziegler

INFLUENCE OF MENNONITES ON OTHER DENOMINATIONS

Chapter 33, on the character of the evangelical Anabaptists, contains various quotations from non-Mennonite authors, some, in fact, from opponents and persecutors who testify to the piety of life and partly to the salutary general influence of the early Mennonite Church. We repeat here but one or two of these citations: The church historian, Ernst Müller, a Swiss Reformed clergyman, said: "They placed the principal emphasis on holiness of life." And Ernst Stähelin, of the same church, professor of church history in Basel, wrote: "Anabaptism, by its earnest determination to follow in life and practice the primitive Christian church, has kept alive the conviction that he who is in Christ is a new creature, and that those who are identified with His cause will necessarily encounter the opposition of the world."

Among the more prominent reformers, Ulrich Zwingli, in his earlier writings refers repeatedly to the beneficial influence of Swiss Brethren teaching upon the Swiss Reformed Church of which he was the founder. In a book written in December, 1524, he frankly ascribes his rejection of the Roman Catholic and Lutheran view of the sacraments, or Christian ordinances, to Swiss Brethren influences. Through his controversy with the Brethren, Zwingli was led to see, according to his own statements, that the Christian ordinances have a symbolic meaning and do not possess the virtue of bringing the sinner into the right relationship with God. He says: "Those who oppose infant baptism have brought to light the good point that cleansing from sin cannot be ascribed to baptism nor to any other sacrament, but that the sacraments are signs [rites] to be observed by the elect of God." In his *Book on Baptism* Zwingli refers again and again to the good results of his controversy with the Brethren. He says:

> We are now face to face with the question of the effect or nature of baptism. Here I unhesitatingly concede to the opponents of infant baptism that the controversy about baptism has had good results. The first point gained is that the human [Roman Catholic] additions to the act of baptism, such as conjuring Satan, smearing with saliva, putting salt into the mouth of the infant, have been shown to be vain inventions.—The other point which has come to light through this controversy is that we have learned to realize that the act of baptism does not wash away sin, as however we have until now imagined without ground of God's Word.

We were of the opinion that the water of baptism cleanses the infant from sin which, as we now know, he does not have, and that
he would be lost without the application of water—all of which are
errors.

And again Zwingli says:

Not baptism but regeneration saves. Therefore the controversy
on infant baptism has proved beneficial, for we have learned
through it that baptism does not save nor purify.

Thus Zwingli specifically testifies to the influence of Swiss Brethren teaching on Reformed theology on an important point, namely the
conception of the sacraments (ordinances). It is remarkable that without exception historians have failed to take notice of this fact.

Zwingli, although he retained the practice of infant baptism, found
himself unable to give a definition of baptism that would justify this
practice. In his literary controversy with Balthazar Hubmaier, Zwingli gives this definition:

Baptism is a sign or rite laying obligations upon those who accept it and indicating that they intend to mend their lives and follow
Christ.

Clearly this definition is in itself an indication of Anabaptist influence. The definition calls, in fact, for the baptism of believers. Hubmaier, in his reply to Zwingli, quotes this definition and comments on
it thus: "Thanks be to God, the truth has at last come to the light."

Zwingli, according to his own testimony given in 1525, for a time
favored the abolition of infant baptism. The reason why he eventually
retained it and was now defending it in his *Book on Baptism,* was because he had decided upon a union of church and state. For an inclu-
sive state church, such as was established with his approval, infant
baptism was necessary. This decision of Zwingli was a grave offense
to the Swiss Brethren. They definitely disapproved of a union of
church and state.

In the earliest stage of the general Reformation movement, the
evangelical Anabaptists stood alone in the practice of church discipline.
In the Protestant state churches discipline was not practiced. Martin
Butzer, the most prominent leader in the Protestant Church of Strasburg, was through Anabaptist influence led to see the imperative need
of church discipline. He admitted that without the practice of discipline there can be no true Christian church. Butzer did his best to
introduce discipline in the state church of Strasburg, but his attempts
in this direction were fruitless. At Geneva in Switzerland, John Calvin
somewhat later was successful in the endeavor to introduce church
discipline in the state church.

John Calvin renounced Romanism at a somewhat later date than Luther and Zwingli, namely in 1534. In the same year he went to Strasburg, where the influence of Martin Butzer (indirectly of the Anabaptists) became a prominent factor in his theological development. It was apparently through Butzer's influence that he realized the essential value of church discipline, though he also came into personal contact with evangelical Anabaptists, and in 1539 had a debate with Anabaptists in Strasburg. As a religious leader John Calvin by far outdistanced Martin Butzer. In Geneva, where Calvin became the leader in the state church, he was successful in certain respects in which Butzer had failed, in particular as regards church discipline. His success in this respect was due to the fact that, while in Strasburg and in all Protestantism the church was ruled by the state, Calvin's superior ability found it possible to make the state the servant of the church. To a greater degree than Luther, Zwingli, Butzer, or any other reformer, John Calvin succeeded in the attempt of making the state do the bidding of the state church. Calvin was leader of the church as well as virtually the political ruler. In Calvinistic Geneva the church had the power to dictate to the state and to have the state enforce its decisions as regards discipline, including rulings against worldliness in dress. Transgression of church regulations was punished by the magistrates. Thus the union of church and state at Geneva was of a somewhat different nature from that found in Lutheran and Zwinglian states.

John Calvin, in 1544, published a book in which he attempted a refutation of the Swiss Brethren Confession of Schleitheim which, as he stated in the preface, was sent him from a very great distance. In this book Calvin approved and commended the teaching of this confession regarding the need of church discipline, but made the assertion that "these unfortunate and ungrateful people have learned this teaching and some other correct views from us." Apparently Calvin was not aware that this confession of the Swiss Brethren dated back to the year 1527; that is, to a time when he was yet a Roman Catholic and his age was scarcely eighteen years.

The rite of confirmation, though never practiced in the Mennonite Church, was yet, incredible as it may appear, introduced in the Protestant state churches indirectly through Mennonite influence. Among Protestants confirmation was first introduced by Martin Butzer in Strasburg. Butzer freely recognized the fact that "it would be more scriptural to baptize believers only." He nevertheless retained infant baptism for the reason that the existing union of church and state required it, and the civil authorities would not consent to its abolition.

In the controversy on infant baptism the Swiss Brethren and some of their sympathizers pointed out to Butzer that the possibility of personally accepting the obligations involved in church membership is entirely absent in the baptism of infants. In the Roman Catholic Church the realization of this fact had led to the introduction of the rite of confirmation, and this rite was now introduced by Martin Butzer in the established church at Strasburg. Eventually it was practiced in all the Protestant state churches. Butzer wrote at a later date: "Since in our time the people are baptized in infancy and cannot personally confess the faith when they are baptized, confirmation with its oral confession is necessary."

It is a matter of common knowledge that the principle of separation of church and state and liberty of conscience was advocated by the early leaders of the evangelical Anabaptists, including the Mennonites. The little land of Holland, where the Mennonites were more influential than in any other country, was the first country to recognize and embrace the principle of liberty of conscience. About the time of Menno Simons' death persecution began to abate in Friesland and other provinces of Holland. Although the laws demanding the persecution of the Mennonites remained, as it were, on the statute books, some of the magistrates as well as an increasing number of the population were reluctant to see the cruel execution of innocent people who took their religious convictions more seriously than any other class and were ready to suffer martyrdom for their faith. By the year 1567 a number of Friesian cities, such as Harlingen and Franeker, had large Mennonite congregations. There can be no doubt that the grant of liberty of conscience by the Dutch government is partly to be ascribed to Mennonite influence. The Mennonites were not politically active yet protested effectually against the prevalent religious tyranny. The very presence of the numerous Mennonites who were recognized as good citizens was a strong argument for toleration. By the year 1581, under the benign reign of William of Orange an attitude of general toleration prevailed in all parts of Holland.

The modern Baptist Church is of purely Mennonite origin. The first congregations given the name "Baptists" were in fact Mennonites.

The earliest Baptist congregation was organized in 1609 by John Smyth in Amsterdam, Holland. Smyth and his followers had been Puritans but had, with other Puritans, separated from the state church of England and become "Independents" (Congregationalists). In consequence of persecution they had sought and found refuge at Amsterdam, where they came under Mennonite influence. A group of these people—the "Pilgrim Fathers"—somewhat later emigrated from England to America.

During Smyth's sojourn in Amsterdam he was led to see that infant baptism is without scriptural authorization. He also disowned the Calvinistic doctrine of predestination as held by the Congregationalists. While he had been largely influenced by the Mennonites, he differed from them on the points of nonresistance and swearing of oaths. Eventually John Smyth made a strange resolution. He decided to baptize himself, and proceeded to carry out this intention. Subsequently he baptized forty-one others.

Finally, through further study, Smyth became convinced of the orthodoxy of Mennonite teaching on the points in which he had differed from it. He now felt that his self-baptism was unjustifiable, and applied for admission to the Mennonite Church. With about forty persons of his group he subscribed to a Mennonite Confession of Faith drawn up by Hans de Ries, the most prominent Mennonite elder of that period. This confession consists of thirty-eight articles and contains statements of the distinctive doctrines of the Mennonite Church, such as nonresistance, rejection of the oath, suing at law, the demand of church discipline, and others.

In the Mennonite congregation in Amsterdam which received John Smyth's application for admission there was disagreement as to the validity of his act of self-baptism; hence action in this matter was delayed for some time. Smyth died in 1612, before he was received into the Mennonite fellowship, while the rest of the group, about forty persons, united with the Mennonites. Later they returned to England.

Another confession of faith, consisting of one hundred articles, was drawn up by a member of this group, and published under the title, *A Confession of Faith of Certain English People Living at Amsterdam*. This confession likewise teaches Mennonite doctrine throughout. These people were Mennonites in doctrine and practice, and evidently desired to be known as such. The Mennonites of Holland called themselves *Doopsgezinden,* a term difficult to render into English. The literal meaning is "baptism-minded." Another name often used for the Mennonites in Holland was *Doopers*. This is the equivalent of the German word *Täufer* (Baptizers or Baptists) which was in general use in Germany and Switzerland. From the earliest times the Swiss Brethren were known as *Täufer*.

The group formerly led by John Smyth followed the Mennonites in the practice of baptism by effusion. At a later date, after the rise of the Calvinistic Baptists, they became known by the name of General Baptists for the reason that they taught general election; that is, the doctrine of free will and free grace, disowning the Calvinistic doctrine of predestination. A church of Calvinistic Baptists was established by John Spilsbury in Southwark, London, in 1633. They were called Particular Baptists, since they defended the doctrine of particular election. In those early times the mode of baptism practiced by all Baptists was effusion. No Particular Baptist Confession before 1644, and none of the General Baptists Confessions previous to 1660, specifies dipping or immersion as the mode of baptism.

Before the rise of the "Friends" (Quakers), about the middle of the seventeenth century, the Mennonites and Hutterian Brethren stood alone in testifying to the Christian teaching against war.

APPENDIX D

HALFWAY ANABAPTISTS (HALBTAEUFER)

The Halfway-Anabaptists virtually constituted an indefinite religious party within the dominant state church. They were disappointed with the Protestant state church, and were convinced that the evangelical Anabaptists exemplified true Biblical Christianity. But in face of the fact that the Anabaptists had been in many cases summarily sentenced to death, these people hesitated to unite with them; they did not have the courage of their conviction. Nevertheless they gave the Anabaptists assistance and rendered them service in every way possible. They did all within their power to make life possible and endurable for them. They would give them food and shelter and warn them of approaching danger, regardless of the fact that by so doing they themselves became transgressors of the civil law and made themselves liable to severe punishment. The designation "Halfway-Anabaptists" for these people was used in decrees against them. They were very numerous in certain states and sections, such as the Tyrol and various parts of Switzerland.

The following is an authoritative description of the attitude of large portions of the population, and of the Halfway-Anabaptists in particular, to the Anabaptists in the Tyrol, the formerly Austrian province due east of Switzerland. This account is taken from an important official report made by Tyrolean magistrates. It is dated October 17, 1539, and has this title: *Report Concerning the Reasons why the Anabaptists have become so numerous in this province, and why, notwithstanding all possible diligence of some of the magistrates, they could not be suppressed.* This report indicates the almost insurmountable difficulties confronting the persecuting authorities, in consequence of the friendly attitude of a large proportion of the population toward the Anabaptists. The document shows how deeply the Anabaptist movement had taken root among the general population. The said report follows.

The common people take an entirely favorable attitude toward the Anabaptists. They are kindly disposed toward them and take side with them. Even such as are not of the Anabaptist sect and were not baptized by them give them lodging, food, and aid. And although there are those who, because of fear of punishment or on account of abject poverty, abstain from rendering them such aid, they nevertheless permit the Anabaptists daily to walk to and fro among themselves at will. They do not report Anabaptists to the magistrates or government, and do nothing toward having them arrested.

If the magistrates are informed of a place in mountainous parts or elsewhere where Anabaptists sojourn, or where they have a meeting; if any such information comes to the magistrates, and if they plan to make efforts, by the help and assistance of the population, to fall upon them suddenly in order to seize and arrest them, and if the magistrates then order some of their subjects to proceed in all quietness with the officers of the law to such a place, and to assist in surprising and arresting the Anabaptists, then if those who receive such orders cannot excuse themselves and cannot in some way persuade the officers to permit them to stay at home; then even those that accompany the officers to such places will not move a hand to assist in apprehending the Anabaptists.

And even when any Anabaptists are close to them and they could easily lay hands on them, they will let them run unhindered into the forests and mountains, and thus make their escape from the magistrates. They excuse themselves afterwards saying that they had not seen any or had not been able to outrun them. And sometimes those who have been ordered to assist in arresting the Anabaptists will warn them of the coming of the officers.

Again, although the citizens, especially in the summer season, may not permit the Anabaptists to enter their homes [since houses in which Anabaptists had been given lodging were to be burned to the ground], they permit them to stay close by their houses on their grounds or in near-by forests and mountains, where they let them build booths and huts, and permit them to move about at will. They do not report to the magistrates any Anabaptists, much less do they give information about places where they abide, or where they have their meetings, but they, on the contrary, will give them aid and information to enable them to escape. And food and all necessities of life are brought to them at day and night. All this is contrary to the mandates, orders, and prohibitions issued by the government.

In various parts of Switzerland, also there were indications of the great numerical strength of the Halfway-Anabaptists. In the political district of Burgdorf in the Emmental, canton Bern, they were so numerous that the ministers of the Protestant state church in this district, assembled in conference, expressed the opinion that the Halfway-Anabaptists surpassed in point of numbers the loyal members of the state church. This was in 1670, after about a century and a half of persecution in Switzerland.

The attitude of the Halfway-Anabaptists toward the evangelical Anabaptists (Mennonites) is described in some of the pertinent historical source material, such as the above-quoted report of Tyrolean civil authorities, in the prayer book entitled, *Ernsthafte Christenpflicht* (the Christian's Solemn Obligation), and the book, *Probierstein des Täuferthums* (Touchstone of Mennonitism). On the latter see Appendix C. The first named book was evidently the earliest prayer book used by Mennonites. The first known edition was printed in 1745. There may have been earlier editions, and some of these prayers may have been circulated in manuscript form before the publication of the book. In the first century and a half of their history the Mennonites apparently did not use prayer books. Whatever may be our opinion concerning the use of prayer books, we will admit, after examining this book, that it gives unmistakable evidence, direct and indirect, of spiritual life on the part of the Mennonites in that period. Thus the book is of considerable value as source material on Mennonite history. We shall here in particular point to one or two characteristic features of these prayers.

The Halfway-Anabaptists are repeatedly referred to in this book. They are designated as *die treuherzigen Menschen* (truehearted people). Their attitude toward the Mennonites and the services they rendered them are described in some of the petitions contained in the prayers of this book. We quote from these prayers:

"O holy Father in heaven, we pray Thee for all truehearted people who love us and do good unto us, and render us services of mercy by providing for us food and nourishment, housing and shelter. O Lord, do Thou recompense them richly with all that is good. And since they hear Thy word gladly but have little strength to surrender themselves to obedience, we pray Thee to grant them that they may through Thy Holy Spirit have ingrafted in them Thy word which is able to save their souls."

"Be merciful, O loving Father to all upright, kindhearted people who through Thy grace and for Thy name's sake render us help and at all times come to our assistance by giving us place and shelter. O Lord, do Thou repay them with all blessings and give them what they may have need of in every respect."

"We pray Thee also, O holy and righteous Father, for all kindhearted people who speak well of us and show us mercy by giving us food and drink, housing and shelter. O Lord, be Thou highly praised for working the desire to do this in them. Recompense them, Lord, both here in time and in the life to come."

The same book also indicates that the evangelical Anabaptists obeyed Christ's command, to pray for those who despitefully use and persecute the Christian. The book contains prayers for their persecutors, and there is evidence that at various times they experienced remarkable answers to such prayers.

At the time of the Amish division (1693-1696) the question whether the Halfway-Anabaptists should be considered as saved was to a small extent a point of controversy.

The remarkable fact that for more than two centuries the combined efforts of both the state and the heads of the national church in Switzerland failed in the attempted extermination of the Mennonite Church must be largely ascribed, under God, to the influence and efforts of the Halfway-Anabaptists.

A NOTABLE TESTIMONY TO THE LIFE OF THE ANABAPTISTS OF SWITZERLAND IN THE 17TH CENTURY

An important testimony to the life and character of the Swiss Mennonites two and a half centuries ago is found in a book written by George Thormann, a minister of high rank in the Reformed state church, and published in 1693 by the magistracy of the canton Bern in Switzerland. It is a book of over 700 pages, entitled *Probierstein des Täuferthums* (Touchstone of Anabaptism). The book was written at the request of both the ecclesiastical and civil authorities and was issued from the government printing office at Bern. The author in the preface expressed alarm at the great numerical increase of the Anabaptist people.

Earlier Swiss Protestant writers had been untruthful and unreasonable in their accusations and denunciations of the Anabaptists. The books of these writers, in consequence, proved offensive not only to the Anabaptists themselves but also to those who were personally acquainted with them and their doctrine. The author of this book having decided to guard against making the same mistake, says repeatedly that his readers are informed as concerns the doctrine of these people and their commendable daily life and conduct. He makes no effort to show the Anabaptists in a bad light.

The author bears strong testimony to the fact that the membership of the national church were deeply impressed by their earnestness and piety.

He writes: "Among our country people the opinion prevails in general that whoever sees an Anabaptist, sees a saint, a person who is dead to the world, having experienced true conversion, and that there are no more earnest and consecrated people than they. Is it not so, dear brethren?" And again: "If among all Christian communions there is one which seems to be upright and give assurance of personal salvation to the soul, it is certainly that of the Anabaptists. And this is true to such an extent that their religion appears to very many of our country people as by far the surest way of salvation." "I have observed," the author says further, "that the people of our country districts indicate a very high esteem for the Anabaptist people. Their regard for them is such that many look upon them as saints, as the salt of the earth and the very kernel of Christendom. Their opinion concerning them is so favorable that many believe a good Christian and an Anabaptist to be one and the same thing. And thus many of our people are altogether confused in their consciences and are troubled by the question whether they should not join themselves to these people, without regard to the consequences."

People in general, according to this author, said: "Observe how they are continually mistreated, insulted, sought, and persecuted, and how cheerfully and steadfastly they endure it all. Is not God showing His almighty power and the sustaining grace of His Spirit in these people? . . . How is it that, notwithstanding all that has been attempted against them, it was found impossible to suppress their church, and their religion is, on the contrary, increasing more and more?"

And again, according to our author, the people said with reference to the so-called "Anabaptist Hunters" (a special police force commissioned to spy out and arrest them): "As God converted Saul of Tarsus to the Christian faith, who had raged so terribly against it, so also He has changed the hearts of a number of men who formerly were willing to be used by the magistrates in the persecution of the Anabaptists so that now, instead of doing them evil, they themselves have become Anabaptists, and have steadfastly held to that doctrine to the end of their lives. Is not God through such occurrences giving witness to all the world that this doctrine is of God?"

While earlier writers of the state church had asserted that the Mennonites' profession of nonresistance was only a clever cloak to hide their sinister, rebellious intentions, George Thormann does not make any such charge against them. He says on the contrary: "They are conscientiously opposed, not only to taking part in war, but even to bearing arms; they forbid this to their people as a great sin." He did not believe, he says further, that the Anabaptists of Switzerland had any evil intentions, nor "such un-Christian, mutinous, evil designs" as the Anabaptists of Münster. And yet, he adds that neither he nor they themselves but only God knows what they might do if they had opportunities for such madness as had the Anabaptists of Münster.

The latter part of the book contains earnest challenges to the readers of the book to follow the good example of the Anabaptists. The author says: "Is it commendable in the Anabaptist people that they show earnestness and zeal in their way of serving God? Do the same among us, dear brethren. . . . Is it a fine thing that the Anabaptists abstain from glib talking and do not talk much of worldly things? Do the same in the strength of your Christian calling. . . . Do they give a good example by not being easily provoked to anger? Do even the same, dear brethren; avoid anger more and more. . . . Is it good and praiseworthy that they do not indulge much in worldly enjoyments

and in vain pleasures of the flesh? Do likewise, dear brethren. . . .
Is it good and commendable that they shun the public inns and drink-
houses, except in cases of emergency, and that they strictly guard
themselves against taking much wine? Well, do the same; shun all dis-
orderly, intemperate, ungodly conduct. . . . Is it praiseworthy in
them that one does not hear them use profane language or swear? Do
again the same, for this is the will of God toward you, as well as toward them."

George Thormann's book gives a valuable description of the life
and walk of the Swiss Mennonites of that period. Contrary to his own
intentions, he has done the Mennonite Church a distinct service by
writing this book. It throws welcome light on the question how it is
to be explained that the state and the national church of the canton
Bern found it impossible to exterminate the Mennonite Church. About
two centuries of strenuous effort on their part toward this end proved
a failure, because many of the general population sympathized with
those who endured persecution for their faith and conscience, and
gave them assistance and help in every possible way.

NOTES AND REFERENCES

NOTES AND REFERENCES

1 For an exhaustive discussion see the article by H. Böhmer, "Waldenser," in *Realencyklopädie für protestantische Theologie und Kirche*, by Herzog-Hauck, Vol. XX, pp. 799-840.

2 *Martyrs' Mirror*, English edition, Scottdale, Pa., 1938, pages 284-287.

3 *Het Bloedigh Tooneel der Doops-gesinde, en Weereloose Christenen*, Dortrecht, 1660, I p. 318.

4 *Encyclopedia Britannica*, 14th ed., Vol. I, page 858.

5 An interesting side light on the existence of evangelical churches before the period of the Reformation is afforded by the following incident which seems to be well authenticated. In 1540 three men of Thessalonica visited some of the Swiss Brethren congregations in Moravia. They represented a Christian body in the city just mentioned, and had learned that there was in Moravia a Christian congregation of similar faith and practice as theirs. They made the long journey to Moravia to confer with that church and were first directed to the Hutterians from whom they differed on the point of community of goods. Finally they were led to the Swiss Brethren congregation at Pausram in Moravia and found that a virtual unity in faith and practice existed between their brotherhood and this congregation. The existing unity of faith was celebrated in a united communion service before their departure. See *Ausbund, das ist etliche schöne Lieder*, Germantown, 1785, Dritter Anhang, das sechste Lied.

6 Saxony was then ruled by an elector, that is to say, by one of the princes —seven in number—whose prerogative it was to elect the emperor of Germany.

7 Conrad Grebel was united in matrimony with Barbara ———, in February, 1522.

8 Manz was the son of a priest at the cathedral of this city.

9 This name, by which he became generally known, was given him because after his arrival in Zurich he often wore a blue coat.

10 Grebel's letter to Münzer is printed in Cornelius, C. A., *Münsterische Aufruhr*, II, pp. 240-249, and in *Gedenkschrift zum 400-jährigen Jubiläum der Mennoniten*, pp. 89-102. An English translation by Walter Rauschenbusch was published in *The American Journal of Theology*, IX, No. 1.

11 *Heinrich Bullingers Reformationsgeschichte*, I, p. 238.

12 Wolkan, *Geschicht-Buch der Hutterischen Brüder*, pp. 34, 35.

13 The original titles of these books are: (1) *Welche ursach gebind ze ufrueren*, etc.; (2) *Von dem touff, vom widertouff unnd vom kindertouff;* (3) *Von dem predigamt;* (4) *Ueber doctor Balthazars touffbuechlin waarhaffte, gründte antwurt.*

14 The *Ausbund* contains an important hymn (No. 6) of twenty-four stanzas written by Felix Manz. A translation of this hymn (not in verse) is found in *Martyrs' Mirror* (1938), p. 415.

15 A long hymn in the *Ausbund* (No. 132) describes the martyrdom of Hans Landis.

16 The pamphlet is reproduced in *Martyrs' Mirror* (1938), pp. 1115-1118.

17 First Timothy 1:5.

18 The Schleitheim Confession was also printed in the French language, and later (1560) was published in Dutch. A reprint of the original edition, edited by Walter Köhler of Tübingen, appeared in 1908. An English translation based on Zwingli's Latin text in the *Elenchus* was printed in the book by W. J. McGlothlin: *Baptist Confessions of Faith*, Philadelphia, 1911, pp. 3-9.

[19] This letter, together with a touching description of Sattler's martyrdom is found in *Martyrs' Mirror* (1938), pp. 416-420.

[20] Compare Romans 13:4.

[21] Sattler is the author of Hymn No. 7 in the *Ausbund*.

[22] The second martyr from among the Swiss Brethren was Johannes Krüsi who was burned at the stake in Lucerne on July 27, 1525.

[23] *Vom Tauf, vom Wiedertauf und Kindertauf,* (1525). Cp. note 13 above.

[24] The *Ausbund*, earliest hymnbook of the Swiss Brethren, contains a hymn by Otmar Roth of St. Gall (No. 58).

[25] See page 74 above.

[26] As a matter of fact, the ministers of the Protestant state church, with very few exceptions, had formerly been priests. They were not re-ordained by the leaders of the Protestant state church, but had become Protestant preachers through obeying the orders of the Council to accept the new creed and order of worship. In the last analysis these men were ordained on the authority of the head of the Roman Catholic Church, the pope, whom the Reformed theologians believed to be Antichrist.

[27] The report of the debate was printed by Froschauer in Zurich, 1532, a small-sized volume of 308 pages, entitled *Handlung oder Acta gehaltener Disputation und Gespräch zu Zoffingen inn Berner Biet mit den Widertöuffern.*

[28] *Martyrs' Mirror* (1938), p. 1129. So impartial a historian as Ernst Müller was inclined to doubt that the number of the martyrs in this canton was as great as given in the *Martyrs' Mirror*. More recent investigations have however verified the substantial correctness of this list. The thirty-three martyrs mentioned by name are:

Hans Hansmann (Seckler) of Basel; Hans Treyer and Heini Seiler, hatmakers from Aarau; they died in July, 1529. In February, 1530, Conrad Eicher of Steffisburg was martyred. On January 11, 1535, Moritz Kessler of Sumiswald met the same fate. After him there was Ulrich Schneider of Lützelflüh, and a "young man from Wallis." On May 2, 1536, Moritz Losenegger; on July 7, 1537, Bernard Wälti of Rüderswyl; then Hans Schweizer, of Rügsau, and on August 28, 1536, Georg Hofer of Obergallbach of the principality Signau; in the same year Ulrich Bichsel, Barbara Willher of Hassli, Barbeli zur Studen of Sumiswald, Katharine Friedli Imhof, Verena Iseli of Schübach in the principality Signau, and Ulrich von Rügsau. On March 28, 1538, Seidenkohen of Constanz. On April 16, 1538 Peter Stucky of Wimmis, Ulrich Huber of Rötenbach in the principality Signau; then in August Hans Willer, Elisabeth Küpfer of Sumiswald; on September 17, Peter Wysmüller of Wimmis. On November 8, Steffen Rügsegger of Signau, and then Rudolf Iseli of Tannental. On June 3, 1539, Lorenz Aeberli of Grünau and Hans Schuhmacher of Wynstägen by Safenwil. On May 1, 1542, Peter Anken of Siebental. On September 17, 1543, Christian Oberli, and then Hans Anken of Amsoldingen. On July 30, 1566, Wälti Gerber was put to death with the sword. The last martyr of the Brethren in Bern who is known by name was Hans Haslibacher. *Mennonitisches Lexikon,* I p. 171; Ernst Müller, *Geschichte der Bernischen Taüffer,* pp. 78, 79.

[29] Among the earliest Mennonite families in the canton Basel the Hersbergers, Schaubs, Treyers, Rysers, Burgins, and Rohrers deserve mention. Through four or five generations the Hersbergers were prominent in the Mennonite annals of Basel. Friedli Hersberger fled to Ohnenheim in Alsace. The Hershberger family is today numerous among the Mennonites of America.

[30] Assuming Kessler's statement that the people of Teufen deposed Jacob Schurtanner to mean that they shunned the services at the parish church, they only followed the advice given by Zwingli in his book *The Shepherd,* published March 26, 1524, which he dedicated to Jacob Schurtanner. In this book Zwingli had written: "If the shepherd (pastor) is false, do not listen to him, and if all parishioners recognize him as false, dismiss him by a unanimous vote. If you cannot do this, refuse unitedly to hear him."

[31] Horsch, J., "An Inquiry into the Truth of Accusations of Fanaticism and Crime Against the Early Swiss Brethren," *The Mennonite Quarterly Review*, (1934), Vol. VIII, pp. 18-31.

[32] Horsch, J., "The Faith of the Swiss Brethren," in *The Mennonite Quarterly Review* (1931), Vol. V, pp. 25, 26.

[33] Harold S. Bender made a collation of existing manuscript copies of the Strasburg discipline of 1568, which was published in the original and in translation in *The Mennonite Quarterly Review*, Vol. I, January, 1927, pages 57-66.

[34] This confession of faith was printed in full in *The Mennonite Quarterly Review* (1938), Vol. XII, pp. 167-202.

[35] This work, entitled *Taufbüchlein*, was reprinted in full in *Gedenkschrift zum 400-Jährigen Jubiläum der Mennoniten oder Taufgesinnten, 1525-1925*, (1925), pp. 134-178.

[36] Author of the hymn No. 57 in the *Ausbund*.

[37] Author of hymns No. 68 and 69 in the *Ausbund*.

[38] The title is: *Ein Göttlich unnd gründtlich offenbarung: von den warhafftigen widerteuffern: mit Götlicher warhait angezaigt*. 1527.

[39] Leopold Schneider is author of a hymn in the *Ausbund* (No. 39).

[40] The *Ausbund* contains two hymns of Blaurock (No. 5 and No. 30). The first is an impressive hymn of faith in thirty-three stanzas. The second is Blaurock's "swan song," written as he faced martyrdom for his faith. See the *Martyrs' Mirror*, 1938, pp. 430-432, for an account of Blaurock's martyrdom, and a prose translation of these two hymns.

[41] Fischer, C. A., *Vier und funfftzig Erhebliche Ursachen Warumb die Widertauffer nicht sein im Land zu leyden*, Ingolstadt, 1607.

[42] The translation of the Prophets which was published in April, 1527, at Worms, filled a real need. The translation of the Bible into German by Luther, and that by the Zurich theologians (known as the Froschauer version) were printed later than this. Many editions of the Worms translation of the Prophets appeared at different places.

[43] The reader will call to mind what was brought out above, that Zwingli publicly taught this view of baptism for a few years. In fact, both Hubmaier and Conrad Grebel confessed in later years that it was through Zwingli's influence that they were led to see the unscripturalness of infant baptism.

[44] The original title is, *Vom christlichen Tauf der Gläubigen*.

[45] Revelation 14:1.

[46] Ezra 4:24.

[47] The quotations from Obbe Philips are translated from his *Bekentenisse*, as republished by Samuel Cramer in Volume VII of *Bibliotheca Reformatoria Neerlandica*, pp. 89-138.

[48] The original title of this important work by Menno is, *Dat Fundament des Christelycken leers op dat alder corste geschreven*, M.D. XXXIX. (without place of publication). Menno himself later calls this book "Mijn Fondamentboeksken" (*Opera Omnia*, 1681, p. 235).

[49] At this time already in both the Netherlands and in Germany the laws demanded capital punishment for all Anabaptists whenever the civil authorities would find it possible to lay hands on them.

[50] *Complete Works*, I, p. 7. All further references to the writings of Menno Simons, unless otherwise stated, are to the English edition, *The Complete Works of Menno Simon*, Elkhart, Indiana, 1871.

[51] *Works*, II, p. 11.

[52] Their martyrdom is described both in the *Martyrs' Mirror*, p. 468, and in the *Ausbund*, hymn No. 16.

53 *Works,* II, p. 11.

54 *Works,* I, p. 7.

55 At least seven different portraits have been claimed as likenesses of Menno Simons. None of them is an actual portrait. One of these pictures was discovered some thirty years ago in the Mennonite Church at Haarlem in Holland. It was a painting bearing the inscription "Menno Simons." Numerous reproductions of this portrait were made and disposed of as the likeness of Menno. Some years later, however, a Dutch visitor noticed a duplicate of this painting in a gallery in Italy, this time labeled "John Calvin." Upon investigation it was found that the picture was neither that of Menno nor Calvin but of another prominent man of the Reformation era.

56 The complete works of Dirck Philips were recently (1914) published in the original language (Dutch) in Vol. X of the *Bibliotheca Reformatoria Neerlandica.*

57 Compare *The Mennonite Quarterly Review* (1933), Vol. VII, pp. 105-107.

58 Compare his chapter in the *Foundation* entitled, "To the Corrupt Sects."

59 The title in German is: *Christliches Gemüths-Gespräch von dem Geistlichen und seeligmachenden Glauben,* etc.

60 Jacob Denner published a large volume of sermons, which was reprinted at Philadelphia, Pa., in 1860.

61 A similar service was rendered by the Mennonites of Danzig during the siege of that city by the Russians in 1813.

62 This confession of faith is printed in *Martyrs' Mirror,* pp. 373-410. It was first published in English (1837) at Winchester, Virginia, by Peter Burkholder and is sometimes referred to as the Burkholder Confession.

63 See the preceding note.

64 These two confessions are printed in *Martyrs' Mirror,* pp. 27-38.

65 In a note found in the *Martyrs' Mirror* (p. 44) it is stated that this confession was unanimously adopted by the congregations in Alsace, the Palatinate, and Upper Germany. The date when this took place is not stated.

66 At least fifty-three editions of this book have been printed in the Dutch, German, and English languages. The latest German edition was printed at Scottdale, Pennsylvania, in 1919.

67 The last edition of Deknatel's Sermons appeared in 1835 at Allentown, Pa.

68 *De Doopsgezinden te Amsterdam, 1530-1930,* by F. Dijkema.

69 The *Ordnungsbrief* of 1779 was published in the original German in *The Mennonite Quarterly Review* (1937), Vol. XI, pp. 165-168, under the title, "An Amish Church Discipline of 1779."

70 The history of this division has been well presented in an article by Milton Gascho, "The Amish Division of 1693-1697 in Switzerland and Alsace," in *The Mennonite Quarterly Review* (1937), Vol. XI, pp. 235-266.

71 An electorate was a province ruled by an Elector, that is, by one of the seven German princes whose prerogative it was to elect the Emperor.

72 For the names of Swiss Mennonite refugees in the Palatinate after 1664 which later appear among the Mennonites of America see below. Appendix A.

73 See the article by David G. Rempel, "The Mennonite Migration to New Russia (1787-1870)," in *The Mennonite Quarterly Review* (1935), Vol. IX, pp. 71-91, 109-128.

74 The Pietists, it may be noted, were zealous members of the Lutheran or Reformed Churches who, besides attending the regular worship in their churches, met in private assemblies for prayer and Bible study.

75 The group led by Isaac Peters is known today as the Evangelical Mennonite Brethren.

[76] They cited particularly Isaiah 26:20, 21 and Revelation 12:14.

[77] This is an organization of representatives from most of the Mennonite bodies in America, with headquarters at that time at Scottdale, Pa.

[78] See Van Braght, T. J., *Martyrs' Mirror* (1886), pp. 467b, 596a, 605b, 651b; *Het Offer des Heeren* (1904), p. 528.

[79] See *Martyrs' Mirror* (1886), pp. 495, 547; *Het Offer des Heeren* (1904), pp. 330, 630, 633.

[80] *Martyrs' Mirror*, pp. 465, 500.

[81] *Works*, I, pp. 195, 196.

[82] *Works*, II, p. 104.

[83] *Ausbund*, hymn No. 31, stanzas 3-5; as translated by Henry S. Burrage, *Baptist Hymn Writers and Their Hymns*, p. 9 (Portland, Me., 1888).

[84] After the first edition of *Het Offer des Heeren* in 1561, at least ten more editions appeared before the year 1600.

[85] Four editions of this work were printed between 1615 and 1631 at Haarlem and Hoorn in Holland.

[86] The state church authorities at Dortrecht put forth efforts to prevent the first publication of the *Martyrs' Mirror* in 1660, but without success. The work was reprinted in 1685. It was translated into the German language for the Mennonites of Pennsylvania, and printed at Ephrata, Pennsylvania, in 1748. A reprint of this translation appeared at Pirmasens in the Palatinate in 1780. In America four reprints of the same translation, and three editions of an English translation of this work appeared, the latest English edition in 1938, at Scottdale, Pennsylvania. Besides, an abridged edition in the Dutch language was printed six times between 1671 and 1769. Later an abridged edition was printed three times in Pennsylvania.

[87] *Works*, II, p. 243.

[88] *Works*, I, p. 75.

[89] *Works*, II, p. 10.

[90] *Die Lieder der Hutterischen Brüder*, pp. 650-652.

[91] Luther's *Works*, Erlangen edition, Vol. XI, pp. 488, 490.

[92] First Corinthians 5:11; Second Thessalonians 3:14; Romans 16:17.

[93] In this connection it is of interest to note that in the observance of the communion among the early Swiss Mennonites not all church members in regular standing were invited to participate. While all had the privilege or right to do so, the invitation to take part in the communion service was extended only to such as were resolved to give up, if need be, everything, even life, for the sake of Christ and the evangelical truth. A willingness to do so was expected of all members of the church.

[94] *Doopsgezinde Bijdragen*, Leiden, 1876, pp. 16ff., contains the full account given by this chronicler.

[95] *Works*, II, p. 135.

[96] *Works*, II, p. 279.

[97] *Works*, II, p. 445.

[98] *Works*, II, p. 277.

[99] *Works*, I, p. 284; I, p. 250.

[100] This letter was printed in *Doopsgezinde Bijdragen*, Leiden, 1894.

[101] *Works*, I, pp. 240-268.

[102] A marginal note in the Dutch edition of Menno's *Works* of 1681 (page 489) says: "The Upperlandians are known in the upper countries and Moravia as Swiss Brethren." And in an appendix to the Dortrecht Confession, printed in 1666, the statement is made that "the Swiss Brethren are also called Upper Germans," or Upperlandians.

103 *Works,* II, p. 292.

104 *Works,* II, pp. 283-295.

105 The citation from his *Reply* (*Works,* II, p. 295), given in the article on Menno Simons in the *Mennonitisches Lexikon,* is not to the point. This book of Menno is not addressed to the Upperlanders but to Sielis and Lemke personally.

106 *Works,* II, p. 204.

107 *Works,* I, p. 38.

108 *Works,* I, p. 124.

109 *Works,* II, p. 345.

110 *Works,* I, p. 161.

111 *Works,* II, p. 38.

112 *Works,* II, p. 243.

113 *Works,* I, p. 254.

114 Second Thessalonians 2:4.

115 *Works,* I, p. 241.

116 *Works,* II, p. 188.

117 *Works,* II, p. 49.

118 *Works,* I, p. 31.

119 Jeremiah, chapter 31; Hebrews 8:6, 7.

120 *Works,* I, p. 65.

121 *Enchiridion,* p. 323.

122 *Works,* I, p. 242 and II, p. 449.

123 *Works,* I, p. 81; II, p. 435; I, p. 81.

124 Hauck-Herzog, *Realencyklopädie für protestantische Theologie und Kirche,* I, p. 482.

125 *Works,* I, p. 36.

126 *Works,* I, p. 155.

127 *Works,* I, p. 158.

128 *Works,* I, p. 32.

129 *Works,* I, p. 158.

130 *Works,* II, p. 59.

131 *Works,* II, p. 316.

132 *Works,* II, p. 264.

133 *Enchiridion,* p. 114.

134 Compare in Menno's *Works,* II, 164; II, p. 525; II, p. 330; II, p. 153; II, p. 375.

135 *Works,* II, p. 184.

136 On Adam Pastor see further chapter 25 and footnote 57 above.

BIBLIOGRAPHY

BIBLIOGRAPHY

NOTE: No attempt has been made to compile here an exhaustive list of the source materials used by the author in the preparation of this volume, nor of the numerous works that deal with the material covered here. Such an exhaustive list would include perhaps a majority of the eighteen hundred or more titles listed in the *Catalogue of the Mennonite Historical Library in Scottdale, Pennsylvania* (1929), as well as some unique materials found in other historical collections here and abroad. The items listed here comprise a selected reading list of outstanding books and articles available to those who are interested in further reading about the history of the Mennonites in Europe. They are meant to serve the general reader. Except for certain standard reference works, the preference has been given to literature in the English language, especially articles from periodicals presenting the results of recent research not accessible elsewhere at this time.

A. In the German Language

BECK, J. v., *Die Geschichtsbücher der Wiedertäufer in Oesterreich-Ungarn, betreffend deren Schicksale in der Schweiz, Salzburg, Ober- und Nieder-Oesterreich, Mähren, Tirol, Böhmen, Süd-Deutschland, Ungarn, Siebenbürgen und Süd-Russland in der Zeit von 1526 bis 1785*. Wien, 1883.

Beiträge zur Geschichte der Mennoniten, Festgabe für D. Christian Neff zum 70. Geburtstag, (Schriftenreihe des Menn. Geschichtsvereins, No. 1). Weierhof (Pfalz), 1938.

Beiträge zur Geschichte der rheinischen Mennoniten, (Schriftenreihe des Menn. Geschichtsvereins, No. 2). Weierhof, 1939.

BRONS, ANNA, *Ursprung, Entwicklung und Schicksale der altevangelischen Taufgesinnten oder Mennoniten*. 3. Auflage, Norden, 1912.

BERGMAN, CORNELIUS, *Die Täuferbewegung im Kanton Zürich bis 1660*. Leipzig, 1916.

CORNELIUS, C. A., *Geschichte des Münsterischen Aufruhrs*. Leipzig, 1860.

CORRELL, E. H., *Das Schweizerische Täufer-Mennonitentum*. Tübingen, 1925.

DOLLINGER, ROBERT, *Geschichte der Mennoniten in Schleswig Holstein, Hamburg und Lübeck*. Neumünster i. H., 1930.

FRIESEN, P. M., *Die altevangelische Mennonitische Brüderschaft in Russland im Rahmen der Mennonitischen Gesamtgeschichte*. Halbstadt, Russia, 1911.

Gedenkschrift zum 400jährigen Jubiläum der Taufgesinnten oder Mennoniten (1525-1925), herausgegeben von D. Christian Neff. Karlsruhe, 1925.

GEISER, SAMUEL, *Die Taufgesinnten-Gemeinden.* Karlsruhe, 1931.

Geschicht-Buch der Hutterischen Brüder. Macleod, Alberta, 1923.

HEGE, CHRISTIAN, *Die Täufer in der Kurpfalz.* Frankfurt a. M., 1908.

HEGE, CHRISTINE, *Kurze Geschichte der Mennoniten.* Frankfurt a. M., 1909.

HÄNDIGES, E., *Die Lehre der Mennoniten in Geschichte und Gegenwart.* Ludwigshafen a. Rh., 1921.

HRUBY, FRANTISEK, *Die Wiedertäufer in Mähren.* Leipzig, 1935.

HORSCH, JOHN, *Kurzgefasste Geschichte der Mennoniten-Gemeinden.* Elkhart, Indiana, 1890.

KRAHN, CORNELIUS, *Menno Simons (1496-1561): Ein Beitrag zur Geschichte und Theologie der Taufgesinnten.* Karlsruhe, 1936.

KELLER, LUDWIG, *Die Geschichte der Wiedertäufer und ihres Reiches zu Münster.* Leipzig, 1880.

———, ———, *Ein Apostel der Wiedertäufer* (Hans Denck). Leipzig, 1882.

LOSERTH, J., *Der Anabaptismus in Tirol.* Wien, 1892.

———, ———, "Der Communismus der mährischen Wiedertäufer im 16. und 17. Jahrhundert," in *Archiv für österreichische Geschichte.* Wien, 1894.

MANNHARDT, W., *Die Wehrfreiheit der altpreussischen Mennoniten.* Marienburg, 1863.

MÜLLER, ERNST, *Geschichte der Bernischen Täufer.* Frauenfeld, 1895.

MÜLLER, LYDIA, *Der Kommunismus der mährischen Wiedertäufer,* (Schriftens des Vereins für Reformationsgeschichte, No. 142). Leipzig, 1928.

MÜLLER, J. P., *Die Mennoniten in Ostfriesland vom 16. bis 18. Jahrhundert.* Emden, 1877.

Mennonitische Geschichtsblätter, herausgegeben vom Mennonitischen Geschichtsverein. Weierhof, 1936-

Mennonitisches Lexikon, edited by Christian Hege and Christian Neff. Vol. I, 1913; Vol. II, 1937; Vol. III, in progress. Frankfurt a. M.

MURALT, LEONHARD VON, *Glaube und Lehre der Schweizerischen Wiedertäufer in der Reformationszeit.* Zürich, 1938.

ROOSEN, B. C., *Geschichte der Mennoniten-Gemeinden zu Hamburg und Altona.* Hamburg, 1886-1887.

STAUFFER, ETHELBERT, "Märtyrertheologie und Täuferbewegung," in *Zeitschrift Für Kirchengeschichte,* 1933.

WISWEDEL, W., *Bilder und Führergestalten aus dem Täufertum.* 2 vols. Kassel, 1928 and 1930.

WOLKAN, R., *Die Lieder der Wiedertäufer.* Berlin, 1903.

ZIEGLSCHMID, A. J. F. ed., *Die älteste Chronik der Hutterischen Brüder.* Philadelphia, 1943.

——————— ed., *Das Klein-Geschichtsbuch der Hutterischen Brüder.* Philadelphia, 1947.

B. In the Dutch Language

CATE, S. BLAUPOT TEN, *Geschiedenis der Doopsgezinden.* Leeuwarden and Amsterdam, 1839-1847.

KÜHLER, W. J., *Geschiedenis der Nederlandsche Doopsgezinden in de Zestiende Eeuw.* Haarlem, 1932.

SCHYN-MAATSCHOEN, *De Geschiedenis der Mennoniten.* 3 vols., Amsterdam, 1743-1745.

VOS, KAREL, *Menno Simons (1496-1561).* Leiden, 1914.

C. In the English Language

BENDER, HAROLD S., "Conrad Grebel, First Leader of the Swiss Brethren"; "The Theology of Conrad Grebel"; "Conrad Grebel as a Zwinglian"; in *The Mennonite Quarterly Review,* 1936, 1938, 1941.

————, ————, "Conrad Grebel, Founder of Swiss Anabaptism," in *Church History,* 1938.

BENDER, HAROLD S., *Conrad Grebel 1498-1526, The Founder of the Swiss Brethren.* Goshen, 1950.

————, *The Anabaptist Vision,* Goshen, 1944. (Reprint from the *Mennonite Quarterly Review*).

BRAGHT, THIELEMAN J. VAN, *Martyrs' Mirror* (1660). English edition, Scottdale, 1938.

DOSKER, HENRY E., *The Dutch Anabaptists.* Philadelphia, 1921.

COUTS, ALFRED, *Hans Denck, 1495-1525, Humanist and Heretic.* Edinburgh, 1927.

EVANS, AUSTIN P., *An Episode in the Struggle for Religious Freedom: The Secretaries of Nuremberg,* 1524-1528. New York, 1924.

FRIEDMANN, ROBERT, "Anabaptism and Pietism"; "Spiritual Changes in European Mennonitism"; "Dutch Mennonite Devotional Literature from Peter Peters to Johannes Deknatel, 1625-1753"; in *The Mennonite Quarterly Review,* 1940, 1941.

————, ————, "Conception of the Anabaptists," in *Church History,* 1940.

FRIEDMANN, ROBERT, *Mennonite Piety Through the Centuries, Its Genius and Its Literature.* Goshen, 1949.

HEATH, RICHARD, *Anabaptism from Its Rise at Zwickau to Its Fall at Münster.* London, 1895.

————, ————, "The Anabaptists and Their English Descendants"; "Hans Denck, the Anabaptist"; "Early Anabaptism"; "Living in Community, a Sketch of Moravian Anabaptism"; "The Archetype of 'The Pilgrim's Progress'"; "The Archetype of 'The Holy War'"; in *Contemporary Review,* 1891-1898.

HORSCH, JOHN, *Infant Baptism: Its Origin Among Protestants and Arguments Advanced For and Against It.* Scottdale, 1917.

————, ————, *Is Dr. Kühler's Conception of Early Dutch Anabaptism Historically Sound?* (Reprint from *The Mennonite Quarterly Review,* 1933). Scottdale, 1935.

————, ————, *Menno Simons: His Life, Labors, and Teachings.* Scottdale, 1916.

————, ————, *The Hutterian Brethren: A Story of Martyrdom and Loyalty, 1528-1931.* Goshen, Indiana, 1931.

————, ————, *The Mennonites, Their History, Faith, and Practice.* Elkhart, 1893.

————, ————, *The Principle of Nonresistance as Held by the Mennonite Church.* Second edition, revised and enlarged, Scottdale, 1939.

NEWMAN, ALBERT H., *A History of Anti-Pedobaptism from the Rise of Pedobaptism to A.D. 1609.* Philadelphia, 1902.

PHILIPS, DIETRICH, *Enchiridion, or Handbook,* (1564). English edition, Elkhart, 1910.

REMPEL, DAVID G., "The Mennonite Migration to New Russia, 1788-1870," in *The Mennonite Quarterly Review,* 1935.

SIMONS, MENNO, *Complete Works.* Elkhart, 1871.

SMITH, C. HENRY, *The Story of the Mennonites.* Berne, Indiana, 1941.

SMITHSON, R. J., *The Anabaptists: Their Contribution to Our Protestant Heritage.* London, 1935.

WENGER, JOHN C., "The Life and Work of Pilgram Marpeck"; "Pilgram Marpeck's Confession of Faith, 1531"; "The Theology of Pilgram Marpeck"; in *The Mennonite Quarterly Review,* 1938.

————, ————, "Pilgram Marpeck, Tyrolese Engineer and Anabaptist Elder," in *Church History,* 1940.

————, ————, *Glimpses of Mennonite History,* Scottdale, 1940.

WENGER, JOHN C., *Glimpses of Mennonite History and Doctrine,* 2d. ed., Scottdale, 1947.

————, *Doctrines of the Mennonites,* Scottdale, 1950.

VEDDER, HENRY C., *Balthasar Hübmaier, the Leader of the Anabaptists.* New York, 1905.

INDEX

INDEX

THE AUTHOR

Born at Giebelstadt, Germany, December 18, 1867, John
Horsch came to the United States in 1888 to escape compulsory military training, against which he had religious scruples
of conscience.

He served successively on the editorial staff of the Mennonite Publishing Company, Elkhart, Indiana; the Light and
Hope Publishing Company, Cleveland, Ohio; and from 1908 to
1941, of the Mennonite Publishing House, Scottdale, Pennsylvania.

He was a devoted student of Mennonite history from his
youth and for fifty years a prolific writer on subjects relating
to the Mennonites, their history and principles.

He was author of numerous books, many pamphlets and
tracts, and uncounted articles published in English and German periodicals both here and abroad.

Mennonites in Europe is the crowning achievement of a
busy lifetime devoted to the study and interpretation of
Mennonite origins and the history of Mennonites in Europe.

The author passed to his reward on October 7, 1941.